Routledge Revivals

Alienation from Schooling

Originally published in 1986, this book presents three full case studies of secondary school communities in Australia: one city school in a working-class area, one community school serving a wide, more rural area, and a school with an academic tradition in the suburbs of a large city. The material is drawn together to discuss and describe the issues revealed by the studies: these include discipline, boredom, staff-student relations, and the relevance of school work to the outside world. The book includes interviews with both students and teachers, recording the reactions of students to the way they are being taught, and their views on whether it is worth working hard at school when there is no certainly of a job at the end of it.

The philosophy of the teachers emerges in the interviews, as do their views on the prospect of changing students' attitudes from those acquired at home, and on the need for vocational rather than academic courses. What also comes out in the interviews is their realistic attitudes to their students' future job prospects, and their views on alternative courses which could prepare the pupils for life rather than for a specific job.

The book also includes an account of how the case studies were undertaken and reported. The methodological chapters set out some of the dilemmas and the possibilities in the study of such complex human situations.

Alienation from Schooling

Edited by Peter Fensham

First published in 1986
by Routledge & Kegan Paul

This edition first published in 2018 by Routledge
2 Park Square, Milton Park, Abingdon, Oxon, OX14 4RN
and by Routledge
711 Third Avenue, New York, NY 10017

Routledge is an imprint of the Taylor & Francis Group, an informa business

© 1986 Selection and editorial matter, Peter Fensham, all other matter © 1986 Routledge & Kegan Paul

All rights reserved. No part of this book may be reprinted or reproduced or utilised in any form or by any electronic, mechanical, or other means, now known or hereafter invented, including photocopying and recording, or in any information storage or retrieval system, without permission in writing from the publishers.

Publisher's Note
The publisher has gone to great lengths to ensure the quality of this reprint but points out that some imperfections in the original copies may be apparent.

Disclaimer
The publisher has made every effort to trace copyright holders and welcomes correspondence from those they have been unable to contact.

A Library of Congress record exists under ISBN: 85008176

ISBN 13: 978-1-138-29812-5 (hbk)
ISBN 13: 978-1-315-09856-2 (ebk)
ISBN 13: 978-1-138-29856-9 (pbk)

Alienation From Schooling

Edited by
Peter Fensham

Routledge & Kegan Paul
London, Boston and Henley

First published in 1986
by Routledge & Kegan Paul plc

14 Leicester Square, London WC2H 7PH, England

9 Park Street, Boston, Mass. 02108, USA and

Broadway House, Newtown Road,
Henley on Thames, Oxon RG9 1EN, England.

Set in Times 10 point on 11
by Columns of Reading

Introduction and Chapter 5, selection and
editorial matter © Peter Fensham 1986
All other material © Routledge & Kegan Paul 1986

No part of this work may be reproduced in
any form without permission from the publisher,
except for the quotation of brief passages
in criticism

ISBN 0-7102-0163-X

Contents

List of contributors		vii
Foreword		ix
	Part I	1
1	Introduction *Peter Fensham*	3
2	Greenfield A case study of schooling, alienation and employment *David H. Tripp*	27
3	Addison Hills A case study of alienation and transition from school *Stephen Kemmis*	160
4	The Purdah experience *Colin Power*	199
	Part II	261
5	Across the States A response to the studies from within the project *Peter Fensham*	263
6	Policy response to the case studies *Jean Blackburn*	284
7	Some methodological, substantive and theoretical aspects *P.W. Musgrave*	289
8	Case studies and what we already know *D.S. Anderson*	303
9	Reflections on methodology *S. Kemmis, C. Power and D. Tripp*	323
10	With critical friends, who needs enemies? *Lawrence Ingvarson*	344
Index		351

List of Contributors

Peter Fensham is Dean of the Faculty of Education at Monash University, Victoria. At the time these studies began he was Professor of Science Education at Monash. In addition to research in that field he has been involved in a number of studies relating to social justice in education.

David Tripp is a Lecturer in the School of Education at Murdoch University, Western Australia. His first research studies involved an evaluation in Britain of the Thinking curriculum project based on De Bono's work. In Perth he has undertaken a major study of the impact of television on children.

Stephen Kemmis is Associate Professor in Curriculum Studies at Deakin University, Victoria. His main interest are in educational research methods, curriculum ideologies, curriculum innovations and educational reform. At the time of the study reported here, he was concluding a period of investigation of case study methods in educational research and evaluation; subsequently, he has been involved in investigating action research as a potential form for a critical educational science.

Colin Power is Professor of Education at Flinders University, South Australia. His early work was on interactions in science classrooms. More recently he has contributed substantially concerning paradigms for educational research. He led the team that evaluated the Australian Studies of Student Performance Project. He is a past President of the Australian Association for Research in Education.

Contributors

Jean Blackburn is a Visiting Senior Research Fellow at Adelaide University. She was a commissioner of the Commonwealth Schools Commission in Canberra from 1973-80. More recently she has been the Chairperson of the Ministerial Review of Post-Compulsory Schooling in Victoria.

Peter Musgrave is a Professor of Education in the Faculty of Education at Monash University where he was earlier the Dean of that Faculty. He is best known for his book *The Sociology of Education* but has written extensively about the curriculum and its social roles. His current interest is children's literature.

Don Anderson is a Professorial Fellow in the Department of Sociology, the Research School of Social Sciences, Australian National University in Canberra. He has had a long standing interest in processes of socialization and professionalization. He has carried out many evaluations and at present is an editor of the National Clearing House for Youth Studies with a focus on youth policy, and education and training.

Lawrence Ingvarson is a Senior Lecturer in the Faculty of Education at Monash University. He has major interests in the professional development of teachers, in strategies for school improvements, and in the processes and roles of evaluators in curricular and other educational programmes.

Foreword

The research reported in this book is about a social condition that will come as no surprise to readers who are directly involved in the process of schooling. It is particularly familiar to those engaged in those systems of public or mass education which have no choice about who they must try to educate. Our accounts are attempts to describe alienation from schooling so that this widespread condition may be better understood.

Our studies would not have been possible without two primary sources of cooperation. The first source is made up of the communities of three schools, particularly the staffs and students. Many of them are indeed 'subauthors' of quite a lot of our text. That they were prepared to share their lives at school with us, and thus with a wider world of readers was a contribution for which we are deeply grateful.

Second, there would have been no project without the support of the Australian Education Research and Development Committee (ERDC) and its Chairman, Dr. S.S. Dunn. Case studies of the sort we were proposing (and particularly the exploration of their amalgamation) was, at the time (1979/80), both risky for us to undertake and for a national body in Australia to support with public funds. In addition, we were asking for funding in a manner that would release the three major investigators from some teaching duties so that they could undertake the time consuming case studies themselves. Despite the obvious economic advantages in this procedure it was also new ground for an Australian granting body. ERDC took this risk and found ways to account for the released function.

Since the study was completed after the work and life of ERDC had become one of the unfortunate victims of an

Foreword

indiscriminate political hatchet operation, we want not only to express our own thanks to the former members of this body, but also to record how much we believe they contributed in its short life to educational research in Australia.

The book has also enabled us to record how we undertook the study. We are grateful to our publishers for this since we believe there is a great need for a continued debate in educational research about how its products relate to their production.

Because it is about what we were doing and how we went about it, the book reports something of our own personal pilgrimages during the period of the project. Undoubtedly these would have been different had we not worked together.

As a project group we all had support from our respective institutions and we particularly thank those persons who contributed to the recording, typing and collation of the case records and the reports of the case studies that emerged from them. Special thanks goes to Ms Elaine Scott of the Faculty of Education, Monash University, whose interest and care adds much to any manuscript like ours she undertakes to prepare.

Finally, we are most grateful to a number of professional colleagues who agreed to react to aspects of our handling of the study. Lawrence Ingvarson, Paige Porter and Don Hogben acted as critical friends during the study itself. Peter Musgrave, Don Anderson and Jean Blackburn responded to the reports of the case studies.

Peter Fensham
Colin Power
Stephen Kemmis
David Tripp

Part I

Chapter 1

Introduction

The two substantive issues in this book are alienation from schooling and transition from school to the world of work and not-work. Their relevance to the social, economic and educational scene in Australia in the 1980s needs no justification. By the 1980s the unemployment among school leavers in Australia that began to increase through the mid-1970s had become an accepted feature. Alienation from schooling – a not uncommon experience for some students in any age – took on a new significance for school families and school communities when the customary 'escape route' for some disenchanted students to the world of work and the rewards of employment was cut off.

Likewise, a new phase – the transition from school to the world of work (and not-work) – had become a major concern of State and national policy makers and of some school administrators. The two topics – alienation and transition – were now of direct interest to thousands of students, their parents and teachers, and of long term concern to an Australian society unaccustomed for two generations to taking such things seriously.

The research orientation the four co-authors brought to the study of these issues is associated with the case study methodologies of persons like Stake, Stenhouse, Smith, Walker, etc. All four of us had had associations with two great centres of such research and in each of these, new but rather similar questions about the methodology were being asked during 1978.

At the Center for Instructional Research and Curriculum Evaluation at the University of Illinois, Robert Stake, Jack Easley and others were grappling with the problem of reporting a research project on the impact in schools of the curriculum projects of the National Science Foundation. The project had

Introduction

been based on eleven case studies by ten different researchers of school situations across the USA.[1] At the Centre for Applied Research in Education in the University of East Anglia, Lawrence Stenhouse and others were beginning a series of case studies in schools undergoing change in order to explore the potential of indexed case records. These sorts of research questions attracted us and influenced the shape of the project we wanted to carry out in Australian schools. The research reported in this book was thus guided by both methodological and substantive concerns.

Foremost among its *methodological* concerns are:

1 Questions about the relationship between the *case record* (the data from which a case study is prepared) and the *case study* (the 'product' of the case study research which will be used to summarize the findings and make them available to others within or outside the situation studied).
2 Questions about the amalgamation of case records and case studies into reports which might be used as bases for policy making.
3 Questions about the susceptibility of case records and case studies to independent summarization by persons not involved in the generation of the case records or the case studies.

Foremost among its *substantive* concerns are:

1 Questions about the *transition* of students from school to work.
2 Questions about the *alienation* of students in secondary school, especially in relation to an economic situation where career aspirations and job opportunities may be out of touch with one another.

While a number of hypotheses might be formulated in each of these five areas of concern, it was our intention to treat them as open-ended areas for investigation. Our understanding of the case study approach was that it works through issue identification, progressive focusing and exegesis of the situation studied. To define our hypotheses before embarking on the case studies or entering the case situations would be tantamount to pre-judging the issues and wrongly focusing the studies.

Alienation and transition

Despite the fact that alienation represents a pervasive theme in

Introduction

analyses of Australian life, understanding of its determinants and manifestations remains quite limited. Conceptualizations of alienation have been proposed from historical, philosophical, sociological and psychological perspectives; yet comparatively little research concerning the phenomenology of alienation or its amelioration in school contexts or at the school–work interface has been conducted in Australia or elsewhere.

Our interest in this project was to allow the communities of the schools in our studies to define these phenomena and the constellation of issues and events that make them up. The purpose of our study was not to check off a list of features that we, or someone else in other research, believe may be associated. A number of other Australian studies using the checklist approach were in fact underway at the same time.

To a greater or lesser degree, every high school in Australia faces the problem of coping with groups of students who reject its values, programmes and norms. Although the term 'alienation' has taken many interpretational twists, the process and the problems are real enough. In time, the enthusiasm with which a number of students begin high school turns to apathy or even uncooperative, hostile and antisocial behaviour amongst the 'toughs' and the 'stirrers' in the school.

In a society in which social acceptance, individual worth and status are largely a function of one's occupation, the problems of youth alienation are likely to be exacerbated when young people are not being helped by the society and its institutions to assume what is, to them, a meaningful and satisfying occupational role and, even worse, are being denied hope of occupying such a role.

Many studies of alienation in secondary school to date have tended to view alienation as a static phenomenon which can be measured empirically and is causally connected to other measures, e.g. of organizational structure and functioning. Such studies may provide evidence in support of some grand unifying theory but they throw little light on alienation as a process involving both teachers and students seeking to find meaning and purpose within an institutional context. If we are to understand the process, it would be helpful to have detailed case studies of the ways in which teachers are attempting (i) to grapple with the manifestations of alienation within the constraints of the classroom; (ii) to modify programmes and teaching so as to recognize the vocational aspirations of all students; (iii) to invent new programmes aimed at assisting students in the transition to work

Introduction

and (iv) to build self-respect and meaning amongst students who expect, and are likely, to be the losers in the occupational stakes. Schools need the support and help of critical friends who can help them in the diagnosis of their particular problems, in the making of judgments about strategies which might be worth trying, and in the monitoring of the consequences of the strategies decided upon. Such studies of alienation in school and of the transition to work should be of value to educators in helping them to identify problems in their present practices and to pinpoint some of the causes of these problems, as well as expanding the range of possibilities entertained in negotiating new patterns of schooling with students, parents and employers.

We were conscious in the climate of 1980 of the interest of policy and programme makers in these topics but our research was not for policy makers. It was research at the level of schools. Concerns like those of alienation and transition can look very different from the perspective of policy makers. Our interests were the concerns at the level of schools. What is good; what is bad; what is enjoyed; what don't they like; what is possible; what doesn't work; what is necessary; what are the options? As students, teachers and school administrators were studied, how do these different groups and persons answer these questions and what issues emerge from them as important? Our study was primarily to hear what the persons in three Australian high schools had to say (if anything) about these topics and to record faithfully the essence of their messages and their contexts.

Before proceeding to more detailed aspects of the project it will be useful to enlarge on the rationale for each of our methodological concerns.

Case records and case studies

Lawrence Stenhouse[2] has distinguished between *case records* and *case reports* as part of his recognition of several pressing problems that confront case study researchers as they attempt to relate their observations and their collected data to a final report. There are problems of selection of matters to include in the report: for example, these matters are inevitably drawn from a wide range which might have been so treated. There are also problems of interpretation of the data: whether participants' understandings of the situation are congruent with those of the case study worker, and whether the interpretations finally presented are credible and consistent with the range of data available. There are problems of presentation since individual fragments from the records may not adequately capture the underlying feelings or issues.

Case records are 'messy' accounts. They are unsuitable for dissemination. They may include private musings by the case study worker. They often include data about participants which cannot, for reasons of discretion, be made available to others. They are chaotic conglomerates of different kinds of data which only take on any shape through the progress of the case study worker's understanding of the case and through progressive testing of the adequacy of interpretations against the accumulating data.

The usual situation in case study research is that it is only the case report that has a disseminable form and is available to readers (or viewers) as the final outcome of the study. Because of the 'messiness' and the political sensitivity of the case record, other independent researchers are rarely given access to the original data, and hence cannot judge its reliability, the adequacy of the interpretations, or the methodological rigour of the study. This state of affairs has given rise to a certain 'unrespectability' of case study work, suggesting that the study is not subject to the usual canons of scientific inquiry and may therefore be an unreliable or untrustworthy account. Stenhouse argues, using the analogy of historical research, that this criticism is unwarranted.

Thus he suggested that case records could be indexed and stored in archives, and that other investigators on some approved basis (e.g. membership of an approved group, or after some interval when the sensitivity of the records might be expected to have diminished sufficiently) have access to the records for purposes of checking the adequacy of the study in the light of the record, or in order to explore their own interests in these data. Another suggestion is that case study workers should have 'critical friends' who have access to the case records and the developing interpretations of the case study workers as a way of 'guaranteeing' the adequacy of the study.

Both these suggestions have limitations. Archives may be difficult to keep; they pose problems about access; they make the lives of those studied the potential subjects of future histories, thus according them a status entirely out of keeping with the normal conditions of social life; and they are aggrandizing to the researchers who 'keep the keys' to the archives, giving them rights and responsibilities over the lives of others which are

Introduction

power-conferring and open to abuse. 'Critical friends' may be friends more to the researchers than to the researched. They are open to methodological or substantive 'capture' by the perspectives and interpretations of the researcher. They must be bound by the procedures governing the case study worker if they are not to become potential 'leaks' and so undermine the protection these procedures afford to those studied. Thus, the use of critical friends requires still further procedures to govern the way they act with respect to the study. They may also offer only a rhetorical 'guarantee' of the quality of the study since they cannot make the grounds for their approval or disapproval of the study open.

In the present research, attempts were made to address these questions. For the purposes of the study, the three case study workers were to attempt to share their emerging archives in the course of their work, and a 'critical friend' to each case study worker would also have access to the archives of the developing case studies. It was hoped that it would be possible to form some views about the efficacy of both kinds of procedure by critical appraisal of their effectiveness as potential 'guarantees' of the quality of the case studies generated in the course of research.

Amalgamation of case records and case studies

There are obvious difficulties in compiling either the case records or the case studies generated by different case study workers into single summarizing accounts. There are problems of lack of overlap in observers' experiences on site in their respective cases, differences in data collected, differences in interpretation, problems of accumulating apparently similar data across sites, and the like. One of the most interesting problems has to do with the 'tacit' case record – the experience of the case study worker of the situation being studied – and the way this tacit knowledge can be drawn into the open and articulated as different case study workers compare field experiences, or when the project co-ordinator has also been involved in them through a site visit.

There is a tendency among some social science researchers (positivists) to think that there is a social situation to which any observer can have only partial access. They see case records and the reports of case studies as too eclectic on the one hand and as just random fragments on the other. These are some of the reasons, perhaps, that many of these sorts of researchers find

Introduction

case studies unsatisfactory. It seems to them that case investigators bit off more of the situation than they can chew, and then have difficulty in digesting their findings into reliable and valid reports. Contrary to this view, the present investigators take the position that the meaning of social situations is always relative to their contexts and to the individuals involved. Unless acknowledgment is given to these features of the situation it will not be possible to describe or to understand what is happening. The observer in a case study accepts that he/she will not have unlimited control either over what is observed or over what can be reported. While the dimensions in which an observer may choose to begin to observe are decided by the observer (this is true for natural situations as much as it is for these two approaches to social ones), the situation which is observed is reported in terms that are the results of negotiations about what is happening in it. This means the report will itself depend upon the precise forms of the interactions between the observer and the observed, and between the observer and other observers in and around the situation (e.g. participants, sponsors, potential readers of reports).

If we accept the importance of the social negotiation of meaning, case study research poses unique and interesting challenges. In particular, there is the challenge of creating a case study which is justified by the process of the study and by its case record. Each case study worker confronts the question of what knowledge can be justified as true belief within the constraints of his/her own study. The case study worker requires a very high degree of self-critical awareness to reach the stage of reporting a case study with some confidence that the 'findings', i.e. the case study, can be justified by the research process and the evidence available.

When different case study workers research different situations with parallel 'elements' (e.g. the same concerns at stake) or when they study the same situation from their own particular perspectives, the question arises of how the resulting studies can be judged with respect to one another. There is, in principle, a test of how well justified and critically-evaluated each study is in its own terms, and there is an empirical test about the degree of overlap in findings. But non-overlapping findings pose the problem that it may not be possible to tell whether the observer's own perspective (or research strategy) or the situation is responsible for the divergence in findings. At once we find ourselves asking the positivist's question: 'Which view is more

Introduction

true of the situations?' But we have already denied ourselves this mode of resolving the problem in our methodological tenet about the social negotiation of meaning. We may make some appeals to the case records or to the observer's statements of process to discover whether the evidence seems adequate for an interpretation to have been reached, but we cannot make a final determination of the 'truth' of the findings by appeal to some 'independent' source of uncontaminated data, since we have already posited that no such independent and uncontaminated sources of data exist. (If we did have access to reality through such channels, then case study, and all other forms of research, would be unnecessary.)

The present study will also attempt to form some views about these processes. In putting case study workers together to share their studies and asking a co-ordinator to try to reach a common account of issues through accumulating findings across cases (noting common threads and themes as well as differences which appear to be due to observer perspectives, research techniques and contextual differences) we hoped it would be possible to derive some insights about the justification of findings in case study work. We were also interested to discover the extent to which other case study workers' perspectives, research techniques and situations for study can throw light on one's own, and the extent to which a particular study can be enriched and more fully justified by creating a community of inquirers working within shared frames of reference.

Independent summarization of case study material

Reference has already been made to the difficulty of amalgamating case records and case studies by those involved in their production. A further problem arises in situations where an independent person has the task of amalgamating the case material, for example, in the case where an administrator wants to reach a summary statement about some policy area given several accounts of particular situations relevant to the policy determination. (Such situations occur frequently in national (or State) agencies where it may be necessary to pool material gathered in the various States and territories (or different school types or systems) where somewhat different situations and constraints exist, or in such a situation as may be faced by the Schools Commission when it attempts to summarize learnings

Introduction

across a certain band of innovations projects, for instance.)

The current problem is this: given nothing but the case studies (or even given the case studies and part of the case record), is it possible for an independent person to write an account which does justice to the understandings of the case study workers and participants in the situations studied, and yet reaches an adequate summary position? Moreover, if such a summary is prepared with policy recommendations, as is frequently the case, are the recommendations appropriate in the light of the understandings reached by those involved in the studies?

We must recognize that the independent writer of such a summary of this kind may have a separate perspective from those in the research situation or from those that are in the situation as it exists without the case study researcher. (This is compatible with our general views that observation is always affected by the perspective of the observer, and that, hence, it is important to negotiate the meaning of situations). In other words, something may be added to the case studies themselves in reaching a summary of this sort – something which has an existence independent of the conditions of the studies themselves.

The Stake and Easley CSSE project for the American National Science Foundation also provides a model for our situation in the present investigation. Certainly the investigators in that project were aware of the policy implications of their work and of the problems of producing an executive summary which could take account of material in the case studies and the case records. We hoped it would be possible in the present investigation to subject some of these problems to more systematic critical analysis and appraisal.

Summary

In keeping with our methodological perspective of case study research, our analysis of each of the five stated concerns on page 4 was to be exegetic, allowing our understandings to unfold in the light of our observations and the issues raised. We had no doubt that we would develop insights into each of these concerns. Each would be a subject for explicit investigation and we would collect data on each in the course of the research. Each issue would be addressed during meetings of the investigatory team, and they would be reported in the methodological chapters of our publications. It was our expectation that our understanding of

Introduction

these issues would evolve in the course of the investigation. We also expected that as our understanding evolved, we would find more precise language for expressing the problems.

This state of affairs we regard as entirely 'natural' and appropriate in case study research and in critical analytical work of the kind we proposed for the project. We mention these points only because it may be thought that we were already at a stage where the problems were sufficiently well-defined and articulated for the research purpose and process for us to be simply resolving them by empirical investigation and the collection of appropriate data. On the contrary, the present study was an attempt to disclose the nature of the problems themselves, to articulate the issues involved, and to reflect critically on the issues and the methods used in the studies.

The overall design of the project

Three separate case studies were to be undertaken, one each in Victoria, South Australia, and Western Australia. Each would be by an experienced case study worker. Each case study worker would use a 'critical friend' who would have access to the case record and the case study (as it developed) and who, it was hoped, would facilitate the critical–reflective process of the 'imagination of the case and the invention of the study.'[3]

During the progress of the studies, the project team would meet together from time to time to discuss methodological points and to share their relationships with their sites, their accumulating data and their interpretative responses.

Each study was to be produced under principles of procedure designed to protect participants in the schools studied from abuse of the knowledge generated. These principles concern the independence of the case study worker, the confidentiality of data, the negotiation of boundaries of the studies, the negotiation of release of reports, and the role of the critical friend in each study. The draft of these principles that was given to the schools is attached as an Appendix to this chapter. It was initially thought that the principles to be adopted would be reached by negotiation of this draft with at least some of the participants at meetings just prior to the case study work in each site. In practice, the draft was agreed as a basis but its meaning in detail had to be negotiated with various participants from time to time during the study.

Introduction

After the initial case records had been assembled (and perhaps during the 'data-collection' phase), each case study worker was required to produce a draft case study report. This was negotiated with participants in each situation so that it could gain endorsement as a fair, relevant and accurate account of the 'case' at each site. Once having achieved participant confirmation in this way, the reports would then be released among the project team workers. This limited release paves the way for the amalgamation report. Simultaneously, the reports would be released to any independent reporters to form the basis of the summaries and responses.

In the preparation of the amalgamation report, the project co-ordinator met with the case study workers to discuss the separate studies and to begin to formulate the amalgamation report which would be written by them. This summarizing report from the project was also to be given to schools along with the case studies for the other sites.

It was hoped that several more independent persons could be found to write separate summaries of the three studies. The persons sought for this task were people experienced in policy roles, people familiar with the broad research literature on these substantive issues and people in touch with the other contemporary Australian research into the substantive concerns. Indeed, a lot of time was spent on planning an over elaborate process that hoped to involve policy-type persons in responding to the reports of the project in two stages. In practice this part of the design could not be followed through and only one of the policy responses turned out to be what we had naïvely expected.

The project team was also to report on its methodological concerns.

Some 'warts and all' of the design

The project itself began with a planning conference over three days at Phillip Island. Among the many aspects that were discussed by the project co-ordinator (P.J.F.) and the three investigators was the kind and degree of interaction that should occur between them during the project. After much argument we chose to interact primarily, as stated on page 8, about process rather than product. That is, as opportunity arose (with each other on any occasions, on site visits, at planned project discussions, with critical friends, etc.) to share the experiences

Introduction

and the problems of conducting case studies. We chose during the on-site period (extending to about nine months) not to interact very deliberately about emerging issues or other outcomes of the studies.

It is important to note that we could have chosen to interact about the product. As issues emerged in one study they could have been relayed to the other two investigators for exploration at their sites. Checks could have been made of what constituted in each site the associated constellation of factors and effects. Such comparative case studies would be interesting ones to undertake in multiple sites, but they would constitute a very different project from our own.

The schools and 'being there'

In choosing schools for the studies we decided that they should be government co-educational high schools of reasonable size that were not obviously undergoing major change or innovation for purposes which might overshadow our interests. Each investigator followed the customary procedures for his State. In Western Australia Greenfield school was suggested by the Research Division of the State Department of Education. Addison Hills was approached directly by the investigator who knew something of the school through an earlier contact of a colleague. At Purdah, the investigator had had a previous association with the school and his re-entry was also supported by the South Australian Education Department.

Each of the schools was primarily a 'local' school drawing the great majority of its students from the community of families who lived in a defined geographical area. Addison Hills, because of the Victorian binary system of high and technical schools, did not have all the students of this district. Each school had to take all the post-primary students in their area except for the few who went to non-government schools (or the technical school in the Victorian case).

The formal cues that the schools were given by their investigators about the projects' intentions can be read in the Appendix to this chapter. It may also assist readers as they turn to the reports of the case studies in Chapters 2, 3 and 4.

As mentioned earlier this document for the schools was not just an explanation of the project. It was also a contract that set out the terms of the project, and it was on these that powers in

Introduction

the schools – principals, teachers or councils – decided whether to allow the study to proceed. Although it was undoubtedly read by a number of the adult participants at this point of entry to the school, many subsequent participants including all the students would have had only an oral statement from the case investigator rather than this contractual document. Case study researchers place a considerable emphasis on negotiating terms and rights of persons in their studies. When whole schools are involved the usual procedures like those in this project are biased against students being accorded the same status as the adult participants such as principals, teachers or council members.

The project co-ordinator also wrote directly to each principal stressing the project's overall or national perspective and offering himself as an external reference point if any difficulties arose between a school and its investigator.

It was planned that the co-ordinator would also visit each site briefly at a point when the study had progressed suitably and at the convenience of the school. In fact, site visits were made only to Greenfield and Addison Hills. The planned visit to Purdah was postponed, then cancelled when conditions at the school reached a state that made the continued presence of the project on-site unhelpful. During the two site visits, the schools were observed and short interviews were held with the principal, a number of teachers and some students in several classes.

On the one hand, the site visits by the co-ordinator provided proof to the schools of the project's wider existence. On the other hand they also provided some proof that the schools of the studies did exist and that the studies were in fact taking place.

In operation in their schools, the three investigators had very different styles and they were, no doubt, perceived differently. Colin Power was carrying out a study at Purdah (South Australia) that, to some extent, was based on a familiar and understandable process. He was interviewing large numbers of students from whom answers to questions were presumably being sought – traditional and customary practices of educational research. Stephen Kemmis at Addison Hills (Victoria) was much more low key and confusing – chatting here and there rather than anything that would seem like systematic interviewing or the obvious collection of data. David Tripp seemed to have an agenda at Greenfield (Western Australia) and its members were aware that they were data providers and in some cases data analysts as well. His use of the word processor to feed back rapidly conversations or descriptions confronted the teachers with themselves. Thus

Introduction

there was a co-optive element in David's approach that could disturb in a way the other two styles did not. His teachers no longer gave opinions that disappeared into the usual anonymity of research. Their words and behaviour came back as the base for the next interaction with this new sort of researcher. The initial agreement to participate turned out to be more than they probably expected. A few then contracted out but to do this again meant a confrontation of an uncustomary type.

Colin Power also had a share of the problems of 'being there', but unlike at Greenfield these had little to do directly with the case study or his style of carrying it out. Purdah was going through a tense period in its own life and Colin and the continuation of his study in the school became victims of that.

The site visits provided some direct contact with two of these styles. The apparently casual contacts with the adults and the students at Addison Hills contrasted with a certain formality of contact at Greenfield and the pressure that David Tripp's co-optive arrangements exerted there. On the day of the site visit to Greenfield one of the vice-principals plucked up the courage to say he did not wish to discuss one of the word-processed transcripts nor to be involved any further in the study.

Critical friending

To explore the idea of critical friends in case study research to which we have already referred, each case investigator identified and enrolled a colleague who was interested. Two of these, Lawrence Ingvarson with Stephen Kemmis, and Don Hogben with Colin Power, had also experienced their nurturing within the close family of researchers at Urbana and Norwich. Paige Porter with David Tripp was well aware of case studies from literature and discussions with exponents of the method. We hoped that these persons would support the investigators in their uncertain, insecure and often embarrassing work, as well as being an external reference for the sieving of data that otherwise may have been in danger of distortion and loss because of the vagaries of the researchers' best intentions and worst prejudices.

Our experience of the role has a sweet and sour flavour. Each partnership was different because the six people are very individualistic. Each had his own research style and had the critical friends been the investigators they would have approached the study differently. So we were likely to re-enact the contemporary debate in research circles about the fact that the case study method not only allows but may even encourage this intrusion of the person into the research process.

It had been agreed in the original planning that the particular aspects of critical friending that we hoped to explore would be best served if the critical friends interacted only with the investigator, his data and his response to them and to their gathering. That is, the critical friends would not visit the sites or accompany the investigator as he observed classes or conducted interviews. We were not using them to validate data or to be part of its triangulation.

Stephen Kemmis's low key entry to Addison Hills was essentially untraumatic and although he did not record large amounts of the data he collected, he quickly began to reflect on what he observed and heard. Since he did not overtly intrude this on his participants, there was little to discuss with Lawrence Ingvarson about the dynamics of 'being there'. Their meetings were about the transformation of data to issues and how best these could be communicated.

David Tripp had a more complex entry to Greenfield and as has been mentioned, his research style involved a contentious process of data sharing with the teachers. 'Being there' was to an extent always problematic and Paige Porter was used by him as a support for it. The sorting and interpretation of data was also active from early on in the contact with the school, so there was always an agenda for meetings with the critical friend.

Compared with these two approaches, Colin Power's style of research led to a greater separation between data collection and its interpretation and analysis. While he was at the site he was basically collecting data by processes that produced them in large quantities of words. His problem of 'being there' was not directly related to his project so also did not generate the need to interact with his critical friend. Don Hogben was engaged by Colin only during the analysis stage of his overall investigation and by that time the bank of data to be checked from interviews and observations was overawing for anyone other than its author. For Colin, it was still at a formative stage. To Don it seemed like a summative task and his interest in the role had been a more formative one. They thus found little about which they could usefully react with mutual satisfaction.

For each of the pairs, finding time to meet turned out to be difficult even when the intention and wish to do so existed. Thanks to the co-operation of ERDC, the research granting

Introduction

body, some functional release from regular responsibilities was available to the investigators for their studies. Despite this, the case studies were done over a number of months in 1980 and into 1981 as just one activity among a number that engaged all the project team during its lifetime. When David and Stephen had visited their schools and were eager to talk something over, their critical friends' programmes usually made such a meeting not possible.

So two pairs functioned to some extent but much less than we originally envisaged. The critical friends met together in November 1980 and a week later the whole team spent a number of hours together discussing the project and how its progress might best be presented at the conference of the Australian Association for Educational Research.[4]

Lawrence Ingvarson and Paige Porter also participated in the second project conference at Phillip Island in 1981 and they were a great help to our confidence as the reports of the studies began to take shape. These long exchanges together, twice at Phillip Island, and on four or five other occasions throughout the project enabled us all to grow a little taller in our understanding of this sort of research, the skills it involves and the articulation of its processes.

Prologue

The looseness (not sloppiness) of our type of case study research has raised many questions about it. Is it worthwhile? Does it contribute things that other research approaches do not? Does its depth make up for its lack of extent?

Without the commitment to a very explicit design, and the absence of the press of 'gathering in the sample', we found we were freer to join in this critique as well. Our answers beyond those that speak to our inner selves are set out in the reports themselves (Chapters 2, 3 and 4), in the amalgamation (Chapter 5) and in the methodology (Chapters 9 and 10). These are what we wish to share with others. Readers will be free to find from them their own answers to the questions.

As a further contribution to this discussion we invited a number of others to write down their response to the three case studies. We are grateful to all these persons and pleased to include some of them in this book – in Chapters 6-8.

In Chapter 6, Ms Jean Blackburn, a member of the Australian

Introduction

Schools Commission from its inception in late 1972 until 1981, responds to the three case studies from that extensive experience of policy formulation and implementation. In Chapter 7, Peter Musgrave, Professor of Education and former Dean in the Faculty of Education at Monash University, reviews the three case studies from the perspective of social research into schools and schooling. In Chapter 8, Dr Don Anderson, Professorial Fellow in the School of Social Sciences at the Australian National University, compares the studies to other Australian studies on the two substantive concerns. He directs the National Clearing House for research into these two fields.

The book thus has three parts. In Part I the project is introduced and its three studies reported (Chapters 1-4). In Part II there are four responses to the studies, one from within the project by its co-ordinator and three by outsiders using different perspectives (Chapters 5-8). Finally in Part III the project team reports on its experiences and on the methodological concerns of the project (Chapters 9-10).

Notes

1 *Case Studies in Science Education*, CIRCE and the Committee on Culture and Cognition, University of Illinois, Urbana-Champaign, 1978.
2 L. Stenhouse. 'Case study and case records: Towards a contemporary history of education', *British Education Research Journal*, 4(2), pp.21-40, 1978.
3 S. Kemmis, 'The Imagination of the Case and the Invention of the Study', in H. Simons (ed.), *Towards a Science of the Singular*, Occasional Publication No. 10, Centre for Applied Research in Education, University of East Anglia, Norwich, 1980.
4 P.J. Fensham *et al.* 'A Report on the Case Studies of Alienation from School', pp.512-29 in *Youth, Schooling and Unemployment*, the proceedings of the annual conference of the Australian Association for Research in Education, Sydney, November 1980.

Appendix – The account of the project for the participating schools

Alienation from schooling
A Research Project funded by the National Educational Research and Development Committee

Many schools in Australia and in similar countries overseas find that a number of their students, around the school leaving age, lose interest in study and become disillusioned with schooling. 'Bored with school', 'turned-off learning', 'crapped off with teachers', and 'year-10 blues' are commonly heard. In their turn, such students raise teaching and curriculum problems for the teachers and administrators of schools and school systems. Some schools seem to manage to minimize these problems whereas in others they become acute, leading to disruptive and difficult behaviour from students and loss of morale and the sense of effectiveness among teachers.

Until the last few years, these conditions were largely of a temporary nature because students suffering them, in due course either 'escaped' from school into a new phase of living in a job, or found a new zest for learning in the final levels of schooling or in vocational studies. The serious contraction of employment opportunities for school leavers tends to differentially affect the students who most experience this 'alienation' from education.

Transition from school to employment is now not an alternative pathway of personal development for a large number of these students, and they are now staying on at school despite their sense of estrangement from its teaching and learning activities.

This study is an attempt to focus on this phenomenon of 'alienation from schooling' and how it occurs and is dealt with in a school community. It is one of three parallel studies being carried out in 1980 in Western Australia, South Australia, and Victoria. Each of the studies will be of a school that is set within its own community and is part of a particular State system of education.

The purpose of the study is not to map the extent of the problems nor to attempt comparisons of how schools in the same system cope with them. It is rather to describe as fully as

Introduction

possible, in the time available, the phenomenon in the particular context of each of the schools. We are thus *not* concerned with choosing a 'representative' school *nor* with choosing three schools in a system for comparison. Three States are involved because a group of us in these States is interested and experienced in using the research methods for such descriptive case studies and because these methods seem particularly appropriate for the study of school alienation.

The primary aims of the study are to produce the three individual Case Reports. Secondary ones are to draw what lessons we can from the common methodology and to see to what extent there appear to be, at a broad level, issues and contextual factors that are recurring themes in the descriptions.

The secondary aims will be reported in an Amalgamation Report and an Executive Summary. The former will seek to report the cumulative experience of the three case studies and to provide a richer account of the issues involved. The latter will be more concerned with policies relating to alienation that could be proposed at both the local school and wider levels. In this way all three sets of reports may be useful examples of the bases on which existing policies and practices (school and wider ones) can be reviewed or new ones can be established.

Methods of the project

The case study approach is being employed rather than survey analysis or experimental research approaches. This is because the researchers wish to understand the nature of school alienation as it exists in a school. This phenomenon is not yet adequately understood for us to depend upon survey analysis or the other techniques as the basis for describing or explaining it. In short, case study may help us to define the problems and issues related to school alienation in the real life context of individual schools whereas the contemporary general conceptualizations of it may constrain this definition.

Several advantages of case study work lead us to prefer it for this investigation:

1 It places great importance on the perspectives of participants (teachers, students, school administrators, etc.) rather than the theoretically-derived perspectives of the observers in reaching definitions of the phenomenon.

Introduction

2 It can draw upon and distil the language, ideas and interpretations of participants in its process and reports, rather than use and develop the specialist language of the researchers.

3 Unlike some other forms of research, the case study process offers many formal and informal opportunities for participants to have a substantive input into the study, shaping its conduct and content.

4 Case study work is interpretative, but the interpretations of the case study worker are chastened by those of participants. It involves face-to-face negotiation of meanings between the researcher and the researched.

5 The methods of case study allow the researcher to work with participants in coming to grips with the constraints, opportunities and circumstances of particular school contexts; case studies are less likely to focus on an ideal world (outside the practicalities of real situations) or on an abstract realm of *all* schools in *all* times.

6 Case study methods may generate insights into school situations which can be fed back into the schools; one criterion of their quality is their recognizability to participants as accounts of the school situation; another is their utility for participants as 'food for thought' about the particular issues faced by particular schools in particular contexts. If case study workers are reclaiming meanings from the experience of participants, they are also claiming that the insights gathered or formulated will feed further reflection within the schools.

7 Case study work does not depend on standardized research techniques. It employs informal interviews, informal observation, document analysis and participatory experience in the setting, as some of its primary data-gathering techniques. The data is refined by 'triangulation' (cross-checking between perspectives, data-sources, circumstances and times) and processes of *negotiation* by which participants may check the fairness, relevance, and accuracy of the researchers' accounts.

Introduction

Personnel

The investigative team consists of

(i) Co-ordinator, Professor Peter Fensham (Monash University), who will visit each site once during its study, and who is responsible for the Summary report;

(ii) Dr David Tripp (Murdoch), Dr Stephen Kemmis (Deakin), and Professor Colin Power (Flinders) who will carry out the individual studies and together compile the Amalgamated report;

(iii) Dr Paige Porter (Murdoch), Mr Lawrence Ingvarson (Monash) and Dr Don Hogben (Flinders) who will act as 'critical friends' for the three case study investigators.

The case study worker will spend about two days per week in the participating schools over about a term, or an equivalent number of days in a more intensive period.

The 'critical friends' to the case study workers will help to ensure that the school case studies are justified in two senses: first, in terms of the relationship between interpretation and evidence (do the interpretations stand up to critical scrutiny?), and second, in terms of the ethics or politics of the research (how disruptive is the study? Is it fair to participants *vis-à-vis* the researchers? Does it protect and fairly represent those studied when it is more widely reported?).

Involvement in the project

In order to clarify what is undoubtedly a difficult and complex problem the case study researcher needs to gain access to the individuals in a school community with direct experience and/or insights into the problem. In order to do this, the case study researcher obtains information from representatives from all groups in the school community, and in a variety of different ways. The collection of this information, checking the interpretation of events and perspectives, and negotiation of what is to appear in reports take time. Members of the school community (teachers, administrators, pupils, etc.) will be approached to participate in the following ways:

Introduction

(a) interviews: staff and students will be approached to give their views of the nature, causes, and strategies for the amelioration of school alienation. Each interview will generally take from half to three-quarters of an hour. The number of interviews will vary depending on the interest and involvement of staff and students;

(b) observations: the researchers would like to be able to observe or to tape (audio and/or video) classes and other settings (e.g. background) in the school. Field notes and tapes will be used largely as a stimulus for an exploration of alienation phenomena. Teachers will have an opportunity to explain their strategies for overcoming problems of alienation, and to discuss with the researcher the reactions of students;

(c) records and meetings: the researchers also need to be able to give an account of the development of school policy dealing with issues arising out of problems of alienation. Therefore, they will negotiate with school personnel access to records and meetings where such issues are discussed.

The extent of involvement for any individual will vary according to the willingness of the individual concerned to be interviewed, observed, or to release documents, and the experience of the teacher or pupil with respect to the issues being addressed.

Participation rights

At each stage of the project the researchers will be obliged to explain fully to participants the nature of the co-operation required, and the possible costs and benefits to them. Teachers and students have the right on this basis to choose not to participate in the study or, having initially agreed to participate, to withdraw.

Given that there will be three forms of reporting in addition to the basic case records, the rights of participators in relation to all these need to be explained.

A   The *Case Records* will be available only to the researchers and critical friends. Participants will have the right to see those sections of the case record in which interviews with

Introduction

them or observations of their lessons are recorded, but to no other sections of the record.

B *Case Studies* contain the researchers' interpretation of the ways in which teachers in general and the school as a whole have responded to problems of alienation and school-to-work transition. Because the researcher's values influence the shape of his account, the content and release of the case study are open to negotiation. Where individuals or groups in the school disagree with the way in which the researcher has interpreted the situation, either that conflicting interpretations on a given issue exist will be acknowledged in the report, or the school and the researcher will negotiate a mutually acceptable way of presenting the issue. In the released form of the case study, the degree of anonymity will be open to negotiation.

C The *Amalgamated Record and Summary* will be made available to the school community for comment and feedback prior to its release.

Benefits to your school

Benefits will accrue to the school, its staff, and pupils in two ways: first there are the general benefits of the activities of the project itself, and second there are the benefits of reports on currently important issues.

With regard to the first, there is immediate benefit for the image of the school in the local community simply in that it will be seen to be actively participating in national research on problems of public concern. In the school the researcher, by talking to staff, can help people to clarify their own ideas and sharpen their perceptions. Also, through talking with a number of different staff the researcher can act as an initiator and facilitator of inter-staff dialogue, helping to communicate individual concerns.

Schools will have the benefits of three reports, one being their own case study, the others containing the cumulated experience of the three case studies. The researchers are anxious to help the schools use the reports effectively in the formulation of policies which will ameliorate alienation amongst students continuing at the school, and help those students likely to encounter difficulties on leaving.

Introduction

The school report itself will help by offering an analysis of the current situation, but it is also hoped that staff will take up an invitation for further discussion of the document later in the year, for the formulation of policy options and strategies of action. Such discussions could be the focus of staff in-service activities.

Chapter 2

Greenfield
A case study of schooling, alienation and employment
David H. Tripp

Forethought

> *Julia:* He was very clever at repairing clocks; And he has a remarkable sense of hearing – The only man I ever met who could hear the cry of bats.
> *Peter:* Hear the cry of bats?
> *Julia:* He could hear the cry of bats.
> *Celia:* But how do you know he could hear the cry of bats?
> *Julia:* Because he said so. And I believed him.
>
> T.S. Eliot *The Cocktail Party*, I.1.

Introduction

In this study the researcher was one of the participants, one who collaborated with the school staff to realize the primary methodological aim of the study, namely, to present participants' views to their satisfaction. Negotiation was the means of collaboration, and the way this was agreed is shown in Appendix 1, but briefly it took place in the following manner. First we met to discuss the issues and I wrote a report of that discussion. That report was then discussed and the second discussion similarly reported. This process continued until we were satisfied that the report was an accurate statement of our ideas and the way in which we had put them. Thus we collaboratively found areas of consensus and conflict, agreeing to differ where the latter could not be resolved. This cycle of negotiation was the prime driving force of the study as participants were forced to clarify ideas, to reconsider their statements, and particularly to try to resolve the contradictions which always seem to emerge in a wide ranging discussion.

This way of working produces what I call 'jointly authored statements' and these form the bulk of the data of the study. Although I did the drafting, other participants redrafted passages themselves or told me what changes they wished to make. These statements should not be seen either as transcripts of discussions or as written statements: they lie somewhere between. There is implicit in each statement something of their being. 'Not what we said, and not what we'd have written' but, 'What we're prepared to have written about what we said'.

In these statements we have quoted our 'tidied' speech where we feel we have said things forcefully or lucidly, otherwise we simply paraphrased the main points. Where subsequent negotiation altered what we originally wrote, we rewrote the statement so that the amendments are not visible. However, sometimes in our amendments we provided new information or disagreed with a point we wished to retain. In these cases we retained the original and inserted the subsequent amendment. The descriptive introductions for the staff were not negotiated but were selected from my own personal impressions.

My original idea was simply to present the jointly authored statements as the case study but two considerations intervened. One problem was sheer length: the combined statements ran to some 50,000 words. The other problem was that I wanted to say things about the issues which would not only have been submerged by negotiated discussion, but would also have been placed in a misleading context. They would have appeared to have arisen during discussion rather than arising from my subsequent analysis of the written statements. So my analysis was not negotiated, though participants were given the opportunity to comment upon it (Appendix 3).

The point of the analysis is not to summarize the main points of the joint statements, for summary is inimical to portrayal. To collate 'the facts of the case' is to decontextualize them whereas portrayal demands description in context. Negotiation produces carefully worked 'artifacts', and I would have liked to maintain their integrity by presenting each in its entirety. As this was not possible, I have indicated where dictates of length required cuts to be made in this report by a row of dashes, – – – –
and readers should note that this final editing was not negotiated

with the participants concerned as it occurred over a year after the original sitework.

The criteria by which I selected what to include in this report were first, relevance to the issues themselves or the context of the issues or the discussions. Second, whether they reflected upon, or were reflected in, my analysis of the case or reflected upon my analysis of the case. So what the reader is presented with is all the information which I thought to be relevant to the focus of the study, and an account of my analysis of it. So my analysis should be seen as additional to the jointly authored statements, not as an abbreviated substitute for them, and the reader should place my analysis alongside the joint statements as a personal statement from the researcher.

The way in which the data were collected also affected the final form of the study. Whereas I invariably used a tape recorder for my interviews with staff and my lesson observations, I seldom used a tape recorder when talking to pupils individually. This is one reason why the bulk of the data included here is from the school staff, rather than the pupils. Also, the method of negotiation itself was more appropriate to members of staff than pupils, and in this respect the study tended to proceed with the initiative coming from the staff: their statements were checked with pupil viewpoints rather than the other way around. The occasions where the reverse was true were lesson observations where I tended to collect comments from pupils which I subsequently asked staff to comment upon. Thus it is that this case study essentially expresses the viewpoints of the teaching staff and my commentary upon them. The study should perhaps therefore be subtitled: teachers' perceptions of the problem.

This was not my original intention, but because of the difficulty of meeting the same students on a number of different occasions, it was much harder to pursue particular points with individual students over a period. Exceptions were when I casually talked with pupils during lessons, but I managed to speak to some students (particularly those I saw regularly in Year 10 Social Studies) in other subject lessons, and I maintained contact with them over most of the year. I tended to paraphrase the input of their comments in my notebook at the end of the lesson, rather than to try to get down verbatim quotes, which accounts for the relatively sparse direct quotation from students in this study.

Readers may approach this study in different ways. They may read my summary and check both their and my understanding by reading the participants' statements and other data; they may

David H. Tripp

read the data to form a personal analysis, which may then be checked against mine. Either way, an index has been provided to enable the reader to quickly locate relevant passages in the data. Thus a possible third way of reading the study would be by using the index to access particular topics in the data, though this is not recommended as a sole reading as it would decontextualize the issues.

There are, of course, a number of issues and problems relating to the question of the method and procedures of the study, most important of which is the school's response to the report (Appendix 3). Apart from those discussed above, I have drawn attention to some others in the notes, and in a separate methodological paper.[1]

Greenfield: the case-study school

As I guaranteed the school anonymity it was very difficult to write an accurate description of the school and its locality without thus exposing the school to identification by readers who are either familiar with the area or with the school itself. Thus, I have limited myself to a very broad outline.

First, an important feature of the school is that it is located in what has traditionally been a working-class area. A sizeable minority of the pupils come from Housing Commission flats and houses, which is indicative of the low incomes and social problems associated with the area. Another sizeable minority of the school's population comes from migrant families, only just over half the pupils coming from families where both parents were born in Australia. The predominant countries of immigration are Britain and Italy. The school has about 900 students and numbers have been fairly stable over the past few years.

Second, both staff and pupils are acutely aware of the effects of the poor quality of the buildings, and of the difficult conditions under which they have to work (such as noise from other classes, and traffic) which affect the morale of the school. A second problem with the school buildings themselves is that they are so designed that the administration is at one end of the building complex, which is laid out in a traditional grid, thus isolating the further reaches of the school from the school office, canteen and staff room. The result is that there is greatly reduced staff presence in the farther parts, and that students and staff often have to walk the length of the school in order to see someone or carry a message.

The school was not chosen by the researcher, but was suggested by the Department of Education. It was, however, a wise selection in view of the topic investigated, and the extremely cooperative, frank and interested staff.

The data: Section 1
Some pupils' views

This section is composed of some of the comments made by pupils which I managed to tape record or to write verbatim into my notes. Some of them I have commented on, but many are self-explanatory. Two other sections of pupils' comments follow, one an edited transcript of a discussion about a videotape I made of a Social Studies lesson, the other extracts from a discussion with a small group of the School Council.

As the presence of a tape recorder or notebook seemed to inhibit conversation I abandoned them both early in the study, preferring to make notes afterwards. I also found that the more formal class discussion did not work. On three occasions I took over a class without the presence of the teacher, but found it was not possible to establish an open atmosphere in the brief space of a lesson, in a school classroom, with myself obviously in the role of a teacher, leading the discussion. Twice also I attempted small group discussion but found pupils so unused to being left alone and responsible for their own group discussion that I abandoned that technique too. What I have presented here, therefore, is some of the relatively small amount of pupil discussion which was recorded verbatim.

Able pupils

The pupils had been given a duplicated map of a country and told to colour in the areas of high, medium and low population density. This task took most pupils the whole of a double lesson, mainly according to the observer's interpretation, because the pupils in this class were allowed to socialize whilst working. I called this style, 'Music While You Work' because the continual movement and interchange pupil-to-pupil and pupils-to-teacher seemed to make an otherwise boring task enjoyable.

Such a situation, however, was thought likely to be a source of dissatisfaction amongst the more able pupils. Two groups of pupils were interviewed during the lesson and, in particular, it was two girls who enjoyed and were good at Science who said that they liked the Social Studies teacher but hated the subject. These pupils saw what happened in Social Studies as a function of heterogeneous grouping (it was the 'dumbos' who stopped the teacher doing anything worthwhile with them).

Two comments revealed their basic dissatisfactions: 'You can't get anything done' and 'There's only boring stuff to do'. Questioning about the first comment revealed that the able pupils felt that they were being disadvantaged by the casual friendliness of the social interaction in the class in that they were not going to receive good Achievement Certificate results if they were not made to work hard. They felt that other pupils in other classes would do more work and thus have the edge on them. This they contrasted sharply with their Science and Mathematics teaching, where they felt they knew where they were.

The second comment revealed the lack of extension of ability in the work set, which (and the observer saw little to contradict it) they said was what the basic students were also expected to do. Although the former of these two points was not necessarily true, it undoubtedly had an effect on the second, which means in effect that they were being alienated by the sense of frustration engendered by the lack of worthwhile learning.

Basic pupils

The teacher writes on the blackboard:

> 'A man buys a suit marked at $55.
> He is given a discount of 20%.
> (i) Find the discount.
> (ii) What does he actually pay for the suit?'

The teacher works out the problem on the blackboard, speaking each part of the working out as he writes it:

> *Teacher:* ' . . . so I change the 20% to .20, and multiply by 55 . . . '
> *Pupil:* (When the teacher finishes) 'Does it matter if you change the $55 (to .55), and multiply by 20?'
> *Teacher:* 'You always change the percent, not the money, right?'

The answer was not unreasonable, but it was not an answer to the question asked. Obviously it would not make any difference which number of the sum were divided by 100, and it would seem likely that the pupil who asked the question was near to having, or did actually have, a genuine insight into the nature of the

David H. Tripp

process about which he was seeking further understanding or confirmation. The student was in fact asking a question of a high cognitive order, but the reply he received was of the lowest.

Furthermore, it is quite clear to the student what he is supposed to do (to stop thinking about what he is doing, not to ask questions about it, and to do what he is told) although it was not said in so many words, and the teacher's tone was kindly, almost patient.

At the risk of over-analysis, there are a number of possible factors aggravating alienation here. First, there is the teacher's (not unfounded) low opinion of his pupils' ability. Behind his answer to the pupil who asked if it was the same to change the money rather than the percentage would seem to lie the idea that if this (unable) pupil would only concentrate on learning an operative version of the discount algorithm, then he would at least stand a chance in the exam; but if he is going to spend time looking for other (less correct) ways of doing the same thing, he will confuse himself, and if he (the teacher) gave a full answer to the pupil's question, the rest of the class would be as confused as he is. Talking to the teacher after the lesson, he had this to say:

> It's as much retention as an ability problem. It's not that we haven't taught them things like multiplication; we do, we teach them multiplication over and over again, and they can do it; but come back next week and they've forgotten again. You just have to carry on with those who can.
>
> Take these problems we were doing today. I've already done it twice with them, and now we're doing it again because they'll need to be able to do it for their exam. But even if they could all do it now, in a fortnight only half of them still could. You just have to do the same things over and over again, and hope that some of it sticks so they can do something in the exam. That's all we do now, just revise stuff we've already done, and hope they can remember it for long enough.

The above kind of opinion was expressed by different staff, but it can only be criticized in terms of the underlying assumptions: namely that there should be an examination; that the examination should emphasize such things as discount algorithms, and that algorithms are best learned for examinations as rote procedures. Given these assumptions the teacher was doing a good job: he was not allowing the students to become confused with reasons for dividing by 100, but told them simply to remember to move the decimal point on the percentage; so the sad response to the only interesting question asked during the whole lesson inevitably follows those assumptions.

In general, the teacher feels he has little choice in the matter, because to change the content and style of his teaching would mean changing the system, and without such change he sees no need to change himself when such a change would lessen his effectiveness within the present system. Hence, the comment by another member of the Maths staff that, '. . . concrete activities are no good for teaching theory . . .' also makes sense. And this is the point: it is more pertinent to criticize individual teachers for lack of effort to change the system than to criticize the teaching of individuals: their teaching is more a product of the system (as indeed they themselves are), than their own free choice even when the manner in which they teach is likely to exacerbate the alienation of the less able pupils.

Relevance I

Pupil 1: It's all the same, you just learn nothing.
Pupil 2: You just learn about Perth, . . . [suburb], Australia, and that, nothing interesting.
DHT: Haven't you learnt about America?
Pupil 1: I want to go to the US.
Pupil 2: Yeah, Disneyland.
DHT: What else would you like to see?
Pupil 2: Dunno. What else is there?

Values teaching

The lesson consisted of a duplicated sheet of questions for the pupils to fill in. The topic was the sports carnival the previous Friday. After the forms had been filled in, the teacher moved on to a discussion of their points.

Several things emerged from the discussions: First, the teacher was overtly didactic in the lesson, ensuring that certain points were made. To do this he used the usual question and answer technique in which he selected the 'right' answers. That is not to say that he did not let everyone make the points they wished to; he simply praised some answers more than others, and went on questioning until someone produced the one he wished to hear and comment upon.

David H. Tripp

For example:

> *Teacher:* Why do runners run, do you think? What makes them take part?
> *Pupil 1:* It's to try themselves out.
> *Teacher:* To compete, you mean, to see how well they do?
> *Pupil 2:* Thrills.
> *Teacher:* For thrills? Because it's fun? Yes, or just for the enjoyment. Anything else?
> [Pause]
> *Teacher:* Well, I think it's also because it's important just to take part, to do your best. But there's something else too. Yes?
> *Pupil 1:* So you can see how good you are?
> *Teacher:* Well yes, but it's also so others can see how good you are. It's an opportunity for those who are good at it to display their ability. That's important to them. You can display your ability if you're clever in class, and the carnival enables those who are perhaps not clever in class to show that they are good at other things.
> *Pupil 3:* What if you aren't clever and you're not good at sports either?
> *Teacher:* Then you should watch and support those who are. That's why everyone has to go to the carnival.

Quite clearly points are being made which have nothing whatsoever to do with English, the 'discussion' is used as a platform for inculcation of certain attitudes. It is interesting to note that whereas in at least one other subject area staff expressed the idea that it was in English that the aim of passing on middle-class values was most vehemently rejected, it was in fact in such English classes that it was most explicitly pursued.

With regard to the question of alienation, there are a number of messages likely to be rejected by the pupils in such a lesson. First, there is only the pretence of discussion: it is in fact semantically a monologue in which the teacher so controlled pupil comments that only one 'voice' came through.

Second, pupil 3 would hardly be pleased with the answer to his question which in effect expressed the feelings of the class, some of whom had absented themselves from the carnival, an action which appeared to be the trigger for the topic and direction of the discussion.

Third, the larger question as to whether the topic was useful or perceived to be worthwhile by the pupils, is perhaps more important than the way in which the class was conducted. A teacher in English classes has the whole world of literature to pass on, or the chance to develop the innate abilities of his pupils to express themselves and to develop ideas. With such a multitude of possible learnings (which the pupils will never encounter unless in their English classes), what makes the teacher devote thirty-five minutes to an expression of his reasons for attending an event that many pupils quite clearly found boring and irrelevant?

Developing attitudes

> Chris came into the department staffroom saying,
> 'Julie Jones says her Dad's going to come down here tomorrow and break both my arms and legs!'
> Interested chorus of 'Why, what've you done to her?'
> 'I told them to do nine of the twelve questions for homework and she did all twelve, so I took a mark off her score'.
> In response to general censorship, he replied, 'Well, it'll teach her a lesson. When she does the exam she'll have to do exactly what she's told. She won't forget that now'.

Relevance II

On working out the relationship between house prices and the age and location of suburbs:

> *DHT:* Didn't you find all that interesting and useful?
> *Pupil:* Useful if you want to buy a house.

Boredom

The students enter the classroom very quietly, sit down, and get out their books without any interpersonal communication. The teacher begins the lesson without any words at all: he simply turns to the blackboard when the class is still and writes on it:

1 Find:
 15% of $25
 = 0.15 × $25
 = $3.75

He speaks as he writes . . . 'Change the fifteen to point one five . . . '. The students are then asked to copy it down and work it out in their books. When the teacher thinks adequate time has elapsed, he asks a student the answer. Receiving the correct answer, the teacher asks if anyone had a different answer. Several hands go up, and he says: 'Well, here's another one for those who didn't get it', and he blackboards another like the first.

Staff–pupil relations

>   *Pupil:* He's a real . . . I used to like [school subject] but now we've got him, I always try not to go.
>   *DHT:* But I thought you said he was great at camp . . . was real fun, and sang songs, and things . . .
>   *Pupil:* At camp, yeah, great, but I hate him in lessons.

Relevance III

This conversation in a Maths class was with a boy I had interviewed earlier in another class. He could do discount problems, and seemed pleased to be able to do so, although he had not got them all right.

>   *DHT:* You can do this, can't you. Not easy is it?
>   *Pupil:* Not bad at Maths.
>   *DHT:* Do you enjoy it, Maths?
>   *Pupil:* It's O.K. Teaches you how to do things.
>   *DHT:* It's useful to you, is it, to be able to work out discount?
>   *Pupil:* Dunno.
>   *DHT:* Well, say you're buying something in a shop and there's a sale on, you can work out what you'd have to pay for things.
>   *Pupil:* Not like this though.
>   *DHT:* What do you mean?
>   *Pupil:* Well, you kind of know, don't you, how much it is if it's 10 per cent off, or 25 per cent off, you get to know.
>   *DHT:* But isn't it useful to be able to check it?
>   *Pupil:* Not necessary, you always work it out on the till, that shows you.
>   *DHT:* What do you mean, you work it out on the till?
>   *Pupil:* Like at Kentucky Fried. I work there, and they give

you a discount off your food. Just the food, not the cans and things, too many of them disappear. You put it into the till and the discount, and it works it out for you and writes out the ticket.

Once again the impossible task of making school-work relevant.

Work experience

I was discussing the General Studies course with a group of year 11 pupils when the following exchange took place:

Pupil 1: I wanted to learn something useful, you know, something what might get me a job, or a better certificate anyway.
Pupil 2: Yeah, I came back because I wanted to learn more. I got an Achievement Certificate, but in Maths we just do what we did last year, and there's no point in it.
Pupil 3: And Science. In Science all we do is look through the newspapers for jobs. I didn't come back to get a job, I could look through the newspapers at home.
Pupil 2: Yeah, and then he [the Science teacher] thinks it's a good idea if we all go off and do more work experience. It's just work, y'know, not paid properly or anything.
Pupil 3: He asked me what kind of a job I'd like, and I said motor mechanic. He said he had a mate with a wrecker's yard. It was miles away. I didn't want to work then, I wanted to learn. But that's it about this place, you want to learn and they make you find jobs, and that's what they think of you, y'know, wrecker and all that. I want to be a motor mechanic, repair things. He said, 'O.K., you go to the wreckers then'.

Ears

'You don't listen to teachers . . . not if it's not about your lessons'.

Relevance IV

The second half of this lesson was an exercise in filling out an application for a driving licence form. The question of relevance was foregrounded by the fact that the teacher did not reproduce the form which the pupils would actually have to fill in, but took the one which was reproduced in their text book. It was the New South Wales form.

The problem was in fact simply an exercise: pupils did not simply have to fill in the form, they copied their answers down into their copy books, answering questions such as: 'If your name is Elizabeth Jones, but everyone calls you Beth, what do you put as your given name?' That was not a problem for any pupil in the class, not relevant to their filling in the form, but nevertheless had to be answered by all the pupils. The message therefore appeared to be: 'Here is another irrelevant exercise masquerading as a useful one'.

If the aim of the lesson were to teach pupils how to fill in forms for others who had difficult names, then how much better to have set up a simulation where pupils took the roles of old people, young children, and migrants on the one hand and customs officials, policemen, and survey interviewers on the other and explored the difficulties some names posed.

Individual attention

As I walked around one Maths class, a girl asked me to help her with the problems. She had got every one of them wrong and quite clearly did not understand what she was supposed to be doing. As I began to explain, a glazed look appeared in her eyes which told me she was not really attending although I was speaking to her individually, so I wrote out the calculation she would have to do and asked her to work it out. She began to do so, but added instead of multiplied. 'It's multiply' I said. 'Oh, yes' she responded, sounding surprised, but doing nothing. 'Go on then, multiply by that'. She hesitated and then began putting digits in the answer line and smaller digits attached to the top row of the sum. 'What are you doing?' I asked, 'Shouldn't that be nine?' 'Oh yes' she said, and wrote in the nine, then stopped again. 'Can't you do the rest?' 'No', she said, 'I can't multiply long sums'.

School knowledge

The Year 10 Social Studies class began a new topic today: 'Race'.

Greenfield: schooling, alienation and employment

The teacher put the following on the blackboard:
(a) P.68. Explain what is meant by the term 'race'.
(b) Write down the four major racial groups.
(c) Activity Book, pp. 69,70, nos 1,3,4.

Pupils were expected to read the textbook and answer the questions as the teacher walked around the room, helping as necessary. Many pupils had difficulty finding the information, so as soon as one found it, most of those who could see copied the answer into their books. In answer to the first question all pupils copied down the definition of race from the text, which included words such as 'genetic', 'inter-related', and 'traits'; and below was a list of criteria of race which included terms such as 'cranial capacity'. No pupil I interviewed knew any of these words.

After a quarter of an hour the teacher went through the answers orally. When the text-book definition of race was given back to him he asked what 'genetic' meant. 'Eugenics' was called out. The teacher did not respond at all. Then a pupil asked, 'Could anyone start a new race?' 'I suppose they could' was the response.

Belonging

I waited outside the classroom where I was about to observe a lesson. Against the wall under the verandah were some lockers. As classes changed, a few pupils eddied out of the stream to stop by their lockers. One took out a book, another ate half an apple, a third simply opened his, ran his fingers over the contents, then locked it again. These lockers weren't simply for keeping things in: they were private space in a public institution. They were for keeping in touch with oneself.

Relevance V

Today I followed a group of basic year 10 pupils through all their lessons. I didn't do very well. In English I couldn't think of anything to write; in Maths I couldn't do the networks; and in Science I got only five out of fifteen questions right in their test of 'Light'. Some of them had difficulties too. One of the questions was, 'How does light travel?' The teacher wanted 'in waves' but

David H. Tripp

we all put 'in straight lines', so he let us have either. Does it matter that I don't know what they're expected to learn? If so, does that mean that it must also matter for them? Then how can they be shown that it does matter? If it does not, then why are they learning it?

Year 10 pupils discussing a Social Studies lesson

I had been into this class on several occasions, and earlier that morning had made a videotape of the first thirty minutes of the lesson. The following discussion took place during class time in a small room where we could view the lesson and discuss it in private. The transcript included here is heavily edited from more than half an hour's talk. Editing in this case means not only that much has been omitted, but also that the sequences have been re-ordered so that the somewhat haphazard development of the group discussion here appears orderly and logical.

DHT: Do you like Social Studies?
Pupil 1: It's good. It's not really working because you can do maps and stuff like that, and that's good stuff, that's not boring.
Pupil 3: Yes, you don't have to think all the time, and you don't have to do homework, and that's good.
DHT: Hold it, you're saying too much now. You like Social Studies because you don't do homework, and it's nice copying things into your books, you enjoy doing maps and things . . .
Pupils: Yeah, maps and things like that, projects.
DHT: Yes, you enjoy that. But you do projects and things in Science too?
Pupils: Nup!
Pupil 3: It's entirely different, though, isn't it?
Pupil 5: You should come to school to do the work, you shouldn't have to take it home with you, that's homework.
Pupil 1: In Science you've got a whole lot of calculations to work out, you have to really think with your brain, and if you've missed out on a few lessons and stuff like that, you can't pick it up, but with Social Studies you can.
Pupil 1: It's easy.
Pupil 3: It's good.
Pupil 5: Fun.
DHT: Do you think that you get through less work than you

Greenfield: schooling, alienation and employment

do in Science or Maths?
Pupil 1: No, we don't.
DHT: So those maps you did: (just colouring in those areas on the maps, that's all you did in a double period, saw the film and did some colouring) how long would it have taken you to do them if you'd been working on your own?
Pupil 1: If you just concentrated on your work it wouldn't take long.
Pupil 2: But it'd be so boring you wouldn't . . . you'd keep stopping, having cups of coffee, getting a biscuit . . .
DHT: Now wait a minute: you said you enjoyed doing it [colouring maps], now you say it's boring . . . ?
Pupil 1: Just sitting on your own at home it would be . . .
Pupil 3: . . . getting monotonous.
DHT: So you're saying the work is boring and monotonous but that when you can do it together . . .
Pupil 1: . . . it's very good.
DHT: . . . in that class, it's very good?
Pupils: (General agreement).
Pupil 3: That's what happens, . . . makes it nice.
DHT: And the other thing is that you said you didn't really have to think about it, but you just enjoyed copying . . .
Pupil 1: . . . you do have to think about it, but you can . . . [inaudible].
DHT: Did you have to think about anything in yesterday's lesson, do you remember?
Pupil 3: You've got to think about where everything is . . .
Pupil 1: . . . about what colour to use . . .
Pupil 1: . . . about what's swamp.
Pupil 1: The other thing is to find out if yours is right. You check with someone else's and if theirs is different you call Mr Dee, and he comes and tells you you're right, so (laughter) you tell them they're wrong.
DHT: The thing which struck me first of all as I watched the film, was the amount of noise the whole time.
Pupil 1: Like talking?
DHT: Yeah.
Pupil 1: Well, we were discussing the work, weren't we?
DHT: Well, were you discussing the work?
Pupils: (General disagreement)
Pupil 1: You get the ability to do your work, you know, and if you're just doing your work you've got to talk about something, so you talk about what you're going to do tonight,

and you interrupt it with, 'Well, you've got to do this . . . and you do it like that'. But you still do your work, you've got a good working atmosphere. There may be too much noise, but people finish their work and they enjoy it at the same time.
Pupils: (General agreement)
Pupil 3: Yeah, people finish their work and they enjoy it at the same time.
DHT: Yes, it's very relaxed, isn't it?
Pupils: (General agreement)
DHT: But there are obviously people who . . . let's watch it (turns on video) whenever I had the camera on there were people who weren't working . . . someone chatting there . . . walking about here . . . someone else getting up now . . . you look at these two here . . . There are about a quarter of the people who aren't working.
Pupil: But you still get the work done.
Pupils: (General agreement)
DHT: Another thing that struck me was that it took everyone a very long time to get going, particularly Pupil 1. What went wrong yesterday?'
Pupil 1: I just didn't understand the map.
DHT: What, the printed map he gave you to colour in?
Pupil 1: The map didn't say how you had to set it out on to the map.
DHT: So what Mr Dee did then was he went around to everyone individually. He must have spoken to almost everyone individually and told them individually.
Pupils: (Agreement with statement)
DHT: Is that better than if he said now listen to me and he explained it on the board?
Pupil 4: Yeah, because when he is there you feel like you are a person he is talking to all the time, and when he is saying it to the whole class nobody really listens. You know everyone mucks around and chatters away.
DHT: But you listen in Science and Maths where people teach like this don't you?
Pupil 4: You've got no choice.
Pupils: (General agreement)
DHT: You like Mr Dee, you like his teaching but you won't listen to him if he asks you to listen together.
Pupils: (Agree)
Pupil 4: It's hard to understand because the first time he explains it to you it doesn't really sink in, but when he comes

Greenfield: schooling, alienation and employment

around personally and shows you exactly what he is doing, it does.
DHT: Yeah, he came around earlier and it took you about thirty minutes to get going. You still haven't finished it have you?
Pupils: (Most had finished.)
DHT: Do you find that you spend most of your time just sitting and waiting for him to come around?
Pupils: (All agree that they don't.)
DHT: You don't. He seems to move around pretty quickly?
Pupils: (All agree.)
Pupil 4: Besides that if you get stuck on one thing you just find something else to do to keep yourself going.
DHT: The other thing that you said that you liked about him was that you can ask him questions . . .
Pupil 4: You don't feel embarrassed to. You don't feel embarrassed like with some teachers you would say 'I didn't understand that, Sir' and they would say 'Again', (i.e., sarcastically, as if the pupil never understood anything). They would blast you off for being stupid and not listening and stuff like that.
Pupils: (Agree)
DHT: But do you think that you learn more from people who make you attend all the time?
Pupil 4: No.
DHT: But you listen to them better.
Pupil 4: It depends really on the individual I think. Like if someone is bad tempered and really strict I can't be bothered listening to them.
Pupil 1: And the teacher, he makes it more enjoyable, because in Social Studies, you know, there's not much you can do that makes it more enjoyable.
DHT: Yeah, he treats you well, doesn't he?
Pupils: Yeah. Great.
DHT: Yes, some teachers wouldn't let you move would they?
Pupil 3: No, not in Science.
Pupil 1: No, in Social Studies you don't mind asking Mr Dee all sorts of questions, he won't say you're silly or anything like that; but in Science or Maths, or things like that, you don't want to ask a teacher a question or something like that.
Pupil 5: Yeah, ask Mr . . . a question and you'll get your head knocked in.

David H. Tripp

School council

On two occasions I met members of the School Council to discuss some of the issues that appeared to be emerging. The School Council is an unrepresentative group in terms of the whole school, but in itself represents an entire group within the pupils, as most of the students are lively, capable, and conforming. They're the students who generally do well at school, enjoy school, and want to have direct input into the running of the school themselves. As such, they represent students for whom the school is working effectively.

First, I was surprised by the level of cynicism expressed in response to many of my questions. For instance, when I asked why they were staying at school, they made three points in this order:

1 It is better to say that you are still at school than unemployed when seeking a job.
2 School is somewhere to go, and see all your friends at school and have a good social time.
3 It is worthwhile staying on if you are good, because you can go on to further education.

Two of the year 10 representatives, and one year 11, said that they were only at school because they couldn't get a job.

They were also quite clear about why students left: to get a job was the immediate reply, but a little probing revealed that the only alternative was: 'Because they hate it so much'. With regard to year 11 leavers, one girl had this to say:

> Those that are leaving, they are leaving because they realize that school is not for them. There is not much point in them going on, they are not going to study and things like that, so they might as well go out and get a job now. They waste half a year or something before they realize that school is not the right place for them, and they leave anyway.
>
> *DHT:* They leave because they have got jobs?
> *Pupil:* Yeah, most of them have got jobs and so they leave.
> *DHT:* Could they have got jobs earlier, then?
> *Pupil:* Yeah, they thought that they could do better by staying on, and then they leave.
> *Pupil 2:* Some of them don't really want to come back anyway, they just think it is better to be at school while they are looking for jobs. Then when they get a job, they go.

Greenfield: schooling, alienation and employment

On another occasion we discussed the differences between lower school and upper school. They felt that in the upper school their studies were more organized, they were helped individually more, they found it difficult to meet deadlines, and had to work more on their own. In lower school they complained about not being trusted, being 'treated like kids' and that 'teachers talk at you all the time'. The greatest contrast was in the way teachers treated them in the upper school, 'on a different level, now we are more like friends'. This contrasted with the lower school, 'In ninth year they treat you like cretins. Always making you line up, stand up, all do the same thing together'.

Exploring the differences in preferred learning or teaching styles, it became quite clear that some students liked to be directed and to have facts blackboarded to be copied and learnt; whereas other students complained of no encouragement or opportunity to think for themselves, and of teachers being unable, or refusing, to answer their questions properly.

> They never seem to understand you, not to answer your question as you mean it. They give you an answer but it is not what you mean or it doesn't make sense. You just give up asking questions in the end, and take down all the stuff they give you.

With regard to options, the students expressed clear preference for those that were oriented towards later employment. They complained of lack of flexibility in courses offered, and cited Human Biology and Physical Science as being mutually exclusive, although they are both fundamental to a job like nursing; Maths 2 and 3 and Accounting being mutually exclusive, although the Maths being useful for the Accounting in real life.

Another major complaint was their fellow students. They said that many students tried to denigrate anything positive they tried to do, if not actively to wreck it. There was agreement that they were the few students who were trying to improve things, but that they could not do so unless other students were prepared to become involved. They felt the general student attitudes towards the school and learning were very poor, and that Greenfield had a very poor reputation in the city. I asked those who had part-time jobs if they felt much of a difference between school and work. Their response was unanimous:

> Yes, it's real fun, just like going for a holiday . . .
> Yeah, and you get paid for it!

David H. Tripp

> (Laughter)
> You get paid for having fun.
> Yeah, it always is.
> People treat you, sort of, as if you are older, . . .
> Yeah, the boss is . . . ! (Laughter)
> A lady will come up to you and she will be holding a baby who has got a chocolate, and she'll say 'Give the lady the money', and that's really funny, you're the lady!
> And they are not always at you. They give you a job, and leave you to get on with it, and you do, 'cause you know they can sack you or not give you all your pay, so you get on with it on your own, and it's great.

One of the complaints against teachers was that some teachers held students back:

> If you have got a strict teacher he will keep you at it and you will have to do the work, but you can't do any more. If you have got a slack teacher, I don't mean a slack teacher, I mean one who is not so strict, and you can get on, you can get ahead, not too far ahead, or you can go and do other things as well. But you get a strict teacher, and you just have to do what everyone else does.

The students spoke very feelingly about their sense of Greenfield being a second-rate school to attend. As one girl put it:

> You go to a party, and you say that you go to Greenfield, and all the kids will say, 'Ug, you don't go there do you? How awful. What a terrible place to go', and so on. Everyone you talk to thinks it is an awful place and it's not surprising with the buildings and things.

With regard to the question of job expectation, all of the students were very positive:

> All the people that I have come into contact with have got jobs since they left. There are plenty of jobs about, if you want one.
> *DHT:* What do you mean, 'If you want one.'?
> Well, some people don't want one, they like to mess around on the dole.

The only concern that students appeared to show was that some of their friends that had left and got jobs, now wanted to get better jobs, because they didn't like the jobs they were in, but were finding that they couldn't get employed elsewhere. This was not seen as a problem either, because 'You can always come back to year 11 and 12 if you don't like your job'.

The data: Section 2
Two philosophies of teaching

These two teachers' statements have been presented together so that they may better be contrasted. My analysis of the differences does not do justice to the nuances and the force of their words, and so the reader is encouraged to read them both in full.

The reader will notice that the first philosophy seems to be more clearly articulated, more concisely expressed, and more emphatically stated than the second. This is partly because the difference does in fact exist, and partly as the result of the presentation. Discussions with Barry were more informal, less structured, and have not been reworded to the same extent as the discussions with Malcolm.

Amongst the possible reasons for the difference between the impact of the two statements is the very nature of the differences between the two philosophies themselves. It is part of Malcolm's philosophy to be completely certain that what he believes is right to the point of dogmatism, whereas it is part of Barry's philosophy to keep an open mind, to allow or even encourage other interpretations. Further, it is clear that Malcolm has been working according to his philosophy for many years, whereas Barry is still in the process of trying to work his out, that is, he is in the process of changing his philosophy. To this extent Barry allows some confusions to come through in his statement (such as the question of values). Malcolm, on the other hand, is so sure of his position that he will not be shaken on a fundamental point (such as that it is pupil failure which leads to youth unemployment), in spite of the fact that he appears to me to be adhering to some popular misconceptions.

Malcolm Kramer, Physical Science

> Their problems are connected with their failure. They expect more for less. This is probably a reflection of the fifties and sixties. I know that there was more content in what I did at school than what they are getting now in Science and I suspect it is the same in other subjects too. Ceratinly there is less

content in Social Studies now than there was. The idea of doing something for the pleasure of mastering it is gone. You could appeal fifteen years ago on that basis, but it only appeals to a very very few now. There's more of an encouragement for kids these days to accept anything which is nonsense, like Nostradamus or the Bermuda Triangle, and other sorts of garbage, as gospel. They take any easy solution, anything that doesn't require effort on their part. They can avoid any rigour. Rigour is dull, rigour is a dirty word.

Throughout the site work period I had had several informal discussions with Malcolm, but towards the end I had three discussions with Malcolm alone, for it was necessary to pursue his philosophy, as it was clearly of importance to the school.

Malcolm is an unusual teacher in that, although he has taught for many years, he has combined his teaching with successfully running a small business. Malcolm explained that this experience gave him a broader view of the process of schooling than that of the average teacher, and he is somewhat critical of the way in which the majority of teachers move from their own schooling, through teacher training and straight back into school again, with very little idea of what happens in other spheres of work and society. As Malcolm was brought up in Western Australia and has spent his working life here too, he has made many friends and contacts in the business community and he stresses the value of the dual perspective he thus obtains.

This statement begins with Malcolm's response to a question about what he feels has changed in education over the past decade.

Malcolm: The pursuit of individual excellence has been reduced. This means that a lot of softer options are provided: communications, not English . . .
DHT: Softer?
Malcolm: Softer in that there is a reduction in rigour, and you find, like at this particular school, that there is, outside the sporting area, a strong feeling against individual excellence. This also possibly reflects the views outside the school as well.

I think that it is a spin-off of the feelings we have given them in primary school and in English in high school, that they are individuals with just as much right to whatever they want and feel and do as anyone else, which is something which to my mind comes at maturity, something which comes somewhere between sixteen and twenty-five and for some people, never. It comes with a feeling of being a responsible individual, a free man if you like, a true free man. This seems to be inculcated all the way through these days. It's been going for the last ten years and kids have got ideas and attitudes which are not suited to their abilities or to their role in our society. I don't think the problem can be solved by putting in another fifteen social workers, I think the problem is largely a moral problem and how you solve it, I don't know.

Malcolm's whole philosophy so epitomized the thinking of one group of staff, and was so clearly aligned with some of the views I had heard expressed by sections of the non-educator community, especially businessmen, that I returned for two more discussions in which we explored some of the implications of the philosophy upon classroom teaching.

As far as it is sensible to say that a group of individuals have a common philosophy, the group philosophy of the Physical Science staff is based upon a concern to prepare students for an out-of-school life which is known to be hard. There is a strong emphasis on all students achieving certain basic standards in academic work, attitude and behaviour. The process of teaching these standards is based upon the idea that adults should impose standards upon students until the students are capable of maintaining them for themselves. Malcolm put it bluntly:

> Kids are like sheep: they get lost easily and like to be told where they are. Students are given too much freedom too early, and they don't know how to handle it. Freedom is for people at a certain level of maturity.

We began our next discussion with Malcolm's definition of alienation:

> An alienated child is one who has rejected, or is rejecting, part of the standards, the mores or folk-ways of our society.
> Alienation from school is not specifically something pertaining to school: it manifests itself at school because school is a part of our society, a particularly controlled part of our society, and hence alienation from school tends to reflect, at least in part, the socio-economic society from which that school draws.

This was the most clearly expressed definition, and hence position, on alienation that I encountered in the study. Malcolm quite clearly saw alienation as a phenomenon which is engendered by society and hence which is imported into the school, which

Greenfield: schooling, alienation and employment

may be entirely neutral in the interactions. Certainly the role of the school in aggravating or ameliorating alienation was not of prime importance. We went on to discuss some of the elements of the definition:

DHT: There seems to be a danger in that statement of ignoring the fact that society is a far more diverse affair than we like to think. When you say they have rejected the standards of society, isn't this to ignore the fact that there are a number of different standards in our society, and that the alienated student is in fact adhering to a set of standards that are fundamentally different from those of the conforming middle-class?

Malcolm: Yes, I'm not ashamed of pushing a middle-class barrow at all. I think that what has changed is that in the past parents and children were at least aware of those middle-class standards, whether they chose to adhere to them or not, but now, in the more open atmosphere that is growing up in some schools in some places, they are not necessarily aware of those standards at all, and they appear to take their external values from such things as '96' and 'Airport' and other Sydney-style programs that bear very little relationship to reality or real people at all.

DHT: So you see it as being of prime importance for schools to provide an experience of middle-class standards . . .

Malcolm: Yes. I think so. I have what I am aware is an old-fashioned view, but I see teachers as being partly custodial of our culture, a responsibility that teachers are abdicating in many instances, and although the greatest part of our culture is transmitted through the Humanities, it is significant that this is where the greatest degree of abdication is taking place.

DHT: There are people teaching in the Humanities who would make such statements as: 'You can't impose an external discipline on kids without reducing their self-dicipline, and it's wrong to anyway. All that you can do is to provide a structure which will lead them more to an internal or self discipline'. Is that the kind of attitude which you would see as an abdication of standards?

Malcolm: In part, yes. Before self-discipline there must be a set of standards, morality, set of beliefs, call it what you like, indicating what is considered desirable. One can be quite self-disciplined and be the most immoral, the most dislikeable person around. All that statement says, is that you should be internally self-consistent.

David H. Tripp

> *DHT:* I have some difficulties with that, but what you are saying is that the way to enable students to attain self-discipline is to initially impose your own discipline externally on them. Such external discipline is not being imposed throughout the school, and hence many of the problems which you encounter are the result of you trying to do something on your own, rather than with the support of everyone else?
> *Malcolm:* Are you 'you-ing' me individually, or as a department?
> *DHT:* No, I'm only asking you to speak for yourself.
> *Malcolm:* Well, then, in that case I have to disagree with you because I am not alone by a long way. I'm not imposing standards alone, by any means.
> *DHT:* What then is the group which does attempt to impose discipline?
> *Malcolm:* The Science Department, particularly. The Maths Department partially, at least. Manual Arts, Home Economics, to a degree also. And it's also very significant that many of the people who are trying to do it have been asked to transfer at the end of the year, especially those who are doing it successfully. So you might like to come back again in twelve months' time in order to compare how things have gone.

Returning to the effect of the conflict between philosophies in the school upon the students, Malcolm had this to say:

> Students adopt different standards of behaviour in different subject areas. This is something I expect you are already aware of. They have different expectations, they adjust and they realize that what they can do in one subject area, is simply not on in another subject. This in itself is useful, because the world really is like that. They are at least exposed to different sets of values, and expectations, and that is important. There's no way that a school can bring about a fundamental change in a child's value system, but it should expose them to another set of values which I think is very important, for they have to be aware that they exist.

Discussing some of the more obvious effects of the conflicting philosophies, I pointed out that there were limits to the amount of containment which could be imposed on students:

> *DHT:* The basic problem is that if kids are strictly controlled for one part of the day, or in one place, then they will erupt at other times elsewhere. A strong discipline in one subject

causes problems for a teacher in another subject who wishes students to behave responsibly of their own accord; whilst the converse is that teachers who wish to impose a strong discipline complain when they have the students coming to their classes straight from a noisy, boisterous, perhaps free atmosphere of having done what they liked.

Malcolm: I don't think you have the right idea there. Not about what we're actually doing. We don't march people around two by two and have them sitting there blinking in unison. By the same token, the nature of the situation, and the materials we use, do impose their own discipline, they limit what you can do and what you can't do, which is common of course to Manual Arts and Domestic Science, as well as to Science. We will not put up with paper aeroplanes and kids climbing in and out of windows which, as you wander around the school, you have probably seen for yourself. We will not put up with antisocial acts, acts which interfere with the rights of other children to learn. Inside those boundaries all sorts of things are possible, and do happen, and we have very open, happy, and relaxed classrooms. They're not rigid, they're not authoritarian classrooms by any means; they're certainly directed, but not authoritarian in the sense which I think you were thinking of.

DHT: But it's not something I've simply brought to my perception of the situation, it is the result of what pupils themselves have told me. They constantly complain about such things as 'You can't blow your nose without being sent out', or 'If you ask a question the teacher will hit you'; they refer to the Physical Science staff as a whole as 'the Gestapo'. I've shown them evidence of the fact that when they are given freer situations they do mess about, and take advantage of it, but they generally say they learn more and much prefer it to the rigours of an external discipline.

Malcolm: That's human nature.

[Subsequent addition: 'Incidentally, the term "Gestapo" was used by a member of the English staff about us. The kids told us that themselves'.]

Later in the discussion we moved on to discuss what is taught and its relevance. I suggested that the learning of information in Science classes was often taught at the expense of understanding. Malcolm replied that:

> Knowledge enables one to master and control one's environment. Ignorant people cannot control their environment. They

live in fear of thunderstorms and worship false gods and so on. Knowledge is control and understanding of what's going on around you, the more you know the better off you are. I can't see anything wrong with that, to me that is a desirable, perhaps the most desirable aim.
DHT: Can you defend that view in relation to the Lower School Science syllabus?
Malcolm: Yes, I can, to a reasonable degree, because our Lower School Science syllabus is about one's physical and biological environment. All of it is at a level which is useful to the average person in our population.
DHT: Well, take a topic like Mendel and gene characteristics: I saw several lessons on this which were taught from the book and the blackboard, at the end of which some students said it might be useful if you were breeding plants but it wouldn't make any difference to humans. Why is that?
Malcolm: That could be an error in presentation. I'd certainly present it in a way related to their families and own future children.
DHT: What do you think of the 'Language and Learning' approach advocated by some staff?
Malcolm: Well, these things come and go. Creativity was all the rage for a few years, but I never really took the trend seriously, and now I find that we are expected to teach the basics like we used to. I've just waited and what I've always done has come back into fashion with the real world. Ordinary good teaching has never been out of fashion.

We turned in our final discussion to the question of why some pupils chose to stay on for the academic courses in years 11 and 12, and why other equally capable pupils chose to leave.

Malcolm: Many of our good ability students are leaving at the end of year 10 instead of staying on, and getting the apprenticeships and plum jobs that are about, because of uncertainty about their future. Parents are telling them to go and get a skill now, rather than continue with learning, because they see this as setting them right for the future. Certainly, in this school, we have many high ability students who are not staying on, although they would normally be in an academic stream, because they go and learn a trade. Ten years ago they would have stayed on at school, because it was acknowledged that if a child could, he should stay on longer, even in an area like this. This means that now the entry standards are rising in

Greenfield: schooling, alienation and employment

the trades, and there is greatly increased competition. You see this particularly with secretaries, they really have to be good. It is putting the standards beyond the reach of a lot of kids who previously would have been employed in that area.

This confirms what other teachers have said, though with regard to its effect on the students at school Malcolm disagreed with my suggestion that it meant that many students would not make the grade and hence, if teachers were to tell them, they would become difficult at school. Malcolm put it this way:

I think that there is a grave philosophical error there, because instead of telling these kids that they are going to miss out because of the way they are, you say that, 'Yes, you will miss out unless you adopt these particular strategies and standards of behaviour and attitude; you don't have to be a genius, you simply have to be acceptable'. It's not got all that much to do with intelligence, it's presentation.

DHT: But isn't that just raising the standard all round? It wouldn't make jobs, and you would still have the same number of unemployed kids.

Malcolm: That's it. Very few people are attempting to point out to kids in an area like this, that if they are more conformist members of society, then their opportunities for employment will be greatly enhanced, but no one seems to think that that's worth worrying about, no one seems to think it is worthwhile.

DHT: You are just raising the level of competition. If the kid who presents himself well gets a job and another kid doesn't, it hasn't made any more jobs available.

Malcolm: You owe it to your kids to give them an edge over those from somewhere else. It's not the teacher's role to make jobs, but part of their function is to make the kids employable.

DHT: But you are going to have two kids from this school going for the same job. I still don't see that's any solution to their employment prospects. Many kids are unemployed, and yet we still say to them: 'You do the right things, and you'll improve your chances'. The effect of this, I am sure, is that it encourages kids who do try to do the right things to think that they will all get jobs. It's a con, because many of them won't.

Malcolm: The point you're missing is that those who do do reasonably well, not marvellously, just reasonably, and if they present themselves well, they will get jobs. There are jobs there if they're prepared to do what's necessary to get them.

[Subsequent addition: 'The real problem is the compression of

David H. Tripp

wage scales which means that it costs an employer almost as much to employ a more mature person as a junior. But employing a junior is a much greater risk. It not only involves training, but the older person has a stake in our society, is perhaps a housewife and a mother, they are more stable, responsible and experienced in life, and so are better prospects for the employer. It is the aim of schooling to ensure that school leavers are, as far as possible, similar in these respects.']

Finally we moved on to the problem Malcolm encountered when he was trying to help the year 11 General Studies pupils to find jobs or to do further work experience. He found that they would not go to a job if it was outside the immediate district, or if it was not precisely what they wanted. He quoted for instance, a boy who was interested in cars, and who wanted to be a motor mechanic: Malcolm found a wrecker's yard through a friend which would take the boy on work experience with the possibility of full-time work afterwards. The boy refused to go saying it was too far from home, and he could not be bothered.

Malcolm: They often have too high an opinion of themselves. They think they can do what they like and everything will come good. They don't seem willing to start at the bottom and work up to something good, they must have it from the beginning, or they simply won't start at all. They think unemployment is preferable to employment in a job which they don't want. That's a luxury they and we cannot afford.

– – – –

Barry Frayen, Social Studies

They are so passive. They won't say anything. You say to them: 'What do you think about this?', 'Huh, uh, boring'. 'What do you want to do?' 'Dunno, can't be bothered thinking . . . '. Seriously, that's all you get from them. 'Dunno, can't be bothered thinking'. So they have lost their motivation for learning a long time ago. They have been branded as basic level students, they know that they are basic, they see no way out of it and they know that a lot of them haven't been able to get jobs at the end of the year. So what's the use of education? Got to come to school but that's all.

Barry is in his early thirties, very Australian and apparently marked for promotion. Having just completed two years' secondment supervising the school experience of trainee teachers for a university whilst also finishing his part-time B.Ed. degree, he is temporarily at the school as the acting senior master of Social Studies.

Tall, athletic and fair, he appears to have achieved a personally very satisfying life-style, balancing the professional life of teaching with share-farming with his brother-in-law. He lives on a large block in the hills which he feels distances him sufficiently from the daily pressures in school to ensure proper relaxation.

I did not manage a discussion with him until the second term, when his period as acting senior master had finished. When I saw him he had become a kind of special floating Social Studies teacher whose task it was to produce a new course for the lower school years. This special role had been designed for Barry by the superintendent, who was concerned to try to close the gap between pupils' capabilities as measured by the Board of Secondary Education Comparability tests, and the standard of the everyday work being produced in class.

Also, he was concerned about the problem of 'so-called basic' pupils who were not learning much from the way Social Studies is presently taught. In fact, Barry suggested that the superintendent's primary concern was the manner in which Social Studies was actually being taught in the State, 'appallingly'.

Barry added two other reasons for a new approach in his statement to the Department in support of his project:

(a) That pupils fail to see the relevance of Social Studies to themselves and their life, and
(b) that they have problems with or understanding the curriculum.

[Subsequent addition: 'The concern is at the total lack of student involvement in decision making in the classroom. The Social Studies approach to teaching the subject is content orientated, and only pays lip-service to higher levels of learning'.]

Barry's approach is to try to:

(a) change the teaching approach so that it is student orientated, not teacher orientated;
(b) develop attitudes in students which help them to be aware of the value and relevance of Social Studies to them as individuals.

David H. Tripp

Barry and the Superintendent's concern with regard to teachers is that they are programming content alone: although other aims and objectives may appear in the programs, what is happening in class is that the pupils are doing busy-work, and none of the other aims is being taught. Barry has interpreted this project as essentially being based in a 'language and learning' approach. This was the reason why Barry was chosen by the superintendent: he had been trying to develop a new approach to teaching Social Studies as an answer to some of the problems outlined above. He had been reading the work of academics such as Douglas Barnes, James Britton and Nancy Martin, and had been examining such projects as the Curriculum Development Centre's 'Language in Learning' project, and the local Department's 'Language across the Curriculum'. At the intellectual level Barry articulated the philosophy more or less according to the Base Paper for the CDC project, quoting the following sections to me:

> We take as our first general principle the belief that learners must take an active part in their own learning, and must not be merely passive recipients of instruction. We probably learn most effectively when we are puzzled or curious, or when confronted with a problem which genuinely challenges our understanding. We will then proceed to explore our inside and outside worlds to resolve the problem or gain satisfaction.
>
> This will involve intention and expectation on the part of the learner, a willingness to make guesses or to form tentative ideas, and an ability to select relevant data from the flux of our experience. We will then try out our newly-reached understanding, and reflect on the consequences.
>
> Such learning is most likely to happen in a sympathetic environment, where we are encouraged to explore and are not inhibited by the fear of making mistakes or exposing our inadequacies.

As we are both familiar with the philosophy behind this approach, we did not spend much time probing it, but concentrated upon the particular difficulties he encountered in the application of the ideas to Social Studies.

― ― ― ―

In developing the new course, Barry made the assumption that the content should relate to the pupils' experiences and life out of school, on the basis that they would be motivated to work on obviously 'useful' topics, and that they would be able to 'language' such topics with their existing knowledge and ability. This position raised a number of questions about the nature of the course. For instance, Barry gave me some notes taken by another teacher from a senior welfare officer as to what the concerns of the Social Studies project should be. The suggestions are that a "better name' for the course would be 'A Citizenship Course', and this was developed as follows:

> Reading should be aimed at reading roadsigns, road code, which must be followed by a written test to obtain a driver's licence. This would perhaps be sufficient incentive. Other suggestions included: Voting enrolment cards; application forms for sick leave, social services, and insurance claims; banking deposits, cheques, and withdrawals; consumer protection; checking prices in supermarkets . . .

A discussion then ensued about the role of the school and the home and Social Studies in particular. I objected that the above was hardly Social Studies in the sense that Social Studies was an amalgam of History, Geography, Sociology, Economics, etc., and that the idea of Social Studies as a discipline seemed to have been lost.

[Subsequent Comment: 'Agreed – students already see Social Studies as a fill-in, a non-essential'.]

Barry argued that such a course of 'survival skills, would 'help kids to fit better into society', and that the skills of Social Studies could as easily be learned upon that kind of information as any other. I argued that Mathematics and Science should be equally involved in such a course (price comparisons, technological superiority, etc.), but that in schools those subject teachers did not have the time to teach such a course as they were busy teaching their pupils about their disciplines as such, and such questions and activities as the proposed course embraced were in fact equally based upon those other disciplines.

Barry responded with the notion that the content was only a part of the course: that what was learned from that content was the most important outcome, and what was learned was a function of how it was learned. Thus it was more important in such a course to take pupils out to see three different rivers, each one an example of a different stage of development, than it was to blackboard the information and test pupils on their learning of it.

David H. Tripp

As an example, Barry took the case of learning about local government: one approach would be to blackboard the hierarchy of a shire council and then to look at what they did; the other would be to ask pupils to find some instance of the activities of the shire council for the following day, and then get the pupils to find out who made a decision and what the machinery was which enabled the decision to be made and enacted, to produce the results observed by the pupils. Thus the pupil who observed that there was a sign on the oval stating that no ball games may be played between 6 and 7 pm which was signed in the name of the shire council, would use that as a starting point from which to investigate the role and structure of the shire councils.

I suggested that such an approach had nothing to do with the content being taught but was a function of how the teacher construed the notion; also that Barry's examples were clearly Social Studies topics in a way that the 'Citizenship Course' topics were not.

I raised the problem of pupils becoming unable to do any academic course once they were in an alternative course, and Barry suggested that one possibility would be to have a special year's course to enable them to upgrade in terms of essential knowledge to take CSE* courses after year 10.

The disadvantage of the extra year to an academically late maturing pupil would not be so great as the disadvantage to such a pupil and others who are at present alienated by academic courses unsuited to their needs. Barry's feeling was that pupils in the alternative course might well wish to stay on to do the extra year if they had enjoyed their schooling, and thus more pupils would eventually do CSE work.

Further, an upgrading year would also advantage some pupils from the academic streams who needed the extra time and revision. The converse may also be true: that some pupils from the alternative course may not need the extra year's upgrading, particularly if there was more scope for individual work within the alternative course.

In a later discussion Barry gave me a progress report on how his

---

* The Certificate of Secondary Education (CSE) was a certificate of school achievement in Western Australia at the time of the study, that included results in school-based subjects not recognized for university entrance purposes.

language and learning negotiated curriculum project was going with the Social Studies classes.

– – – –

Barry: ... by next Monday they have got to have the official notes on that [topic] and the writing has got to be in their own words. How they take their notes is they read a section, they close the book and they then write down what they feel is important. They are allowed to copy figures and facts but they are not allowed to copy any direct words. So it's all got to be as much as possible in their own writing. That group is going quite well although the hassle is the kids are finding that doing their own work with you not supplying all the input is hard and the self-discipline is lacking. They are orientated towards the teacher being the source material for everything and just sitting there and just taking. They are finding it difficult with the freedom. Consequently there has been a lot of wasted time and I . . .

DHT: Can you give me concrete examples of what kids do when they find it hard, or when they can't find things if you don't give them stuff?

Barry: If they are working in a group situation they tend to get off the topic very quickly and they will sit there and talk and chat away a whole period. The kind of thing I find is that they will decide to do a heading page so they will spend a whole period writing a pretty heading page and then wonder why I say they can't do that now.

What they can't get used to at this stage is to write in their own language as they would say it. It's just straight verbalization. that's what they are finding difficult. But they are so used to producing for me or for the teacher that producing for themselves and not the teachers is so foreign to them.

As I was saying to a kid the other day, I said 'Look, I don't want to read what the author has written, I can go and get the book and do that myself, what I want to know is what you have learnt, and you can only do that by putting it down in a way you think yourself'. But I think the major thing is that some of them just get totally lost. They are not equipped. Like they will come to me and say 'Can I do it all from this book?' or they will find that there is a paragraph or a page on sewing machines and how they have changed, so they will say, 'Well, I will change my assignment to sewing machines' because they have

David H. Tripp

found a page they can copy out. Can you see what I mean? Rather than looking at the overall thing and saying, 'Well, I need some material on this', they are saying, 'Well, what's the material I've got? I will modify the whole of my assignment to use it'.

Barry's whole approach has been on the way of working and the skills which are to be achieved through that way of working, rather than upon 'essential' Social Studies knowledge. So Barry feels that the only progress he has made to date is,

> They are starting to talk about themselves, the kind of problems they have, and that they are not simply individuals, but that wider issues do affect them. To develop and utilize this interest, I have taken as a topic 'The Individual', showing them that an individual is also a member of society and how society affects him or her, beginning with simple ideas such as peer group pressure.

We began this discussion by talking about the changes Barry had noticed in the experiment he had made with the language and learning approach in Social Studies. His main point was that the cognitive level was raised and students found the work much more interesting.

As a result of Barry's experience he suggested very strongly that a change of approach had indeed reduced three major causes of partial alienation:

(a) pupils being bored by too simple work;
(b) pupils being unable to cope;
(c) pupils not seeing the relevance of learning.

He thought the major success was that pupils were working better at their own level, they were doing less time-consuming but more difficult and interesting activities, and they related what they were doing much more to their own experiences. On top of that, Barry stressed the importance of having turned learning from a passive to an active process, and suggested that school might be very different if that were the same throughout their education.

On the question of relevance, Barry felt that students defined topics as irrelevant when they could not see how they were related to themselves. As long as information was presented in an abstract fashion, however relevant it was in reality, students could not perceive the relevance.

[Subsequent comment. Barry: 'Not so much that students couldn't see how it might relate to themselves, but more, that if they felt it did not belong to them in some way, then they refused to relate to it'.]

As an example, he said that a teacher who was doing the early history of Western Australia would probably choose the topic book and get students simply to work through that. An alternative approach was to get the students to discuss the names of the local area, streets and features that they all knew and find out how they got those names. When they found a name that interested them, then students were very keen to go to work to find out more. Why Stirling named an area Riverton fascinated some students who went on to find out a great deal about Stirling and the early days of the State. The point he made from this was that it gave the students a feeling of personally owning the learning. They were finding out things that the teacher did not necessarily know, which the teacher had not simply given them to absorb, and they had some say in determining the kind of things which they learned.

One of the difficulties of trying to adopt and develop a new philosophy is that it is not possible to work out all facets of all aspects before beginning to operate according to the new philosophy. Barry came up against this problem on several occasions, the most obvious of which was when he decided to tackle the question of personal values with a year 9 group. He was aware that values intruded into both life and language but was not aware of the extent to which his own values intruded into his teaching. The fact that our discussions clarified this question for him indicates the importance of support for the innovating teacher.

We became aware of the problem after Barry had held a parents' meeting to explain what he was trying to do. The discussion turned to his topic 'Values and Society'.

Barry: So what I did was show them the SEMP film called 'Greg', and the parents very readily laughed at it and said 'Isn't that terrible? Isn't that horrible? The poor kid, what's he going through?' Then I turned around and said to them, 'Okay, what about what you are doing to your own children?' I said that I included myself, as a parent having kids at school. I said that in the same way as Greg's parents are passing their values and attitudes down to Greg, we (as parents) do the same thing, but ours is a different set of values and attitudes; and I said, 'Are we any more right than they are?' I said what I hoped to be able to do with the kids would be to give them the ability to examine their attitudes.

It's not just attitudes towards family, it's attitudes towards other people, it's attitudes towards life! I mean that when Greg in the film says, 'I'm going to get to twenty-three and then I guess I'm going to have to have a wife. Probably she'll want a home so I'm going to have to settle down and give her a home. Then she'll probably want babies too, so I've got to give her kids and give her a decent income', it's all in neat little packages! What we try to do in Social Studies is broaden the kids' horizons so that they see more of society than the little piece they know. That's when the parents got a bit upset. I can understand, I guess, why they did.

DHT: What sort of comments did you get?
Barry: Things like, 'You have no right to ask the kids to even think about what their attitudes are. They have just got to accept these things because we are the parents and we set the values and attitudes for our children, and they just have got to accept them'.
DHT: To know the values they are learning is to give the pupils the wherewithal to question them?
Barry: That's right, and 'You don't have the right to give the kids the ability to question our attitudes'.

My point was that the kids are eventually going to question their values anyway, as you haven't given them any kind of mechanism to work rationally with. The result could be a kicking over of the traces, a rejection of everything valued by the parents, and pupils going to extremes. But at least if you have shown them that there are other alternatives just as attractive and just as worthwhile, there is more chance of them doing something worthwhile than there is the other way. But the parents still felt it was far too threatening.

The whole idea of the exercise was to try to get parents to think about the problem. It was to try to show them that they do have a big influence on the kids' values. I tried to point out three things: that kids' values and attitudes are developed from home, from their peer group station in our society and then from school, but school generally reflects the other two. How can we just let kids quite unthinkingly build up attitudes which, if we had examined them, we would not wish our children to develop?

It's just like, I said to one parent, 'If you're driving down the street and every time you see a policeman's car you say 'Oh, a ruddy cop, I'll slow down', you are building up in your kids a negative attitude towards the police and law reinforcement', and she said 'Yes, but that's only to you that that's a negative attitude – to me it might be the right attitude because the police are no good', and she was quite genuine about it. At that stage I terminated that discussion because I . . .

DHT: Yes, quite a values clash. I think your comments have underlined a number of things. Michael Butt was saying that one of the problems (he was talking about under-achievement) is the fact that some teachers have very low opinions of the pupils' abilities, and that these opinions are often held simply because they do not understand the kids' experiences and values. You are coming up against the same problem from a different perspective: whereas some teachers don't know about or understand the kids' home experience, others do but reject it because they find it 'worse' than their own, and they would wish to change the kids' values, imposing their own. Now, is showing kids how to question their inherited values any different? After all, your attitude is that the police are useful and necessary to the community and that they do a reasonably good job. Don't you want the kids to question what in your eyes are questionable values?

Barry: What I was pointing out was that we as parents and teachers develop attitudes in kids. I wasn't making a judgment on whether their attitudes were right or not.

DHT: No, I think you are. You are, in that the values you are asking students to challenge are their home values. What it comes down to in the end is that the school has values, and it is bound to put those values over in its teaching. But it is perhaps self-deceiving to say that you are going to teach the kids to question their home values without looking for any changes in them. Why don't you teach kids to question values passed on to them by getting them to question the school's values?

Barry: I think it is important for us as teachers that we show kids that there are attitudes and values in the community other than their own; that people think differently to them and they are people just exactly the same, and that there are alternatives and they should be able to look at them and evaluate those values.

The year 10 issue is attitudes to work. Now one of the parents came to me yesterday, have in mind he is a staunch Liberal man, and said to me 'I think it's a great idea conditioning changes in kids' attitudes'. Now he got the wrong impression altogether. He said, 'I'm on a committee of business men who want the school to change kids' attitudes to work, so we can develop in them good attitudes to work so they want to work and are willing to work. We can't get kids to work eight hours a day, they work two hours and then they just mess about. We want you to teach these kids attitudes so that they don't do that and they can sit there and do what they have to do. That's important. That's an attitude which we have learnt over years. It's a good attitude and you should be responsible for giving it to kids'. The principal came in here and he backed me right to the hilt and said 'That's not just conditioning, that's brain-washing. You can't do that to kids'.

Towards the end of the year we returned in our discussions to the outcomes and problems of the more general aims of the course he was developing. Barry was basically responding to what he termed the 'busy work' approach to Social Studies. He saw this as an important factor in alienation and said:

> What worries me, you walk into a Social Studies class and you find that about 40-60 per cent of the kids are just switched off, just sitting there, colouring in their maps or whatever, but what does it really mean? They don't have a clue what it is supposed to mean. So what is education all about? If the kids do not know what they are supposed to be learning, well then they are bound to leave anyway, aren't they?

As a factor of alienation, Barry suggested that a prime cause was the way in which teachers treated students.

> I really feel, that although the system is not right in many other ways, most alienation comes back to the fact that teachers do not take the time to find resources and examples which relate new concepts and information to the students' experience, and they do not take the trouble to continually explain to the

students the relevance of what they are doing.

If you think about education, and what are we educating kids for, almost all of what we teach them is irrelevant anyway in that it is not satisfying any need in the students. The kids are here, and we've got to teach them, if we were really honestly trying to educate children to become more fulfilled people then we should be doing something altogether different. I'm not just saying that of this school, it's common to every other school I've been in. We're really just perpetuating what was done to us in the classroom, and once we've got the hang of doing that we don't have the time or the inclination to sit down and question it.

Going on to discuss teacher-coping strategies, Barry saw heavy discipline as an easy way out. I interpreted this to mean that the teacher always has his or her way, it is not difficult to establish or maintain, and no risk is involved. On the other hand, the teacher who does allow students to make some decisions about their learning and their classroom behaviour has to work extremely hard all the time to operate a system of checks and balances to control the greater excesses of irresponsible behaviour, while still allowing students some freedom of choice and expressions.

The data: Section 3
Other teacher statements

This section contains statements from teachers in the core subjects, that is, Science, English, Mathematics, and Social Studies. They are included under the different subject headings more for convenience of access than for any other reason. These statements have been heavily edited for this report.

Anne Marlowe, Senior Mistress of Biology

It was clear both from my observations and from the viewpoint articulated by Anne that she is unusual in her approach to teaching in comparison with other members of the Science department. Anne is, in fact, virtually on her own, but it is important to note that whilst it is true to generalize with regard to the teaching styles in the different subject areas, such generalizations need to be interpreted in the light of the spread of opinion within each subject area. Anne in fact teaches in a manner more akin to the 'English' philosophy than that of the Science department at Greenfield. It was largely to make this point about the variety of styles within each subject area that I included her statement in the study.

It was difficult to find somewhere to talk as we were in the Science block and the traffic noise penetrating all the rooms not only required us to raise our voices, but drowned out my tape recorder. Finally we squeezed into a space between two sets of shelves where Anne has a desk, and the shelves muted the traffic to a dull roar.

Anne is senior mistress of Biology, and has arrived at that station by the unusual route of English teaching. It was at once clear that Anne places prime importance upon social relationships, as she set me at ease by saying how she would like to help, and then asked me the first question. She is a slim, vivacious woman approaching forty with short blond hair and bright blue eyes with a distinct twinkle; she smiled at me and the world in general.

> *Anne:* Obviously the problem [of alienation] does exist, and that is something which has concerned many of us for a long time. I have been quite well aware that the academic schooling

that we offer is quite unsuited for at least, maybe, 50 per cent of the students who undertake it. I have made some attempt (when I say I, I mean we, the school) at providing an alternative course but, having been involved in it in one school from the Science point of view (Mirrabooka), I felt it was a waste of time, because nobody developed the course . . . it was just a fill-in, and what you did when you weren't doing 'the important work', which was teaching the academics (I'm being sarcastic here). I felt really bad about it, because it was taken by people who had time, not those who were really committed, and it was just totally unsuitable.

Very often people say these are the dummies. What's the good of educating them, they'll only forget what we're trying to tell them. They won't learn anyway, they're only filling in time because they can't get a job. I honestly feel that the school has the wrong attitude, not the kids. The kids who come back maybe think oh well, school's good, you can muck around at school. Maybe there must be a proportion of students who feel like that. And we give them a watered down version of the academic course. It's no use to them whatsoever.

Well, as I say, most of us have a certain class background, for us it's a common background. But the sorts of backgrounds of the students in this school will be totally alien to us except for maybe a few TV shows, maybe a few books, but the everyday living in the sort of household of these children we teach would be like visiting a foreign country. It's all very well to say oh, he's got problems, Dad drinks, but it's very difficult for any of us really to understand that problem and to know how to compensate for it, deal with it, understand it, accept it.

Anne did not think that there was a shortage of information about the students in this school which was preventing staff from knowing and understanding what the students' backgrounds and particular problems were. But she did feel that it was a problem for teachers to get hold of the information, because they had to make an effort to find it, and it was difficult to know what one had to know about which pupils until one knew what there was to know. This implied that everything had to be known about all the students before a teacher could make up her mind whether the information was important or relevant or not. (Anne:.'Not everything, but everything that is known by people in the school, nurse, guidance officer, deputy principal, parent interview, etc; making the effort, having the interest'.) So it was the amount of information to be gleaned from a number of different sources, that constituted the problem. Anne also suggested that the majority of teachers felt that they were teaching perfectly adequately without knowing much about the background of individual students. 'Can you force teachers to take an interest in their students at a personal level? I don't think so'.

A problem with the pastoral side of the school is that much is left up to the year co-ordinators, who receive minimal remuneration and no credit for promotion, but are simply allowed six extra free periods off per week.

> *Anne:* I consider that six periods on top of their other free time are totally inadequate for the incredibly difficult job they've got. I think again this is another example of a token system.
> *DHT:* It's not really taken seriously. People will say the structure's there but it's not sufficient to enable it to work efficiently.
> *Anne:* Yes, that's exactly it. It's a very, very difficult job and to be totally effective, it must not be just slotted into free periods.

In fact, Anne's point could be summed up by saying that, it was not that the structures were not present but that they were not working efficiently. She gave this example:

> *Anne:* A crisis occurs and a student needs help, you can't say come back in period six. Well, of course, you can, you have to, but it's ineffectual when you say 'Come back in period six, I'm sorry', or 'The bell's gone, I'm sorry, I've got to go to a class now, stop crying, here's a tissue . . .'
> It seems to me that rather than have a separate course, we should have teachers who are trained, or motivated, to relate to their students.

This appeared to be a very telling remark. It suggests that even the needs of the academic students are not being met in the best ways, and that one of her objections to an 'alternative course' is that such a course focuses on the deficiencies and needs of the pupils rather than the deficiencies or responsibilities of the teachers. In fact, what Anne seems to suggest is that there are ways of teaching courses which would render an alternative course unnecessary.

When asked if it were possible to recognize students who would be difficult in year 10 as early as year 8, Anne thought that it was. With regard to students who were achieving well early on, but who dropped out later on in the school, she commented:

> They simply tend to look bored and the ones who are achieving and who are well behaved in the class can so easily develop into the behavioural problem or develop non-achievement, stop achieving well, because they're bored. Nobody takes any notice of them, they're so good. 'Oh, I don't want to hear your answer, Michael, I know you know it', and it's a terrible put-down for them.
>
> *DHT:* Do you think it's possible to treat pupils as individuals in class?
>
> *Anne:* I'm well aware of the fact most of us, me included, teach to the middle ability of a class, and unless the high achiever can find some way of entertaining himself or herself, and unless they're really well motivated to do what's required and then extend themselves or do what's provided for them, they are certainly going to be very ordinary. They'll never develop into self-motivated learners. May I say here that that's the great criticism I have of our education system at the moment. We produce 'yes' persons and persons who seek rewards from teachers like 'Gee, that's good (tick), ten out of ten'. We don't encourage them to seek rewards for themselves and I feel that is because we seek only academic excellence, not personal development.
>
> Of course, this carries on right down through the school, down to the child of very low ability. He or she sees him or herself as a failure for not getting ten out of ten, or because they're 'in basic', they're a 'dummy'.

The important question raised here relates to the hidden curriculum: students are trained by teachers to respond to

David H. Tripp

teachers on academic criteria. This actually works against their responding to teachers as people, and regarding themselves as worthwhile individuals in school on grounds other than academic ability.

– – – –

Anne: I maintain that 50 per cent of my problems in the class are my fault. They are, there's just no doubt about it. I can be an absolute so-and-so.
DHT: If you feel that something is your fault, can you also account for why you allowed that to happen?
Anne: Yes, because if I'm not fully prepared, it's easier to dominate a class.
DHT: Shut them up, and make them listen to you?
Anne: Yes, or if I'm having a bad day, then I just hook into my teaching role – I just function automatically. It is not easy to function pleasantly all the time and to maintain good relationships. That's one of the hardest things human beings can do I feel. It's easier to plan roles than to be real people.

I feel defeated by the system. And yet we bumble along and we keep going, it's a great juggernaut that you just can't stop, and all efforts to modify it are so token. And sometimes I get depressed but what it all boils down to is the fact I just go along with it.

– – – –

Michael Butt, Senior Master of English

Michael is a largish cheerful person with a rich quiet voice, and one imagines he would read well for radio. In conversation he becomes quickly animated, leaning forward to underline key phrases. We sat in the deserted staff room during teaching time, a tape recorder between us, and empty coffee mugs pushed to one side. Michael fiddled with a teaspoon, occasionally waving it in the air as he talked. He is in his late thirties, I guess. He has a good degree in Literature, and has worked in the curriculum branch of the department, a mark of esteem from the superintendents.

Later in the year we talked about his early schooling, and he recounted how difficult he had always found it to write: as a natural left-hander, successive teachers tried to make him write with his right hand, or worse, to hold the pencil in the left hand with a reversed right-hand grip. Now he writes with his left hand curled over the top of the line, but still hesitates over the precise wording, no doubt a legacy from early days when writing was such a laborious task that it had to be correct first time. In his lessons I later noted how patient he was with pupils who could only write slowly and with difficulty.

We began the discussion with my asking Michael to outline the structure of English teaching in the school. Setting occurs in English in year 9. Courses diverge by year 10. Until then, the courses cover much the same ground, though 'at what teachers consider to be different levels of difficulty'. Advanced classes tend to be more 'academic' (literature and structured writing) and basic classes more 'practical' (projects and comprehension).

> *Michael:* We haven't got any wholly advanced classes really, though we ought to have, because in this school there's a tremendous amount of under-achievement rather than lots of dumb kids. Lots of the teachers don't hold that view but I believe it very strongly.

Comparability tests in English show that in years 8 and 9 there should be 17-19 per cent advanced pupils but, on the basis of teacher assessment, there are only 7-8 per cent advanced pupils.

> *Michael:* With a disparity of that magnitude you have to take notice, and that is one reason why I say there is an under-achievement problem, and not just lots of dumb working-class kids.
>
> I don't think the school is meeting the needs of most kids and we have some teachers who have rather a condescending attitude towards them, and the effects of their expectations upon pupils' performance must be considerable.
>
> Things are changing now, however. The principal's influence is starting to spread, and there's a much more positive mood this year.
>
> *DHT:* So you are saying that the under-achievement problem is the result of teacher expectations and attitudes?
>
> *Michael:* No, it's a contributing factor, but there are many other problems. For instance, most year 12 students have to have a job. They are allowed to live at home, but they have to buy their clothes and some will work all weekend to get pocket money. Many girls especially have a hard time. Many of the

David H. Tripp

> families have both parents working, and they have to go home and get tea ready, do the shopping, and baby-sit.
>   Although many parents want their children to do well, they don't realize what this means in terms of homework and study. If you tell many parents that their children should be studying three hours a night five nights a week and an afternoon at the weekend for the TAE* they just look at you blankly and say, 'Well, what do they do at school, then?' [These pupils are then in competition with others who do not have these disadvantages.] So the whole under-achievement problem is very complex here. Look at the buildings too: they don't inspire one to study, so teacher attitudes are simply a part of the problem.

I then asked Michael if he had developed a particular rationale or philosophy of English teaching in particular or education in general.

> *Michael:* My philosophy of English teaching is based on the idea of an integrated language program, which means that you don't teach skills in isolation but you relate their reading to their writing, their literature to their writing, literature to their personal experience . . .

> *Michael:* Another essential of my philosophy is that you have to start where the kids are. Whilst I do believe that older students should be pushed in the academic direction, you must begin, particularly with younger kids, with the language they already have; you must build upon that, drawing upon their experience of the world. And that's very difficult when you teach kids whose experience is very limited. If you stay within that experience you get nowhere, for it's no good saying that because kids are interested in violence and football, that's all that you do with them. If the kids like sexy, gory TV shows, the challenge is to start with those values but broaden their experience, and show them other values. Our role is to have an enriching function, to expose kids to things which are 'better' (though that's a loaded emotive term, isn't it?), perhaps to give them a broader experience of the world, I should say.

When asked about the effect of the job market upon pupils'

---

* The Tertiary Admissions Examination (TAE) was the examination basis for university entrance, etc. in Western Australia at the time of the study.

attitudes to school, Michael quoted the cases of two able girls who, during the past week, were wanting to leave. Michael analysed the situation as being partly the result of their own poor self-image (derived from home values of the status of women), and partly the pressures of school conflicting with boyfriends who resented their doing homework every night.

Michael: But what they are seizing upon is the idea that if they leave now, just four months before the TAE, then, if there are any jobs going, they will get them. It's no good saying to them that the minute they turn eighteen and their employer has to pay adult award wages, they'll be sacked. They don't believe it.

That attitude is the direct result of the job market. We can no longer say 'There'll be a better job for you if you stay on and get a good CSE result'. That's no longer the case, and they know it. If they do stay on, for many of them it'll be for the personal satisfaction. [Or for lack of anything else to do.]

DHT: There are kids in year 8, and even year 9 who are totally lost because they are unable to read. Normally these kids are put into a special class, or into a remedial set, where they have intensive tuition until they can be returned to normal classes. This doesn't happen here, I think.

Michael: We have a dilemma here. If you set up a special class the kids become known as 'the dummies', and this affects their whole school lives, social as well as academic. Other kids won't play with them, they won't talk or dance with them, they won't let them play sport, and so on. They are usually put with a motherly lady, and they become totally dependent upon her, and often opt out of all other contact. Students and staff tend to regard them as oddities, and they come in for all kinds of abuse.

We don't have a special class, so that kids who were in special classes before they came here have vanished into the normal classes. Teachers do not know which students were in special classes in primary school, and many of those kids they regard as perfectly normal. Those who are quite unable to cope are given individual work to do by Jenny (Neitche, the 'enrichment teacher') but they are in normal classes.

In the special class there is no doubt that they made [more?] gains, but at the expense of so much else. Does it matter if you improve your reading age from 7.6 to 8.2 if you're the butt in the playground and everyone taunts you? You still can't read

David H. Tripp

the newspaper and the social implications are enormous.

Staff sometimes ask for a special class, but when you ask them to name the special kids, they get the really chronic ones, but there are the kids who were in special classes before they came here who they do not name as needing special treatment. I think this is very significant.

[Does this mean that there should be a special class, but with fewer kids in it than there were?]

Michael: They are playing with the other kids in the playground, they take part in the sports carnivals, and I believe that they are being much better equipped to go out into the world than they were, because they have the necessary social skills to cope. This is a tremendous advance.

- - - -

Ian Ellis, Senior Master of English

Ian Ellis is a senior master of English. He compared the situation at Greenfield with the situation in country schools with regard to what one knows about pupils:

We simply don't appreciate that children lead lives totally different away from the school. It's much more apparent in the country where one is interacting socially. One does go to the pub and it's the only pub in town and you see pupils in year 11 and year 12 or one plays in the football team alongside pupils. One meets the parents of the pupils at the golf club or some other social function . . . and sees the pupils carrying on a totally separate social life. It's very difficult in a large metropolitan school to see pupils outside of the classroom. It always comes as a shock to teachers who take pupils to an excursion held at night, perhaps taking them to a theatre or to a play to see how different the pupils look outside their normal school crowd with their uniform on. You are then forced to treat them as individuals rather than as school pupils.

Also, there's so little contact with parents here. It becomes difficult to place children in context within the family. One sees only the parents of better pupils and then only once or twice a year and it's impossible to identify the parents when one sees them in the street. One can only identify them when one sees them with the child and you think well, yes, he does look like

Greenfield: schooling, alienation and employment

his father or his mother and if both parents come to see the teacher at a parents' gathering, one gets an impression of what the family life is like for the child. But if that doesn't happen, then there is no real way of judging what the child is like outside the school.

Frank Pollard, Senior Master of Mathematics

It had not been easy to see Frank as he always seemed to be busy; as senior master of Mathematics he appeared to use most of his free periods in administration but it turned out that he was also on several committees, which took up free time. Frank looked fortyish, and it was later clear from the way in which he talked that he had been in the department for many years. He had, however, only recently transferred to Greenfield, and saw both the school and the subject department as something of an interesting and worthwhile challenge. He talked quietly, often with vehemence, always with enthusiasm, though sometimes a note of resignation crept through. My impression was that he was a strong and patient head of department who saw his role as that of changing procedures, habits, and attitudes slowly and incrementally, wearing down problems or opposition, rather than trying to break through them.

I began the first discussion by suggesting to Frank that many of the pupils saw school as a waste of time because they knew at the end that they would not get a job.

Frank replied, saying that although that may be true for the lower end of the ability range, 'students who wish to do anything in the trades know that there are certain levels that must be reached before an interview is obtained'.

DHT: Would it then be true to say that there were not alienated children in the ordinary levels?
Frank: No, that would not be true either. There are definitely kids in there who are term serving, if that's what alienation means, and I think it does. They aren't interested in being at school, they are there for one reason alone: because they have to be. There is a legal requirement for them to be there and, unless they come along with a little piece of paper to show that they are employed, which they can't of course do, then they

79

have to stay here. But not in any one of the cases, and I can think of four straight away, is the student a problem of any kind, a physical problem. It's just that in all cases the amount of work done is only just enough to keep them in their achievement level, they are just term serving, they are there because there is nothing else to do.

DHT: Well, what do you think produced that attitude?

Frank: Well, I think it was just that they didn't see what we were doing as being any use to them. They couldn't see that what I was trying to do, which in the ordinary level stream was to prepare students to go on up into upper level school and even tertiary Mathematics, and therefore covers a fairly rigorous Mathematics course, they just couldn't see that that was at all related to their needs. Yet, there was no way I should have put them onto the elementary course, because it did not match their intellectual capability. It isn't all that much more relevant anyway. I think that's their problem.

It's hard to think yourself into their minds, having come through an enormous amount of education yourself. I'm sure they can see people who left last year, in particular, those they meet down the street and with whom they were school friends and all the rest of it and they say, 'Oh well, school's a waste of time, I've got a job', or 'I haven't got a job and I got ordinary level in everything (or intermediate level) and it hasn't helped me get a job'.

DHT: So this attitude is coming through from various quarters outside the school, rather than these kids having met these problems themselves?

Frank: I don't think they've got any idea of the problems themselves. Most kids plug away getting what they consider to be the best possible education, still thinking that it's going to open everything for them when they get out of school; I think they're up for a disappointment when they finally find out that it doesn't work like that. Everything doesn't drop into your lap, because you've got that bit of paper. Particularly, I think there are kids at both ends of the ability spectrum who haven't met the problem, I'm sure, not for themselves. Although there might be a few who've gone and applied for jobs and things like this during the year 10 as kids do.

I think an important problem in this school making it very different from many other schools stems from its surroundings. What's imported from the home into the school has an effect. I wouldn't mind betting (probably on very unsafe odds) that 90 per cent of the parents of the students here would have been alienated from school themselves. They probably would have left school at the minimum possible age which was probably year 7, although these parents are a bit younger than that, but it certainly would have been at the end of year 9 when the leaving age was 14. And I think that's probably a factor. It may not be the dominating one but it is a factor: 'School never did me any good and it's not doing your brothers and sisters any good either'. So I think it rubs off on kids. And Dad got through. He's a successful man (in their terms of success, of course, and that's subjective) . . . Dad's a successful man and he left school when he was in year 8. I think that's an important attitude.

I then asked about the elementary students and their course.

DHT: Do they ever see things like arithmetic as being relevant?
Frank: No. It is a surprising thing and we have arguments with people about this because they just don't believe me, but we can do topics such as hire purchase, bank accounts, wages, budgeting for food, taxation, and all these sorts of things, and you would think this was right on the ball, because these are the things that the kids are going to have to do in life; but because they're not involved in it right now, they don't see it as relevant. You can teach it, and they might find the benefits next year when they perhaps remember what I said about the difference between reducible and simple interest, but it doesn't help the actual teaching because at the time they don't see it as being any more relevant than anything else which they are doing, like solving a quadratic equation.

It was a conclusion which I was surprised to come to but when I had accepted it, it made sense. The point is they just do not see it as being any more relevant than anything else. So all we can do is teach it in the hope that it will be useful to them later on, and not because it's relevant to them now. What is relevant to school is what's done at school because they're there for a large proportion of their day.

Frank said that the way in which a course is taught is very important, and his philosophy was to 'steer a course between over emphasis on activity, which gets out of hand, and over emphasis on formal work'.

As an example Frank took present year 10 work on measurement.

David H. Tripp

They are approaching it through doing all their own measurements on everything and then converting and manipulating these. Another activity project which Frank runs is one on postal charges. There is a box of letters addressed to destinations all over Australia and the world. The students have a leaflet with the scale of charges, and they have to work out the value of stamps to be put on each envelope.

> *Frank:* The aim of the exercise is to show them how to read the thing. They have to be able to pick up a scale of charges of some kind, measure what they are being charged for and then work out the cost. It will be done with all the kids except the basic level, because I think it's too sophisticated an exercise for them. The advanced classes won't do it either, they just haven't got the time.

– – – –

The second discussion opened with the problem of Mathematics and the Alternative course. Frank said that he felt 'the department is disowning the Alternative Program'. His impression is that the prevailing advice is to 'follow Trade Maths E, and add other topics like Social Arithmetic from Part 4'. Frank thinks that many teachers will continue with this until they are forced off it as it doesn't really suit the students' needs, and only then will teachers gather together a set of resources which are more appropriate.

We then moved on to discuss evidence of alienation. Frank said that it meant 'turned off students', some of whom were 'an overt and deliberate nuisance' and others who were 'totally passive'. Of these latter Frank said, 'As you go around the place you forget that they are there as they wish you to, I think'. These are the low profile students whom other teachers have referred to as 'time serving'.

Evidence of alienation was most obvious to Frank in the levels of underachievement experienced by all teachers in all classes, underachievement being defined as 'the minimum possible amount of work'. More overtly, however, some students made a habit of unpunctuality and truanting, which clearly demonstrated they wished to be elsewhere.

Frank did not think that the answer was to ensure that all students had a more thorough grounding in the basic skills at the expense of other aspects of their education: 'I believe the approach that aims to grind them down and push in more of the basic skills is quite wrong, and compounds the problem'.

Frank sees the alternative, in fact, being to 'broaden the base of the Mathematical experiences offered to students'. He pointed out that there is now room for broader experiences because the drilling by repeated example of the basic operations has now largely disappeared (for instance the hours spent in multiplication of four digit numbers by four digit numbers), leaving room for 'enrichment activities previously available only to the able' to be offered to the less able, too. Frank says this is a result of the basic skills themselves having changed over the last decade:

> The basic skills are no longer the traditional skills, such as multiplying long numbers, all that is done just on two digits now, the long numbers are just for fun, otherwise use a calculator. Calculators and computer programming are now the real skills. The basic skills still need to be taught, but they need to be taught in more interesting ways. For instance, teaching how to plot points on a graph is much better learnt by plotting pictures than straight curves. Doing it that way is 'on turning' rather than 'off turning', so the students learn more because they enjoy doing it.

In contrast to what is possible, Frank feels that much Mathematics teaching was alienating pupils in that it is 'pointless drudgery'. My observations have led me to believe that this applies not only, or primarily, to Mathematics teaching, but is a result of teachers in general simply continuing to do what they have always done without much thought as to how or why it could or should be modified.

Another important point Frank made about alienation was that he believes it to be a disease. By this he means that,

> It may start in one particular subject area, but then it spreads to everything the student does in school. I believe that, far too often, in the past, although this is changing now, the disease has started in the Maths classes. With students being put through hours of mindless but often difficult tasks, they begin to question what they are doing and why they are there, and this leads to poor attitudes when they do not get adequate answers. They then compare that experience with what they learn in other subjects, and they become turned off those too.

In sum, Frank stresses the point that mechanical aids are redefining the basic skills for Mathematics teachers, that teaching

David H. Tripp

can and should be far more interesting and varied, but that so long as what is taught is left up to the individual Mathematics teacher, and that teacher is not given the necessary time or help to change his teaching strategies and content, teachers will continue to do what they have always done, alienating greater numbers of students each successive year as they fail to meet the changing needs and expectations of ever increasing numbers of pupils.

Andy Dee, Social Studies teacher

Andy Dee is the only teacher included in this section as the statement of Barry Frayen, the other Social Studies teacher with whom I worked, is included in Section 2 (Two Teachers). Other information about Social Studies teaching in general and Andy Dee in particular is included in Section 2 (Teaching Style).

Andy is a quiet, cheerful teacher to whom I was directed by the then acting senior master of Social Studies as a 'typical teacher: sound, but not spectacular; no discipline problems; gets on well with pupils who like him; you won't bother him much, either'. And indeed I found him very helpful in everything I asked of him, I liked observing in his classes because he (and consequently the pupils) seemed able to ignore my presence, or to take it for granted, rather.

I spent more hours in Andy's room than in any other single classroom. This was partly because having become known, it was easy for me to maintain contact, and partly because I could talk to the pupils informally, tying the issues to the work they were doing. Also, and perhaps most important, because I found the heterogeneous grouping, the nebulous nature of Social Studies, and the pupil/teacher relationship in the class provided the most complex school situation which I had to come to terms with. I was surprised at the end of the sitework phase to find how apparently lean gleanings of this intensive observation had been, and how indistinct was the little data I had. However, I was aware throughout the study just how often ideas seemed to occur to me in Andy's classes, which I could later make better sense of in other situations. In hindsight I learned much, though I had little down on paper.

In view of the extensive coverage of Andy's teaching elsewhere, all I have included here is my version of our final discussion, the occasion when I asked him directly about the

Greenfield: schooling, alienation and employment

nature of alienation. I began by asking Andy what he thought the term 'relevance' meant to the students with regard to their school work.

Andy: Most of the students look at their school work simply as a means of getting a job. That's it! They seem to have no other criteria. They say that Social Studies will not be useful to them at work, so they won't work hard at it. They don't see Social Studies as learning new information, as broadening their experience, as getting a better outlook on the world, . . . it is just, 'Will this help me in my job?'

DHT: But don't they see a good Social Studies mark as being an indication of their ability which will help them get a better job? Even if it were in Astronomy, wouldn't that help?

Andy: I don't think they see it that way. Most of these students are not going to stay on, they want apprenticeships and jobs, and they are often told by friends and even the Youth Education Officers, that employers will go more on interview and work experience because the employers do not understand or believe in the Leaving Certificate. You can show them a list of jobs with requirements saying so many intermediate passes . . . but it doesn't make much difference as these aren't often the jobs students expect to get, or they think they can get passes in subjects which they see as having more to do with the specific requirements of the job.

DHT: So they don't see subjects which have relevance to their lives as being important? What you seem to be saying is that relevance equals utility.

Andy: Yes.

Andy is obviously dealing with two views of relevance: (1) the students', where schooling is seen as a means to a fairly immediate and tangible end and (2) his own, which has more to do with the development of a better informed individual with a broader view of the world and society. The question as to whether the content and teaching style of Social Studies enables students to understand its relevance to themselves, should be considered (see Barry Frayen).

We then moved on to the question of alienation. In general terms Andy said that the students told him they didn't like school because it was 'boring'. Andy saw the way in which students spend their leisure time as the major factor contributing to their perception of school as boring. He suggested that in contrast to playing 'Space Invaders', and working part-time, school was very

85

dull. Evidence for this was not only what the students told him, but the fact that he finds the only way of engaging their interest and attention is to show them a film or video tape, to go on an excursion, or to get them talking about themselves.

Andy: Show them a film and they're really interested. Hand them out a worksheet and they'll immediately switch straight off it. They're just not interested in books or learning things.

Alienation is just the general irrelevance of what they're taught. A lot of it I can see is not relevant to what they need anyway and at the same time some of the ideas that you try to get across to them, such as that their world is not just Greenfield, that there is more than that in it, other people's lifestyles, other countries that would interest them, they won't take either. There's no background for it. Kids don't read at school or at home.

DHT: But don't they get a lot of that background from television? Even if they just watch 'Kojak' or 'Charlie's Angels' they must learn a lot about America. 'Prisoner', 'Cop Shop', or 'The Sullivans' must teach them a lot about other aspects of Australian society.

Andy: They don't seem to see it as such. It's just the violent and exciting bits that they seem to see. It never enters their head to see 'Kojak' as about New York or telling them something about America. It's just not directed, their television watching, their television watching at home is not directed for any purpose. We do at school, we show them programmes and ask questions, we talk about it before and after, but they don't see it like that at home.

It seems that an important educational opportunity is being missed in that the students' televisual experience is not being capitalized upon by teachers in general. Educational television is well used in the school, but it seems strange for teachers not to employ students' home viewing experiences in their teaching, as this is a part of the students' lives in which the teacher can so easily share.

Andy went on to say that he thought students were incapable of disciplining themselves to work. I then asked why it was that other teachers had decided that this discipline must be imposed externally, but Andy felt that it should not. He considered that it was a matter of balance.

Andy: You have to have a measure of discipline in the class

Greenfield: schooling, alienation and employment

make it work; but if it all comes from the teacher, then, when the teacher is not there they are quite incapable of doing anything for themselves again.

That Andy has this philosophy is borne out from my own observations, for it is clear that Andy has a classroom where students are able and are encouraged to work for themselves, but not forced to perform particular tasks. In fact, Andy aims at a graduated approach to discipline according to the age of the students: he imposes more discipline on a year 8 class (thirteen year olds) but finds that ' . . . from there you gradually ease it and find in fact that students in year 10 will work a lot better when they are not simply working because I am forcing them to'. He pointed out that he does not have most of his classes from year 8 to 10.

Andy: This class I had only this year. This class had three teachers in Social Studies last year alone. Two of the teachers decided they couldn't cope so up and left, so the students got the message that teachers couldn't handle them in Social Studies and really couldn't care very much.

I don't even think it's part of education to sit thirty students in a room for eighty minutes without allowing them to talk to each other. Sometimes they'll talk about their work, and sometimes they'll talk about other things, that's natural and necessary. It's part of the classroom situation that they are interacting and working together. Where that is completely stamped out is an artificial situation.

So Andy revealed a fundamental difference between his approach and that of some other teachers: he sees learning as being a natural process subject to the social behaviour of students; other teachers see learning as best facilitated when social behaviour is suspended, and special rules are applied. Andy sees strict discipline as a major contributing factor to alienation of students from schooling in that part of what it is to be human is being denied.

It is not simply the imposition of discipline however, that Andy sees as aggravating alienation, but the way in which it is imposed. As students challenge the authority of teachers and indeed all adults, teachers who would have total control in the classroom have to find harsher and more violent means of establishing that control. Ultimately, Andy expresses the view that many of the students who are real problems in the school have been made so

87

by teacher attacks on their self-image, their standing with their peers, and their ability at school work. Depending upon their personality, Andy sees students becoming offensive or defensive when subjected to personal attacks.

Andy pointed out that in his own experience he did not feel there was more alienation at Greenfield than at any other school.

> *Andy:* It's strange that in a working-class area you can get a much better relationship with the kids than you can in a middle-class area like Churchlands or City Beach. I've been surprised at the ease with which we can talk to kids here, even in the first couple of weeks total strangers have come up to me and said 'hello'. They weren't in my classes and I didn't know who they were; I haven't seen that happen in many other schools.

– – – –

Finally Andy made the point that, in contrast to many students' experiences at home 'school is a friendly place, it's a place where they are least alienated, they're belted around at home and pushed out of the house, and they come here for a bit of friendship and companionship'. This was repeatedly confirmed by pupils throughout the study.

The data: Section 4
The Alternative Course

This section is about the problems of the existing year 11 General Studies course. First, two short extracts from the field data illustrate quite different teachers' perceptions of the problems of the idea of an Alternative Course. In the first, Fran expresses the idea that the aim of the course should be to undo the pupils' existing view of school work. In the second, Ralph suggests that 'more of the same' is best. Most of this section, however, is devoted to the more general aspects of the course.

Fran Barnes, English

Fran teaches English. She first made the point that the year 11 General Studies pupils 'arrive in year 11 with a habit of bad marks and worthless opinions'. By this she meant that they have a very poor self-image and expect to do badly, as they have done hitherto at academic work. 'They don't want to work, not school work, they are into social relationships and finding out about things'. When I asked Fran what she meant by this remark she explained that the students say that they are wanting to repeat the year and get better grades, but they regard work as being dull, boring, and uninteresting but a necessary evil; when they really enjoy doing something they don't regard it as work, and what they really enjoy is finding out about things that affect them for themselves.

One indicator of their attitude to school which Fran thought was significant, was the activity which she gave them earlier this year: to redesign the schooling system so that it was better for them. What amazed her was that they recreated the existing education system right down to and including details such as 'even having bad teachers. They felt that you would always have some bad teachers in a system, and bad teachers were good for a school because students should learn to put up with them'.

Fran mentioned on several occasions that their concept is that work is nasty, but it is good for you to do nasty things; that there is total absence of a concept of enjoyment or satisfaction through achievement in school work. She put this attitude down to their previous experiences through their school life, and was very critical of the way in which the education system in the State allowed teachers, once initially qualified, to teach for the rest of their lives without any retraining or bringing up-to-date of their existing qualifications.

> *Fran:* Although it is good in some ways for staff to have very diverse learning experiences, unless they are all brought together and up-to-date there can be no coherent philosophy of good practice in a department, let alone in the school. Look at English for example. We have some coming from primary teaching, others from secondary via university, others from colleges. If you mention the words semantics or linguistics, some do not know and do not wish to know. My point is that you can go on teaching the same thing in the same way for a great number of years: there's no refresher course and nothing to make you keep up-to-date. Children are too important to be left to people who have a job just because they are permanent.
>
> Things have changed in the kids' lives, and things have to change at school. You can't just go on doing the same thing because it was good five years ago, let alone fifteen. We need the opportunity for real staff development.

Ralph Mostin, Mathematics and Year 11 Co-ordinator

– – – –

As Ralph teaches the year 11 Alternative Course, I asked him how he saw it. 'Babysitting leavers', he said. So I asked him what he did with them, and he explained that he offered a slightly modified year 10 ordinary syllabus, so that students with elementary passes could improve their grades. He thought that most students who came back to do general studies in year 11 'didn't recognize until too late that they should be in ordinary, not elementary groups'. He stressed that it was not for lack of telling, and suggested that the pupils are incapable of working for long-term rather than immediate goals.

When we discussed the idea of General Studies being a quite different course, not for upgrading at all but to provide students with good academic records in a different sort of course in year 11, Ralph said that he felt such a course 'would be very good indeed, but I think idealistic, it couldn't be run here'.

Several times during our discussion Ralph mentioned 'kids who shouldn't have been there in the first place'. He was talking about students who were not making the grade in advanced classes in the lower school, or in TAE classes in the upper school. He said that traditional methods of teaching Mathematics were the only possible way of teaching large and upper ability classes. We discussed this at some length and, although Ralph said that he felt the 'majority of students would be advantaged by a change to activity and discussion approaches to teaching, especially those of lower ability', yet 'it would not be possible to complete the syllabus in time', using these methods. Ralph saw activities as being useful for keeping students involved (entertained? concentrating? attending?) in the topics, rather than producing qualitatively different conceptual learning outcomes. He also said, 'Activities are for practical topics rather than for learning theory. Theory is much better learnt through traditional teaching'. As the Alternative Course students were there to improve their Leaving grades, a repeat of the previous year was what they needed.

- - - -

Jean Dunn, Co-ordinator of Alternative Courses

Jean was shy and nervous; naturally shy, I think, and nervous of me and because she did not know quite what to expect. This was in fact the first discussion and perhaps I was nervous too.

Normally Jean teaches commercial subjects; she finds herself the co-ordinator of the year 11 Alternative Courses by chance. Having just transferred this year to Greenfield, she was asked on arrival to take on the co-ordinator's role mainly, so far as I can make out, because she had too light a timetable in commercial subjects, and because her subject expertise was of itself seen as a qualification. She has, however, done her best in the circumstances of walking into a job she feels she knows nothing about in a school she knows little about, though she confesses feelings of inadequacy for the task on several occasions.

[Reading this statement nearly a year after having first written it, it now seems very stilted and uneven; but I have left it unaltered because I am not sure whether it was because it was the first discussion, or whether it would have been like that whenever I had written it.]

The discussion opened with a comment I was to hear all too often: 'I have only just come this year, so I don't know if I'll be able to tell you much'. Staff turnover is high, more a problem for the pupils than the administration, I think.

The Alternative Course is also called General Studies, and I immediately asked Jean what her aims were for the course. She replied: 'One, to make students [more] employable; and two, to improve their self-image and confidence'.

Jean considers the main problem with the course is that they have just been treated as another normal class, being rotated around a number of staff who have light timetables. This prevents any coherent content and planning. She, for instance, sees them for just two periods a week. As a result of this, 'I just can't see it being a success this year'. The ideal set-up would be to timetable them quite differently from the rest of the school, with one or two teachers only teaching them the whole time, with a new curriculum organized the previous year and with a room of their own as a base in the school, but another problem is the numbers involved: until the pupils actually arrive, no one knows just how many there will be. This year fewer students (forty) came than were expected (sixty).

The movement of staff, voluntarily and by the education department, has prevented any serious planning. In 1979 a member of staff had begun to set the course up when he was transferred. The job was given to another member of staff who, shortly before the beginning of the 1980 school year, was also transferred. Jean Dunn arrived at the school this year to find herself taking over the course co-ordination less than a week before term began.

According to Jean, pupils' perceptions of themselves in relation to the course are 'that they are incapable of tackling anything else, and accept that they are not going to get a job [quickly]'. In other words, they see themselves having failed at school, and at finding work, but have returned for lack of anything else to do and to improve their employment prospects. Pupils themselves only too readily made these comments later when I met them as a group.

One of Jean's main criticisms was that there was no adequate certificate for people who completed the course. The existing certificate was vague and did not tell employers enough to enable them to recognize that the pupil was more employable than one who had not stayed on. I felt however that in view of the structure of the course this last point was debatable.

Seven staff teach the course, one from each core area and three from the options.

Jean: This means that the whole thing is fitted into the timetable just like an extra class without any consideration given to an actual course for the kids, even though each teacher may try something different with them to what they had done in year 10. My opinion is that if these kids have already had three years of subject orientated schooling and they haven't done well, they're certainly not going to do it this year and built up their achievement levels much. I think the course should be totally different.

But that's it, I can't see the course being successful this year because of the way it's been set up. But hopefully, next year . . .'

Jean had quite well-developed ideas about what the course could be:

1 It would involve more work experience spread throughout the year. At present students are very limited in the amount of work experience they get because of the timetabling of other subjects. They have two weeks at the beginning of the second term. This would enable staff to teach in relation to their work experience throughout the year.
2 There should be more community involvement, both in terms of work and study. The amount they can get in the community is similarly limited by the present timetabling practices. Jean feels that they have a very narrow view of society in general, simply confined to their own standards in their own locality. As an example she quotes that they would not even try to taste Mexican food when it was cooked for them on camp.

Jean has also noted that they are also very insecure with regard to cultural and creative things. They commented at camp, when they were finally persuaded to make some things in clay, that they were glad that no one at school could see them doing it. Jean agreed that this seems indicative of an understanding built up during schooling: that if you are less able, handicapped, or very young, you do fun things with your hands. Jean has not done any drama with them yet but that would be an obvious and interesting move.

3 The building up of self-esteem and maturity. Jean does not see that it is possible to do this with specific activities, but indirectly through the way in which the students are treated and the relationship they have with the teacher. It is therefore

essential to give them more responsibility in the school.
Giving them their own room to decorate and look after would
be giving them a measure of responsibility. Giving them more
responsibility through negotiation of the content of the
course, preferably during the previous year.

Jean asserted that these pupils are well able to handle responsibility if given it. She gave as an example how they had organized a camp for themselves. But it is the pupils in the academic courses who seem to be given what responsibilities there are for senior pupils in the school. Jean stated that, as a result, 'These students see this course quite clearly as the course for drop-outs'.

DHT: What else would be the sort of general aims? The
principal speaks quite freely of things like helping them to
mature and giving themselves better images. How do you
actually see what you do with the kids achieving these aims?
What is it like in terms of activities in the classroom . . . ?
Jean: Yes, it's not what we're doing at present; it's something
which has got to be done. Like I think they need a lot more
responsibility in the schools.
DHT: So is it a general aim to give more responsibility?
Jean: No, it is an aim, I think it is one way of helping to put
up this self-esteem, this sort of thing, the maturity and so on.
I've been trying for ages to get a room that could be their room
that they could do up and look after because they tend to be
pretty careless.

Again, the only room we can have is one which is the drama
room which is being used by all other classes and for
everything else. All the other rooms are being used at some
stage and I think they ought to have one room which is solely
theirs, and this ought to be timetabled in too, where they are
responsible for the decoration of the place and the upkeep of it
and they could use it at lunch times, before and after school. I
know probably at first you'd have problems but I think they are
not given enough responsibility that way. They are still treated
as irresponsible, because they are always the rougher kind of
kids and they don't like authority, obviously after having had
so much of it, but they are never given the opportunity much
to do without it.
DHT: What kinds of classroom activities do you think
develop self-esteem and responsibility?
Jean: It is hard to say in the actual classroom what sort of

activities develop maturity, really I think it is an overall thing that develops in the way you treat them and what you let them do. I know you control them, but I suppose it really depends on the personality of the person who is taking them for these two or three periods.

DHT: How do you know they can handle responsibility?

Jean: I've found that when we organized this camp a couple of weeks ago (I did all the organizing and everything) and told the kids to bring me their money on a certain date, only half of the number who said they were going came along and did it, so in the end I said 'Right, it's cancelled, we haven't got enough people'. So then some of the students actually came to me and said, 'Right, we will guarantee to go around and get enough people to come. We'll make sure they do it'. And I said, 'Alright, then you go and you'll have to reorganize. You'll have to go and see the principal and you'll have to see all these teachers, and you'll have to explain the situation and you'll have to re-get permission and all these sorts of things', and they went off and I gave them a list of all the things that had to be done and they went off and they virtually reorganised the camp all over again. All the things that I'd done in the first place which probably I should have let them do originally, and I thought that that was good. It was a sign of them organizing themselves and showing a bit of maturity.

So whether they could gradually develop this ability, organizational ability, maybe working out some of their own programs and the things they consider would be suitable to them and maybe this could even be done, I would like to see it done at the end of the year, before even. Get together those people who intend to do this and get some ideas from them originally and make it clear that they're going to be doing a lot of the organizing and have the responsibility. The parents, too, I think, ought to be brought in at that stage as well.

Jean was against selection for any alternative course in year 10 because it would cut out late maturers from doing CSE later. On reflection she felt that Social Studies could perhaps be separated in the lower school, and transfer would still be possible to CSE at year 11 because Social Studies was less sequential than Mathematics or Science.

DHT: There seems, from talking to people, to be a quite clear division in the school between those who feel that the curriculum is not meeting the kids' needs, and something quite

David H. Tripp

different should be done in the social skills, and the people who feel that the school should really be doing what it's always done, only better. The kids who can't cope should be given an alternative curriculum, according to both groups; but, according to the second group it is so that the kids who can cope could be taught a more academic curriculum more effectively because the other kids aren't holding them back. Is that the feeling that you've got?
Jean: It's all very idealistic to say that everyone is equal and these kids have got to be given the opportunity to do this and the same opportunities as the brighter kids, but basically I think all they get is failure. So yes, I would say I would be in favour of that, of giving them a particular curriculum based on their needs and the sort of life they are going to have and that sort of thing.
DHT: If it makes sense to do it in year 11, doesn't it also make sense to do it in year 10?
Jean: Except you might get late maturers or something like this.
DHT: . . . who would then be cut out of any academic development later on if they haven't had the groundwork. So there comes a point . . .
Jean: Yes, I find there's a lot of difference between year 10s and year 11s, even in the lower circle kids, they do tend to develop socially a bit more by year 11, particularly from the beginning of year 10 when they are often just crummy little fifteen year olds, but by the end of year 10 they mature a lot. I think if you split them up at the beginning of year 10, it would have the effect of cutting some people out of a chance that they may well be able to use.

Jean has had no experience of doing this kind of thing before. She simply had the emptiest timetable and was working in the other non-academic course (vocational and business studies).

She contacted the department for help, where she was eventually put into contact with someone in Research. He suggested that she organize a committee to plan the curriculum and that once the curriculum had been planned, Curriculum Branch would look over it and help them improve it. Within the school another new teacher has had some experience of curriculum planning and wishes to be part of the team. No provision has been made for any of the staff to plan in terms of time, experience, or advice.

Greenfield: schooling, alienation and employment

Jean has not found the professional reading to be of any help, indeed no one had recommended anything to her. She had, however, had a look at another school and was impressed with what they were doing. It is possible to read on local developments at the Research Branch, where they keep files of the different courses being developed in different schools. She thought this was of very limited value as files cannot be borrowed from the Branch and no time was allowed for her to read them in school time. The understanding she got from the Branch was that the emphasis is school-based curriculum development and she should go away and develop a school curriculum.*

DHT: And what about next year?
Jean: Next year? I don't know. It doesn't look like we'll get much help. I suppose we'll do something like this year. If I'm still here, that is.

---

* Methodological note: In Appendix 2 to this chapter a transcript is included of the last three paragraphs above which I have here summarized. I think the transcript highlights the advantages and disadvantages of summary.

The data: Section 5
Special duties staff

Bob Nichols, Youth Education Officer

I found it difficult to arrange a suitable time to meet Bob. He didn't seem to have any 'free' periods, and there was a constant stream of pupils through his door. Before I went in, he was explaining to a girl just how she should arrange for a job interview with an employer who had asked to see some Greenfield girls for office work. Whilst we talked, two other girls came in to borrow camping gear, and a boy was given directions as to what he would have to take to camp.

Bob gives the impression of great vitality: he speaks rapidly and gestures frequently, emphasizing points; he has a great deal to say. He is also a good listener, adopting an almost caricatured pose of 'I'm giving you my undivided attention'; also he picks up points one makes to elaborate or question them. I enjoyed the discussions and, when writing up later found that, unlike most other discussants, he accepted hardly anything I said without first changing the emphasis or modifying it in some way.*

The role of the Youth Education Officer is somewhat loosely defined. Briefly, he is not expected to teach more than a few periods a week in the school, the maximum being eight. He is supposed, through organizing work experience, counselling, and other courses, to help students bridge the gap between school and work. Bob takes a very full part in many of the more informal aspects of school life, particularly the camps and excursions. He spends much of his time simply being available to talk to students, and feels that he has to avoid the 'teacher image': he tries to get closer to students' thoughts and feelings than is possible when one is also trying to make them perform in school subjects.

The major problem Bob sees with the job is the short secondment (three years) he has. This affects Bob particularly in

---

* Methodological note: In some discussions the process of negotiation was a very real adjustment of meanings and emphasis, sometimes I simply rewrote the original if it was simply wrong, but at other times I retained the original, adding to the text the later comment upon it to gain extra and richer meaning rather than to replace it. The discussion reported here is an example of the latter process.

that he would like to obtain some formal qualifications relevant to his work, but can see little point in doing so when it is likely that he will be back in the classrooms (teaching Manual Arts) before he has finished. He stresses that the job is not one which one can just pick up and perform well in, but one which needs a period (he still sees himself very much as a learner) simply gaining the skills and information necessary to act effectively.

We began by discussing the value of Mathematics in life outside the school:

> *Bob:* I came through a trade, and ever since I left school, I've never had to use anything more than first year (Year 8) Maths. I think that now kids have twigged to it that what they are learning in schools is not relevant to employment. A point I keep making is that we still haven't really connected what a kid learns in Maths with its applications in a trade. When I taught Manual Arts, I found that it took kids a long time to discover that what they were doing in Geometry was in fact what they needed in Manual Arts. Take making a simple billy . . . the circumference formula they learned in Mathematics didn't seem to be relevant to the problem of the size of the bottom of the billy. Although it was the same, they didn't see it. The kids have twigged that most of what they do isn't even fulfilling an educational need, but is just because we have to teach them something because they come to school every day, and that's what fills up the time. Relevancy has disappeared and the kids have twigged to that.
> That's one thing, but the other thing is of course that with unemployment as it is today, many of the kids aren't going to get jobs anyway. They may shuffle the figures around but there will be a lot of kids without jobs.

We discussed several points here, such as the fact that, though the understandings were theoretically the same in the billy example, they were not seen to be the same because they were taught in entirely different contexts and upon different information.

It is probably a matter of students not bothering to learn the geometry taught in Mathematics, because they do not have any need of it at the time, but later, when they need it in Manual Arts, it has to be retaught and they have to relearn it, not because it has not been adequately taught the first time, but because they have decided not to learn it properly. If students do not apply what they learn in one part of the school at one time to

David H. Tripp

what they learn in another part of the school at another time, how are they going to apply what they learn in school as a whole to life?

With regard to the question of students not getting jobs when they leave, it is quite clear that a number of students decide that what they do at school makes little difference to their chances: they are in basic classes for most of their subjects, so the odds are too long to make the effort worthwhile. There is very little indeed for these students in the three years of secondary schooling.

These points demonstrate again how the school has to respond to totally opposed pressures: first we have the traditional commitment to academic learning which was/is always regarded as the key to employment and further education; on the other hand we have the predicament of students who are aware as early as year 8 that their school performance will alter their life very little, and hence for them there is very little point in schooling. Further, it may be said, that upper school, as the curriculum is at present constructed, is not a further qualification for employment in terms of what is learnt, but only in terms of the fact that the more able students tend to stay on, so an employer wishing to employ a more able student would tend to employ someone who had stayed on.

> [Subsequent comment: Bob pointed out that this was not entirely true as staying on for years 11 and 12 would reduce the apprenticeship from five years to three and a half or four, thus making years 11 and 12 more attractive. However, on the other hand, he explained that some employers deliberately avoided students with good academic qualifications:
>
> *Bob:* They find those kids easier to train when they haven't already done it differently at school. Also, of course, some kids who have not got good academic qualifications have been pushed into the more manual options, and they in fact have got better manual skills than the academic stream students.
>
> As an example he quoted a local smash repair firm as such an employer. This means that for some children it is actually an advantage to leave at year 10 rather than years 11 and 12.]

With regard to the fact that running two different courses in the school curriculum (academic and life skills) would mean selecting students from an early age, Bob said that they are being

Greenfield: schooling, alienation and employment

streamed for academic courses anyway and that at present pupils are very well aware of how the way they are streamed affects their job opportunities.

Bob: I've had kids in here at the beginning of year 10 crying because they did not know what they were going to do. I reckon that about 80 per cent of those who are going to leave in year 10 only have a very vague, or no idea at all of what they're going to do.

This would seem to be so, because students have no experience of what they could be, because they have simply been at school. Although work experience goes some way to showing them things that they could do, this is really a very limited scheme. Bob made the point that students do not know if they have the skills or the aptitude to do what they want to do, or what they can do with the skills and aptitude which they do have, or could acquire. Most students simply want to be what a friend, relative, or someone they know is.

[Subsequent comment: Bob gave the example of a girl who said she wanted to be a horticulturist but didn't know what a horticulturist was or what the job involved. She simply knew that a friend of her sister's was a horticulturist.]

We went on to talk about what the real skills were that students need for employment and, contrary to my expectation, Bob said that employers wanted students to have good communication skills. They wanted them to be able to talk over the telephone, to issue directions which were readily understood, and to receive and relay information accurately. Employers wanted students to be able to deal with clients and customers, to work well without misunderstandings with other people. In fact, Bob said that the school was doing so little with regard to these skills that employers tended to look more at the work experience references than the school reports.

[Subsequent comment: Bob pointed out that because employers were using the work experience reference, these references were becoming less like factory reports stressing the good and the bad points of the student, and more like testimonials, and that it should be left for the school to do the references, so that the prospective employer had an accurate picture of performance in the work situation.]

Students were well aware of the irrelevance of what they were being asked to do, and Bob suggested that their response was

David H. Tripp

either to create disciplinary problems in the school, or simply to switch off.

> *Bob:* There are a lot of kids just putting up with a lot of things. In other words they are not discipline problems, but they're just sitting there, they're just waiting and wasting time. I have a lot of kids pass through this office, 300 or 400 a week, and going by general comments, this is the case, they just don't think they're doing anything that is any use to them.

[Subsequent comment: *Bob*: That is not to say it is no use to them, much of it is useful general experience and background information, it's just that they don't see it as such.]

Bob has one period a week throughout the school year for year 10 pupils to get some career education. In this course he aims to broaden their view of the kind of work which they can do, to provide them with some social work skills, to do some basic work on filling in forms, telephoning, etc., and to give students practice at working in a co-operative team learning situation. He is going to begin the course by in-servicing all year 10 teachers and all those taking the year 11 alternative course.

An important issue which Bob seems to be addressing in this course is the problem which students have when they go from a learning (schoolwork) environment in which they are essentially required to sit on their own and do their own work, to one in which they are required to work producing things (employed work) with other people. Bob feels that students need help in acquiring these skills.

We moved on to discuss pupils' perceptions of their employment chances. Bob thinks that the majority of students think that they will get a job of some sort when they leave school, even though they have been told the realities of the situation. Local commonwealth employment statistics, for instance, show that in August of this year there were 240 people under twenty-one looking for a job in plumbing, and that there had been only four jobs available that month. The question then, is when and how to discover which pupils will not get a job, how and when to tell them this diagnosis, how to help them face the situation, and how to enable them to cope with unemployment.

Bob is continually being made aware of just how little thinking has gone into people's career choices. He quotes as an example a large increase in the number of boys wishing to become chefs:

> *Bob:* I always put the question to those boys, 'When you're

nineteen, what are the two most important things for you when you leave school at nineteen?' Almost invariably they say girls and cars. And I say, 'I'm sorry, but you're not going to be able to go out with girls because Thursday, Friday, Saturday nights you're going to be working!' And all of a sudden you've pulled the mat out from under their feet, because right up until the middle of year 10 they're sure they're going to be chefs. Now they're going to have to look for something else. And that's the sort of thing I have to keep telling kids all the time, because they just haven't thought of them. And these are some of the things I'm going to be doing in the career education.

Bob went on then to explain how disoriented students become when they have thought up until the time they leave that they are going to get a job and that it is going to be a particular kind of work. When they find they cannot do the work that they wish to, or that they're not going to get a job, then they become totally disoriented and forget everything that they have in fact been taught, such as the services offered by the Career Reference Centre. Bob says a number of students come back, out of a job, and he asks them if they have been to the centre and they say that they had not thought of doing so, although all year 10 students have been taken there on a visit to see the services offered.

Another problem Bob encounters with the pupils who are leaving is that they have just had no experience in the importance of meeting deadlines and getting forms returned on time. The point is that they have probably never had to do this before. But he has pupils coming on the very day that applications for apprenticeships have to be returned to the firm asking for a reference. Sometimes the principal is away that day and it is very difficult to get his signature.

One approach to alleviating the problem of the unemployed school leaver advocated by Bob, and indeed he is actively engaged in its realization, is to start an employment co-operative which would build and rent BMX bicycles. They are trying to persuade the local shire to build a racing track, and the idea is that students would be able to buy a share in the enterprise that would guarantee them a job when they leave. Bob contrasts this with the 'Young Achievers Scheme' (run by Malcolm Kramer) which is perceived to be more a training and talent spotting ground for large business enterprises. It gives pupils an opportunity to see through simulation how big companies work,

David H. Tripp

and it enables teachers and businessmen to observe how pupils perform in it. Bob is acutely aware of the difficulties many students face because of their background and family expectations, 'What end up as employment problems usually begin at home'.

I asked Bob what he thought alienation meant in the Greenfield context. He gave me an immediate reply.

> *Bob:* Well, we have kids at one of the most active parts of their lives, and we put them in the classroom asking them to sit still and learn but their body says no, I'm sixteen and growing and I want to be doing things.
> This is different from the days of the junior certificate in that the majority of students were doing things outside the school at sixteen, unless they enjoyed sitting down and learning, in which case they became the minority which stayed on.

In other words the problem is that of universal comprehensive schooling to the age of sixteen.

— — — —

Shirley Bowie, Year 10 Co-ordinator

Shirley made it very clear to me from the outset that she did not want to be interviewed because she thought that she could have little to contribute to the study. I was concerned by this for two reasons: (a) as Year 10 Co-ordinator she has a quite different and regular contact with a number of students, particularly those with difficulties, and (b) because reluctance to participate suggested that I was intruding, wasting time, or in other ways not handling the situation well. However, Shirley did give me forty minutes and said she would allow a second discussion to negotiate the first.

We met in Shirley's little office which was set out with chairs so that four people could sit facing each other to talk. On this occasion she sat behind her desk. Shirley's teaching subject is Domestic Science.

I first asked Shirley to tell me what she did in her job, and the extent to which what she actually did reflected what she would like to do in the best of all possible worlds.

> *Shirley:* I think it should involve dealing with students' problems; but it doesn't always appear to be like that. I seem

to deal a lot with absenteeism, trying to catch up with those
that wag it. I feel what we should have is a social worker,
rather than untrained people.

What I would like to do is to find out why students go absent
all the time, why some will miss certain classes, but there isn't
time, and I am not trained for that kind of work.

I asked if there were discernible patterns in absenteeism and
Shirley said that as a subject, Maths was popularly missed and
that, as for times of the week, the last two periods on Friday
were extremely popular to miss. And with regard to particular
pupils she said that certain pupils are *habitués*, and that others
very rarely absent themselves. Shirley repeated her point that
chasing students was not her job, and we went on to discuss the
way in which she had to operate in this capacity.

Briefly, staff hand in lists of students that have been absent
from their lessons during the day, and administration correlates
these with the absentee list, feeding the names of those who
should have been in a particular class back to the year co-
ordinators the following day, and it is then their job to find the
pupil to discover why they missed that lesson.

Shirley has 288 pupils in year 10, which makes it quite
impossible for her to interview them individually as she would
like. She would like to have more information on individual
students, being able to build up a file including such information
as their home background and school problems. Shirley said that
most students' problems do not surface in the present system.

Shirley: There are only a very few students who come over
here to talk when they have got trouble, and that is because
they will hardly come to someone with whom they have had
little contact and do not know. Although I feel that some have
come to me because I had them in year 9 last year. I still
haven't got to know many of them.

I asked Shirley who the pupils did talk with about their problems.
'I don't think they talk to anyone. Probably, if they talk to
anyone, it's Sister. When they are, or pretend to be, sick they go
to her and they have the opportunity to talk'. When I asked
about students talking to the guidance officer, Shirley said that he
was perceived more as someone to talk to about careers, and that

as he was part-time and had only come this year, he was not someone with whom many students would discuss problems.

The contact Shirley has with students at present, apart from her teaching, is that they must come to her for passes to enable them to go home at lunchtime. This is the only reason students have for seeking her out. In order to encourage pupils to see her more, Shirley is in her room with an open door from twenty past eight in the morning to the beginning of school, and every lunch hour.

> *Shirley:* Those that come, they know that I am available, but I only get one or two. And those that do come tend to want to spend every lunchtime here, so it doesn't reach out to everybody, but perhaps not everybody needs that kind of contact: maybe we are getting to the ones that need it, and the others don't.

[This was a significant comment, because it shows that in spite of Shirley's concern she does not really have the information which would enable her to know if she was reaching those students who most needed contact.]

> *DHT:* I suppose the very fact that your job is to chase them up will mean that the absentee students will not come to you to talk about their problems, because you have to discipline them?
>
> *Shirley:* No I don't. I just have to find out why they were absent. I see my role definitely as a helper, not as a disciplinarian. If I come on heavy then they're definitely not going to come and talk about problems.

If it appears that a particular student is continually missing particular lessons then Shirley, without directly questioning the teacher, tries to discover whether there is in fact a personality clash between the student and the teacher, and whether the student should move to another group.

Perhaps the nearest Shirley comes to a disciplinary role, is when she rings the students' parents in order to discover the reason for absence. This would be construed by many students as the same as a telephone call from the deputy head, which is used as a disciplinary measure, putting pressure on the parents to deal with the pupil at home.

Greenfield: schooling, alienation and employment

Shirley cited at least one case in which she felt she had been used by parents to put undue pressure onto a student. Had she known the student better, and the home background, Shirley felt she would have behaved quite differently. Shirley has found that because she was seen by the student as working for the parents, she has lost that student's confidence, and the student has one less person to turn to about her problems. Shirley has now to wait until she can establish a different relationship with the student.

— — — —

Broadly speaking there were two major problems in fostering a trusting relationshp with students: the first for Shirley is to find sufficient time to devote to an individual student:

Shirley: Kids need at least an hour of solid time when you give them your undivided attention. They don't come to the point quickly, you need to talk your way into and around it. I don't get that kind of time with them.

The second major problem is that 'contacts have to grow', and seeing only a minority of the students for brief contacts means that it does take a long time for students to build a trusting relationship with a year tutor. Obviously continuity of staffing through years 8, 9 and 10 would go a long way towards facilitating such growth, but the rule has been that a year tutor looks after the same year over a period and hence looks after different children each year as they move through the school. Shirley has been an exception in that this year she has moved up with the students, and said, 'I wouldn't contemplate starting with a different group this year when I am only just getting to know them'.

Camp was perceived by Shirley, as by all other staff involved, as being 'a time when contacts take a great leap forward', but at camp this can be effective only after some kind of initial relationship has been established and fostered.

I suggested that many students were a problem in the school not because they did not wish to learn, but because they did not wish to learn in the manner in which they were being taught. Although Shirley felt there may be something in that idea, she felt the fact that many kids were staying on who, if they could get a job would have left, was a greater source of problem.

David H. Tripp

> *Shirley:* Some of them are, of course, just lazy, they don't want to work. Also they aren't used to being told what to do; I think that at home some of them are left to their own devices and when they come to school and are required to work, it comes as a bit of a shock. I think the problem is a lot of them have not had the training at home. They haven't learnt to do what they are told when they are told.

- - - -

I asked Shirley to define what she meant by alienation.

> *Shirley:* Absence, rudeness, loudmouthedness, general nuisance, things like spitting, graffiti, and flaunting rules.

The data: Section 6

Jeff Toohey, Principal

Jeff's office is pleasantly informal, with his desk at one end of the room out of the way behind the door, and easy chairs spaciously placed around a coffee table at the other. When I came to knock at the door, I found it half open; Jeff asked me in and he immediately left what he was writing at his desk and we sat opposite each other across the coffee table. He immediately made me feel thoroughly at ease by his informal manner, enthusiasm, and apparent interest in the project.

Jeff is rather an unusually young principal for what is known to be a difficult school, and one which was, before he came, run in a very idiosyncratic fashion. I soon learned from Jeff that his style was 'democratic', and that he had instituted appropriate mechanisms for participation in decision-making within the school. These included weekly senior staff meetings, a school council of elected pupils, consultation in most matters, and making himself very accessible to the whole school.

On the first occasion we met, we simply discussed the nature of the project and its demands on and possible benefits to the school.* Jeff would not give me any indication as to whether I could use the school or not until he had put the proposal to the staff as a whole. This involved my producing a short statement of the aims, scope and procedures of the project, which he then circulated in the satff room a week prior to the matter being discussed in a full staff meeting, where it was accepted.

I did not see Jeff again until I had met several other staff, and had been in the school for nearly a fortnight. When I did see him it was to ask about his view of the Alternative course. He explained that there were in effect three courses in the upper school, academic, commercial, and the general studies course, the latter being seen as the 'Alternative'.

---

* Methodological note: I chose to have as little contact with Jeff as possible throughout the study because I did not want to risk appearing to staff as 'informing the principal'. Although it was unlikely, given Jeff's personality and philosophy, that regular meetings with him would be construed as such it was not until I was well into the study that I was sure of this and by then the substance of the study had shifted away from the concerns of the administration to the perceptions of pupils and staff. Thus I used these discussions with Jeff only as a way of checking his perception of those matters over which he had direct control.

David H. Tripp

Jeff: [General studies is for] a group of students who have returned here virtually because they haven't got a job. In general the philosophy of the course is to give them a chance to mature more, to give them a few saleable extra skills (extra saleable skills!), or I would like it to be, I've got lots of misgivings about it . . . we started out with very good ambitions for it, but I don't know if they've been realized . . . but we're spending lots of time this year working on it to improve it. It's only been going two years.

DHT: So you'd have kids in there who are waiting to leave, so that you'd retain nearly all your academic group, the majority of your Business group, but only a minority of the General Studies group?

Jeff: Yes, except sometimes they will transfer from CSE to General Studies. They've had a go and realize they can't handle it. Most of the CSE who leave will leave at the end of the first term. I've had them come up to me and say, 'I've had a go, but I can't handle it. I'm off'. I think that the leaving rate might tend to slow down because of the unavailability of employment, although a counteracting factor is that while they are in year 11 they turn sixteen, qualify for the dole, and leave school, nullifying the fact that they haven't got a job. The fact that they can't get the dole would be a contributing factor in their staying on after year 10.

Quite clearly tied into the questions about the structure of the alternative course was that of staffing, for both Jeff and other staff (see Jean Dunn) had said that the lack of continuity of responsibility for the course led to most of its problems.

DHT: One thing that seems relevant to the study is the department's procedures for promotion and staffing. There often seems to be little rhyme or reason about who has been posted where and when, and the principal seems to have very little say about who is appointed to his school, or a head of department about who his assistant teachers are going to be. This appears to affect the school in a number of different ways, particularly with regard to the mounting of a course such as the year 11 alternatives.

Jeff replied to the effect that, 'although it has been said that the main aim of the Western Australian education department is to provide a promotional structure for teachers to progress through', my criticism was both naïve and unfair. He suggested that teachers were not moved about without reason, but that the nature of the State and problems of country service meant that teachers did have to be moved regularly. The centralized system was necessary in Western Australia, and one of the necessary features of a centralized system is that individual teachers, senior masters, and principals have less control over appointments. Furthermore, Jeff was well aware of the problem and had made a case in his 1978/1979 school report to the effect that certain schools such as Greenfield, with particular difficulties, should be made Special Appointment schools, precisely to enable the principal and existing staff to build a school with a reasonably coherent philosophy to which the majority of staff subscribed.

This brought us to the next point I wished to discuss, that of the differences amongst the staff in their diagnosis of the problem of alienation from school. Jeff expressed the feeling that a uniform philosophy amongst staff was not in the best interests of the school, and that there should always be a range of diversity. However, problems did arise when staff were so divergent in their individual philosophies that some staff were inevitably working against the aims of others. In this regard he feels it is important for the senior staff to have a greater say in school appointments.

Jeff felt that the philosophy of the school was more of a compromise between opposing views than an eclectic view of the same concerns. Towards the end of the discussion we returned to the problem and I enquired as to his use of the word 'consistency' in staff philosophy which he had used in his report.

> *Jeff:* It's not that I want a team of 'yes' people, but I don't want people who are philosophically opposed, but that's what we have got: we've got complete opposition and in that situation you won't even get consensus, you will just get strife.

When we moved on to the topic of the purpose of schooling, whether it is purely for academic intellectual development or preparing children for life in a wider sense, Jeff drew on the new programme for gifted children to express the idea that the school should be catering for individual differences and it could do so with regard to intellectual development but that, because it was doing so, it should not be seen as the sole or even the main aim of schooling.

He also made the point that vocational training was 'in conflict with the aims of secondary education'. He went on to say, quoting the Dettman Report, that the aim was 'vocational preparedness', which is quite different from 'vocational training'. The training aspects, seen by Jeff, were the legitimate domain of technical and further education. The distinction seemed to me to be in terms of the generality of the education given. Vocational training is limited to the acquisition of particular marketable skills (such as operating a lathe or industrial sewing machine), whereas secondary education has to do with preparing an individual for life (and hence employment) and places more emphasis upon personal qualities than particular operational skills.

Jeff sees that it is possible to rationalize the presence of vocational training courses in the school, as being situations in which personal development may also take place.

Returning to the philosophy of education, Jeff said that his real problem was that there is no occasion when the school staff can get together as a group for an extended period to work out a philosophy of education for the school. Jeff felt that it was an easier exercise to perform in the country than in the town, because the staff were all living locally and involved in the community in a way which the staff of a metropolitan school almost invariably were not.

The last problem to be discussed was that of in-service. I suggested that the real problem was that in-service was an optional exercise and that the very people one felt needed it most were those least likely to participate. Jeff explained that it was up to the senior masters, for they could make anyone go to a particular course.

I did not think that this got around the problem, which was partly the relatively small amount of investment by the department in in-service, which resulted in relatively few courses of short duration being available in the first place. Second, that it may well be that the senior masters are the very people who are in the greatest need of in-service. And third, that it was well known that staff should attend in-service courses in groups if changes were to be effected.

Our final discussion took place late in the year when the alternative course had been planned for the next year. Jeff explained that because of the restrictions in staffing, and because of the lack of other resources, they had decided to integrate it with the existing year 11 courses, allowing the pupils to take four subjects which they could continue to CSE level in year 12 if they so wished, and four other optional subjects. I said that, in other words, the formula had changed, but the basic structure was the same: pupils in the alternative course would be provided with more of the same and treated just like other upper school pupils. Jeff denied this, pointing out that it was a 'general studies' course, and that it was the best that could be done under the circumstances.

Mary Sims, Deputy Principal

Mary was very busy during the week I wished to meet her but she set aside an hour and we sat in her office to talk. This was a mistake for, apart from the noise of a mower just outside the window, the 'phone rang more than a dozen times, and three times we were interrupted by pupils at the door.

Mary is officially termed 'Deputy Principal Female' in the staffing book and, although the lack of punctuation in the title provides scope for the imagination, it describes her duties perfectly. As deputy principal she carries a heavy load of administration, everything but the timetable so far as I could see, and as a woman teacher she is ultimately responsible for everything concerning the girls which male teachers cannot or will not do. These latter duties stretch from the writing on the walls in the girls' toilets to dealing with personal problems from pregnancy to feelings of academic inadequacy to inappropriate dress.

Not surprisingly I found Mary an energetic talkative person who does not suffer fools gladly. Sometimes I felt foolish as I was, and still am, ignorant of many of the less obvious aspects of the running of the school.

Mary's first reaction to my outlining the aims and scope of the project was that the school's problems were imported from society: as there was no prospect of a job for many of the students, there was nothing for them to work for, so they felt school was a waste of time and treated it accordingly. Or, another example was the growing racial problem in the school (thirty Aboriginal students). Because these students tended to be alienated they truanted more and then could not cope when in the classroom, which reinforced their alienation and completed the circle.

Mary felt that there were two groups of students with particular problems: the first group were those of low ability who were having difficulty coping with the demands of school anyway; the second group were students who could do much

David H. Tripp

better but were under-achieving because of other factors.

With regard to the first group, Mary estimated there were about 10 per cent of the students (twenty-four in each year) who were in need of an alternative course comprising mainly basic skills of numeracy, literacy, etc., and social and survival skills. There would be a similar group in each year of students who were not coping with these basic skills. At present these students are not withdrawn from their classes, which means that they get no special remedial programme designed to cater for their needs. It is a philosophy of the principal to have no withdrawal groups, but there must be ways of withdrawing students other than placing them in separate classes. One of the possible effects of the principal's policy is that students are set (by achievement) in their classes for the individual subjects except for Social Studies, for which the classes are heterogeneous throughout.

With regard to the second group of students (those who were under-achieving) Mary felt that the problem lay with the broader community problems, and not with the school curriculum. She felt that the problems that many of the students faced at home in their everyday lives should be left at home as far as possible, and these students should not be deprived of academic success as would be the case were they offered a non-academic course in social skills and personal development. Mary also made the point that students will be leaving school for jobs, where they will have to cope whatever their home background. However, she also recognized that the absence of employment resulted in total immersion in the problems of home life for many students.*

My general impression was that Mary believed that there was no course which could help students with their home problems, and therefore an academically oriented course was the answer in that it at least left open the option for students to gain qualifications which would perhaps better their chances of employment.

We arrived at the conclusion that different groups of teachers in the school were interpreting the same problems quite differently, with different successes and difficulties. For instance, the humanities groups have as a main aim, helping students meet

---

* Methodological note: This statement was written entirely without quotation as an experiment. Because of the 'dead' and formal account, I felt that much of the immediacy and impact of what was said had been lost, and did not employ the same device in other statements. I have, however, included it here as I originally wrote it, as an example of that form of presentation.

their needs with regard to their personal and social life, to which academic excellence is secondary. Other teachers perceive their problems as being the lowering of academic standards and difficulties with regard to this. On the other hand, most Science and most Mathematics teachers have tried to retain academic standards and the pursuit of excellence, which can best be achieved by a traditional discipline, which has led to problems of attitude to work amongst their students, as some Science staff have reported.

Mary sees part of the answer being that the school needs more para-professional help to enable teachers to get on with the job of teaching whilst social workers and guidance officers look after the other aspects of the pupils' welfare.

Mary summed it up by saying that, although she believes the purpose of schooling is academic excellence, she would put 'people first and scholars second'. She elaborated by saying that if the pursuit of academic excellence was going to produce a child with a grudge against society, she would prefer to have a child who was well balanced and socialized rather than one who had achieved good CSE results.

Returning to the role of the school curriculum, Mary said that it was more a matter of how the students were treated than a matter of the content of the curriculum which they were taught. I suggested that there was not a necessary distinction or even a relation between meeting the students' needs and the content of the curriculum, for no one had yet shown that a curriculum based upon the social and emotional needs of the student could or would in fact meet those needs. However, Mary stressed that teachers of the highest calibre could hope both to teach an academic curriculum and meet a student's personal needs at the same time. So it would appear that there could be a practical conflict between the two aims for a teacher who was experiencing difficulties, even if there was not a necessary philosophical one.

One of Mary's greatest concerns was that good scholars were leaving school simply to get away from their own problems. So long as students attended school they were dependent upon home, and with problems such as parental cruelty, physical violence, and incest not uncommon, students had every reason to wish to become independent and leave home.

We spent some time talking about what kind of support Mary gets in her job as deputy principal. It was significant that Mary interpreted support as being the practical, procedural kind (such as in-service courses on aspects of school administration, or more

David H. Tripp

help from Community Welfare) rather than the inner life of the teacher, or the development and maintenance of a philosophy of education. To me this reflected the great day-to-day pressures of the job.

Anne Marlow, Acting Deputy Principal

Anne was made acting deputy principal for a term while Shirley Bowie was on long service leave. As I thought that she might have a different perspective of the school and her work from this new role, I talked to her specifically about this. It was difficult to find a suitable time as both she and I were busy, but I have transcribed below without comment extracts from what she said. I felt that there was little point in glossing her words as she made the points so clearly.

> *Anne:* It's been a real education for me. I've found that what classroom teachers don't know is just what it's like to be a teenager in this district. We think some of them have problems; but we see only the special problems. In fact all of them have problems just through being a teenager. For instance, they literally don't know whether their friend will still be their friend tomorrow. That's not just how I remember being a teenager, it happened to all of us, but now they get into gangs and fight each other, it's almost gang warfare, except that the gangs are always changing.
> What we don't realize is that because we would find their problems trivial to us today, they are not trivial to them. Take name-calling. We think it really doesn't matter much if we're called a 'bitch' or accused of being a 'slut' (that's the worst you can be called, according to them), what matters to us is whether we are what we're called or not. But to them it's really important, so important that they'll fight over it. Problems like that just aren't seen in class, they happen elsewhere, and it's only in this office that they really become apparent.
> Another thing you don't realize is how individually sensible pupils can become senseless in mobs. They aren't really socialized to school values at all, though we treat them as if they are, and one aspect of school values is that their values are trivial and insignificant. Of course they aren't, and that's where most problems arise. That means that what they need is counselling, not discipline. That just makes matters worse,

they need to be listened to and advised and helped, but I find that the great temptation is simply to treat kids expediently. That's all we have time for. Not to listen, but to administer some kind of punishment.

Another problem is that many staff, particularly those who've been here for a long time, don't realize how the area itself is changing. There's a lag in perceptions, but this is becoming one of the inner suburbs where young people, professional people can still afford to buy a house. The old idea of this being a homogeneous lower class area hangs on, and it's communicated to newer staff, and they form opinions about the kids, and so the kids themselves then start to underachieve. How you can begin to change this, I don't know.

Which is perhaps the proper place to end this study.

The researcher's analysis: Section 7

As was indicated in the introduction, this section is in no way a summary or synthesis of all the ideas and information contained in the other sections of this report, and still less of all the data collected during the study. This section is basically my own view of the issues and the school's response to them. I have aimed to provide both an explanation of and a gloss on the previous data sections, but I reiterate, it is essentially my own interpretation. There will be almost as many other interpretations as readers. I make no apology for this as I believe it to be a basic tenet of case study that the researcher both aspire and be limited to such a role.

The problem

> The school must provide kids with the skills and security to face a jobless future. It is a master subterfuge to ask them to give three years to education without the prospect of employment at the end. Schools must change.
> (Neil Douglas, Acting Deputy Principal)

It was clearly stated in the original entry document that the researchers anticipated a connection between pupils' employment prospects and their attitude towards school. In general it may be said that the extent to which such an interaction is amenable to discovery and description is dependent upon the symptomatic phenomena being accessible to the case study worker. The phenomena must either be manifested in such a manner that the researcher can interpret them as symptomatic, or they must be seen by the respondents themselves so they can articulate the symptoms for the researcher to describe. Although the reader will find both sources of interpretation in this study, I had reservations about the extent to which the interaction between alienation and employment was in fact amenable to articulation because of the difficulty of describing the phenomena as they were perceived by the pupils involved. This was not simply a function of the extent to which it was difficult to access the pupils' observations and thoughts, but more a function of the role and importance of schooling in their view of life.

For example, pupils' responses suggest that they see secondary school simply as a stage in life which has to be lived through before it becomes possible to pass on to the next stage. It is as if secondary school is seen as nothing more than the essential means of transport to employment, like catching a bus to another town: the bus changes them in no way, it does not prepare them for arrival at that other town in any way, but the only way for them to get to that town is by riding on the right bus. And this became the problem of this study: to what extent was it possible to discover and describe a phenomenon which was not perceived by a number of those participating in the situation under investigation?

To discover the absence of something which appears to be missing, to define what it is missing from, and deduce its nature can of itself be valuable. That is, if there is a hole in something it is important to discover what it is that has the hole, its location, dimensions, and probably causes. And this was the kind of outcome I expected early in the study. However, I found that pupils did see other aspects of a relationship between school and employment. For instance, even though what they had to do at school was not of itself preparation for employment, they knew that the way in which they did it was. These pupils said such things as, 'If you get better marks you'll get a better job', and 'You won't get an SEC apprenticeship if you're basic in Maths'.

On the other hand, some pupils maintained precisely the opposite view, that employers were just not interested in academic marks, and, 'It doesn't matter how good you are at Social Studies, if you're not good on the job you'll get sacked'. And in a sense, and with reference to some jobs, the view was accurate. The youth education officer could quote local employers (such as a smash repair firm) who said that a good academic record was a disqualification for a job with them because pupils who are good at academic subjects spend more time studying them and consequently less time on manual and craft subjects. Pupils who took this view had school subjects clearly prioritized according to their direct value or utility for their chosen field of employment.
Alienation: Basal or Aggravated?

Another quite different problem to emerge was whether there had been a change in the level of alienation amongst pupils and, if so, could it be attributed to a change in employment expectations when there was no record of the levels of alienation in previous years? So it was necessary for me to make the following assumption: the degree to which potentially alienating factors will alienate is a function of other dissatisfactions. Embedded in this idea is the further assumption that alienation can be characterized as having a threshold below which the pupil tolerates a measure of dissatisfaction, but beyond which the pupil will become alienated. This is, of course, a characteristic not found in, for instance, a Marxist definition in which all subjects are alienated from the state in some degree all the time.

The reason for making this point at the outset is that, whilst it is important to take into consideration all the potentially alienating factors encountered by a pupil, in this study both pupils and teachers used the term to apply only to those pupils who were extremely or violently alienated from school. Alienation was not seen as a continuous feature of being, but as an exceptional state arrived at by a few individuals. I have tried to reflect the respondents' usage of the term by distinguishing between alienation as a (relatively) static state of being arrived at by a few pupils, and the dissatisfactions encountered by all pupils which are the contributory causes of alienation.

Thus I have included in this study observations of what I regard as implicit sources of dissatisfaction. That is to say, aspects of school such as the underlying messages in teacher comments to pupils, which have not been articulated by respondents as causes or symptoms of alienation. These are seen as relevant because they must add to the accumulated dissatisfaction experienced and, hence, ultimately contribute to a pupil passing the threshold of alienation. I have here raised the two fundamental problems of the study (pupil perceptions of the relationships between school and work, and the nature of alienation from schooling) to foreground them as they were from the outset the focus of the study.

Defining alienation

Contrary to normal practice, I did not define what was meant by the term 'alienation' at the commencement of the study, because I wished to discover the meanings that the word had for participants, rather than to impose a preconceived notion. I wished to first discover whether the term had meaning for the participants at all. Had I asked respondents for their definition of the term at the outset, no doubt they would have supplied me with one whether or not it was an accurate reflection of their perceptions. Then, having defined the term, respondents may well have simply found evidence for the presence or absence of alienation in the terms of the definition they had produced.

So, in order to uncover the meanings respondents themselves attached to the term 'alienation', I simply used it without definition, and then analysed the way in which they used it. Immediately it was apparent that the concept was universally held and quite clear to participants because none asked me what I meant by the term. Had respondents themselves been unclear about what I meant, or what they themselves meant by it, or had they a number of different definitions available, it would have been likely that I would have been challenged to explain my definition. However, on reading the report, Fran Barnes pointed out to me that she was operating on my definition rather than her own because the definition she used in our discussions, and hence the definition I assumed she was operating by, was rather her guess at my unstated definition than what I took to be her own unconscious definition. Although one can see how such a circle of assumptions occurred, I do not believe it resulted in substantive error. On the contrary, it was a powerful support for my conclusion that the overt discipline problem was the most common definition of alienation: Fran assumed that that was my definition because it was the most generally held definition within the school.

During the study three broad definitions of alienation emerged from the staff; in all cases they were expressed at the level of particulars (names of alientated pupils, or behaviours indicative of alienation). At one end of an apparent continuum was the pupil who was an overt and disruptive behaviour (discipline) problem, and at the other end was the pupil who was passively uncooperative, who sullenly refused to participate but who did not need disciplinary action as such. The first pole was the common definition of alienation given by staff. Somewhere between the two was the pupil who had opted out, simply withdrawn from the aims and activities of schooling, demonstrating this by habitual absence and underachievement, but without confrontation or total rejection.

The overt behaviour problem was often termed 'bucking the system', and involved misdemeanours such as physical violence to people and property, verbal abuse and taking every opportunity to disrupt lessons. The extent to which this kind of behaviour occurred was seen by staff and pupils alike as a response to teacher competence, not as an indication of the degree to which the pupil was alienated from schooling in general. This may be explained by the fact that this kind of anti-school behaviour is both the most easily controlled by staff, and the most obvious when out of control.

At the other extreme, a change in behaviour was reported when the passively rejecting pupil became 'alienated'. In other words, for the pupil to be classified as alienated, the classifier was recalling some 'baseline' of behaviour from which the pupil had changed. The baseline was sometimes expressed in terms of social features such as communicativeness, but most often expressed in terms of the quality and quantity of work produced. It was, at its least visible, 'dropping out' whilst still remaining within the system. These pupils merely met minimum requirements.

Hence it could be said that teachers allowed pupils to express their alienation in different ways: 'I have no discipline problems, it's the attitude of the kids that's wrong', followed by 'There's nothing I can do about the kids' attitudes, they get them from outside school, it's not the school's fault'.* On the other hand, teachers who did admit to discipline problems generally felt personally responsible for the pupils' alienation. Thus teachers who saw alienation primarily as overt behaviour, named certain pupils as being alienated from particular subjects and particular teachers, rather than from school as such.

In general the definitions fell into two broad categories the first of which included those where the school was seen as having to cope with pupils who were primarily alienated from the whole of society in general, and secondarily from school as a particular part of society. In this view, school was not instrumental in aggravating alienation. Of individual definitions, only Malcolm Kramer's was societally rather than educationally oriented, although in less direct words, the home background and the social class of the pupils were generally blamed for alienation within the school.

The second class of definition was one in which school was seen as being the prime cause of alienation from school in that the school attempted to impose an alien set of behaviours and standards upon the pupils.

It is not surprising that these two quite radically different

---

* Methodological note: Fictitious exemplary statement. Unless quotations are attributed, they are the author giving an example of the kind of statement encountered.

conceptions of the term should clash upon a number of occasions in the day-to-day running of the school. Just to illustrate the point during the year I was on site there was controversy about what to do with the pupils who were not containable in normal classes because of behavioural problems, and the two dominant points of view corresponded broadly to the two conflicting definitions of alienation prevailing in the school.

One faction wanted to form 'a special programme for students whose behaviour is so extreme as to cause physical danger to other students in and out of the classroom'. (Malcolm Kramer) This group's plan was dubbed 'The Gorilla Group' in discussions. It involved taking all the most difficult pupils from the lower school out of their ordinary classes to put them in a separate class under a strict disciplinarian who would concentrate on 'knocking some sense into them' and teaching the basic skills of literacy and numeracy which so many of these pupils lacked. The pupils would attend this class for certain lengths of time during which they would be isolated from other pupils by arriving and departing school at different times and taking different breaks during the day.

The alternative espoused by the opposing faction was a 'Drop-in Centre' to which pupils who were causing trouble could be sent or go voluntarily. A 'pairing' system would also operate, so that a chronically difficult pupil would be the responsibility of a particular staff member, thus giving the pupil someone with a caring interest to whom they could turn. After school the centre would be staffed by trained social workers.

This latter scheme was eventually accepted, and Schools Commission funds obtained late in the year. The incident showed that it was quite clear that although the two groups of staff were equally concerned about the same symptoms, they interpreted them quite differently. This difference is returned to in my analysis of teaching and alienation.

School alienation and employment prospects

For most of this century there has been a common expectation that those who do well at school will get a good job as the direct result of their school achievement. That this is no longer necessarily so is perhaps the greatest problem schools are having to face. Hitherto many of those pupils who did not really enjoy school were content to sit through it and to try to do well simply

David H. Tripp

because it affected the kind of job they could get. One might therefore expect that when the certainty of a job was removed such pupils would become totally alienated from it. Although the potential for such a causal relationship is present, it did not appear to me that this was yet happening at Greenfield. What is happening instead is that the majority of pupils appear to still believe that they will get a job if they satisfactorily complete their schooling and obtain the required certificate.

Indications of the changes that have taken place in the youth employment market are job advertisements such as the following, which appeared in the local newspaper (name changed):

> BYRON'S COFFEE SHOP
> Wanted for immediate start
> Trainee waitress. On the job training.
> Smart appearance and CSE
> Telephone for appointment.

With such intense competition for jobs one would have expected most pupils to be doubtful of their chances of obtaining one. That the pupils did not appear to take the possibility of unemployment seriously was very puzzling to me until I perceived that it appeared to be the result of two processes; on the one hand teachers were sending pupils the message that if they tried hard and did well they would get a job; and on the other hand, no one in the school was telling them personally that they had very little chance of employment on leaving. With regard to the first, I found that in the main teachers are still saying the same things about the importance of schooling for employment that they have always said: pupils are still exhorted to do well so they can get a job. Thus, contrary to much of the evidence on the media and in the locality, pupils believe that in spite of the manifest difficulties, if they respond to the exhortation, it means that they will be the ones to be employed.

To a large extent this is true. In an ever more competitive employment situation employers have to prespecify selection criteria, and what simpler criterion than the quality of school leaving certificate? To have achieved well at school means that the candidate is at least reasonably able, has learned to persevere with dull tasks, and in some important respects has conformed to expectations. Hence the newspaper advertisement above; why take a trainee who has achieved less when there are so many available who have achieved more? Both some staff and many pupils, however, were confused about this important point. They seemed to assume that, because jobs were obtained by the best pupils, failure to obtain a job was principally the pupils' failure. This is to ignore the character of the current situation which is such that there will be failures regardless of how much those who fail have actually achieved. For many pupils their failure is more a failure of the employment system in which they must compete. It is the difference between norm referencing and criteria referencing. I believe the school should clarify the minimum criteria necessary for employment, and hold pupils responsible for achieving these, rather than to suggest that they are personally responsible if they cannot obtain a job. The perpetuation of confusion on this point must aggravate the loss of self-esteem which may result in an unemployed pupil becoming permanently unemployable.

The second point, the matter of pupils not being told the reality of their chances, is hardly surprising as no one can possibly know in advance which pupils will eventually be unemployed. All predictions are based upon past trends. Suppose, therefore, that there is a chronically unable pupil who comes from a family of pedigree dole-bludgers, who is disruptive in a year 9 class. He has nearly two more years' compulsory education ahead of him. Who is going to predict that he will not be able to get a job? With what certainty? And even were accurate predictions available, would it be right to convince him at that age that he was unemployable, especially if there were not a suitable 'alternative' curriculum available? To make the obvious prediction would clearly be to make a self-fulfilling prophesy, and who would wish to be responsible for that? Hardly surprising then that staff do not take it upon themselves to inform individual pupils of the reality of their employment chances.

To summarize the teachers' view, employment chances are seen as a competition where the most deserving still win; they do not expect some pupils to obtain jobs, but nevertheless use the importance of a good certificate to coerce reluctant pupils to work. Clearly, behind this view are two of the most deep-seated value judgments society has of schooling: that it is important to have (or to want to have) a job; and that the purpose of school is both to make potential students into students, potentially employable pupils employable, and to select out those who are neither students nor employable.

The pupils' views appeared to be somewhat different, though not necessarily in opposition to those of the staff. First many asserted that all their friends who had left had obtained jobs.

Deeper probing revealed that they all knew some who hadn't, but these were not mentioned because they also asserted anyone could get a job if they wanted one. Their friends who hadn't got jobs said it was because they didn't want a job.

This argument could not be taken at face value, however, for research on the unemployed school leaver shows that failure to get a job leads, amongst other things, to a crisis in self-image and esteem. The fact that many of those who, according to the pupils, did not want jobs were in fact actively seeking employment suggests that they were probably saying that they did not want a job simply as a face-saving measure. In this respect pupils were being misled by their own peers about their job prospects.

Another commonly held pupil viewpoint was that they would be employed through family or other ties and contacts. Several mentioned that they had uncles who would employ them regardless of how well they did at school; and others claimed that friends could find them jobs where they worked. This is an undeniable factor: it does matter who you know, and a minority of pupils obtain jobs in this manner.

Another group of pupils, perhaps those who caused the greatest anxiety to the staff, were those who left before completing their studies because they had an offer of employment. Michael quoted the girl who left a few weeks before her exams, and staff in every core area cited examples of pupils who could have done well at school had they stayed on but who left early to get a job.

Five common reasons were put forward by pupils and staff for this decision to leave early:

(a) they thought it would be easier to get a job because they could be employed as a junior or under other assistance schemes;
(b) they thought they'd have better chances of employment during rather than at the beginning or end of a school year;
(c) they could gain experience which would give them a lead over other pupils who stayed on;
(d) they disliked school and simply wished to leave;
(e) they had responded to the pressure to do well at school in order to get a job, so getting a job, any job, equated with success.

I could not tell whether any of these constituted either a more important or 'real' reason than the others.

Finally, there was a group of pupils who simply assumed that

Greenfield: schooling, alienation and employment

although the competition for jobs would be tough, they would be the winners, and if they weren't, then it was their own fault. This last group was most closely aligned with the staff viewpoint outlined above.

What then is the relationship between school alienation and the employment situation at Greenfield? If the two are related, then it is a very loose and complex relation. I think this because if there is a group of pupils at Greenfield who are alienated merely because they think they have little chance of a job at the end of it, they did not identify themselves to me, nor did staff indicate that they thought such a group existed. What I found instead were other factors which appeared to operate tangentially to the direct relation.

For example, one boy was copying out all his Social Studies notes into a 'neat' book from rough notes, when all the rest of the class were putting theirs straight into their 'neat' books. 'Why was he doing this? Because he would get better marks if the work was neat. What difference did that make? He wanted to go from basic to intermediate pass. Why was that? Because he had not really tried before and he knew he could do it'. Six months later he was doing no work at all in the same class and disrupting the class at every opportunity. 'What had happened? There wasn't any point in getting an intermediate pass. Why not? Because he couldn't be bothered. Wouldn't it make a difference to get a job? No, he wanted to drive a truck and Social Studies wasn't much use in that'.

I suspect that what he was so studiously avoiding to mention was his main concern, namely that he had begun the year determined to get a good certificate either to have better chances at getting employment or to get a better job, but had realized during the year that the odds were too long against him either making the necessary school progress or of the certificate making much difference to his chances, so he gave up. He would, after all, have been receiving a basic pass in everything but Social Studies. To admit this personally sensitive failure to me would be to destroy his rationalization, 'It doesn't matter and I don't care'.

Another indicator of the kind of tangential relationship between school alienation and employment was the fact that I was often told that getting a job was more a matter of luck than effort. Being in the right place at the right time and knowing the right people featured in the stories they told about leavers who had got good jobs. Never were they said to have worked for and deserved them. I believe this has always been present in both pupils' rationalizations and reality, but there was an overwhelming sense of the hand of fate, that individuals could do little to help themselves. They had to be a winner in the job lottery, had to take what came.

So I sensed a pervasive optimism. Not one pupil anywhere in the study said they thought they would be unemployed on leaving. It might happen that there would not be enough jobs for everyone to have one, but that would be a problem for the others. The basic optimism of human life, I thought, rather than a rational prediction specific to job prospects.

The school is therefore faced with a major problem. Its whole structure, from the organization of classes into similar age groups to the professional expertise of the staff, is specifically orientated towards preparing pupils for employment, either immediately upon leaving or after further training. How then is the school to cope with preparing pupils for any other destiny such as unemployment? Clearly this school (and I suspect the education system as a whole) has no answers. One of the reasons it has no answers is that most pupils still regard the purposes of schooling as legitimate. One of the reasons that they accept its legitimacy is because they do not imagine they will be unable to get a job. One of the reasons why they believe that they will get a job is that no one is telling them that they won't. One of the reasons no one tells them they won't is that no one can predict which pupils will be employed and which won't. As it is only after school that pupils encounter the problem of unemployment, the school does not have to face the inevitable problem that it is failing a sizeable minority with regard to their preparation for life. Hence the very tenuous relation between employment prospects and alienation from school.

On the other hand, it makes sense to suggest that a pupil who is sufficiently alienated from school to fail to achieve the basic minimum necessary for employment, will become unemployed. It is clear from the study that a number of pupils are alienated from school, and that the process of schooling is itself a factor in the degree of alienation. Aspects of these problems are described in the study.

The future is a different matter, however, and although it is not possible to tell if the alienation described here has increased as a result of the employment situation, it is possible to predict that it will increase as an increasing proportion of the least employable pupils realize that nothing they can do during their schooling will significantly enhance their position. Perhaps it only needs youth unemployment to double for this realization to occur; perhaps it is already occurring as a sufficient number of leavers become unemployed for it to be fashionable not to work.

My impression is that the problem is already upon the school. The symptoms are self-doubt and critical self-questioning among the staff. There is an increasing sense of crisis as the tried and trusted aims and procedures of the past fail ever more frequently, but no new answers appear to be forthcoming.

Teaching and alienation

The question of the way in which teachers teach and hence the way in which pupils are required to learn was the starting point of the study. Before site work began I expressed the idea to my co-researchers that as the prime purpose of schooling was learning, the symptoms of alienation from school would be most likely to manifest themselves in the classroom. So it was the classroom where the study began, and observation and analysis of teaching remained an important emphasis throughout.

It is not possible in a summary to capture the nuances of all the points that were made and that are contained in the data record. However, in general terms, I did not find that pupils were alienated solely through particular aspects of teaching, though all objected to some aspect. It was this finding which led me to formulate the idea of potentially alienating situations and the threshold of alienation.* The data on this question are a series of extracts providing a cross-section of incidents which very clearly reveal the multiplicity of factors which caused dissatisfaction to some pupils, and what most clearly emerges is that some pupils will object to the very aspect of teaching which other pupils enjoy.

The second major point to emerge was that most teachers' 'philosophies' of teaching had, in fact, little to do with rationale and theory, but were more akin to simple 'coping strategies'. Teachers found what worked best for them in the classroom, and the efficacy of their practices led them to rationalize and articulate a philosophical position based upon the practices. The

---

* Methodological note: The provisional and uncertain nature of this assertion is the result of the timing of the study. In a period of change trends are unclearly marked or confused. I suspect that had the study been performed a year earlier then no kind of relationship would have been apparent; two years later, and a clear trend would be revealed.

underlying logic was therefore: 'I do X because it works, and because it works I believe Y to be true'. In a minority of instances did the converse appear to hold: 'Because I believe Y, I will attempt to do X'. It is not simply the difference between induction and deduction. The former does not appear to develop beyond a 'rationalized coping strategy' operational within the classroom. The term 'philosophy' is more appropriate to the latter because it is derived from a world view which contextualizes the classroom.

Pupils' comments were in the main upon two aspects of teaching: the means and effectiveness of discipline, and the kind and quantity of learning. Not surprisingly, the two aspects were closely related in pupils' perceptions.

Discipline emerged as an important factor but, contrary to my expectation, the pupils had no absolute scale of the extent to which a teacher can 'keep order': they recognized that one teacher could keep order with ease whilst tolerating movement and talking, and another teacher could only just keep order in a still and almost silent classroom.

Pupils did not, as some teachers appeared to believe, equate strong discipline with good teaching. Although a teacher who could not control a class was said to be a 'bad' teacher, a teacher who maintained absolute control over the same class was not necessarily termed a 'good' one, because pupils also rated teachers on the amount they could learn (not necessarily from the teacher) in the lesson. Thus, one teacher was termed 'bad' because he never gained control and the pupils felt they controlled him; another teacher was termed 'bad' in spite of maintaining absolute control, because 'You ask a question and you'll get your head knocked in'; a third teacher was a 'good' teacher in spite of continual chattering and pupils wandering around the room because ' . . . you've got a good working atmosphere. There may be too much noise, but people finish their work and enjoy it at the same time'. Some pupils said that they would listen to the last teacher when he asked for their attention, but even though they might appear to attend to the second teacher, they might also ignore everything he said. So pupils judged teachers more on how they maintained the quality of a learning situation than on the degree of actual control exerted upon them.

One reason why it was so difficult to attribute increased alienation to the discipline in particular lessons, was that pupils tended to overreact to strong discipline in one classroom, causing problems for less authoritarian teachers in another. Thus, if (as was the case with many teachers) symptoms of alienation were taken to be poor behaviour, attention problems and the like, the very classes from which some pupils said they were most alienated and learned the least, displayed the fewest signs of alienation, whilst the classes they said they enjoyed, and where they learned the most, displayed more.

More important to the concerns of this study, however, was the fact that from both pupil and teacher reports it was clear that different pupils from the same group were 'alienated' by different teaching styles. This was made particularly striking at Greenfield by the apparent division of the staff into two almost diametrically opposed teaching syles, each generally representing a different group of subjects, the Humanities on the one hand, and Mathematics and the Sciences on the other. But it is important to stress that each group of teachers contained the whole range of teaching styles.

It is also important to stress the extent of misunderstanding between the two groups. I was surprised to find that almost all teachers shared some of the same concerns and were often working towards similar ends. Yet repeatedly teachers told me that they had nothing in common with each other. What I found, for instance, was that one teacher accused of 'abdicating responsibility' for the teaching of traditional values was actually diverting from what I considered the legitimate domain of his discipline in order to inculcate traditional values (values learning, p. 35).

On the other hand, it would be wrong to interpret that evidence as indicative of an identical intent. The diagnosis of the problems may have been similar, the ends envisaged may also have been similar, but the means were in total opposition in many respects. Thus both groups believed that some pupils lacked self-discipline; they also believed that it was an aim of education to help them develop in that way; but one group wanted to achieve self-discipline by external discipline, and the other wanted to achieve it through giving the pupils more opportunity to exercise it. Thus the opposing philosophies were often misread by staff to embody different ends as well as means.

In one important respect, however, the ends were different: Malcolm appeared to believe that the primary aim of schooling was to make pupils ideally suited to the demands of the present structures of employment, but Barry believed in developing the capability in pupils for changing the present structures, or at least changing with them.

David H. Tripp

The differences between the two styles is best illustrated by contrasting these two teachers (Barry Frayen and Malcolm Kramer) each of whom displayed the most clearly defined but opposing views I encountered in the school. Their statements in the data (Section 2) show that both these teachers are working with well articulated philosophies and value positions. My analysis below concentrates on the differences.

First, both philosophies aim to prepare the pupils for life. Malcolm sees preparation for life as being the acquisition of school knowledge and traditional academic skills, leading to good passes at the end of the course, and hence to employment or further qualifications, either of which will give pupils a role in society and life. Barry tends to see a good preparation for life as that which enables someone to fit into society in more general terms: one whose personality, sense of responsibility, tolerance of differences, and other personal attributes lead to self-motivated and co-operative individuals who will find their particular role in society at a later stage. This distinction, as with all of the others, is a matter of priority, not inclusion or exclusion, and emphasis: neither teacher would neglect the other's espoused aim, but the priority would be reversed.

Second, both teachers espouse good academic standards, but they interpret the notion differently, Malcolm seeing scholarship as an end in itself (such as the ability to write a well formed essay); Barry seeing study as a means to improve a pupil's ability to communicate over a wide range of forms, particularly orally, putting clarity higher than form.

Third, information is regarded by Malcolm as being of great importance, and the nature of this information is primarily facts which are transmitted directly by the teacher to be learned by the pupils whose role and activities are not negotiable; the facts are regularly tested and revised. Barry places much less emphasis on informational learning, treating facts as data to be evaluated, the evaluative response being deliberately sought. His first priority is the discovery of facts, a process in which the pupil is active both in deciding what information is necessary, then in finding and in using that information.

Whereas the teacher's role is seen by Malcolm as the provider of what must be learned, Barry sees the teacher as the provider of a framework, a resource to be consulted. Hence Malcolm primarily seeks 'the right answer', Barry one of a range of possible answers.

Fourth, there is the quite different response to what I term 'the ultimate curriculum decision', which is whether something which the pupils cannot do or understand should or should not therefore be taught. To teach or not to teach, that is the question! In this case neither Malcolm's nor Barry's pupils can apparently learn through the independent inquiry approach: Malcolm's response is to maintain a more traditional approach, and Barry's response is to try to teach the pupils how to learn through the newer approach. In both cases, however, the short-term outcome which concerns the teachers is a poor attitude to learning.

Although the question as to which approach is likely to lead to better attitudes in the long-term remains undecided, it is pupil response to teaching style which will eventually determine the outcome. An important factor here is that although pupils reject both styles to a similar degree, their reasons for rejection are different in each case. Pupils object to Malcolm's style from a position of knowing what it involves and disliking it; but they object to Barry's style from a position of not knowing what it is, and being unsure of and confused by it. My prediction is, therefore, that Malcolm's task will become increasingly difficult, whereas Barry's will become increasingly easy.

As is to be expected from the above contrasts, alienation from school learning takes two quite different forms with teachers holding the different philosophies: some Science staff reported problems of under and non achievement as pupils did the least amount of work possible, and some very able pupils voted with their feet, leaving school at year 10 when they were quite capable of TAE work; and the Humanities staff encountered more frequent and more overt behavioural problems, and an adherence by pupils to the low-level, undemanding and secure learning tasks, such as the copying of tracts from texts, or the colouring in of maps with no analysis of the meaning or relevance of the features displayed.

These differences also go some way towards an explanation of the fact that different pupils are alienated from different subjects and teachers. Some pupils liked being made to sit still, to listen, copy and learn what they were told to: others liked being told to find their own information and to express themselves. However, pupils commonly expressed more, and more active, resentment at some of the Science and Mathematics teaching than they did about the Humanities. Most complaints about the Humanities teaching centered around confusion about what they were supposed to be doing and not being given enough to do, but not about the way in which they were treated.

However, of all teaching traits objected to, the sarcasm of one Humanities teacher was singled out by pupils as by far the most objectionable: personal attack apparently causing more resentment than any difference in teaching style. This fact, alongside pupils' more general comments, led me to believe that it is not the way in which pupils are exposed to knowledge as such that they respond to, it is the manner in which different ways of exposing them to knowledge determines the role of the learner, and hence the way in which they are treated as persons. Clearly they would prefer to be co-operative partners with teachers than subjugated recipients.

Alienation of teachers

One of the most interesting ideas to emerge from discussions of the report was that some teachers (Fran Barnes in particular) felt that the study of alienation in the school should have included at least a mention of the fact that alienation of the pupils was but one aspect: teachers were alienated from each other too (person from person, department from department, person and department from administration . . . etc. with all possible combinations), and some teachers were themselves alienated from their work. Although alienation of departments was explored in the report in terms of conflicts over the optimum teaching style, problem diagnosis and possible solutions, the question of the relationships of individuals to their departments (usually represented by the senior teachers) and towards the administration (usually represented by the principal) was not pursued, mainly because such aspects did not appear to be close to the focus of the topic of the study. Clearly, however, such considerations must impinge on aspects of the performance and nature of the school, if only in the most obvious terms such as atmosphere and limits to the possible.

In view of the strong objections to this omission from the report, and the surprising degree of disenchantment of those who just one year earlier had high expectations for change within the school, it is necessary to mention their presence here, though I believe that these factors have grown in importance during the interval between the fieldwork and reporting phases.

A second kind of alienation not investigated in the study was that of the alienation of the teacher from his or her work. One result of disenchantment with the system or colleagues can be the loss not only of enthusiasm and professionalism, but of the vocational aspects of teaching. Done well, teaching is perhaps the most emotionally taxing job in our society, and is hence the most demanding of self. Yet it is possible to regard teaching simply as a well-paid job with short hours, high social status, and long holidays. It is appallingly easy for a teacher of the first kind to become a teacher of the second kind, simply because the pressures are too great, the support inadequate, and the rewards too distant and few.

One has to consider in this regard, for instance, that in some subject areas highly qualified teachers with five years' experience will have to wait a further ten to fifteen years before they are promoted and then will in all probability have to uproot their family and leave their friends to work for several years in remote country districts. Also, of course, there are greatly decreased opportunities for teachers to move out of teaching into other kinds of work, either permanently or in order to take a break. In terms of a teacher's livelihood and professional standing there is no formal requirement either to update earlier qualifications, or to change well learned teaching habits.

In effect, there is a 'retreat to the classroom' in which the teacher tends to come to school, avoid involvement with colleagues or wider aspects of the school, teach within the sanctuary of his/her classroom, finding outlets for social, creative, caring, and sporting energies elsewhere. This, rather than alienation between staff, must have immediate and direct effects upon the levels of alienation in school pupils. Most of the examples of teaching likely to alienate pupils included in the report may be seen to stem from this factor. Lack of preparation, lack of attempt to try to understand the pupils, lack of learning situations designed to interest, and teacher-directed classrooms are all indicative of alienation from the work.

It is not easy to suggest remedies, though some have already been canvassed, especially by the West Australian Department of Education. Five year qualifications (renewable licences to teach), special promotions, and secondment to the Research and Curriculum Branches are some. I believe, however, that the most far-reaching and basic reform should be the devolution of many powers to the schools, especially to the principals. It is essential that principals (and others of the school and community) are able to choose the staff of their school, as is the norm in some other systems – such as the UK. This enables teachers to have their work recognized by promotion within the school, and principals to develop a harmonious and supportive team committed to their own philosophy. Under such a system it would appear likely that teachers have to have a greater commitment to their work (they choose and are chosen by the school), and principals have increased autonomy and hence responsibility, and are thus more accountable. However, discussion of such a system is an issue for quite different investigation, and can only be mentioned here.

With regard to transition, it seems necessary to place great emphasis on the question of teachers' understanding and experience of work of the kind their pupils will take up, including unemployment. I do not mean by this that teachers should have work experience of a similar nature to that which they provide for pupils. What would seem to be more appropriate is to provide teachers with the opportunity to visit and study the world into which their pupils move when they leave school. In the same way in which I was able in this research to study, articulate, and learn from some of the problems faced by the case study school without actually becoming a member of the teaching staff, teachers should be able to study and learn about the problems faced by their pupils. Without such information it is foolish to expect teachers to prepare pupils for a world with which neither they nor their teachers have had much contact, and about which they both know very little.

Relevance of the curriculum

Much of the discussion with staff and pupils hinged upon the question of the extent to which the currently taught school subjects were not related to the needs, interests or life of the pupils outside school. This apparently simple assertion turned out to be perhaps the most complicated and irresolvable issue in the whole study.

First, it soon became clear that what staff were calling the question of relevance was rather a question of transfer of learning. That is, whether a type of learning was relevant to life or not in any absolute sense was of secondary importance to whether the pupils could or would apply it to life outside school. Furthermore, the extent to which learning was transferred by pupils was itself a function of the similarity of the contexts of learning and application.

A key factor of this problem was that pupils expected school to be quite separated from the world outside, and they viewed that world quite differently. Teachers spoke of pupils who, they said, were incapable of seeing the relevance of learning (transferring it) even when they were given a task from everyday life which took them outside the school; or that they were incapable of using learning from one subject area in another. These two different aspects may be termed 'external' and 'internal' transfer.

An example of relevance with regard to external transfer was told to me by a teacher who had done a project with a class to choose the best value colour television set and then to find the cheapest place to buy it. He sent the pupils around the shops, they collated the material and found the best price. When the teacher later asked a pupil whose family had subsequently bought a television set how they had gone about it, the pupil said that they'd just 'gone to Vox Adeon around the corner and bought the biggest one'. The teacher interpreted this to mean that the pupils had failed to see the relevance of the exercise. An example of internal transfer was cited as the pupils' inability to use the formula for the circumference of a circle, which they had learned in Mathematics, to measure the length of sheetmetal required to make a billy of specified diameter in Metalwork.

Two important dimensions of relevance emerge from these examples: context and time. The example of the television set well illustrates the problem of context. The exercise could be interpreted as actually irrelevant because it was wrongly based upon the assumption that the aim of buying a television set was a more powerful similarity of the two occasions than the difference between purposes of the purchasers. In effect the pupil appeared to be saying, 'That is how we purchase a television set at school, which has nothing to do with how we purchase a television set at home'. Had the teacher attempted to explain the incident in terms of the social construction of reality or the power and values structure within the family, he may have put the pupil's inability to relate the two events down to quite another cause than the pupil's mental ability. Relevance is a matter of the similarity of contexts, and similarity is a function of how the contexts are perceived by pupils, not a matter of similarity as perceived by the teacher.

It is logical to extend this instance to cover other examples and to question whether a school can ever teach anything but school knowledge. Thus the relevance of school subjects is an important and problematic issue, because pupils apparently reject what is taught in the school curriculum because it *is* a school curriculum, regardless of whatever it contains.

The importance of time is illustrated in the second example. It may be that pupils are habituated into the expectation that what they learn in Mathematics they do not need to use elsewhere. But the learning of the formula occurred some time before they made the billy, so they were required to store the learning for use in another place (unspecified) at another time (unspecified). In the light of this, Frank Pollard's comment (p.81) that in school it is school learning which is relevant to pupils, makes good if somewhat cynical sense about external relevance. One might add to that 'What's relevant to a school subject is that school subject, and not some other school subject' to express in similar terms the pupils' view of internal relevance. Most of the time it appears that the pupils are expected simply to remember learnings without knowing why, where or when they might need to apply them.

The problem appears to be one of how to provide the right learning environment for the learnings which the pupils are to apply elsewhere. Little account seems to be taken of this important aspect of teaching. Consider Andy Dee's comment (p.86) that pupils learn nothing from television which would be useful background to Social Studies, or Ralph Mostin's belief that concrete activities are not good for teaching (p.91). A problem of such magnitude cannot be resolved by the 'one-off' projects of individual teachers: a whole re-orientation of schooling would be necessary to change the pupils' firmly-held set of expectations about the relevance of school learning.

Another dimension of the issue of relevance of the curriculum as an important factor in alienation from schooling was the feeling amongst many staff, particularly some of those in Social Studies and the General Studies course, that what was being taught was actually irrelevant in an absolute sense. The Mathematics class where pupils were working out contingency tables from networks; the Social Studies class where pupils were colouring in the mountains of North America on duplicated maps; the English class where pupils were summarizing the plot of a novel; the Science class where pupils were learning that light travels in waves. All of these could be said to be far removed from the pupils' everyday concerns, and hence said to be irrelevant.

Staff who espoused this view had in mind a curriculum aimed to teach the 'life skills' which the pupils were seen to lack. Life skills consisted of things like estimation of distance and other measures, form-filling, first-aid, mechanical repairs, and letter writing. Advocates of this curriculum claimed that it was relevant to the pupils' needs because what was taught were the kinds of things they needed to be able to do. This approach raised a number of problems both for me and other members of staff. These problems feature in the statements in the data, but my objections briefly stated are as follows: first, that no one has yet shown that a 'needs based' curriculum centred on basic social, emotional, and survival skills could in fact meet those needs; second, in view of the aspects of relevance previously considered, I doubt 'real' life skills can ever be taught within the existing structure of formal schooling because the learning context is inimical to transfer; third, that it would not be possible to select pupils for the course, for by selection some pupils would be denied access to academic schooling and hence to many job opportunities; fourth, that education, not basic training, is the business of the conventional school.

As with the informational content of the curriculum, the processes whereby it is taught affect relevance. Two such factors concerned the actual teaching methods and the kind of learning esteemed in school. First, it is generally true of education that the more esoteric the learning the higher the status in which it is held. This idea has been around a long time but the majority of school learning is still that of 'knowing that' not 'knowing how to'; in fact, school is about learning as such rather than about doing, whereas the majority of work and everyday life requires little learning and much doing. In this sense, the whole aim and purpose of the school system cannot correspond to life experience.

The second point connecting teaching style to relevance and hence to alienation concerns the way in which a traditional approach to academic learning decontextualizes the information. This was most clear in the manner of presentation of many topics observed. For instance, the topic 'nuclear energy' is removed from the sphere of experience by being presented as, 'The nucleus consists of . . . ' not, 'What makes a nuclear bomb work?' and 'Why do so many people die as the result of a nuclear attack?' Similarly, the religions of India taught as 'Buddha lived in . . . ' and not, 'Who's heard of John Lennon's guru?' is to cut pupils off from existing knowledge and understanding. If pupils are denied the opportunity to integrate new information with what they already know, even 'relevant' learning may be made irrelevant. Thus the irrelevance of other learning may be compounded through the way it is taught.

David H. Tripp

The effect of home background

Of all the aspects of pupils' out-of-school experience, their social background was frequently mentioned by staff as important, and some regarded it as the single most powerful causal factor in alienation. The logic of this position is as follows; school is a middle-class institution with a set of middle-class values (such as the work ethic and the value of learning for the sake of knowing), but as the majority of pupils come from homes which are 'working class' where there are quite different values (such as immediate gratification, and the value of 'knowing how' not 'knowing that'), the pupils try to reject the school, and this rejection may be termed alienation.

As two teachers pointed out, what the majority of staff did not recognize was that peer group values and 'human nature' have always been in conflict with school values; many symptoms of a difference in values (such as pupils' difficulties with homework, the way they spent their leisure time, or the television programmes they watched) were attributed to their social class, rather than to other characteristics. Of course there were instances of problems caused directly as a result of the home background, but these may have been less important than the teachers' perception of the pupils' social class leading them to undervalue the pupils' actual ability.

Evidence for this was, for example, English teachers' underestimation of the number of advanced pupils in their classes. Also comments such as 'You have to treat them like eight year olds, they'll never understand this stuff' (of a year 10 basic class and Mendel's Law); or (after the failure of a class discussion) 'They're incapable of talking and listening in a civilized way. They don't do it at home, and they can't do it here'.

On the other hand, one graphic clash of values between the school and the home or business world did occur during my site work (pp.51-4) And there were a minority of pupils who did have real problems at home (such as incest, alcoholism, violence, unemployment, and crime), and these pupils took up a disproportionate amount of the deputy principals' and year co-ordinators' time.

Another aspect of home background was that (as always) the staff as a whole lacked knowledge of what went on in the homes in general, and the lives of individual pupils in particular. This is the inevitable result of teaching being a middle-class profession, but is accentuated by teachers living outside the area in which they teach. This lack of knowledge makes it difficult for teachers either to relate school knowledge to their pupils' out-of-school experience, or to understand pupils' problems, academic and social. This point was made quite explicitly by several teachers, including the year 10 co-ordinator who said that she felt totally untrained for the job, as she needed experience in social work.

The question was, therefore, not simply whether or not the social class of the pupils did intrude into school, but the extent to which it accounted for the symptoms of alienation. My conclusion was that it intruded a great deal less than many staff suggested, and hence had relatively little impact upon alienation.

However, other aspects of pupils' out-of-school lives such as work experience and the part-time jobs figured in pupils' perceptions of school as reference points, and so appeared to be more intrusive. For instance, in contrast to the way they were treated at work, pupils felt 'put down' by school rules and attitudes, and resented it. Pupils spoke unfavourably of the amount of responsibility they were given at school compared with work; they saw school discipline as imposed unfairly and unnecessarily, whereas at work the job they had to do imposed its own discipline, and they were personally responsible for getting it done. Second, they approved of the way they were treated as individuals and adults at work, in contrast to being treated as children at school. Several older girls commented on the differences in the way young male teachers treated them (as children) and the way similarly aged young males at work treated them (as adults, and therefore potential sexual partners).

Overall, little evidence of the intrusion of out-of-school experience in general and social class in particular was found. This is hardly a surprising finding, however, because the intrusion of home life into school is the corollary of the transfer of school learning to life out of school. In view of the minimal occurrence of the former, the equally minimal occurrence of the latter is only to be expected. Furthermore, this view concurs with the way in which pupils see school as a separate stage in life, rather than as a part of their ongoing development. In sum, the school appeared to be a far more separate entity than most staff recognized.

Meeting pupil needs and alienation

I anticipated from the outset of the study that there would be a connection between the way in which the school met the other than scholastic needs of the pupils and the ways in which pupils were alienated from the school. It seemed likely that another dimension of alienation would be the extent to which pupils felt that they belonged to the institution, whether they regarded it, in effect, as their school. I thought of 'belonging' as the opposite of 'alienation' at the outset, but later saw it more as a need in its own right, deserving separate attention.

In the study two key needs were expressed by pupils and staff with regard to the way in which the school cared for them in terms other than teaching and recreation: one was the above mentioned 'belonging', the other I termed 'ears'. 'Ears' was the need for pupils to have someone who would listen to them. Not surprisingly, 'ears' was the most important pupil need perceived by the staff (and never once mentioned by the pupils), and 'belonging' was what the pupils themselves saw as their most important need (and it was hardly mentioned by the staff).

Dealing with 'ears' first, there was at Greenfield a serious effort made to provide pupils with someone to turn to for help with both in- and out-of-school personal problems. The system at present follows a well-established pattern for high schools in Western Australia, namely, form tutor groups, year co-ordinators, and a part-time guidance officer. Twice a week there are 'form periods' when teachers are free to do anything they like with the form for which they are responsible, and they mainly make use of the time for casual interaction with their pupils.

Year co-ordinators have a special allowance of six non-teaching periods a week, and there are three parts to their role: first, to be available in their offices for pupils to just drop in to chat; second, to follow up and help pupils with particular problems, including offences such as absenteeism; and third, to liaise with the form tutors, organizing events and keeping records. Shirley Bowie's statement gives a good indication of the nature of the work, and of the priority she gives to her 'ears' role.

I thought it relevant to the study that both staff and pupils said that the system simply did not work in that pupils seldom came to staff with problems in the way the system allowed them to. I thought this important because it was indicative of alienation from the system for pupils not to avail themselves of the services it offered. All the usual problems were mentioned, such as lack of time, a natural reluctance to talk over personal problems with any adults, let alone teachers, and the duality of roles required of teachers: disciplinarian and friend.

Greenfield: schooling, alienation and employment

Whilst little could ever be done about such factors, it also emerged that another major problem of the system was simply that there was insufficient contact between a particular member of staff and a particular group of pupils over a period. Pupils were put with different form tutors each year (who sometimes changed during the year), and the year co-ordinators themselves also took a different group of pupils each year by retaining responsibility for the same school grade. No teacher could easily establish the necessary mutually trusting relationship with a form or whole year group in such limited time.

One of the suggestions I offered was to take pupils from each school year into the form groups, structuring them vertically rather than horizontally, according to age. In this way, a tutor would have some pupils from each year in the form group, thus retaining contact with them over three to five years, instead of just one. Similarly, the year co-ordinators could move through the school with the same pupils, becoming year 10 co-ordinator the year after being year 9 co-ordinator. In Shirley Bowie's case this had already happened, and she is determined to fight to retain her group again next year.

The problems concerning the 'para-professionals' (as guidance officer and social worker were called) were less a matter of structure and more a matter of finance and departmental commitment. I was amazed to find that in this large school in a difficult area there was no social worker at all, and the guidance officer was only three fifths full-time in the school. Harry Price's statement shows the range of work he had to cover, the main result of which was that he virtually saw pupils only when their problems had resulted in some kind of crisis. He had little or no time for preventative work at all.

The problem of 'belonging' was brought up by pupils on the year 11 General Studies course. They felt they were somewhat special, and were sufficiently responsible to have a place of their own. They felt rejected by the other upper school pupils in that they were not doing 'a proper course', and wanted somewhere to go when they were not in lessons. This was also sought by other pupils, however, and it was clear that they lacked any private space. The form rooms were not their own in any sense other than that they went there for form periods, registration, and the like. They did, of course, have lockers (placed on the verandahs), but they regarded these as inadequate because they could not be made secure from other pupils and so were often vandalized. Nor did pupils feel that their lockers were truly private as they were afraid that staff might search them at any moment, though I found that this was never in fact done. Having a place of one's own for one's own things is a most important factor in belonging to an institution.

The other complaint of pupils was that nothing they learned or had to do at school was theirs either. They wrote, copied, learned, and reproduced what the teachers had decided they should work on, although the syllabus in each subject area offered scope for a great deal of choice. I encountered only two staff (Barry Frayen and Fran Barnes) who made the point that pupils should be given the opportunity to choose what they did and how they did it. Even those teachers, although they indicated that they wished to do otherwise, had not given pupils the main responsibility for their learning: the curriculum and schoolwork belonged to the staff, not the pupils.

In spite of the principal and other staff members' attempts to make the school council of elected pupils a worthwhile and effective body with real powers, many pupils saw it as a club for pupils who were prepared to 'crawl', and they resented the lack of a sphere of operation in the school where they had some rights to be and do what they wanted, which is not easy for a school to give and still be responsible for its pupils. However, if tutorial groups were established along the lines suggested above, it should become possible to allow each group to have special responsibility for its group base. This is frequently done elsewhere.

On the other hand the school was quite remarkable in that there was a great commitment to taking all the pupils away for a week's camp every year. This was organized by staff who gave freely of their own time both in preparing the camps, and in running them.

The camps were seen by many staff as being important primarily for the excellent staff/pupil relationships which were often formed there. It will be seen from some of the staff statements that they learned as much about the pupils as the pupils learned from and about them. Teachers thought that these relationships were carried over by the pupils into the classroom, and so the camps actually were seen to help classroom teaching. I found it puzzling, therefore, to find pupils saying that they thought staff/pupil relationships were poor. Most of the pupils standing for election to the school council included the improvement of staff/pupil relationships as a key point in their election platforms.

Greenfield: schooling, alienation and employment

As is so often the case, however, pupils did not always have the same view about things as the staff. Although there were instances of these relationships being transferred, transfer did not occur automatically or in all instances. Transfer of relationships from camp to the classroom depends upon, amongst other things, the participants being the same people in both situations. Whereas this may seem so obvious as to be trite to an adult, pupil comments suggested that they did not in fact see all teachers as the same person at school as at camp, that is, as an integrated person capable of a range of behaviour, one kind of which was appropriate to school, another to camp, or to semi-out-of-school. Pupil comments quite clearly showed that they regarded teachers as kind of predictable schizophrenics who were quite different people when at camp.

Thus teachers who had established good relationships with pupils at camp felt that these relationships necessarily carried over into the classroom. But some pupils saw the teacher-at-camp as a different being from the teacher-in-class and hence responded as if they were a different person. This is hardly surprising if the behaviours in each situation were so radically different that there was more similarity between the behaviour of Mr X and Ms Y in class than there was between Mr X in class and Mr X at camp.

This point should not, however, be taken as a criticism of the camping scheme run by the school, though it should raise some questions in teachers' minds about the contrast between their camp and their classroom behaviour. Most pupils reported that the camps were the most enjoyable time they had experienced at school.

It is not possible to estimate the alienating effect for certain pupils of the lack of a personally knowing relationship between staff and pupils, and lack of an adequate sphere of self-determination, but these are two areas where it is relatively simple to improve on the current situation.

The Alternative Course

At Greenfield there are two courses which are 'alternatives' to the academic courses. These are the Commercial Studies course and the General Studies course. Both are year 11 courses, the former being aimed mainly at girls who wish to go into office work, the latter at all other pupils wishing to return for another year but not wishing to do either the academic or the commercial course. The concept behind the General Studies course is that it would provide pupils with a genuinely useful year's work that would make them more employable and be closely related to 'life skills'. Not surprisingly such a General Studies course presents problems.

Briefly, the school was faced with about thirty pupils who did not want to take Tertiary Admissions Examinations, but who nevertheless wished to return to school for year 11. Reasons for returning were mainly that they could not obtain jobs with their (poor) Achievement Certificates, or that they could not obtain the jobs they wanted. In the former case pupils simply wished to repeat year 10 work, in the latter to learn other, more job-oriented skills. Some simply wanted to be able to say to a prospective employer that they were still at school, not unemployed. Parents had also pressurized many of the latter group to stay on because they were both working and did not want their children to be unsupervised during the working day.

Although there were sufficient numbers of such pupils, the course was developed very haphazardly, pupils simply being slotted in groups into the existing timetable, where there was room for them. Which staff were to take how many of which pupils was not known until after the start of the term, at which point it was not possible to structure a coherent and integrated course, so staff simply had to find things to do with their own particular classes. This they did with various levels of success. The two Mathematics teachers involved, for instance, decided to divide the pupils into two groups, one simply to repeat the year 10 course, the other to go over more basic skills, like the estimation of distance or the reading of cost tables. In Science, the teacher spent the time job-finding. This consisted of scanning the papers for jobs, writing letters of application, and even organizing some extra work experience for some pupils. Whilst pupils seemed satisfied (if bored) with the Mathematics, the Science scheme was criticized both because some pupils felt that they were not learning anything about Science, and because others did not want more work experience. The difference between the teachers' initiatives and the pupils' expectations illustrated the problems of designing a course which would meet (some of) the needs of (most of) these pupils.

Apart from the very real planning difficulties described above, the course was most severely criticized by both staff and pupils because there was not an adequate certificate available at the end of the year, meaning there was nothing recognized by employers towards which the pupils could work, and around which the teachers could plan. The absence of such a reward was again due to the problems posed by the reasons for which the pupils had returned, which were to repeat year 10, or until they obtained employment. The former group already had a certificate at the end of their course, and the latter group had mostly left school before the end of the year: this left too few pupils in the school to make the investment in the development of an alternative certificated course worthwhile. On the other hand, in the absence of such a course it was not possible to assess demand realistically.

Another problem was that pupils in the course saw themselves as having low status within the school, which was mainly due to the CSE pupils perceiving their course as 'not a proper upper school course', and hence inferior. The pupils in the General Studies course saw their position as being different, rather than inferior, and wanted to have this difference marked by the provision of special facilities for their exclusive use. What they were asking for was a 'den' where they could largely do as they liked, and for which they would be responsible. As it was they complained about not being wanted either by staff or peers, and this was their principal objection to the way they were treated.

Of course, their somewhat precarious position was reinforced by the way in which staff reminded them that if they did not behave and do as they were told, they would be made to leave. Although this also applied to the TAE stream pupils, these tended to be the 'good' students, so staff did not need to make it so explicit to them. Alternative course pupils said that they were being 'victimized' by staff in this respect. Such complaints seemed to me to be rather more specific symptoms of a more general malaise in the course, namely that the course did not really fit any of the existing structures within the institution.

So far as I could ascertain, the single major factor in the problems associated with the General Studies course was a totally inadequate provision for the course in terms of staffing and funding. I was amazed at the apparent lack of departmental support for the course. First, no in-service training of staff was available; no experienced staff were available; there was no departmental advice or support available; no special facilities were available; no earmarked funds were available. Jean Dunn's statement makes such difficulties quite clear, but the more general and long-term implications of such a state of affairs are potentially more serious.

David H. Tripp

Second, there was no central initiative to develop, for instance, a course with a properly recognized certificate, something which could only effectively be done across the system, not individually by each school.

Third, the department offered no help to the school in terms of stabilizing the staff already working on the course. Thus, although the principal began preparation of the course with the co-ordinator in August of the year previous to my study, that teacher was transferred to another school in November. The next teacher the principal appointed as course co-ordinator was also transferred during the summer vacation (January) and so the eventual co-ordinator was appointed less than a week before the start of the new year early in February.

Since the sitework for this study was completed, the department has set up a small advisory section for such courses, but whilst the absence of a career structure for teachers of such courses continues, they will always have a very low priority and relatively inexpert and uncommitted staff teaching them. The course needs to be set up within the school as a properly structured and staffed department, just as most of the optional studies and all the core subjects are. Until this is done it cannot be said that the department has a serious commitment to these courses.

Simply to establish a real alternative course at Greenfield is not the answer to many of the problems of alienation, however, for it would not only leave untouched the problems of lower school pupils, but it would then raise a number of quite different problems. For instance, in many of the statements of the staff, reference is made to the desirability of a genuine alternative to academic courses in the lower school, and clearly there is a great need for it. However, if a 'life-skills' course were to be established for years 8, 9, and 10, two serious problems would ensue. First, the aforementioned problem of selection would arise, if, as some staff advocate, the course were to be aimed at meeting the needs of pupils who would be likely to be unemployed at the end of their schooling. To run such a course would in fact be to select pupils to education for unemployment, in the process of which they would probably become unemployable by virtue of having been prepared for it.

Second, another equally great danger lies in developing a course around the existing 'needs' of pupils as perceived by the staff. The danger is not so much that staff perceptions may be inaccurate, but that a course centred on pupil needs and abilities in their present situations would not only be to operate a 'deficit model' curriculum, but would confirm them in their current situation by better fitting them for it, and denying them any alternative. If pupils are alienated from the present system by being branded 'basic', the possible outcomes of such an alternative course may well be far more alienating than the lack of an alternative to the clearly 'irrelevant', but potentially liberating, existing academic course.

This is, I feel, the crux of the central focus of the study, for it illuminates the impossibility of the school's position: the present structure of the system means that on the one hand it must educate pupils for employment, whilst on the other hand by so doing it deprives the increasing minority of pupils who are destined to spend large portions of their lives in unemployment, of a useful education. Yet it can provide these pupils with a useful education only at the expense of their employment prospects.

The problem of the General Studies course thus has at least two aspects: one as a year 11 alternative, the other as a wholly different view of the aims and scope of secondary education. The problems associated with the former can, and I believe will, be solved in the near future, because they are amenable to relatively simple solutions. Developing solutions to the latter aspect would appear to require the sustained work of perhaps a whole generation of educators, but the obvious place to begin is, I believe, with the existing year 11 General Studies course.

Researchers' conclusion

A conclusion in the sense of closure by proof is precluded by both the nature of case study research and the fluidity of the current situation. Nevertheless, it is possible for the researcher to emphasize the main thrust of his own analysis which may be summarized as follows:

The school is caught in a classic 'double bind' or 'Catch 22' situation which is aggravated by the shortage of jobs for school leavers. It is asked to fulfil simultaneously two contrary and conflicting tasks. On the one hand, society demands that students be educated in the traditional way for employment, although that kind of education fails an increasing minority of students who will face long periods of unemployment during their working lives. So on the other hand there is a call for school to provide an 'alternative course' which would educate those students in such a way as to better prepare them for unemployment. But because the traditional academic curriculum demanded by employers and institutions of further education is a full-time one, a school cannot provide all students with both kinds of education.

The problem with running two mutually exclusive courses is one of selection: someone has to decide which students will be unemployed upon leaving school in order to draft them into the alternative course. Such selection, however, carries with it the massive penalizing effect of predestining those pupils for unemployment by barring them from access to the course which leads to the academic qualifications necessary to gain employment. As no one knows even the grounds on which such selection could be made, let alone the mechanism by which it would be done, it is hardly surprising that no one is able or willing to do it. So of course the school has no answers, there are no answers to a double bind.

So the school is struggling on as best it may in a climate of criticism and reduced funding at a time when what the school really needs is general retraining of staff and a whole new approach to the secondary school curriculum.

Appendix 1: Negotiation of statements

There are two reasons for negotiating documents with staff: First, even if I try accurately to get down onto paper what people really say to me or what I observe, I am bound to have some misunderstandings and misconceptions which will be apparent to my informants but which are not apparent to me. Asking staff to read and comment upon the documents I write gives me a check on the accuracy of my recording of information. Second, everything that staff say or give to me is treated as entirely confidential, intially. So, in order to enable me to use documents in the report or to stimulate and develop discussions, I ask staff to read documents they have given me, indicating what I may not use at all, and what I may only use anonymously. Any parts of documents which an informant has read and not restricted the use of is assumed to be available for quotation to others.

The way I suggest we negotiate documents is as follows: 'I'll give you a confidential copy of the document in question; you read it, first making any alterations to it which express more clearly your meaning and ideas; second, marking on the text of the document those parts which you wish to restrict. Indicate the restricted sections with a double vertical line against the text in the left margin to indicate that those lines are not to be used at all, and a single vertical line against the text in the left margin to indicate that those lines may be used anonymously. Show where the section begins and ends with square [] brackets. For example:

> Miss Budgie: 'The real problem as I see it, is that students bring a sub-culture into the school with them from home, and their home values and attitudes are becoming more and more at odds with what the school is trying to do academically. |[Look at John Julian, for instance: his father can't write and he keeps telling John he needn't learn either.] [Is it surprising that Mr Polly can't control John, or many of the other kids in the class?] I do think we have to take this conflict into account, but we're getting no help from anywhere'.

The marks indicate that the sentence 'Look at John Julian . . . ' may be used anonymously if the boy's name is omitted; and the sentence 'Is it surprising . . . ' may not be used at all. The rest, however, I may use, probably either as a quote in a report, or to stimulate further analysis: ('Miss Budgie says the main problem is a conflict between the home and school in terms of attitudes to learning . . . Is that how you see it too?').

Appendix 2: Example transcript*

Included below is a transcript of that part of the original discussion with Jean Dunn of which I gave a summarized account in the last three paragraphs on pages 96-7.

DHT: Have you personally had experience in doing this before?
Jean: No.
DHT: Any comment? It is typical or . . .?
Jean: I suppose in lots of ways it is typical of the deparment. As I said before, because I haven't had the training, and plus the fact that I was supposed to teach them. Then of course that class disappeared because there weren't enough kids. I think it is typical in lots of ways that the school system is run to cater for the organization of the administration, rather than for the kids.
DHT: Is there anywhere you can turn for help?
Jean: I've been to see the Research people, **** is the fellow in charge of a section in the Research Branch and I have had a talk to him.
DHT: In the Research Branch? Or Curriculum?
Jean: No, he's in Research. His main thing was just advice, to sit down and work out an actual curriculum.
DHT: Have you got one then?
Jean: No, we haven't got one yet, because this was only a couple of weeks ago.
DHT: What help would you get with that, say in the Curriculum Branch?
Jean: Apparently Curriculum Branch will assist as far as looking over what we plan and making suggestions but we still have to plan it all.
Jean: He emphasized the business of it being school-based and you must work it out and then, as I say, Curriculum will have a look at it, comment on it.
DHT: They didn't give you a number of plans to choose from . . .?

---

* Methodological note: This transcript has been included because it raises the issue of the extent to which data have been lost in my account, which has in effect distanced the reader from reality, the reality of both the confusion and force of spontaneous dialogue. If this is a transcript, then perhaps my account should be terms a 'transkipt'.

Jean: No, nothing like that.

DHT: And no real help in planning it?

Jean: Well, this is what I was hoping to get when I went there, but no, I can go and have a look at the file, anyone can go and look in their files and see what they've done at this or that school, activities virtually. I don't think there's actually a curriculum in those files. The way he spoke he said they were more or less activities that they've done, ideas for lessons, but then I haven't looked at it yet.

DHT: I'm just trying to work out the real extent of what you are being asked to do. Have you had any experience in planning a curriculum?

Jean: No, I haven't personally. There is a fellow in the school who says he has had some experience, he's just new here also, and he is keen to work on something in the curriculum. So he, the principal and I and anyone else who is interested are going to sit down as soon as we have got a spare moment or two and try to start planning – (Note: it is now four weeks into term.)

DHT: How is he involved, the teacher with curriculum experience?

Jean: I can't remember his first name. He says that he has had some experience. I don't know how much and he is interested in working out a curriculum for next year.

DHT: And so you are going to have a Syllabus Committee, you and the principal and –.

Jean: Once we have planned it, it has to be a school-based thing, then we can take it to Curriculum and they will look at it and give us suggestions and so on.

DHT: When do you do that?

Jean: In our spare time. Whenever we can get organized to do it.

DHT: And the principal is going to support you in that obviously?.

Jean: Yes, he is going to take part in it too.

DHT: Other staff know this is happening?

Jean: Well, they don't know anything much about the curriculum bit yet. Once we figure on getting it started, I assume we will ask other staff who are interested to join us on the committee. It's just a matter, quite frankly of one thing and another, you're on this committee and that committee and it's a matter of finding the time to do these things. They take a hell of a lot of time.

Appendix 3: Response to the draft report

I would prefer not to attend the Tripp Report Seminar. I have nothing good to say about the researcher's treatment of a very worthwhile topic.

I have written to Dr Tripp, spoken to him on the 'phone and as requested written comments in the report. I have refused him permission to use what he thought I had said in the last part of our discussion. He revised the first part but did not return for a revision of the second half before I went on leave. [i.e. a renegotiation of the previously negotiated statement. DHT]

Inaccuracies, irrelevancies, subjective comments, sexist language, unsuitable style and selection of temporary staff to comment from Social Studies made me lose faith in Dr Tripp's work. I considered it a waste of time reading further when the research worker had lost credibility for me.

I could be biased in commenting on his report of the discussions with me, but examples which made me devalue his reporting elsewhere were:

1. School anonymity page 30. [Examples subsequently deleted to aid anonymity. DHT.]
2. Inaccurate and irrelevant – the Guidance Officer. 'Harry's small room is centrally placed between the staff toilets and the staff common room'. [Example subsequently deleted in shortening report for publication.]
3. Subjective:'. . . but that must have been too much for him as he chose to withdraw from the study . . .'.
4. Sexist description: 'She is a slim, vivacious woman . . . short blond hair, bright blue eyes with a distinct twinkle, she smiled at me and the world . . .'
5. If a report is worthwhile it should not need embellishments like weak humour or deliberate variety. Relevant or not, two staff members' ages were given as 'approaching forty' and '. . . in his late thirties'. [They were the same age. DHT]

These are just a few of the points which have destroyed my faith in Dr Tripp's report. I am reluctant to waste more time on it although the topic is a most important one. (Mary Sims, D.P.)

David H. Tripp

> I've not read it myself, but it's clearly rubbish from what's being said about it by those who have. (Several staff, reported)
>
> It was an excellent report. I have no complaints about how I was portrayed, he got it right, that's how I am. And I did say all those things. Perhaps I like it because he put so much of what I said into the report. (Anne Marlow)
>
> I'm new here, but when I read it I could see it . . . that's how it is, it's just like that, I think. (Anon)

As expected, reactions were varied and sometimes extreme, but the following general categories of criticism emerged:

Research Method

It was quite clear from the first two of the three reactions above, that a number of staff did not understand the nature and purposes of case study. Little could be done about this, as the attempt to explain something of the matter in the entry document (Appendix p.21) seemed to be generally unread or not understood.

Omissions

Two omissions were considered sufficiently important to significantly alter the substance of the report. First was the fact that no comments from the least alienated pupils appeared. This was thought to have been guarded against through the interviews with the school council. However, a teacher who had been involved with the council made the point that, contrary to my expectation and impression the 'best' pupils were not generally those elected to the council.

On the face of it this omission is important because it suggests an imbalance in the report; however, as the report is focused upon the alienated pupil, the fact that it is mostly alienated pupils who appear, is important principally in terms of the portrayal of the school, and is of less consequence in terms of the manifestation and analysis of alienation.

The second omission was permanent staff, when acting staff were included. In the absence of the permanent staff from the school, or their withdrawal from the study, inclusion and hence emphasis of the acting staff was inevitable. With regard to the statements of the acting staff, it appeared to me at the time, and this is clearly reflected in the report, that the acting staff were much more aware of and reflective about the school, its systems, pupils, and the problems it faced than were many of the permanent staff. This was probably the result of their temporary position: they were themselves in the process of understanding and observing people and events and trying to make sense of their impressions. To say this is not to negate the criticism, however: it is probably true that I tended to use those respondents who were most involved with, and forthcoming about, the issues, and this very factor must slant the study to an indeterminable degree.

A third omission amounting perhaps to a misrepresentation, was an important point made by the year 10 co-ordinator with regard to the 'ears' analysis (p.142). She pointed out that potential alienation was often mitigated or avoided because pupils who were not seriously alienated did talk to staff, and were helped by them. Whereas I tended to characterize the 'ears' relationship with staff as one where the pupils who did not really 'need' to talk to staff were the ones who did, but the pupils in most need of adult friendship chose not to talk, hence becoming more alienated because their needs went unmet. In fact many 'good' pupils could have become alienated had staff not ensured that channels of communication were open, so that their needs were met. This is an important concept, because it shifts attention from the problem of existing alienation to prevention of its occurrence. Clearly the more effective pastoral care advocated for alienated pupils would also enhance this process.

Inaccuracies

Several minor inaccuracies and factual errors were written into the draft report, but all that were brought to my attention were corrected in the final version. One kind of inaccuracy, however, proved to be a major factor in the rejection of the whole report by some staff members. This was that at least one respondent in general, and several respondents in particular, represented themselves (and others) in such idealized terms that their colleagues could see little truth in the statements, and following the logic of 'If the researcher's got **** so wrong, what other errors of which I am not aware are present?', dismissed the whole report as literally incredible.

Whilst I have sympathy for this natural reaction, it does represent a misunderstanding of the nature of the study. It was explicitly stated in the introduction that the statements were what the respondents were 'prepared to have written about what they said'. Implicit in this is an assumption about the status of subjectivity and hence about the relationship of the statements to some standard of truth external to each respondent.

The intended method of dealing with this problem at the outset of the study was that the draft report would bring the more important conflicts in the respondents' views of reality to the surface, and the conflicts could perhaps be resolved, or the existence of irreconcilable positions would be recognized and their nature described. In the event I discovered the choice was between facing a respondent with colleagues' responses, some of which were really accusations, in order to negotiate a version of truth acceptable to both parties; or leaving the statements as negotiated with each respondent on the grounds that the study thus provided an accurate description of the way each respondent chose to view or present him or herself.

Methodologically there are good arguments for both strategies and the consequently different versions, but in the event I felt bound by ethical considerations to choose the latter approach. To bring such interpersonal staff differences to the surface would be likely to damage irreparably the strained but nevertheless functioning relationships which are necessary if any school is to operate effectively.

Perhaps the only point of a methodological nature which should be made about this problem is that it does indicate the extent of the difficulty faced by a researcher trying to penetrate a school. Such were the professional standards and colleagial loyalties within the school that I gained no inkling of such a problem during the fieldwork phase. It seems that the impact of printed statements made staff feel bound to try to balance the picture through the addition of their views of each other's views. From the researcher's point of view it was very frustrating to have had information withheld, and then to have had his report rejected because he was unaware of the withheld information.

Methodological conclusion

Overall I was happy with the report as such, but very unhappy with the apparent lack of understanding with which it was received. I felt that I was dealing with an immediate emotional and personal reaction rather than with the more rational 'emotion recollected in tranquility' which should follow. As one teacher put it, 'I think the main problem is that people haven't come out as important as they see themselves', and evidence for this was criticism such as that I had been very uneven in the amount of space and detail devoted to the introductions of different respondents. Of course, some reacted against the report on the very logical grounds that they did not like the conclusions. I use the word 'like' deliberately, as there was little or no engagement with or criticism of my account of the substantive issues in the report. Similarly, those who liked the report offered little analysis either of where or in what terms it was strongest.

What really concerned me was that so few teachers would take part in discussion of the report either with me on a personal one-to-one basis, or by attending the seminar held at the university to discuss it. In the end I have to admit that the majority of those who were against the report would not communicate their concerns or their reasons to me, and hence the proper speculation with which to end is, 'To what extent are teachers alienated from researchers in general, and to what extent are some of the teachers at Greenfield alienated from me in particular?' It is a matter of regret that a second researcher was not used to answer this relatively simple question.

On a more substantial point, it is usual to end a study with a recommendation for further research, and I do not wish to make this report an exception. I have two recommendations: first, with regard to alienation and transition for some research into the nature and extent of teacher alienation from work. My second recommendation is for further methodological investigations into the participants' response to this kind of case study, to the procedures of the research, and especially of participants' responses to the final report.

Note

1 D.H. Tripp, 'The Case Study Interview: Validity, Structure and Record'. Paper presented at the Annual Conference of the Australian Association for Research in Education, Adelaide, 1981.

Chapter 3

Addison Hills
A case study of alienation and transition from school
Stephen Kemmis

Section 1: Background

A landscape: The bus

They could hear the drone of the diesel from about three-quarters of a mile away. High in the sky a small, straggling, flapping flock of ibis turned and wheeled, suddenly smooth in flight. The boy's eyes followed the movement – that gliding movement of the ibis was like stretching in bed before getting up. The girls were talking still behind him over towards the old yew hedge outside the house. The grass between the hedge and the road was spiky, tawny in the yellow sun. There were five of them at the corner, meeting as they did each schoolday, from three households a quarter of a mile apart.

Out of the corner of his eye, he saw the four girls shift their feet and begin to move to the roadside. The sound seemed further away, coming from a hollow between the hills. The road was a line finger-painted straight down the gentle slope of the land and into the hollow. It emerged as suddenly as the bus from behind the brow of the nearest hill. The bus arrived in a roar and a cloud of yellow dust and pulled in to the side of the road. A popping sound as the pneumatic doors slapped open, then a hiss. Soft crunch of feet on the dry grass, hard crunch of the gravel, then the smooth feeling of the rubber and metal step under his feet.

There is a babble of greetings and news. The girls find their friends towards the front and waiting vacant seats. The boy pushes down the aisle to the boys at the back. The bus rocks

Addison Hills: alienation and transition from school

unevenly down the unbroken macadam. His feet brush the soft school bags, feeling books beneath the yielding plastic. He swings and flops into his seat.

All different despite school uniforms. Fifteen conversations. Sport, spunks, Mr Morgan's maths class. Homework bobbing uneasily on a knee, the answers coming in a chiding stream from friends who did it last night. A stand of spindly gums. A clump of grey sheep in the corner of a paddock as if pushed there by the speed of the passing bus. Solid cornerposts with neat lines of the barbed wire stretching away from the road. A drive lined with old pines; the house hidden among greenery.

The road tilts down a long, smooth slope, runs straight ahead, then sweeps in a broad curve into the town. The bus and the chatter gather momentum down the hill. Conversations crackle among the seats, flickering out and drawing in other speakers, then changing direction suddenly to flare up elsewhere in the bus. Down the main street the conversations go on, heedless of the houses, the rows of trees lining the street, the cyclists pushing against time towards the school.

The engine grinds into low gear. The bus swings into line behind five others already disgorging knots of students laughing, slouching, converging on to the path towards the building. Several boys are throwing a ball on the playing field. The boy knows them all. One plays on his district cricket team.

The doors pop and hiss. There is an unsteady clumping of feet down the aisle as the bus empties, the conversations breaking up into groups of students who trail down the path across the playing field. At the other side of the playing field, three uneven strands of students enter separate green doors to clatter into corridors, fiddle with locks and open lockers. It is 8.30 a.m. Within minutes the three other buses are drawing up outside the school, each unloading its community into the school grounds.

Today he has Social Studies first period. The neighbourhood survey. Who's got answers for the questionnaire? Tomorrow woodcraft elective is first and there will be more time for talk around the benches. Roll on tomorrow! For now, up the corridor to room twenty-eight, upstream through the throng, scrape old chairs and tables, and questions about the community. 'What do you mean, "neighbourhood", Mr Pointer?'

This is a story about a quiet corner of Victoria, except it isn't in a corner, like most places in Australia which are either on the edge or in the middle somewhere. What makes it a corner, I suppose, is that it isn't a centre like Sydney or Melbourne or even

Stephen Kemmis

Perth or Adelaide. And it is out in the countryside. It is a place where people seem to care more about what they *are* to other people than what they *do* to them. I say 'seem to care' advisedly, because I know, as they do, that what they do to them is pretty important for survival. It's just not so easy to get on with one another without a bit of rigging of the game.

Like other people in other quiet corners of the State, people in Addison Hills have each other to get along with, then they have each other as a community (people to talk about and people who talk about them), and then they have The System, which they don't talk about much even though it pays them. Some people in Addison Hills may find The System boring but others find it frightening. Quite a few come to Addison Hills because it's not the city. Some come to retire (even people in their thirties who are still working), some come to its quiet charm, some come to be part of a community with other people like themselves and with dreams like their own dreams. When you get enough people like that together, some of the dreams start coming true.

I grew up in a big city, and have spent most of the last ten years of my life in provincial cities of 100,000 to 150,000 inhabitants. I know that a lot of the people who come to Addison Hills are escaping from cities. I suppose all of us can see what they're escaping from, and lots of us would like to escape from it too. It's not exactly the twentieth-century-Western-military-industrial-state, but it's something a lot like it. (A good friend of mine has just moved into Addison Hills and he says it's a matter of lifestyle.)

In big cities you can't really escape, you just find a place in the vortex. In provincial cities and in the suburbs, you don't really need to – you can find a calm spot where the twentieth century doesn't swirl around you quite so giddily. In places like Addison Hills, you can escape *to* something: a place in the country, a community. In the suburbs, you can only escape *from* the city. It is the difference between an orderly withdrawal and a private defeat. When Moses went off into the desert with his friends and followers, they all knew they were going somewhere. I suppose they often had good times as they wandered about, wondering whether the land of milk and honey was just over the next hill. And they had some time to think it over so they knew how they could form a community when they got there. At the same time, I'm sure they developed a taste for travel and for dreaming about a better future, but that was also something to share with friends.

Addison Hills is not the land of milk and honey but it is the

Addison Hills: alienation and transition from school

place where these people have arrived and put down their roots. And they can share a dream and each others' human ups and downs. What makes me sure that it isn't the land of milk and honey is that Addison Hills doesn't supply all its own milk and honey and all the other necessities of life. Most people still have to work in the city. They still have to keep in touch with The System. Perhaps that is why they don't like to talk about it too much. It reminds them of the incompleteness of the escape. But that is also one of the things that makes Addison Hills so charming and so interesting. There are different layers to life in Addison Hills that need uncovering, different strands that need unravelling.

Addison Hills High School has about 600 students and fifty staff. Nine buses bring its students from five other towns and the countryside around Addison Hills to the school, each carrying about forty-five students. These 'bus-groups' preserve the identities of the surrounding towns. In the early years at the school, students tend to form groups based on their home towns; by the later forms, the groups are more mixed. The communities all have their own identities and characters; certainly the students identify with their home towns. Football and netball in the area are organized around town teams which compete in parallel competition, town against town. These rivalries are central to the life of the area.

The communities are friendly. The Churches are losing their influence of some years ago; in the bigger towns the Red Cross is winding up for lack of support. Local discos are run by the Apex Club. But the family remains strong. Some families choose to live here, owning hobby-farms and choosing fairly long-distance commuting to the city over suburban life; others have been on the land here for generations.

The students are polite, described by their teachers as 'docile' or 'conforming'. They are unlike urban students whose style is more of a challenge: a test of strength. The area, the school, and the students make Addison Hills a pleasant place to teach. Although about a third of the teachers are in their first five years of teaching, many have been here longer, a couple for twenty years. The principal is one of these two.

The school is an academic high school, defending a good record of Higher School Certificate (HSC*) passes. There is a

---

* The Higher School Certificate (HSC) is the examination basis for university entrance, etc. in Victoria.

technical school in another town twenty miles away, but students must make a deliberate choice to go there: for many, it means even further to travel to school. There are no buses to the technical school from the towns around Addison Hills.

Unemployment in the area is high, especially among youth. (In August 1980, there was an average of sixty-eight applicants competing for every junior job in the major town nearby.) But the unemployed are not as visible here as they are in the city. Because unemployment is high, students are staying on longer at school. Years 11 and 12 are noticeably larger this year.

The school has a work experience program which most students enjoy. For some, it is an immediate springboard to work; for most, it is a way of coming into contact with the world of work and learning or rebuilding expectations about what it demands. Many students are waiting in the school for work to turn up. Some leave without jobs, but are already part of the two-way information networks in the community which signal both opportunities and intentions to leave. Some students are said to choose 'the dole' as an acceptable alternative to work. There may be a few for whom this is true, but it seems to be a myth: it is said of others, rather than about friends or oneself. Some students at Addison Hills are 'turned off' school. They are so in varying degrees. Some are not at all 'turned off', others would rather not be at school. A school survey shows that the school has a problem in this area: many students do not feel well-served by the school's present curriculum and organization.

Teachers at Addison Hills are worried that some students are 'turned off'. They attempt to provide options within the academic curriculum which can excite interest, but they cannot remake the school. They do what they can for students, but they cannot relax expectations of performance to the point where they allow students to have unrealistically low expectations about Year 12 and HSC.

The school should not, however, be seen as the sole or even the primary source of disaffection for these students. Other forces shape students' worlds and create alternative images of what they are and can be. Home, friends and community offer alternative forms of life which contend with the image of the school as a place to be and as a preparation for work or further education. While still in school, students are not just students, just as when they leave school for work they will not just be workers. Other roles and other ways of being shape their views of themselves and of the relations they have or might have to society at large. At

Addison Hills: alienation and transition from school

Addison Hills, 'society at large' can be a community which is understood in a very immediate way. It provides both a place to be and ways of being.

Sergeant Bruce, in charge of the police station for the past fifteen years, tells me there are three kinds of people in the town of Addison Hills. There are the 'old' town people who have been there for years with their families, and the people associated with the CSIRO Research Station who come for a few years at a time. And there are the 'newcomers'. The 'old' town people are as much a part of the town as its wide verandahs and picket fences but, like these, they are in disarray. The town has changed over the last two or three decades: too close to the city to avoid change, too far away to be assimilated. Always dependent on the surrounding area for the fortunes of their town, they have been left behind in the change of occupational structure of the area and not able to keep control over the changing character of the town. Some of their youth are ones who get themselves into trouble, Sergeant Bruce says. There is not enough for them to do, he thinks. 'They should go down to Melbourne and see another side of life'.

The CSIRO people fit in to the town only to the extent good taste requires. They keep pretty much to themselves. They need services and provide a range of jobs for others in the town. Their children go to the local high school.

The 'newcomers' are coming to stay. They are impressing a new character into the town and the soft earth of the hills around. Drawn by the five, ten, and twenty-five acre lots, the recreational opportunities of the area and its country-town charm, they preserve some of the old but, against expectation, have been most responsible for changing it. They work outside the area but come here to live. Their children belong here, to the town, and to the patchwork background of the land. The land supports the bucolic dream of community they came to find.

Most of the teachers and many of the students at Addison Hills fall into the last group. They come to settle and belong. They come because Addison Hills is the place it is. As a result, there is a low turnover of staff at the school. Two teachers have been on the staff for twenty years. They are part of the community; more recent arrivals have an interesting role on its fringes.

By 3.15 p.m. the boy feels the end of the day approaching. The cadence in the teacher's voice is changing, betraying a knowledge that the period will soon end, though half-heartedly urging continuing attention. Already his friends are becoming conspicuously restless and inattentive, anticipating the catharsis of the bus journey. Desks are already cleared of books; bags are packed. When the bell rings at 3.20 the students seem already to be on their feet. Chairs are lifted onto tables in a clatter and in moments the room is cleared. Solitary teachers pick up books and go.

Six minutes later, the last bus is drawing away from outside the school, carrying the students away in clouds of eager conversation. A single boy in tracksuit is running on the playing field. A knot of teachers gathers in the lower staffroom for coffee, a little marking or preparation; some are gone almost as quickly as the students.

For me, the school has a striking sense of emptiness. But for teachers and students at Addison Hills, the contrast of this transition is familiar; measured against the length of the school day it seems abrupt, but to them it is as familiar as the exhalation of a breath.

An etching: A place in the country

Addison Hills High School sits well back from the main road into Addison Hills, in the fork between the main road and Hill Street. It is screened from both roads by trees, on a site that rises away from the fork. In the corner nearest the fork are playing fields. Behind the playing fields are the buildings, single storeyed, but hugging the hillside, the ones behind looking over the roofs of the ones in front. Many of the classrooms have views over the very pleasant rural landscape. It would be extremely attractive as a housing development site. Because it is set back from the road, at first glance the site seems spacious.

The buildings belong to two major periods: a fifteen-year-old group of buildings on the upper part of the site, showing signs of age, and a new group of attractive concrete block buildings lower down. From the outside the new buildings are as dramatic as the polite taste of the Schools Buildings Branch will allow, their sharp geometric lines contrasting with the natural dishabille of the trees. The new buildings were opened last year by the Minister. The school appears to have done fairly well in its bids for building funds through the Regional Buildings committee.

The school council has had troubles in developing the site. The basketball court was recently resurfaced a week after the lines had been re-marked, the oval was freshly topdressed with soil that turned out to be full of onion weed, a new tennis court was laid east–west so that sun is a problem for players, and a proposed new hall will claim a basketball court (maintaining a tradition in the school: the last extensions claimed an earlier one).

The grounds were once rigidly divided into boys' and girls' areas with a common courtyard in the old section; now most of the grounds are 'open', though there are still areas which are segregated by sex. (The school oval is one of these . . . available, as might be guessed, for boys.)

In the end, teachers and students confirm that the site is cramped. The impression of openness given by the playing fields turns out to be false. The buildings press towards the back boundary fence. The playing fields must be supplemented for physical education by the space at the community sports centre half a mile away.

Inside, the old buildings have the homely, familiar, slightly decaying quality one associates with secondary schools which have to survive heavy use by adolescents. The new buildings have a colder, almost clinical quality about them. The concrete block corridors reach away from the eye in undisturbed perspective; overhead, the box construction of exposed ventilation shafts creates images of the bronchial tubes of some giant, stationary robot breathing air on behalf of the building's inhabitants. The buildings are alive with transmitted sound, not altogether suited to the teachers' tastes. In the older buildings, footsteps are muted drumbeats on the wooden floors; in the newer ones, linoleum damps the sound of footsteps but the concrete walls give back the sound of voices and the clatter of desks. Carpets on some of the new classroom floors make islands of stillness for students and teachers alike. Each room makes its own use of the country light pouring in at the windows; in this room, cramping it along bookshelves and laboratory benches; in that one, allowing it to strike pristine angles and poses along the sparse linoleum-tiled floor; in another, playing with it across a pageant of indoor plants and paintings hanging from the ceiling beams and walls.

The new wing makes a gesture towards adornment through art, but its walls are still fairly bare. Some art works do hover shyly on the concrete wall – some student works, some standard prints and one or two works of local painters. As in most schools, these works tend to gather in the more publicly-accessible regions of

Stephen Kemmis

the school – the foyer and towards the principal's office.

To me, the library is the most pleasant room in the school, though still on the edges of acceptability in terms of space for student and teaching use. Its facilities and collection do not appear to be outstanding, though the views from its windows are. For me at least, the temptation would be to look at the views rather than absorb the culture of words and pictures its shelves contain. That Addison Hills is a rural school is confirmed at every window.

Section 2: Students

Snapshots: Students and transition

Len is looking for work. A good-looking, able boy though probably a bit of a 'stirrer', he would take a job now if the right one came up.

I met him in the year 10 Home Economics elective. We formed an instant bond of friendship when I was moving among the class, mostly girls, trying unsuccessfully to strike up informal conversation. He touched my shoulder lightly and told me my fly was half undone. (The fieldworker died a thousand deaths.)

Len had a job in a take-away food bar over the Christmas holidays and liked it. When he came back to school for year 10, he signed up for Home Economics. His teacher tells me he is good, especially at the theory but he has ground to make up since he didn't do the subject last year. There are five boys in the class of twenty. For his work experience week, he worked in a restaurant. He points out that since he is only fifteen, he is too young for the dole. He also tells me that none of his friends have left school to go on the dole.

Brad wants to become an army officer. Apparently his family have links with the armed forces. He is now in year 10 and hopes to go on to year 12 and then to Duntroon. If he can't go there he will look for work in a bank. He will do his work experience in a bank this year. 'Deep down', says Brad, 'most kids really want to be at school and not leaving'. School may not be great, he tells me, but at least it is known. And of course most of his friends are there.

Jenny, one of the girls in the year 10 woodwork elective is uncertain about her career – perhaps office work (she likes typing at school), perhaps teaching. She wants to go on to HSC but isn't sure that she'll do well enough to make it through the system. She is open and friendly, but I have the feeling she is uncomfortable to be confronted suddenly by the future my question evokes. She is obviously happy at school. Her father has a senior job with one of the local shire councils, and her brother works there too. It is the practice of this council to allow the children of ratepayers to do work experience in its offices and so Jenny will do her work experience there.

Ann is described for me by her friends as 'an A student'. She wants to do HSC, but is completely uncertain about what she wants to do beyond that. She did work experience in a local real estate office. She knows that wasn't what she wants to do.

Susan wants to be a nurse. She says that she is 'only an average student', but she expects to stay on to year 12. 'Do you need a good HSC to go into nursing?' I asked her. She replied, 'If you do, I may not do nursing after all'. She hasn't yet found out what is needed to enter nursing, but would like a work experience placement relevant to nursing as her first choice. I have the sense that Susan, too, is uncertain about her choice – uncomfortable even to be talking to me about her career.

Kathy comes forward quietly as I speak to the others. She finds a space in the conversation to come in and the others bow to her certainty and experience. She is an unusual case in that she left school and then returned. She left at the end of year 9 when, like others, she was able to find a job through friends. She worked in a pet shop – she likes animals. She is a quiet, slightly shy girl, but seems confident about her ability to do a job. The pet shop was a small business run by two women. Kathy was 'squeezed' between them: they had different views of what she should be allowed to do and countermanded one another's instructions. Kathy felt that she was developing responsibilities in the care of the animals and in the business side. She was learning from one of the women how the books were kept. Perhaps these two were not aware of the effects of their conflicting expectations of her or of the effects of treating her sometimes as a responsible staff member and sometimes as a child to be told what to do.

One day one of the owners interrupted her as she worked, complaining of the job she had done cleaning an area of the shop. 'Get it cleaner or you won't be here next week', the woman threatened. Fed up with her treatment, Kathy made her own stand: 'Okay, I'm going now'. Seeing Kathy's resolve, the woman immediately regretted her threat and tried to convince her to stay, ending in tears. But Kathy had had enough and left.

She says she could have got another job through friends of the family, but decided instead to return to school. She says now that she enjoyed the 'freedom' of her job and the sense of 'self-sufficiency'. Outside work, her time was her own and she had her own money. Returning to school late in first term of the following year, Kathy says she felt 'some pressure'. But it was not hard to get back to school work. This year when the others go out on

Addison Hills: alienation and transition from school

work experience, she says she will not go.

She has no definite career plans and no particular educational goal. One feels that she has returned to reassess her situation and regroup her reserves before making another foray into the world of work.

Talking to the year 10s, I spoke to a potential builder (whose father is the Woodwork teacher at Addison Hills), a potential ship's officer (with a grandfather who had been at sea), a potential chef (whose father is a baker, and who is going for an interview next week about an apprenticeship in a local restaurant), a potential lawyer, a potential ranger (a girl who organized a program of nature study for primary school children at a school nearby), a potential electrician's apprentice (who worked with a local electrician on work experience but couldn't get an apprenticeship with him because business was bad), a potential theatrical make-up artist (she knows it's a long shot but wants to try), a potential pilot. . . . There are a few common choices, too: among them are office work, catering, and teaching. No one chooses the dole, though unnamed students are reputed to leave for that reason. No one chooses jobs in supermarkets, but several students have left Addison Hills for jobs on check-out counters or in local groceries.

Summing it up, the students tell me that they recognize their career choices are pretty open at year 10, but say that most have a clear idea of the kind of thing they would like to do. They also said that what they did at school did not seem relevant to their career choices. They wondered whether the curriculum represented the preferences of teachers rather than the needs of students. They said that work-related schooling might be more relevant to them than general schooling. They would like part-time schooling and part-time work if it were possible to arrange.

They see the school as HSC-oriented. Some, but by no means all, want to go on to year 12. The ones who expect to leave earlier find the school unsuited to their needs. (The school encourages these students to go elsewhere.) The students want a more varied curriculum, with elements of both technical and high school offerings. Some of them chafe under the academic orientation of the school.

The choices they make about careers seem often to be based on some personal knowledge – perhaps a relative's occupation, or work they see going on around them in the area. Perhaps the ways they define their needs in preparing themselves for these occupations are also based on what is accessible to their experience of work and the careers they have seen. So a tension can arise between what the students think is needed and what teachers believe – a tension between student and teacher perception of needs. This tension might be reduced by negotiation about careers and what is needed for entry to them. Work experience is an attempt to broaden the terms in which careers are considered. Curiously, however, work experience seems as effective in causing a student to revise a career choice as in confirming it or enriching understanding of its demands. Perhaps more effective.

What is clear, however, is that choosing a career, for these students at least, is very much choosing a *life*. It is a very personal matter, tied up with a present sense of self and anticipations of what one wants to be. In this, the school's processes for career preparation (the curriculum, work experience) seem institutionalized, even bureaucratized, contrasting with the personal process of choice of a way of life. One asks why it is that school itself does not engage this personal dimension, drawing the students into a continuing process of self-examination and consideration of their place in the social world. School seems to have asserted its place on the personal/institutional continuum, and to have come down firmly on the side of the institutional.

Snapshots: School leavers

A boy and a girl left between year 11 and year 12. Both were expected to do well in the HSC. Jan was offered a job in a bank. Given unemployment levels around Addison Hills, it was better to take the certainty than to finish school with only possibilities. Richard left with no job to go to. During the Christmas holidays his mother and a brother had been killed in a car accident.

Howard from year 11 left mid-year. A consistent behaviour problem (and also, perhaps, a victim of his peers), he ended his school career one Friday when he was caught firing rockets in the school grounds, set fire to the goalposts on the playing field and brought a railway sleeper into the corridor. Howard will be missed by some of the year 10s: his behaviour enlivened the day. 'Howard was our Messiah', one told me.

Alistair went on work experience to a large department store. The store offered him an immediate job and promised him a place in its executive trainee scheme. He stayed on.

Addison Hills: alienation and transition from school

Toni, a bright girl who had just begun year 12, left suddenly after the first few weeks of first term. (She is one of three year 12 students who left early in the year; twenty-nine remain.) She had always wanted to teach physical education. She and her boyfriend, a physical education student at college, had been going out together since she was in year 7. Her boyfriend left her. She took a job on the checkout counter at a local supermarket.

Jane, the oldest of eight children, had trouble getting on with her parents. After a row, she left home. She was in year 10. She has part-time work in a department store in a nearby town.

Colin left school earlier this year to take a job as a shoemaker's apprentice. A friend had left the apprenticeship for another job and recommended Colin to the shoemaker as a new apprentice.

As I hear their stories, I see that some are pushed out of school, some are pulled out, some jump, and some fall. The stories don't convince me that they are driven out – at least not in the simple sense that some critics of secondary schooling would argue (that schooling is boring, irrelevant or punishing for students).

The students tell me the curriculum is irrelevant to some of their needs, but it seems to breed a sense of disengagement from school work rather than a sense of repulsion. Other factors – in their families, immediate opportunities, sudden changes in their life-world or perceptions of themselves – seem to precipitate their decisions to leave. The perceived irrelevance of the curriculum to their needs may be a precondition for leaving, but it doesn't seem to be sufficient. If it is perceived as irrelevant, and if it does breed a sense of disengagement from the life and work of the school, the curriculum may 'turn kids off school'. The satisfactions of life and an active sense of engagement must be found elsewhere.

Within this school, 'clown' and 'stirrer' roles may offer alternatives to engagement in the tasks the school defines. Friendships in the school, too, engender some sense of belonging – to the school as a social group, if not as a 'work-place'. Because it is a rural school, urgently bussing its students in and out at either end of the school day, it does not readily provide sources of identification in extra-curricular activities (especially school sport).

Outside the school, there are strong sources of identification. Because the area is fairly closely-settled, there are strong town affiliations for sport and recreation. And these young people know that there is useful work to be done around the community – the work of the rural community is 'visible'. Moreover, they have personalized access to some parts of its economy. Extended networks of contacts through families and friends to local tradespeople and small businesses make it possible for the community around Addison Hills to 'look after its own'.

A portrait: Alison

We sit in a bare room under clinical fluorescent light. It is one of three counselling rooms in the school. The door is labelled 'Conference Room'. It is closed behind us. Inside, there is a smell of new carpet, stark concrete block walls, a desk and two chairs. I sit where she can see the sketchy notes I take as she talks.

I watch her eyes through the discussion. They are more anxious to engage than to disclose. My judgment is that she confuses the limitlessness of being listened to with being understood. Different moods compete in her as she speaks. Today is, after all, the last day of her schooling. Sometimes she seems to frighten herself with what she says. Sometimes she is almost coquettish. Sometimes she rolls her eyes away in a private smile; she cannot believe her own boldness as she measures the distance between what she has said and what she cannot or will not say.

In the end, I am sure of two things. First, she has told me her story in the hope that others will learn by it – mostly, I know, she hopes that schools might be different. Second, I know she has been saying into being someone not quite herself. In speaking to me, she is aware that she is part person, part myth. Her story is meant to instruct.

Thirty years ago her father left strife-torn Hungary. For some reason, I imagine him crawling at night across a field to a frontier and freedom. His hands are strong and youthful. Today, in my mind's eye, they appear strong still, but they carry a story of hard work etched in tiny cracks on the fingers and palms. Her mother was a stenographer. Her job brought her close into a world of words and voices. In its way, it was a world of certainties unlike the world outside, stilled by routines and records, predicting pieces of the future. It was a world to respect. She married Alison's father and gave up her job outside the home. Twenty-eight years ago, Alison's older sister, Caroline was born. Twenty-

Addison Hills: alienation and transition from school

four years ago brother Peter was born; brother Michael twenty. Three years later, so was Alison. Now she lives at home with her parents on a twenty-two acre farm near one of the towns on the peninsula. She is happy and unhappy there. She is close to her mother, more distant from her father. She has a horse and loves riding. The house is cold in winter and she hates winter mornings; there is a pump shower outside. It is winter now.

When she was in fifth grade, she went to private elocution lessons in the town. Her mother, ever respectful of the power of language, wanted her to go. A school friend, Janet, went too. Their brothers were also friends at school. Janet was two years older than Alison but only one year ahead of her at school. First Alison learned her vowels and consonants, then short pieces by heart. She did well, pleasing her teacher and her mother. Then she took up drama – her performances in church and school plays suggested she had some talent.

At twelve she was a 'tomboy'. With her brothers' friends she learned to shake a fist or give a shove. She can still be a toughie though nowadays she can be more subtle. Soon she was mending cars with her brothers' friends. 'Cars are easy', she says – she could be a mechanic. She knows more about cars than many, maybe most boys. The world opened slowly as the boys became her friends too. They became a group. One became her first boyfriend. She went with the group to his parents' farm at Apollo Bay. Sunday school provided another group of friends, as did Brownies: she is still a leader with a local Brownie group.

For the first few years of high school a group of girls was at the centre of her school life. There were ten of them, paired within the group. Alison and Janet are a pair. Janet is her closest friend at school, but she sees more of Lisa outside school (although Lisa goes to the same school). And even Janet can prove difficult when it comes to boys. Somehow, it seems, Janet likes Alison's boyfriends. In fifth form, her closest friends are still girls. She finds boys fickle friends (and sometimes 'rats').

Two years ago an Aboriginal girl, Rhonda, joined the group. She went to school on the bus with Alison, and Alison befriended her. The bus is a meeting place for many of the children at the school: they come from the five towns and from the farmland between the towns. Rhonda had a hard time at school. Some called her names, but Alison defended her and even showed the others an angry fist. Rhonda grew closer to Janet at school but seemed not to settle in. Once they went to a football match and Rhonda saw a group of boys from her old school. Alison went over with Rhonda and their own group to meet them. They seemed a pretty rough sort of group – not the kind of people Alison liked to mix with. After two weeks, Rhonda left school to look for work. Alison doesn't see her any more.

At primary school Alison did well. At high school, she was 'average'. Her teachers liked her; she treated them boldly as people. She is not accustomed to bowing to authority. Even so, the teachers made her uncertain, seemed somehow to criticize, to find limits around the things Alison knew. She did well in practical subjects. She lost interest in home economics and began to do less well – though she cooked at home from the age of seven. In accounting, she understood the book-keeping: it was 'logical'. She could explain it to her friends. But she didn't like the teacher and she didn't work as she could have. She didn't do well on assignments or exams. She was involved in the making of two films at school which she enjoyed. Both films won prizes for the school: two cameras, other film-making equipment, school work seemed irrelevant. In life, things are 'logical'. It all comes down to logic, Alison says. 'Logic' has to do with concreteness and practicality.

She kept on with her drama privately for a while, but had to forego it last year when her private teacher left for a year overseas. Alison's career interests changed with her appraisal of her work at school. At different times, she has wanted to be a psychiatrist, an architect, a speech therapist, an accountant, a motor mechanic. Drama remains a strong interest. But formal qualifications seemed a barrier to many of the things she wanted to do earlier.

She had a Saturday morning job in a local haberdashery. She was valued there – knew her way around the shop and the merchandise. She made five dollars a week. Then she had a job over Christmas with her brother selling car parts. Customers thought she didn't know anything about the goods – she let them think as they liked. She earned twenty dollars a day.

She saved a good deal. In the May holidays she went to Sydney, Brisbane, and Canberra with her sister, now a nurse. These days she is closer to her sister although eleven years separate them. And somehow Alison finds herself more at home with boys than her sister seems to be. In Sydney she met a really nice guy who was staying in the same motel. He seemed about nineteen; she looked it. He came over to where she sat watching television with her sister. She blushed to the roots of her hair and tried to keep on watching. He struck up a conversation. Her

Addison Hills: alienation and transition from school

sister went off to bed and they walked and talked for a while. In fifteen minutes they knew each other's backgrounds. He was seventeen. Now she can't even remember his name but she has gone out with a boy in Melbourne just because he reminds her of the boy in Sydney.

Four weeks before our conversation in the conference room, Alison was going to her Saturday morning job in the car with her mother. As they came onto the road from the drive, she saw her cat lying dead on the roadway. She asked her mother to drive on, and she kept busy all morning. When she came home she went straight out to the road, picked up the shattered body and buried it under the blossom tree. She cried all afternoon. Tears welled up in her eyes as she told me about it. 'A part of me died at that time', she said, 'a bit of security'.

Our meeting in the conference room was on a Thursday. The Monday before, going home from school, Alison made up her mind to leave. She announced her decision at home that night.

I met her first on the Tuesday at recess. I was standing near the school canteen with Stan, one of the teachers. Alison and Janet came over to talk, and Alison gave Stan the news. She was leaving. That day she picked up the school forms and told her friends. On the Wednesday, she stayed home. She came in on the Thursday only to pick up her mid-year report and say her goodbyes. Her report says too much about what she hasn't learned at school.

On that Thursday, she was thinking of a career in drama. She planned to take a course in the city. She did not know exactly what course to take or what institution to go to, though she knew that drama is a big field with many different kinds of work associated with it. She would continue to live at home – she did not yet want to leave ('I think I will always have a taste for farm life, but I would like to change really'.) She expected to go into the city each day to find part-time work, see people who might be able to help her with her planned career, find out about a course. She needed part-time work to cover the bus fare. She hoped to travel each day with Janet, who was also on the brink of a decision to leave school. Janet would be going to the Commonwealth Employment Service to find a job.

On the Friday afternoon after I spoke to her, Alison tried out for a job in a local shop near the haberdashery. The owners knew her and her family. They were pleased with her work and offered her a permanent positon. She started full-time the following week.

Stephen Kemmis

I dropped in to see her at the shop two months later. She was still 'looking into' the possibilities in drama. Maybe something will come of her hopes there. But life had begun to take a new shape – with her fledgling financial independence, out of work hours were swept up with discos, plans, and friends. She was still in touch with school friends, some of whom (like Janet) had by then left too. The community keeps them together. She gave me the impression that she had been freed from a certain kind of humiliation.

As we talked it out on the Thursday in the conference room, it seemed to me that Alison has surprised herself by deciding to leave. Suddenly school seemed no longer necessary. And, equally suddenly, she seemed to have gained control over her identity. School had been a waiting room for Alison, not a preparation for the things she wanted to do. She has found herself outside the abstract blueprints for life and career offered by the school.

How could Alison make up her mind to leave so suddenly? (We spoke about it further when I visited her at the shop, and she confirmed then that it was a sudden decision.) There was the very immediate realization that her mid-year report was likely to be poor, that she wasn't doing well at school. Perhaps she had had enough of being cast in that role. But that didn't seem new or different – the last two or three years had been like that. There was a recognition that what the school offered didn't seem relevant to her own career aspirations. If drama was the way ahead, she felt she didn't need the school to continue. (At the beginning, her drama study had been outside school.) She spoke at length about the process of learning at school what she couldn't do (my words, not hers). The part of her life of which she seemed most proud was outside school – being a leader at Brownies, being competent in cooking and as a mechanic, being 'logical'. She had come to terms with an Alison who had a place in her community and with her friendship group.

But perhaps the most significant event she spoke of was her trip with her sister. She was treated as an adult; people meeting her expected her to be one. And she found she could respond appropriately. Even her peer group was unnecessary – she could sustain the role alone. She began to see the process she had been going through at school – one of gradually being 'frozen out' of school life – for what it was. And she found that the Alison she wanted to be existed not just as a possibility but as a reality. She could recast herself and her relationships with her family, her friends, the community, and the school.

Addison Hills: alienation and transition from school

This dramatic reconstruction of affiliations and categories for understanding the world is the personal face of *fan-shen*. *Fan-shen* is a term used to describe a phenomenon common when people become radicalized in revolutionary societies. (The origin of the term is Chinese.) As a social phenomenon *fan-shen* is the reconstruction of social categories and forms of life which occurs as people come to terms cognitively with a new way of understanding the world. While up until that time, the order of society could be taken for granted in terms of one set of categories (like status, authority, and deserved rewards), it is suddenly understood differently (for example, in terms of systematic exploitation or the recreation of unequal opportunities).

Alison experienced *fan-shen* in stepping from one framework of understanding, in which she understood herself as dependent and as dependent and determined by others, into others, in which she could see herself as independent and an influence to be reckoned with. It is a radical reorientation, though not necessarily radical in the political sense. The elements of Alison's disaffection were present long before the event, as moments in the process of growing up. The trip (and perhaps also the death of her cat) were catalysts which redefined her for herself as newly adult, as someone who could cope.

To what extent is she coping now because of and to what extent in spite of her experience of school?

Fan-shen

>A child
>I am my family,
>Friends, community.
>They see me for what they are.
>Skeins of influence
>Run between us.
>Growing up
>I discover it is so:
>I too have power to act.
>They see me for what I am.
>As someone for myself
>I am someone for others.
>I wake to the world as new.

Section 3: Teachers

Snapshots

Tom teaches Maths. He is acid-witted, slightly cynical. He has the combination of verbal wit and precision of mind that suggests he might be better cast as a lawyer. Talking to me in a friendly, half-mocking tone, he caricatures the kids, their families, the school.

The work he put into teaching the students, and the annual play reveal that his cynicism is as much a comment on his own idealism as on the failures of the school, its organization or the community. The fact that the students like him puts paid to his pretended image of tyrant. What's more, from the sacristy of the Mathematics department, he flirts with ideas of reformation of the curriculum.

Tall, blond, bearded Stan is a mathematician and strong Victorian Secondary Teachers Association (VSTA) member. He is uncomfortable with the curriculum and with the docility of the staff in the face of organizational problems. He is friendly to students and sometimes has them home for dinner. He relates to their needs, perceptions, and problems.

His ear is finely-tuned to the community. He wants to understand it. He put me in touch with Sergeant Bruce for a view of transition from the community. He repeats the Sergeant's belief that these students need to leave the community for a while, go to Melbourne and put its possibilities in a wider perspective.

He is ready to accept that the school has a responsibility for the fact that some kids get 'turned off'. It is not just them, their families, their peers or the community. The problem is how to respond, and how to establish commitment to that response in the school. Rural life claims the allegiances of some staff; they are not ready to remake the school. So the struggle is always incomplete, indecisive and inconclusive. Change is long in coming and the challenges grow more pressing day by day. He works on the school council's Curriculum Committee, but it could not dictate change even if it could decide what needed to be done.

For all that, I would not judge him as likely to become cynical as a way of distancing himself from the problems. In that cynicism we find the alienation of the teacher from the school. His political commitments suggest that he would regard relenting in the struggle as capitulation.

I wonder where he was in 1970, when the VSTA was staging some of its most celebrated battles. Were those his formative years?

Reg is owlish and stringy, looking younger than his age. He listens. He is a social scientist, and active in the staff association. He sees a need for greater coherence in the curriculum, a more intensive engagement of students in its tasks. He sees a need for reconstruction.

These teachers are among the 'reformers' in the school. To me, they are the 'young Turks'.

There are two other groups of teachers I find it harder to talk to. One is the group I would characterize as the 'cynics'. They are negative about the school either because they never cared much for the work, or because, after learning through bitter experience that ideals can be blunted on the stone of corporate inaction, they became cynical. They do not commit themselves easily to new proposals for change and nowadays tend to go along with the system.

The other is a group I would characterize as 'the establishment'. It is a smaller group than I had imagined, but it contains some more senior staff. For them, the character of the school is given by the fact that it is a high school. They do not question the legitimacy of its academic orientation.

The cynics care little for power within the school. They exert their influence by dampening the positive proposals of the other two groups, by living with the system. The establishment is more powerful, though at times it is under siege. In the end, it can rule even by inaction. The 'young Turks' are relatively powerless, even as a group. But they can and do shape the languages in which problems are discussed, and in this way they throw doubt on the wisdom or legitimacy of present ways of working.

Addison Hills, like most schools, is not staffed by reformers because there are few opportunities and few rewards for reform. The bureaucracy of the school's organization casts a cold shadow over the torches of revolution. If things are to change at Addison Hills, the would-be reformers have a big task ahead. Like most schools, it is not organized so that it can be easily galvanized into action. The impetus for change, it seems, must come from outside the school, if change is necessary. Perhaps it is the conditions of work which breed inertia, perhaps it is something to do with the training or placement of teachers. Or perhaps it is something to do with their characteristics as a group. Perhaps it is to do with the way schools are managed.

Certainly the organization and staffing of Addison Hills is resilient to attempts at change. It has survived with relatively few modifications for years. Staff relationships in the school are not, by and large, collegial. Teachers are distributed between students across the timetable; subject departments are not strong sources of social or political affiliation. But it would be wrong to think that management in the school is simply hierarchical or directive. Lacking both structures for participatory decision-making or a strong management hierarchy, the power for change in the school has become diffused and ultimately defused.

The teachers, by choice or by habit, have been disenfranchised as forces for change in the curriculum. They are powerless to meet its challenges. If students are out of touch with the curriculum as it is offered, not much can be done. The school lacks the mechanism, and, perhaps, the will to engage the problems, analyse them, respond with strategies for action and learn from their effects in practice.

A diptych: Sally: Actor and director

Sally M_____ is known to everyone as 'Mrs M'. It was a while before I could work out who she was on the staff list. She is young and lively, with light brown hair and a ready smile. She likes the students and they like her. She has a natural intensity which gathers attention.

I have come to her classroom to watch her teach a current affairs lesson. At least that has been the effect. I have the impression that we are both rising to the occasion; she is going through her paces. Asked to judge her performance, I call it 'deft'. We both know that it has been an artificial lesson. We confirm it to each other afterwards. (She calls it 'stilted'.) It is hard to be watched at work teaching and relating. The only model of the outsider in the classroom available at Addison Hills is the (dimly-remembered) Inspection.

The performance carries messages even so: she is demonstrating some of the skills she actually possesses, not artifices produced for the occasion. I draw the inference that they have been

Addison Hills: alienation and transition from school

developed in use. And 'going through her paces' is the right way to put it.

Today's item from the newspapers is the bombing of a synagogue in Germany. Who did it? Yes, maybe, no why not? Why in Germany? What about the second world war? What did Hitler . . .? How many Jews? But who now? What is the PLO? And where is Palestine? Mr Grant will talk to you about Israel and show his slides next week. And how should they be punished? Is it a crime when it's political? And what else could they do?

And then to oilseed, the topic of the week. Oilseed, too, is a rapid-fire succession of questions. I am not sure whether it ended up being an interesting topic. The staccato style made the lesson a fencing-match and I became transfixed by the parry and the thrust. Unlike me, the students were on their toes. They could be asked next. I wonder if the long-term effect on the kids is much learning about terrorism/wars of liberation or oilseed, or whether it is about the fencing match. (It was a great duel. What was it we were fighting about?)

Sally teaches English and Drama. This current affairs lesson is with her form group. It is outside the most serious work of her day. Nevertheless, I begin to see how this pretty, vulnerable woman keeps control over the barbarian horde of the class. Verbally, she engages them and then outfences them. (Parry, thrust, touché, on guard!) If it were true of all her teaching (and I know it is not), it could be a great impediment to education. The questions move so fast that the answers barely have a chance to squeeze in between them; the kaleidoscope of information being shaken again and again before we have a chance to appreciate the patterns.

I labour the point not to score against Sally, but to puzzle over the effects of this demand for control. Staying alive in a roomful of adolescents requires skill. The survival skill she demonstrated shows that the need for control (on Sally's side) and the expectation of control (on the students') together conspire against learning, though it favours the development of agility in at least some of the students. It requires a great deal more agility on the part of the teacher; Sally plays Errol Flynn playing Robin Hood against all the Sheriff of Nottingham's bully-boys.

One of Sally's real strengths is in Drama. She runs elective courses for years 8, 9, and 10 in film-making. She helps the students find a theme, develop it, write a script, plan shooting, act it out and edit it. (Alison was in Sally's elective.) The class has won prizes for its efforts.

Sally helped the students to make 'The Half-Sucked Peppermint' a couple of years ago. It is a melodrama about a girl who found schoolwork 'a strain'. So she left school but there were no jobs anywhere. She finds out about the kinds of work that might be available (the school's Careers Centre does service as the CES) but all to no avail. Tempted away by a villain in full-dress vampire uniform (put on your top hat, your white tie and your tails), she meets an untimely end. The villain carelessly leaves peppermint wrappers lying about and so is tracked down by the relentless police.

The film is jammed full of messages from its student makers. The girl is a beauty. She has, from the perspective of her fellow students, the glamour that is 'star-quality'. (She is Toni who, two years later, actually left school at the beginning of year 12 and took a job in a local supermarket; life imitating art.) The film contrasts school with a nightmare of unemployment. The star imagines herself into a series of job roles, but doesn't get any of the jobs. Each of the imagined roles is portrayed in a deliciously stereotypic way: cleaning-woman, nurse, conductress, model, waitress, jockey, farmer, labourer (a few blows for the women's movement in there). The message seems to be that school is, after all, the right place to be. 'Out there' is a nightmare of unfulfilled ambitions and potential obliteration. Even star-quality or the CES can't save you. Perhaps the film's implicit message is that school is a nightmare too, but one to be endured if the nightmare beyond is to be avoided. The devil you know . . .

Sally's film-making elective provides an opportunity for students to express themselves through drama and, in this case, to work through some pressing questions of identity. Though 'The Half-Sucked Peppermint' suggests that they are more conscious of their inability than their ability to cope, at least they have had the chance to raise what are for them important questions.

On one side, we see Sally the survivor, playing a role for the house; on the other, Sally the director, pulling the roles and the performances from the students. A change of scenes, or two parts of the same picture?

Addison Hills: alienation and transition from school

A portrait: Rob

Rob moves into the staffroom like an athlete, surefooted and certain. He is listened to in conversation. The stranger notices that first, because Rob is quiet and unpretentious, though not reticent to speak. He is suntanned, with a wiry build on a sparse frame. At first I suspect him of eating yoghurt, but he turns out to have sandwiches which he always eats at recess, leaving himself with an immediate sense of loss and a presentiment of an unfulfilling lunch-hour. His hair is dark, slightly unruly against his attempts at neatness. His dress suggests that he chooses his clothes in the morning more because they are appropriate to the weather and near at hand than because they are appropriate to each other. I recognize faint echoes of the Irish-Australian larrikin and bushman. (His reading of C.J. Dennis and Henry Lawson or mine, I wonder.) Rob is in fact a gentleman hobby-farmer. His independent source of income is the school.

He teaches science. I can see he enjoys the teaching and the science. Watching him at work, I have the impression he is teaching the students something he wants them to know, though his style is laconic more than charismatic, gently controlling rather than permissive. That strikes a chord, too: something about his expectation of repressed self-control in the kids suggests a religious background, part of the Irish-Australian myth.

Significantly, he is teaching about alternative sources of energy. Students are working in pairs (though perhaps it is meant to be individually, Rob doesn't seem to mind the hum of conversations around the room once everyone knows what they're meant to be doing). They have workbooks with questions, resource books, and Rob moving around the room as a resource person. I am not sure that they realize that this is 'relevant' science. I wonder whether they have missed the fact that it is socially-relevant and potentially relevant to them: maybe they have not yet experienced the drill of the more formal lecture-dictation science lessons which used to predominate. (Perhaps some will meet that kind of science teaching as they prepare for HSC.) They are on the near side of inquiry, my guess is that Rob's style favours guided discovery teaching (leading kids to truths where he knows they can be found) rather than completely open-ended inquiry (making their own knowledge out of their own experience).

The room looks slightly 'literate' for a science lab. The books, posters, and materials around the room give it a warmer atmosphere than the more clinical science lab. I say 'literate' because books are obviously a real resource here; the prac. work and chalk-and-talk lessons are obviously not expected to be self-explanatory. But Rob shares his lab with other teachers (and the students), so the influence is not all his.

It is a science lab, though. Tall teacher's desk on elevated dais at the front; tall, blacked benches with gas taps, sinks, and the smooth arcs of chrome taps rising above them; tall, heavy wooden stools. Rob defies the compulsions of the fixed furniture and raised dais after a few minutes of introductory instructions, answers a few questions standing on floor level beside the magisterial front bench (still keeping touch with its mystical authority), then breaks free to wander among the students' benches (speaking from experience, on his own authority). His open, conversational manner is betrayed by this symbolism of higher authority (conscious and deliberate or unconscious and accidental on his part?) but I doubt that it is lost on students. Their questions seem to be more heckling and more ironic at the start of the lesson when he is behind the front bench; when he comes to their benches they seem less ritually-bantering. But, at least towards the back where I am sitting, they seem to take the work slowly; interested but not keenly so. The pace is comfortable, and the students allow themselves distractions.

It is likely that Rob will take this group of students on an excursion to his house, as he has done with other groups. He and his wife built a mud-brick house on their farm. It took a Christmas vacation and his long-service leave to build. He talks with enthusiasm about different sizes and mixtures of mud-bricks, about how to taper a wall, about the different thicknesses required upstairs and down. There is no doubt that it is his and his family's house.

The farm and livestock also provide significances for Rob that transcend his teaching. He speaks with honest, unsentimental respect of the local tradesmen and fellow-farmers who have taught him their skills. He is an invaluable source of intelligence about the community, sharing its values and knowing its networks. These significances – self-reliance, interdependence, community membership – suffuse his teaching with conviction. My guess is that the farm and the house represented an opportunity for retiring from a school whose values differ from his own into his family and the community, but that the effect has been different. An analogy may illustrate what I mean.

Addison Hills: alienation and transition from school

John Berger, in his book *A Fortunate Man: The Story of a Country Doctor*[1], describes the central character, Dr Saussure, as a young doctor who regarded himself early in his career as an adventurer against disease. Later, Saussure realized that his work was not a battle against disease, but about first 'recognising the truth about a man' and then finding ways to restore him, as a whole, to health.

Perhaps Rob's case is somewhat similar. It would be a romance to say of him that he is teaching students, not subjects. But I think it would be fair to say that he does not see himself as an adventurer against ignorance. For Rob, subjects have become vehicles for something else, not ends in themselves. He has a guiding notion like Saussure's notion of health, which can only be expressed indirectly, by contrast with ill-health. In a manner of speaking, and perhaps without conscious acknowledgment of his purpose, he is teaching about a way of life.

If this is so, his withdrawal into the farm and the community represented an opportunity to establish his convictions. He has stepped outside the value-framework of the school and into a value-framework nourished by at least some members of the community. Now his teaching provides an opportunity to express new values; in this sense, he represents an important link between the community and the school. It is a link that both he and the community respect.

Section 4: Curriculum and organization

Still life: Teachers, curriculum, school organization

I first met the staff at Addison Hills High School when a group of us from the university were asked to address a curriculum day at the school. One of the 'young Turks' on the staff came to the university where we discussed possibilities for the day. Apparently, the 'young Turks' on the Curriculum Committee were anxious to generate change in the school but they were finding it difficult to generate interest elsewhere in the staff. The curriculum was fairly stable, with innovation on the edges rather than at the core. The school was proud of its academic character and the curriculum was designed to be academic. At least some of the staff regretted that there was not a technical school closer at hand which could pick out some of the students less suited to the curriculum it offered. An elective system had been introduced to give all students an opportunity to take some non-academic subjects – perhaps the electives did provide something more appropriate to the interests of the 'non-academic' students – but the mainstream curriculum did not. (Once you divide students under labels 'academic' and 'non-academic', this problem won't go away: some suit what's offered and some don't. You've given up on a curriculum for all.)

The younger members of staff seemed interested in more far-reaching change. At the curriculum day, we visitors didn't provide the means to achieve it. We did draw attention to changes in the labour market and occupational structure, we did attempt to get workshop groups working on the identification of issues needing attention in the school, and we did generate some response. But, like many such days, it seemed to fall flat. We talked too much; the staff had too little time to get into ways of reorganizing themselves to deal with the issues.

I felt bad about it. Perhaps it was a confirmation for the staff that little, if anything, can be done to improve schools: academics turned out not to have usable answers either. Since then I have thought a good deal about the powerlessness of curriculum days to generate changes in schools. And I know we have better ways now to help staff to organize so that they can begin to make changes reflectively and effectively.

Addison Hills: alienation and transition from school

Part of the problem is that a day is too short to get much real work done on difficult organizational and practical problems. It takes a long time to build an organization in a school capable of transforming it. Consciousness-raising and working skills are needed. And a willingness to actually change what one does oneself. It isn't enough to tamper with school organization or the curriculum, though those things often do need changing. It is hardest of all to recognize that the living structure we are part of is the problem.

I have always liked the idea that genes use individual organisms to reproduce themselves. It makes as much sense as seeing reproduction the other way around. The same can be said about relationships in the classroom. School organization and curriculum reproduce themselves through teaching relationships, just as teaching relationships reproduce themselves through school organization and curriculum. Changing schools means changing teaching relationships and changing teaching relationships means changing schools.

Teaching relationships are what most teachers most value in our schools. And they want them to improve. So they usually prefer to start by changing organization and curriculum, because it seems that those changes will compel changes in teaching relationships. It seems to make sense because it looks as if it is the present system which constrains changes in teaching relationships. But when people make suggestions for changes in school organization and curriculum they are often disappointed. They have still left unchanged the thing they most wanted to change – their teaching relationships. They hoped the changes they made outside the classroom would cause changes within. But the very fact that the changes proposed outside did not simultaneously require changes within suggests that it would be possible for old relationships to survive in the classroom. And old ways are very resilient.

Why are teaching relationships so hard to change? Because they are very personal ways of coping with very difficult and sometimes risky human relationships. They are supported on the teachers' and students' sides by expectations built up over years of being in school. And they already carry their own baggage of time-honoured educational values to justify them (the value of the teacher as *an* authority and therefore as *in* authority, for example). So creating change means that whole groups of teachers and students have to learn to work together in new ways. And that means changing one's students *and* one's colleagues. And before you know it, you are requiring whole new ways of doing schools and schooling, and it is not very clear exactly what those new ways of working should be. So things fall back towards what they were before. Catch 22.

On top of all that is the problem that teachers aren't very good at actually running schools as organizations. Mostly, schools are very private from the teacher's point of view. The main thing is an identity for oneself as a teacher in one's own performance in the classroom; there is only minimal negotiation with colleagues about broader matters of curriculum and school organization. Many problems are dealt with on a hierarchical departmental system of authority, many other problems are skimmed over because meetings to work on issues are often held at the end of an exhausting day's teaching (managing roomsful of slightly rebellious students) and because people have conflicting ideas about what the issues are and what needs to be done. I suspect that teachers dislike conflict more than people in more aggressive occupations like business or politics. So they are inclined to reach for the resolution of problems quickly for the sake of peace. And so lots of problems don't get worked out thoroughly.

In this view, collegiality is a personal, not a professional matter for teachers. A staff has friendship groups as its informal structure, but its formal structure can be anything from rigidly departmental and hierarchical to amorphous and anarchic. Collegial responsibility in the professional domain seems relatively rare in schools and the profession. When you add to that the problem that new arrangements in a classroom or a department or the whole school have to be 'sold' to the school administration, colleagues and the school council, all of whom have their own ideas about what 'needs' to be done, you get a formidable array of wet blankets to meet the fires of enthusiasm for change, even when change is believed to be for the better by those promoting it.

Whole schools and educational systems will run quite smoothly on this wet blanket principle. From the spark of a new idea through to a flaring of enthusiasm in a department, the administration can just wait until an idea burns itself out. New ideas in schools can simply be tolerated to death. One simply agrees to wait until everyone is willing to act together to implement the idea. And since the debate can go on interminably, the wet blanket of time will eventually suffocate the light and heat of a new idea. The trick is never to *commit* a group or the

Addison Hills: alienation and transition from school

school as a whole to trying out the new idea and working through the 'bugs'.

The younger staff members at Addison Hills probably have the impression that someone made the school what it is today. That encourages them to believe that a small group could make it something else. In fact, the curriculum and organization of Addison Hills, like most schools, is what was left over after the things that couldn't be made to happen didn't happen. It is the total of all the expectations and aspirations and ways of doing things that could evolve without a battle ever being fought and won (a bloodless curriculum, one might say).

I like the story of Kutuzov in *War and Peace* whose self-appointed task in the war against the French was to prevent the Prussian generals with their new-fangled ideas of military science from committing the Russian army prematurely to bold strategies which could fail and leave the army without the resources to fight again. He preferred to wait until the *will* of the Russian army was resolute: only then could Napoleon be defeated. Perhaps Addison Hills is like that. Perhaps now is the time when the staff is ready to work through the problems. If it is the time, we should be able to feel a thrill of common commitment running through the troops. It wasn't there when I first went to the school for the curriculum day.

The bloodless curriculum, the unresolved conflicts of the staff meeting, the wet blanket principle: they are no more characteristic of Addison Hills than a hundred other high schools in the State. The profession of teaching is experienced by practitioners as something in classrooms – in teaching relationships. The profession does not prepare its practitioners adequately for the battles outside the classroom walls. And it turns out to be almost impossible to make changes to one's own teaching without changing the school at the same time. The curriculum, school organization, teaching, and learning hang suspended in a balance of forces. A compromise. A still-life composition.

Section 5: Community

A wall map: The hobby farm community and its school

Addison Hills is a modest-sized town around which are scattered five slightly smaller towns. The towns are separated from one another by distances of twenty kilometres or less. Between them, the spaces are filled by farms, hedgerows, stands of bush, dams, and marshes which support white-faced heron, white-necked heron and ibis. There are a number of large farms, but there is a large and increasing number of hobby-farms, quiet during weekday hours but stirring with life in early mornings and late afternoon and intense with activity on weekends. There is building, fencing, and the care of stock to occupy the family in work, and riding, inter-town sport, and visiting friends to occupy its members in relaxation.

Much is shared between these families in the buying and selling of hay, in arrivals and departures with small truckloads of sheep or goats or cattle, almost as small as the nuclear families who live out this dream of rural domesticity in the tracts of time between sleep and the grind of office work in the city some 45 kilometres away. The families who live here have reached back to an ideal of a time remembered or imagined as kinder than the world today, the ideal of the common industry and shared personal destinies of the family farm. They search for a continuity between the self, the family, and the community. In their search, they have established a new sense of community on the borders of technological, bureaucratic society. It is, in the term coined by the sociologist Ferdinand Toennies, a *Gemeinschaft* ideal of community, characterized by common caring and sharing, as opposed to a *Gesellschaft* ideal in which the community is regarded in terms of a matrix of organizational roles.

It would be true to say that these families had established more than a *sense* of community: indeed, they have established a community. In static terms, much is shared in terms of values; but, more dynamically, the community also comes alive through the social interactions which support the small enterprises of the farms. The economic interactions are neither cold nor crucial: other income (often two other incomes) provides the basic operating capital; the small-scale economy is essentially a lifestyle, signalling an identity with the dream and an affiliation between dreamers. This is not to romanticize or trivialize the sharing: on the contrary, it is to underline its ideological element. Sociologists write of the privatization of individual consciousness in modern societies. Work and formally-structured social relationships fragment communal ties; social organization appears sharply divided from the private world of the individual, and the personal relationships of the family. The workaday world is technologized and bureaucratized. In repudiating the large-scale ideology of the mainstream culture, even the privatized culture of suburbia, the hobby-farmers of Addison Hills make an ideological statement of affinity and belongingness: belonging to the land (though tenuously), to the family, to one another.

Arts and crafts, too, play an important part in this community, demonstrating that things can be home-made with skill and beauty. Clothes, ornaments, and household utensils are badges and signs which express the commonality of values.

Another element of the relationships between these families is important. It is that belonging to the community is personal, yet not depending on immediate geographical proximity. The hobby-farm economy creates an *extended* sense of community. Affinity is not established in concrete locations like the office or the supermarket though in these places, affinities and friendly rivalries are evident. Nor is it established through organizations whose members must be present for the group to exist (the club, the team, the church), though these organizations may celebrate it. It is established through a fluid set of interactions, all recognizable as parts of the same life-world, not compressed uniquely into regular times or places for its observance. Space separates the farms; economic exchanges take place outside the rigid time-frames of the nine-to-five world; travel is a part of all interaction beyond the family. Nevertheless, the sense of belonging is compelling for individual identity. Against the fabric of this community, individual identity is expressed and common bonds established through comfortable rituals of participation and recognition which accompany all meetings, however accidentally they occur in time or place. This is not a formal social organization which compels, coerces or subjugates, making its members instruments of its own dynamics.

Here, towns are reference-points in space, not in an economic framework. They provide a basis for only some of the economic transactions of the inhabitants of the area. The economy of the area depends on the resources brought into it through the other jobs of the hobby-farmers. More importantly, the towns impart names for local-ness, the *local* shop, the *local* team. They are convenient labels under which accidental memberships can be gathered and affiliations formed. The area as a whole has an ideological unity; within this unity, the towns group and differentiate people almost accidentally for personal and recreational purposes. Local churches, local clubs, local teams, local dance-halls provide focal points for spiritual and community life, and provide opportunities for equally-accidental rivalries, for formal invitations, and for more organized interactions at the community level. Weekend sport brings a loosely compressed ebb and flow of travel and interaction as whole towns meet in football and netball matches: home this week, away next; training on weekday evenings nourishes these local identifications.

The high school is in one sense an intrusion into this community. It is a reminder of the larger economic context beyond. It organizes movements of children across the area as a whole for another kind of purpose, the purpose of the still wider community and economy beyond. It formalizes and compresses social relationships in anticipation of life beyond school, which intimates for most of the children at least, the larger economic and political framework they must enter in their turn. It brings the children into contact with the universalizing, the abstract, the technologized, and the bureaucratized society-at-large on whose borders these hobby-farmers live. For parents, the school thus plays a paradoxical role: it brings their children into contact with the modernized culture they have chosen to repudiate, but simultaneously provides the essential skills for living and working in the wider culture which are necessary for building the economic base of the hobby-farm economy.

Young children go to local schools. Many go to one-teacher or two-teacher primary schools. For the younger children, town schools and one- and two-teacher schools in the spaces between towns provide an extension of the family and its values into the community, confirming belongingness. The more child-centred ethos of the primary school affirms the values of personalized interaction. Most of the older children go to the high school which homogenizes the town affiliations and rivalries. For students at the high school, belongingness becomes suddenly problematic, maybe even threatened: the school belongs to the mainstream society and foreshadows its impersonalization. In throwing the students together, it begins to obliterate the distinct characters of the separate towns. And it values a different kind of thinking, abstracted and universalized away from personal experience and the recognized expertise and wisdom of known people, towards 'subjects' and the formal culture of words in books, a property too commonly owned to be distinctive of the local culture.

High school represents a challenge: It is a clash of cultures. For some students, it can be handled pragmatically as a development out of the local community with its immediacy of belonging into the wider world. It opens the door to lifestyles not available locally, to the riches of the wider culture and to careers. (And, should a school-leaver so choose, it can provide the basis for his or her own participation in a hobby-farm economy.)

For others, the culture-conflict is more personally precarious. A range of service jobs in the local economy are available which do not require conspicuous success at school, in local shops and businesses, even the local councils. But this entails dependence on local opportunities and the modest local economy. There are very few jobs in the service economy of the area which will give them access to the lifestyle of their parents.

For some, contact with the universalizing culture of the school can even be painful: personal relationships based on mutual concern and support are replaced with more impersonal, task-oriented relationships; competition is suddenly more serious (a competition for life-chances); what can be seen and understood in the context of the local may become blurred and indistinct in the context of more general society. Needless to say, these shifts of perspective may carry an implicit threat as the certainty of the known and local is placed in a wider context of the abstract, formal, and general.

In the school, the myth of the hobby-farm community is strong. But the school cannot but unmask the myth: at most, the hobby-farm economy is revealed as secondary and peripheral, a refuge. By the standards of the wider society, a choice to remain within the local economy may seem to be a 'soft' option; within the local community, access to the hobby-farm economy by ownership is limited to those who can afford the land, so school-leavers choosing to stay within the community may have no other choice than to enter the service economy, accepting the restrictions on material success that this imposes. And yet, for the students themselves, a choice to stay is an affirmation of one's own past and of the values of one's own community. It is interesting that many of these students choose jobs in trades, whose work and practitioners play a visible part in the maintenance of the hobby-farm community and its economy. The local fencing contractor has relevant and needed skills, a family who has a fence put up appreciates his expert judgment: 'a good fence'.

Access to the hobby-farm community can be bought only by those in a position to repudiate the values of the wider community: those with the material success the mainstream economy provides. Many students who choose the myth rather than the mainstream economy will not be able to become fully-paid-up members of the dream. Even so, they may recreate the values of the community in a more pragmatic sense than the hobby-farmer can do: by full-time participation and dependence, not by choice.

What can education do in this hobby-farm community? Whose interests does it serve? How should the curriculum be constructed so that it engages students? These are pressing questions for Addison Hills High School, the first is just a local variant of a more general question about the relationship between education and community.

On the one hand, we might see education as a way of preparing students directly for participation in their local community. Many in Addison Hills, as elsewhere, see this option as narrowing and presumptuous, a patronizing or even dangerous role for the school which may set its sights only on the local, denying students access to wider perspectives on their culture and society, possibly lowering aspirations to the ones the local community can support. This is the criticism of those who see the school as having a role in extending students' interests and perspectives beyond the local. On the other hand, we may see education as concerned with the liberation of the individual from parochial perspectives, as an entrée to a world of ideas which transcend local concerns. But it can be argued against this view that such an education runs the risk of ignoring immediate and local student concerns in the interests of those 'wider' values and interests. Some say that the curriculum at Addison Hills is already running this risk, neglecting the well-springs of students' interests in the interests of disciplinary knowledge and the selection processes of HSC. These are the critics who challenge the school's 'academic' orientation.

A third view is possible. According to this view, the curriculum is a concrete expression of a three-way negotiation between the interests of the individual, concerns provoked by the wider society, and already-available knowledge. In this view, the knowledge-content of the curriculum is not sacred or given, it merely gives flesh to the intersection between local and more

Addison Hills: alienation and transition from school

general concerns. It is only a medium, to be given meaning in the context of the negotiation between individual and general concerns. This is the view of the teachers at Addison Hills, but they (like most) find it difficult to remake the curriculum of the school to reflect it.

The aim of this view of curriculum is to stimulate concern in students for understanding and interpreting their own interests in the context of wider concerns and interests, to see themselves in a social and cultural (and economic and political) framework. To achieve this aim, the curriculum must be remade constantly for the contemporary students, and in the light of the relationship between the local and wider communities. Some things will remain as worth learning and being taught; some processes of negotiating the curriculum (identifying student interests, analysing social structures) will recur. But much of the *practice* of curriculum will become fluid, and that disturbs expectations about the stability of school 'subjects', the division of responsibility between subject departments and year levels, and the organization of staff and students. Being both unfamiliar to many teachers and more demanding of individual and group effort, it is not a form of curriculum process that is welcomed by many. The organization of Addison Hills High School, and the expectations which sustain it, mitigate against this form of curriculum. The structure of secondary education in the State similarly discourages it, though new arrangements through the Victorian Institute for Secondary Education make it possible (school-based subjects and approved study structures for year 12).

The case of Addison Hills suggests that teachers stick with a bloodless curriculum because of the way their school operates as an organization. This is true of many high schools in Victoria. As a consequence, the school preserves a kind of disengagement of student interests from school interests. This may be construed as 'alienation', if we agree that alienation consists of the disengagement of personal interests and local concerns through institutional processes.

Happily, the students at Addison Hills seem *not* to be alienated in another sense, that of feeling that they have no place where they belong. Here among the hobby-farms, there are plenty of opportunities to belong to a community and to feel a sense of growth within it. There are alternatives to school as a source of identity. The paradox the school faces is of reconciling growth within the community and growth beyond it. And that is a question of curriculum.

Stephen Kemmis

Note

1 John Berger and Jean Mohr, *A Fortunate Man: The Story of a Country Doctor*. London: Writers and Readers Publishing Cooperative, 1976.

Chapter 4

The Purdah experience
Colin Power

Foreword

This case study sets out to portray how students and teachers in one school are tackling the problems created by mismatches between themselves as persons and the demands of the environment in the transition from school to work. In that it is the story of one school, the generalizations presented refer to that school and not to others. It should also be pointed out that the case study does not seek to describe all aspects of the school life. Given that the focus is on an area of difficulty for schools, the report does have more to say about the problems and limitations of the school than its strengths, strengths which, in the view of those in the area it serves, have earned the school a good reputation. Given the limited and somewhat negative focus of the study, blanket judgments about the school on the basis of the evidence presented are inappropriate. Also, given the sensitive nature of the problem investigated, it should be noted that the names used throughout are fictitious.

The case study should be seen rather more as providing an opportunity for members of the school community and for outsiders to develop a clearer understanding of the complexity of the problems being tackled by the school and how the culture, constraints, particular circumstances and organizational needs of the school have come to shape the ways in which teachers and pupils view the problems of the school and of young people in transition. These have led almost inevitably to 'alternative' programs for 'non-academic' students as the institutionalized response to perceived problems.

In writing the report, details of methodology have been briefly outlined at the appropriate points in the report. Extensive use was made of interviews with administrators, teachers and pupils; observations of curriculum planning meetings and to a lesser extent, of lessons; questionnaire data and documents. While data were collected from all 'types' of classes, somewhat more time was spent talking with and observing pupils in 'non-academic' classes and their teachers, given that the account seeks to present the problems from the perspective of those most intimately affected by them. Rather than study intensively a few students or classes, an attempt was made to capture the views of the majority and to synthesize and cross check information from a variety of sources. The time spent with any one individual or class was, therefore, limited. Hence, individual positions have not been explored in any depth.

It should be noted that the report not only reflects the beliefs and values of those observed and interviewed, but also those of the author. Therefore, the reader is advised of my belief that greater attention needs to be paid to the unintentional effects of educational policy and practice, and to questions of justice and quality in our efforts to ensure that all young people are provided with the knowledge and skills judged to be of such value as to necessitate their inclusion in any secondary school program.

Introduction

To a greater or lesser degree every school faces the problem of coping with students who face difficulties in adapting to its academic and social demands, become dissatisfied with, and eventually reject, its policies and programs. At the present time, in response to a perceived increase in the level of dissatisfaction with conventional high school programs, an increasing number of schools are engaged in the process of developing 'alternative' structures and programs. Purdah is one such school.

Initially it was my intention as a case study worker to focus upon the phenomenon of 'alienation'* as it manifests itself at Purdah, seeking to understand how teachers and students define the problem and to resolve it. However, in 1972 Purdah was

---

* Methodological note: 'Alienation' has been defined in general as a tenacious sense of estrangement or separation of the individual from society or its institutions which manifests itself in feelings of powerlessness, meaninglessness, isolation, and normalessness.

The Purdah experience

converted from an academic to a comprehensive high school. As the case study progressed, it became increasingly clear that the phenomenon I was interested in was embedded in, and represented one facet of, the broader problem of coping with the whole range of 'non-academic' students now attending the school.

The problem of 'non-academic' students can be seen as a failure either of the school or the students to adjust. Either way the problem cannot be understood independently of the constraints and peculiarities of circumstance of the school, and so the case study begins with a description of the school setting. Next the various ways in which administrators and teachers are trying to come to terms with what is for the school a serious, but not well understood, problem are detailed. This is followed by an account of the development of a school-based 'alternative' curriculum aimed at alleviating some of the difficulties facing 'non-academic' grade 9 and 10 students and teachers at Purdah. Finally, student attitudes and views regarding school and work are mapped, with particular attention being given to seeking to understand the phenomenon of being 'turned off' school as seen by students.

The school setting

To the casual visitor, Purdah High School is likely to appear to be fairly typical of the government schools established in the 1960s. It is one of many suburban high schools built in the post-war period to cope with the dramatic expansion in demand for secondary education. The school, which was established in 1961, seems to fit with the character of the area. It serves an area of Adelaide wherein pockets of well-kept houses of middle-income, blue and white collar workers are interspersed with the flats and the small factories of a light industrial area. In terms of almost every demographic characteristic, the area is at the median level.*

---

* Methodological note: According to the 1976 Census, the modal household income in the area served by Purdah was $10,500. Approximately 31% of the employed population were in manufacturing or construction, and 21% in wholesale or retail sales. The zone ranks almost at the median level in terms of overseas born residents. Of these, the principal groups are English, Greek and Italian. Most were post-war migrants who established themselves in permanent homes around Purdah in the 1960s after a period of living in temporary accommodation.

The school is tucked away in one of the side streets off the main road. Its manicured lawns, rose gardens, and trees blend with those of houses in the street. The first building one notices is an impressive, multipurpose school hall. A sign announcing 'Bingo here every Wednesday at 7.30' suggests that, like so many State schools, the facilities of the school are being used by local community groups. The office block and solid two storey classroom blocks are similar in style to those of other high schools established in the 1960s and early 1970s.

During the 1960s the school grew rapidly in size, attaining its peak enrolment of about 1500 in 1972. The rows of ageing temporary wooden classrooms hidden at the back of the school are remnants of this period. In the 1970s, enrolments remained high. Facilities were gradually improved. The school now has modern, well-equipped specialist facilities (laboratories, technical, home economics, and resource centres).

Until 1972 Purdah was a traditional academic high school. The school retains many of the traditions and values of its past. The large gold-lettered board in the front foyer still serves to honour academic success. About 30 per cent of the grade 8 intake eventually sit for the matriculation examination at the end of year 12. The school principal, Mr Jeffries, makes a point of ensuring that parents, students, and teachers are aware that the school is not neglecting its academic standards and values:

> A traditional part of the Annual General meeting is the presentation of awards to top matriculation students. Mr Becker congratulated the students and presented these awards. Overall 60% of students who sat matriculated, and there was an 84% subject pass rate.
>
> (Principal's Annual Report, 1979)

Amongst the seventy-nine staff members, the majority also value academic success. Most teachers in the school would prefer to teach brighter academically-oriented classes. Matriculation classes tend to be taught by the older, more established teachers in the school.

The authority structure within the school is, as it has always been, hierarchical*. In the main, the principal, deputies, and subject seniors are responsible for the formulation and implemen-

---

* Methodological note: The case study project had to be negotiated with the staff as a whole at two staff meetings as well as with the principal before these meetings.

The Purdah experience

tation of school policy and programs. However, the school does have a fairly active staff participation in curriculum development. In the Handbook of South Australian government schools, the school describes its policies as 'conservative'. Thus, homework and regular examinations are still seen to be important aspects of school life; classrooms and the timetable are organized on conventional lines; the school has a house and a prefect system, and an attempt is made to insist on the wearing of school uniforms.

The curriculum

In 1972, in line with the recommendations of the Karmel Report[1], Purdah was converted into a comprehensive high school. In time, the facilities, curriculum, and ethos of the school have changed as the school adapted to the increasing numbers of students with abilities, values, aspirations, and home backgrounds at variance with those of the staff establishment. Going comprehensive meant the addition of technical, home economics, and commercial subjects to the curriculum – and facilities for the teaching of these subjects. There has been a constant decline in demand for, prestige given to and (according to some teachers) standards within, traditional academic subjects. On the other hand, the emphasis given to art, music, drama, physical education and vocationally oriented subjects (technical studies, home economics, commercial studies) has increased. The proportion of children who are migrants or the children of migrants has steadily increased so that they now comprise approximately 32 per cent of the student population. Since a significant proportion of these are the children of Greek-speaking parents, modern Greek was added to the curriculum in 1978. French and German are also offered throughout the school. Students are selected into these classes on the basis of a language aptitude test.

The first changes to Purdah's curriculum then involved the addition of commercial, technical, and home economics courses (and subjects) to the program. Officially, classes have been organized on mixed ability lines for grade 8 students not taking a modern language, and on course lines thereafter. By the mid 1970s the proportion of students staying on to year 11 and 12 had increased, but many students also had difficulty coping with PEB* courses. As a consequence, two types of 'alternative' courses

---

* The Public Examinations Board (PEB) was the examination basis for university entrance, etc. in South Australia at the time of the study.

were introduced at the year 11-12 level: the 'Alternative Course' and the 'Work Experience' course.

The alternative course has as its basic aims:

(a) To further develop basic competencies and to offer instruction in specific vocational skills.
(b) To enrich personal development and broaden life experience in such areas as decision-making and financial management in order to promote responsible self-management.

Hence there is within the program a heavy emphasis on vocational preparation (technical studies, numeracy, literacy, career education) and 'relevance' (e.g., the general theme of alternative Science is 'Science for Living'). Students completing the program tend to enter the year 12 secondary school certificate course, or to seek to enter the work force (e.g., apprenticeships).

The Work Experience course is becoming increasingly popular amongst students whose prime objective is to enter the work force but whose intentions have been thwarted by conditions in the labour market. Mr Garrett, the senior teacher in charge of the program, suggested:

> All many of our students want to do is to leave and get a job. They hope that the school will help them to do so. They need something which will be of positive value in getting a job. The best we can do is to provide an alternative to PEB and to give it a structure and goals in its own right. Work experience students can see the value of the program in that they are getting skills and experience wanted by employers. So far we have been pretty successful; seventeen out of twenty in the work experience program last year got a job.

At the other end of the school, a small group of teachers had become increasingly concerned about the capacity of year 8 students to cope with the academic and social demands of high school life in the conventional, large mixed ability classes, to which they were allocated. Two teachers (Mr Rudder and Ms Draper) set up a program that would serve to ease their transition into secondary school. In 1979 grade 8 students who were considered by their primary school teachers to be 'at risk' during transition by virtue of their level of school achievement or social development were placed in what is termed a 'mezzanine class'. (The term was coined from architecture where it refers to the middle or in-between floor of a building.) The basic reason given for the innovation is as follows:

The Purdah experience

A significant proportion of students entering year 8 do so because of their age, not because they are *ready* in terms of basic skills and maturity . . . the assumption is that students beginning year 8 have a certain level of achievement, confidence and maturity. Initial expectations of these students are too high.

(Course statement, Mezzanine class)

According to Mr Rudder, the enthusiastic young architect of the program, about one third (i.e., about seventy students) of the 1979 intake were classified by their primary teachers as being 'at risk'. A small number (fifteen) were placed in the slow learner category and formed a special class run by a special education teacher. The others formed two mezzanine classes of about twenty eight each and were taught for most subjects (thirty-one lessons out of forty) by the one teacher. The emphasis in the program was on basic skills, gradual introduction to secondary school life, pastoral care and influencing personal development. An evaluation undertaken within the school concluded

This approach has proved successful, basically because of the Primary school single teacher approach with an emphasis on pastoral care, but *mainly* because the two teachers involved are of the highest calibre and totally enthusiastic about *their* project.

A case study of one of the mezzanine classes was undertaken by three M.Ed. students at Flinders University. On the basis of the cognitive and affective measures taken, the team concluded that the year 8 alternative classes had been successful in improving self-esteem and attitudes towards school, but that the intellectual needs of the mezzanine class are at present being imperfectly met.* Mr Rudder would argue, however, that the progress of his students has been satisfactory. He sees the evaluation evidence supporting his claim that the grade 8 innovation had been most successful, and that it should be extended to years 9 and 10, since only a small number of students in the alternative classes in his view would be able to cope with a standard year 9 non-language class. Moreover, there were now alternatives open in years 8, 11, and 12 but not for 9 and 10. The target group has from time to time been variously described as including those who are 'basically reluctant learners', 'immature

---

* Methodological note: Report to the school: *A case study of a Mezzanine class.* Flinders University, 1980, 10, 113-16.

with poorly developed social skills', 'non-academic students likely to leave school at age 15', or 'students with basic skill (social and academic) difficulties'. A 'clearly set out, realistic, "life-oriented" course over several years' was seen to be needed by these students. In the latter half of 1979, a committee met weekly after school to plan the year 9 component of this course. The case study worker attended most (six) of these meetings, the proceedings of which gave insights into what are seen by staff to be potential problems within the school and ways of handling these. Further insights were obtained by interviewing teachers, students, and observations of classes.

In essence, the analysis undertaken suggests that at Purdah:

1 Social problems (alienation, boredom, deviancy, etc) and learning problems are not seen within the school as distinct, but are loosely related.
2 One source of these problems lies in the inappropriateness of academically-oriented courses and mixed-ability teaching arrangements in the school.
3 One possible solution is to introduce a range of 'alternative' programs within the school tailored to meet the needs of groups reasonably homogeneous in ability, development, and interests.

The extent to which alternative programs have been institutionalized as the school's response to potential problems can be seen in Figure 1 which shows the course structure in 1980.

There are essentially two teacher reactions to this restructuring of the curriculum. One group of teachers takes the view that comprehensive secondary schooling implies schools within schools aimed at meeting the vocational and educational aspirations of different 'types' of students. The other group has difficulty in accepting 'non-academic' students and programs and resents the changes that have taken place since 1972.

Several of the academic teachers are most concerned about the erosion of academic values and traditions of the school:

> Our status as an academic high school is being eroded by the up-grading of local technical high schools into high schools so that the better students are more thinly spread among institutions. The larger percentage of Southern European migrants with their lack of intellectual values have affected the school. Teachers are continually required to pitch their efforts

The Purdah experience

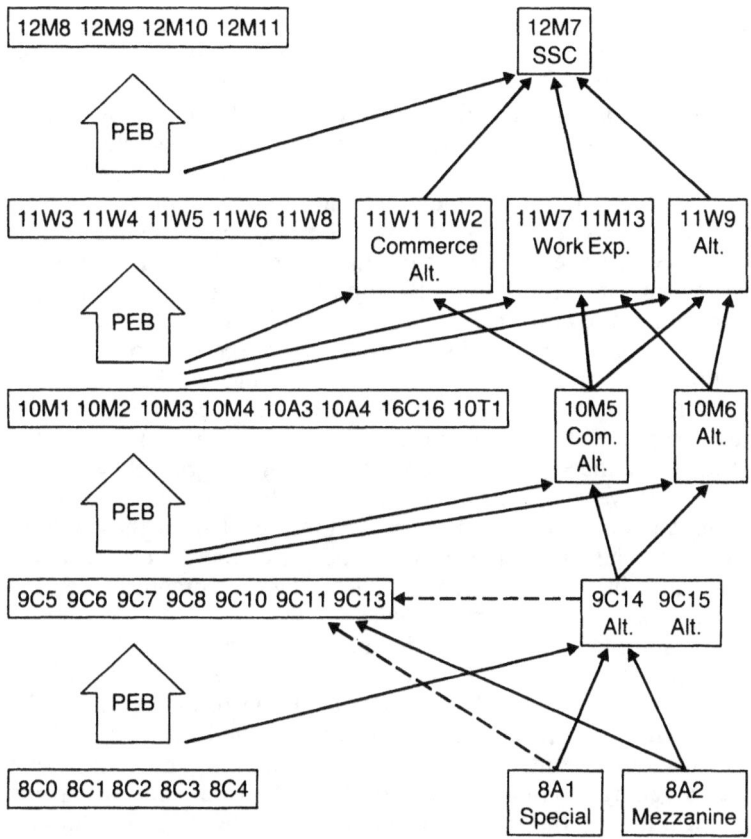

Figure 1: Class organization and student pathways 1980

at a middle level of performance and so the brighter ones are largely unchallenged, if not downright bored.
(Languages teacher interview, CR6.068)

Similar concerns were expressed by other members of the academic 'old guard' of the school. They are concerned about the lack of intrinsic motivation amongst the brighter students in the school. They are opposed to the development of a form of schooling which, in promoting vocationalism and pastoralism, confirms and compounds ignorance and dilettantism while stroking and leading would-be learners into a comfortable and complacent acceptance of human limitations and social realities. Like Hirst they espouse the ideals of a liberal education by suggesting that they are 'concerned with the comprehensive development of the mind in acquiring knowledge [and] aimed at achieving an understanding of experience in many different ways'.[2]

Furthermore, many of these teachers are not convinced of the liberal intent of comprehensive education, the provision of a comprehensive education suitable for all young people. Some teachers interviewed admitted that they believe in streaming ('they sort of stream themselves don't they?') and accept that the curriculum for lower class streams should be quite different from that of upper streams in terms of its purposes, content, and approach. Three teachers went on to suggest that the most prestigious subjects (i.e., the PEB oriented, academic subjects) are incapable of comprehension and appreciation by less talented students. Others (e.g., the History senior) disagree; they believe that effective and creative teachers can help 'less-able, working class' students enjoy and absorb a great deal from the study of literature, history, science, and other disciplines. For them, the ideal of a liberal education for all during the compulsory period of schooling is one worth striving for.

At Purdah, the appropriateness of existing and planned curricula for years 9 and 10 students who are seen to be 'at risk' of becoming 'alienated' while at school and of facing difficulties in the transition from school to work, emerged as a central issue in early discussions with the principal, deputies, and staff. There was a general consensus that provision must be made within the curriculum for the diverse needs of the wide range of students now coming to the school, even though some teachers expressed regret over the changes in the social composition of the student body. Most in the school accepted that alternative courses and alternative subjects within courses were needed. However it was not clear

(i) what the ultimate purpose of the non-PEB classes was;
(ii) what content should be included in year 9 and 10 alternative courses;
(iii) how alternative courses should be taught and evaluated;
(iv) who should actually teach the courses;
(v) who the courses were to be designed for;
(vi) how students were to be selected for alternative courses;
(vii) how to ensure that students could move from an 'alternative' to a 'regular' program.

The Purdah experience

School rules, norms, and socialization practices

As has already been stated the authority and power structure of the school is hierarchical, with the principal at the head. The deputies, the counsellor, and the seniors also play a significant role in dealing with the more serious breaches of the school rules, and in their formulation. Areas of particular concern in 1980 related to the public image of the school: the wearing of uniforms, standards of dress, smoking on the way to or from school and rules regulating dismissal from the school grounds.

Teachers are still expected to ensure that rules are enforced and standards of behaviour and dress are maintained. Hence the strong pleas by one of the deputies at a staff meeting prior to the prefect induction ceremony for the enforcement of uniform rules and for care that students behaved appropriately because 'the school is on show for the whole community'. Over the years the school has adapted to its students by changing the curriculum while retaining its social expectations; while failure by students to adjust to curriculum demands may lead to further curriculum changes, inappropriate social behaviour generally leads to censure rather than modification to school rules.

During 1980 renewed efforts were made by the administration of the school to establish and maintain standards of dress and behaviour, particularly when they reflect on the community image of the school. The tone was set by the principal on the first day of school:

> Once upon a time there was a proud Headmaster who was asked by an equally proud mother whether his school would be a wise choice for her son George. 'Of course!' replied the Headmaster, 'In the past we have produced two Prime Ministers, three Premiers and a Governor-General'. 'Well I'm not sure' was the mother's retort, 'Our George wants to be a taxi-driver'.
>
> In the final analysis it is the man (or woman) not the job that counts. The quality of life in your future society will depend, as always, upon the quality of its citizens, the individual men and women who shape it.
>
> I hope I leave you with at least a glimmer of understanding that your school is really an opportunity for learning how to live the good life in a civilized society.
>
> (Principal's address, Assembly, 11.2.1980)

The emphasis on standards at Purdah is not unlike, and can be linked with, the return to conservatism which has occurred in many western nations in the past decade. At Purdah, the swing back to a more restrictive pattern of schooling has been in response to the perceived demands of parents, employers, and governments for schools to produce an employable product, i.e., workers who are literate and numerate, have appropriate vocational skills and work experience and who show respect for authority, courtesy towards others, persistence and industriousness.

In the area in which Purdah is situated there are three or four State high schools and an independent school to which parents might choose to send their children. The area is one of an ageing population so that enrolments at Purdah, like those in many South Australian high schools, are declining. Added to this, the decision by the State Education Department to allow parents freedom of choice of secondary school (the 'dezoning' policy) irrespective of place of residence means that high schools have become increasingly sensitive about enrolments, since falling enrolments bring with them displacement of staff and reductions in resource allocations. At Purdah, staff reductions in 1979 (six staff were displaced) due to declines in enrolment have brought with them tensions within the staff, conflict and uncertainty as well as a renewed emphasis on standards as a means of creating a favourable image of the school in the local community and thereby making it attractive to parents.

While teachers accept the regulation of student behaviour within the walls of their classroom as a basic responsibility, occasionally a teacher would admit that he or she found it difficult to maintain order in one of the 'alternative' or lower stream classes. At a more general level, many teachers in the school believe that the policing of standards of dress and behaviour in accordance with school rules (explicit or implicit) has become increasingly difficult. One detects a sense of resentment and frustration amongst teachers. The principal also feels that the socialization role of the school in developing character and commitment to the school as an institution is being eroded by groups and forces outside the school. Outside pressures were seen to have particularly adverse effects on particular groups in the school, especially a group of Greek boys who 'want to be big wheels at school' and who are 'influenced by green pastures outside the school'. The principal was also convinced of the part that could be played by school sport in promoting identity with, and preventing alienation from, school.

However, once again this was seen to be an area in which outside groups (e.g., football clubs) were at variance with what the school was attempting to do:

> In an overall program we have to be concerned with the totality of the students, that they're interested in the program, that the program makes a boy feel for his school, even love his school and is proud to play for his school. We've lost a lot of that over the years. Schools' sports teams are in a shambles. Our Saturday morning sports competition has suffered greatly from the attraction of local clubs outside
>
> (Principal)

Many of the principal's concerns centred around the lack of acceptance of authority within the society as a whole and the school in particular:

> Many of these students who are different don't feel anything for the school. It's just a prison camp to them and they jump up and down in the classroom. I think the reasons are to do with changes in social attitudes. Adults in the community are less conscientious about work, more concerned about industrial conditions, and much less willing to accept authority. Students tend to follow their example in schools. However, parents still expect the school to instil the work ethic and maintain firm school discipline. This is rather too much to expect without community example and parental acceptance of the school's authority.
>
> (Principal)

Like most large high schools, Purdah has attempted to establish and develop pastoral care and counselling systems to facilitate its role as an agent of socialization. The caring nurturing role assumes a significant part of the work of the school counsellor to 'clients' of this service and that of teachers such as Mr Rudder who work largely with students in the alternative classes (the mezzanine classes, the work experience class, etc) with which they are identified.

Section 1: Teacher perceptions of student problems at Purdah

Fourteen staff including the principal, deputies, seniors, and teachers of regular and alternative classes across a range of subjects were interviewed to determine their views of the problems to be faced in coping with students who are either unwilling or unable to deal with the demands and expectations of the school. The students had broadly divided teachers into those who appeared as person-oriented and approachable teachers and those for whom the subject was the beginning and end of their involvement with the class. This broad distinction was immediately obvious in conversation with staff and in meetings attended. Conceptualization of problem students in the school reflected the interaction of these frameworks and position within the school.

(a) Administrative perceptions

Mr Jeffries estimated that only a very small number of students at Purdah are really turned off school, namely the handful of students who are 'very often aggressive and unruly in class' and who are 'really determined to strike out at school' to the degree that they become a problem for the central administration. Given that most behaviour problems are handled by the teachers, the deputies, and the counsellor, it is only the most serious and persistent offenders with whom the principal must deal. Mr Jeffries did acknowledge, however, that there are degrees of school rejection and that the students with whom he was concerned were those who are extremely difficult to handle. When questioned about the origin of the problem, Mr Jeffries was reluctant to give a blanket answer. There were, in his view, a number of possible causes and each case had to be treated individually. In some cases school rejection could be attributed to home circumstances (e.g., marital breakdown, alcoholism, unemployment), in some, to something which happened at school (e.g., conflicts with other students or teachers).

In the final analysis, Mr Jeffries took the view that outside influences cause some students to see school as a meaningless institution and to believe that there are greener pastures in the adult world (work, money, discos, etc). At the suggestion of

The Purdah experience

friends who have left school, older brothers or sisters, parents, the media, or members of an ethnic group, some students come to believe that what is being learnt at school is 'rubbish' and that they will 'pick nothing up from school'. Mr Jeffries was not only concerned about the devaluation of the content of schoolwork, he was also worried about the decline in standards of behaviour and the lack in acceptance within the community of the authority of the school. In his view there are a number of forces in society working against what schools are trying to do, these in turn increase the likelihood of conflict and alienation from school. To solve the problems, Mr Jeffries would like to change the nature of the social pressures on the student body, but to do this would demand 'changes in the whole society and the authority of the school'.

Given that the roots of the problem are seen to lie outside the influence of the school, Mr Jeffries sees limits on what the school can do in preventing and handling the problems created by alienation. Students who become a nuisance in and out of the classroom 'initially are sent to a deputy or to the student counsellor'. Unruly students become 'very expensive of time' because they go from counsellor to deputy to counsellor to deputy to principal. The answer finally is either to encourage the parents to allow the student to leave to seek employment or to suspend the student. Mr Jeffries believes that some 'types' of students, particularly those who have been through the courts and those he is currently forced to suspend, ought to be in 'halfway institutions' rather than Purdah.

Schematically, Mr Jeffries' conception of the problems of school rejection at Purdah can be represented in Figure 2.

Most of the students who come to the attention of the administration are located in lower stream classes. While teachers generally are in favour of streaming, finding teachers willing to take classes containing less able and troublesome students is not easy. Amongst teachers there is a stigma attached to alternative classes. A common view is that such classes are little more than 'watered down courses for remedials'. From the viewpoint of one deputy, the school is now suffering from the fact that its teachers are not well prepared to cope with non-PEB students. Existing avenues for professional development are limited and confined largely to the informal sharing of ideas and experiences in the context of planning the alternative course for year 9 and 10 students. This school-based curriculum development project has involved only concerned teachers, while allowing the remaining

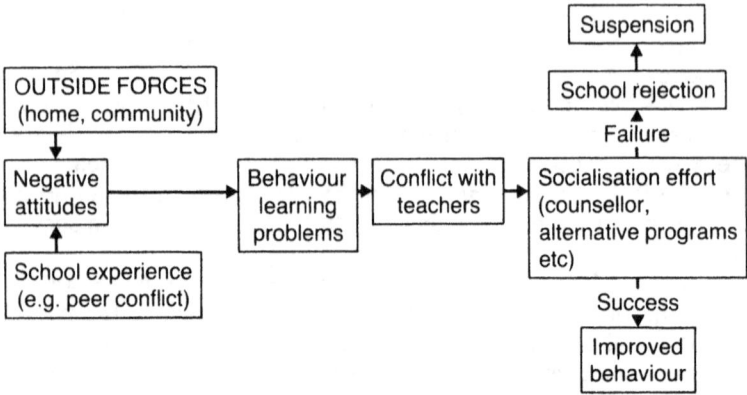

Figure 2: A conception of the dynamics of school behaviour problems

80 per cent of teachers to avoid any serious attempt to reflect upon, discuss, and seek to find answers to the dilemmas posed by going comprehensive.

While recognizing that there is a problem, many staff nevertheless see the school as an academic institution. The purpose of secondary education and of Purdah, the ultimate endpoint, is, as it has always been, the PEB. Some seniors and one deputy principal had difficulty in dealing with the conceptualization of secondary education which underlies alternative programs in the school:

> For the PEB you're working to an end point, aren't you? You've got a building program going on. This is another thing wrong with the constitution of alternative courses, there's no real end point for the alternative classes, just for getting out into work and have money of my own.
>
> (Deputy Principal)

(b) Academic teachers' perceptions

There is a general consensus within the staff that the majority of students who reject schooling are those in lower stream classes who experience failure and frustration because they are unable or unwilling to cope with the academic demands of the school. In

The Purdah experience

that Purdah was formerly an academic high school, many of the teachers are conservative in approach and espouse an essentialist philosophy. In this view, the function of secondary schooling is to transmit the cultural heritage of the society. The curriculum, therefore, should reflect the major forms of knowledge – the academic disciplines, for these are the best ways of cultivating the intellectual powers which have enabled mankind to progress in the past and to cope successfully with current problems. The emphasis in teaching is on the mastery of content and academic excellence. From the essentialist viewpoint, however, there are limits on the degree to which this excellence can be achieved by all. Not all in society value, or are capable of acquiring, the high culture of the middle class. There are those (particularly from working class, migrant families) who come from a different cultural tradition and hold values, norms, and vocational aspirations at variance with those of the school.

In the perspective of academic teachers, there is a clear separation between manual and intellectual labour, with students oriented towards one or the other. There are then at Purdah, two castes, two types of students with 'academic ability' the curtain dividing them. The division is recognized by almost all teachers within the school:

> It almost seems as if there are two kinds of students, academic and non-academic. It seems as if the curriculum is what does this division for us.
>
> (Deputy Principal)
>
> There are two divisions, academic and other ability. No matter what we call it, that's what it is.
>
> (Chairman, alternative year 9 curriculum planning meeting)

The conversion of Purdah to a comprehensive high school and social changes have created two serious problems for academically-oriented teachers. First, the tensions created as a result of the breakdown of the family unit were seen to underlie disruptive behaviour in class, rebellion, and truancy. Second, the combined effects of intellectual poverty, the debasement of the value of education in the home, and inadequacies in primary schooling were seen to leave many students without the solid foundation of basic skills and knowledge needed for any chance of success in regular courses at high school.

Given that most teachers agree that there are indeed two 'types' of students, it inevitably follows that, in their view, the non-academic students ought *not* to be in an academic program.

The academically-oriented teachers had grave difficulty in accepting and adapting to mixed ability classes. Repeatedly they found themselves being forced to sacrifice their ideals (the quest for academic excellence). In their view, mediocrity rather than excellence has become the norm at Purdah. Teachers complain that they must pitch their teaching and assign tasks at the 'middle level of performance' thereby failing to challenge and meet the needs of the bright. In their view, some form of streaming ('they sort of stream themselves don't they?'), of separating students by type and ability is essential. Few academic teachers have accepted the ideology of comprehensive education: the old divisions remain in patterns of thinking and in the inner workings of the school.

At Purdah, the major mission of these teachers is still as it was in the 1950s 'to squeeze the maximum examinable talent from the top end of their streamed innards'[3]. Academic teachers have barely begun the task of thinking through the shape and feel of the 'equality of access to knowledge' curriculum advocated by Lawton[4].

Purdah, like other State schools throughout Australia, has been left unaided to struggle with problems created by the egalitarian policy of providing a comprehensive secondary system in a competitive society. Within the school, there is a good deal of conflict, confusion, and uncertainty about how this can be done and hence about the purpose of secondary schooling. For some teachers, a competitive system is essential in the quest for academic excellence. Taken to its extreme, this position implies that success at school must be a luxury reserved for an academic *élite* and segregation, failure, and alienation for the remainder the price that must be paid. How then can secondary school contribute positively to the development of all?

> Non-academic kids are not successful in the PEB so the question is what do we do with them, how do we get them to have some sort of success?
> (Senior Maths teacher)

This problem is one which academic teachers tend to avoid. They would prefer not to be forced to teach 'non-academic' students, and to leave the task of devising courses and reward systems for them to other teachers in the school.

Where forced to teach 'non-academics', those teachers defined by their pupils as 'strict' by mid-year had begun to 'pick' on the rebellious and to give up on the 'remedials'. Most abandoned any serious attempt to do justice to their discipline. In most cases, the teachers seemed content to keep the class busy by giving them plenty of activity. There was usually some attempt to develop basic or manual skills, but not to present the significant ideas, concepts and knowledge of the discipline:

> Q 'Why are they learning Science anyway?'
> A 'I don't know, I have no idea. I suppose my only answer would be that it perhaps makes them realize they've got to read instructions to make things work. That's about all I can say I just really don't . . . I suppose I could be cynical and say I'm occupying them in a more or less organized way'.
> Q 'You feel you're not doing anything educationally worthwhile?'
> A 'Well not in the theoretical, probably from a theorist's view I don't, but I do think they learn to handle equipment . . . I don't think they would ever really understand anything terribly scientific. I don't think they've got the genetic ability there to start with'.
> Q 'So all you're really trying to do is to keep them happily occupied?'
> A 'More or less, yes'.
>
> (Science teacher, grade 9 Alternative class)

Academic teachers also found themselves forced to abandon or compromise what was for them, standard teaching practice. The demand level and expectations are lowered almost to the point of non-existence in lower stream classes:

> I'm finding a problem in marking in that they look for marks yet my standards of marking are so far removed from anything else that I don't like marking them. I'd much prefer to make individual comments. . . . Homework which I tend to avoid, school policy is homework right across the board this year. I tend to set very little because I find the confrontation of chasing people up creates a worse atmosphere than the positive results to be gained by those who do it. Perhaps that's opting for the easy way out, but I find that a real problem.
>
> (English teacher, grade 9 Alternative class)

The researcher's concern about the extent to which academic teachers were adequately prepared to cope with non-academic classes was confirmed in several interviews and classroom observations. In the case of the more experienced and effective academic teachers, the major problem in teaching lower stream classes seemed to be unfamiliarity with appropriate curriculum materials and remedial teaching procedures. These teachers also found that the range of abilities within year 9 Alternative classes was much greater than they had anticipated. While they believed in streaming and the notion of alternatives, they were critical of the selection methods employed in grade 9, finding that the mix in the alternative classes included 'behaviour problems' ('these students are very demanding of time because they are "volatile" and need to be kept occupied') and 'quiet but slow' students. Teachers complained that the troublesome students consumed so much time that they were forced to ignore the latter group. Humanistic and pragmatic teachers of academic subjects were less concerned about academic success than their peers. They saw their role as primarily one of promoting individual fulfillment. In the words of one teacher this means 'meeting the student where he is and taking it from there'. These teachers operate on the assumption that the basic source of school rejection lies within the school, not in the home. Students come to reject school because the goals, content, and approach in academic courses are inappropriate, causing teachers to write off students who are unwilling or unable to cope and students in turn to reject the school and its programs.

Humanistic teachers assume that most of the students who are not coping with school have the ability to achieve more than they have in the past if they are given specialized pastoral care; their weaknesses in basic skills are remedied; and if courses are adapted to ensure that students see the relevance of what is being taught to their purposes and experience success. The class teacher of one grade 8 Mezzanine class put it this way:

> It's to provide a stable home base and fatherly care for children with a wide range of abilities, whose basic literacy and numeracy skills are poor and who are immature and disorganized. The first priority no matter what, is to get the message through that I care, that I'm interested in them as individuals.
> (Mr Rudder, grade 8 Mezzanine class)

At grade 8 level, the organization of content of the curriculum for alternative stream students is under one paternal teacher. The intention is to eliminate some possible causes of school rejection by ensuring that legitimate purposes of young people are not thwarted by the school, that they are helped to achieve success, an identity, and their vocational goals.

Some of the most unfortunate situations arose when a teacher

The Purdah experience

lacking the skills and knowledge to deal with a difficult class was allocated to a lower stream or alternative class. Inevitably, the teacher was unable to cope, was defenceless and became estranged from the class:

> I find them completely uncontrolled. They're not remotely interested in history and I've never taught history before in my life. I've been left completely by myself. I struggle along trying to teach them about the Romans and Vikings but they're not even interested at all. Most of the things I've tried haven't worked. I have not tried many strategies. They're not interested in school or education anyway. A lot of them are from fairly miserable backgrounds. There's too many of them in the classroom, the classroom's revolting. They'd rather be out getting a job or doing something practical. I know it's a pathetic thing to say but I, you know, it's just that my heart is not in it. They respond to very clear rules but I feel stupid all the time saying if you do this you're going to get words, words, you know, or something. I do quite a bit of that. Maybe I'm just a chaotic type of teacher.
>
> (Lower school Alternative teacher)

Lesson observation and interviews with students in this class confirmed that it was indeed chaos. The students saw the teacher as 'weak' i.e., unable to control them, 'warns but never does anything, inadequately prepared, boring, and inconsistent in dealing with students'. The rules of the game are that one can 'muck up' in the weak teacher's class, have 'fun', or simply 'loaf'. On the other hand, if the teacher is 'strict' students had learned to conform as passively as possible, to do no more than go through the rituals of meeting the teacher's demands. The 'good' teachers are, on the other hand, 'those you can understand', 'explain things clearly', 'will have a joke' and 'control the class properly'. The perceptions and lessons of the 'good' teachers were quite different from those of the teachers classified by students as weak. A parallel class to the one previously cited ran smoothly. The students were kept busy and worked quietly and consistently, extracting information about barbarian food, housing, and agriculture, and completing questions and drawings. The teacher was clearly in control and students co-operated in the activities of the day. At least some of the dissatisfaction amongst lower stream students would seem to stem from inappropriate and conflicting demands, expectations and practices of teachers.

(c) **Non-academic teachers' perceptions**

Interviews with year 11 Alternative class teachers revealed that in their view students in that program were essentially those who were looking for employment but unable to obtain a job. The alternative class teacher saw problems for both the alternative and the work experience programs in the school. The year 11 alternative class contained students who were seeking to complete the SSC in year 12, some seeking an easy year and some who were unable to get into the work experience program. In his view, it was not simply enough to occupy students' time until they obtained employment. Only those students gaining the SSC were likely to profit from the extra time spent at school given the entry requirements for TAFE courses and other further education programs. In his view, the alternative program should have a structure and goals in its own right.

In 1979 the Work Experience program had been quite successful: 85 per cent of students in the program had obtained a permanent job. However, alternative students doing SSC were likely to be left behind in job markets, employers preferring students from year 11 Work Experience programs or PEB students (three good students left just before matriculation to obtain a job).

Deteriorating conditions in the job market were seen as creating new problems for schools. Cases were cited of disenchantment with work experience in other schools because students felt they were leaving programs without qualifications recognized by employers. In other cases, schools were competing actively for work experience places and selling their products. One prestigious school was reported to have been successful in convincing Myer that its SSC course produced an employable product. Under these conditions Purdah faced some difficulties in convincing all of its year 11 students that the courses provided are worthwhile. Within courses, greater attention was being given to job skills, career education, consumer economics and to the development of a broader view of adult life in order to help young people to make wise choices and establish better employer–employee relationships.

Alternative year 11 students most likely to create problems were those who thought the alternative course 'would be a bludge', expected to be 'baby sat', had a 'chip on their shoulder because they couldn't get into Work Experience' and were dissatisfied with Technical Studies because they were looking for

The Purdah experience

narrowly vocational skills. Apparently the teachers involved had difficulty in convincing students that the program would develop relevant skills and that the ability to express oneself clearly, to write and to cope with new demands were important in adult life. The Work Experience program was more successful. Students saw the program as being relevant to their vocational purposes. Moreover, the contexts in which skills were learned were frequently outside the school – in the workplace or in further education (Work Experience students are able, because of the flexible timetable, to attend 'link courses' conducted by the WEA).

Physical education and technical teachers were less likely to highlight the differences between academic and non-academic classes, although they did find that the latter were more difficult to handle:

Q 'In what way?'
A 'Well just behaviour, little things, they find it difficult to sit still and listen to instruction; just general – they're more restless altogether'.
(Year 9 Alternative class Phys.Ed. teacher)

The behaviour problems commented upon were confined largely to truancy, although this was a relatively minor problem because

Usually they enjoy P.E. because it's physical, it is active, and they are doing things most of the time – it's not that they're sitting in their desks.
(Year 9 Alternative class Phys.Ed. teacher)

Section 2: Curriculum development at Purdah

In the past three years Purdah has been actively expanding the range of alternatives open to young people at the school in order to cater more adequately for students unable to cope with PEB-oriented courses. Teachers, like Mr Rudder, have taken the view that the typical academic program unwittingly reinforces feelings of inferiority, frustration, and alienation amongst non-academic students. If there are two 'types' of students in the school, the solution clearly is to have two types of curriculum – an academic and a non-academic (or alternative) program. In analysing the situation and planning the curriculum, the position arrived at is close to that put forward by Bantock[5]. Bantock contends that, as not all children can be brought to the same level of achievement, there is need for a dual curriculum, one selected from the literate culture of the meritocratic middle class, the other from the oral 'folk' culture of the working class. While the hallmarks of inherited social class may not be so readily discernible in Australia as in the United Kingdom, there are nevertheless social, ethnic, and economic indicators that serve to identify an established Australian 'working-class' and a set of ability, motivational, and behavioural markers used by schools to identify the non-academic children from that class.

By 1979, the existence of Mezzanine classes in grade 8, Work Experience and Alternative classes in grade 11 and an SSC course in year 12 at the school had established a pattern. Purdah was, in effect, becoming two schools – an academic high school and a non-academic (technical/vocational) high school. The process of division continued during the period of the case study when alternative courses for year 9 were planned (late 1979) and established (1980).

The advocates of alternative courses in the school were convinced of their success (with some reason) and wished to ensure that an alternative program was available for grades 9 and 10 'non-academic' students. In July 1970, the principal approved a request from Mr Rudder (the architect and teacher of the grade 8 Mezzanine class) to design a continuing program for grade 8 Alternative students. On 31 July, interested teachers were invited to a meeting to 'consider the education of less able students' at Purdah. An *ad hoc* committee was formed with Mr Rudder as

The Purdah experience

chairman.* Membership was varied and variable. The committee included subject and year seniors, counsellors and interested subject teachers. Meetings were held throughout third term on a weekly basis, but not all members were able to attend and other teachers with a particular contribution to make attended by invitation. Various kinds of expertise and orientations were represented in the group – seniors who had detailed knowledge of PEB requirements and the constraints of time-tables, facilities, and finance; Alternative course teachers with knowledge of the content covered by grade 8 students and the students most likely to enter Alternative year 9 courses; school counsellors with experience of handling problem students; work experience teachers with a knowledge of vocational opportunities and requirements. The case study worker attended meetings of this committee as an observer.

The first two terms of reference (see Appendix) of the committee were:

1 to evaluate this school's current courses and curriculum arrangements for students suited to a secondary education alternative to PEB studies;
2 to recommend to the principal changes aimed at developing and improving the school curriculum for students (a) in the long term; (b) in the short term.

Mr Rudder's proposal outlined his views on the placing of students from the three grade 8 alternative stream classes in year 9. Students were to be selected for alternative classes on the basis of opinions of their teacher, consultation with subject seniors and performance. He expected students going into the course to be 'basically reluctant readers, poor spellers, immature, and to have reading, listening, and mathematical problems'. The main point he argued was to ensure that the course and teaching arrangements recognized that the students in the program are 'non-academic types who are very likely to leave school at age fifteen or soon thereafter'. The students were seen to have basic 'social and academic skill difficulties' that need attention. In his view the curriculum committee needed to develop a 'clearly set out, realistic, life-oriented four year course'. The steps suggested were:

---

* Methodological note: According to Mr Jeffries this did not spring entirely from the grassroots. He and a deputy had attended a Curriculum Development Conference and had settled on 'alternative courses' as a suitable area for development and evaluation.

223

1 specify the basic skills considered to be essential for all students leaving at the end of four years of secondary school (These skills were described as 'survival skills');
2 assign skills to particular year levels;
3 sets of 'essential, practical, life-oriented' knowledge should next be set out and assigned to year levels;
4 then, particular concepts, experiences and attitudes (again 'essential' concepts only) should be set out and assigned to levels.

The dominant person in the initial meetings of the committee was Mr Rudder. As chairman, he had set the agenda for the development task and saw his role to be that of steering the committee through it.

Skilbeck[6] has suggested the following five stage model of school-based curriculum development:

Stage 1 *Situational analysis*
Review of the change situation including *external* (culture and social changes, educational system requirements and the change in subject matter to be taught) and *internal* (pupil needs and abilities; teacher values and expertise; school ethos, resources; perceived shortcomings in the existing curriculum).

Stage 2: *Goal formulation*
Statements of the kinds of learning outcomes anticipated; preferences, values and judgements about the directions in which educational activities will go.

Stage 3: *Program Building*
Design of teaching-learning activities including selection of content, structure, method, sequence, materials, textbooks; personnel selection, deployment and role definition; timetabling.

Stage 4: *Interpretation and implementation*
In the design phase, consideration of anticipated problems in installing the new program e.g., clash between new and old, resistance, confusion, etc.

Stage 5: *Monitoring, evaluation and reconstruction*
Design of communication and monitoring systems, course evaluation and pupil assessment procedures; plans for review and reconstruction.

There is a temptation to suppose that curriculum planning ought

The Purdah experience

to proceed in a logical, linear fashion from goals to evaluation. In practice, this is rarely the case. Skilbeck, for instance, claims that his intention was simply that of encouraging teams of curriculum developers in schools to see the process as an organic whole and to work in a moderately systematic way.

Comparing Mr Rudder's plan with that proposed by Skilbeck, we can see that he assumed stages 1 and 2 had been more or less completed and that there was consensus about the shortcomings of existing academic courses. He had proposed, therefore, to begin immediately at Stage 3, selecting and placing by grade level, specific skills deemed to be 'basic', 'practical' and 'life-oriented'. But as Skilbeck and others have noted, curriculum developers often develop different stages concurrently and rarely proceed in a logical, linear fashion. The planning process began at Stage 3 (as intended by the chairman, Mr Rudder) but in the first meeting, two teachers took the committee back briefly to Stages 1 and 2. In the second meeting further clarification of the situation, goals and target group was sought, and decisions about the number of teachers to be involved and class size were made. In the third, the timetable and constraints imposed by the principal on grouping of students dominated the discussion. Subsequent meetings were devoted to the identification and sequencing of items of 'essential' knowledge and skills identified by staff and subject seniors. At times, however, the committee returned to the task of defining the purposes of the alternative curriculum and exploring different ways of proceeding with the curriculum building task. Inevitably, however, the thrust throughout the committee's deliberations was the seeking of solutions which would take care of practical affairs and, as far as possible, maintain the existing organizational structure and functions intact. It would seem that when the crunch comes, the needs of the institution and those in power within it are likely to take precedence over those of its clients.

Purves[7] has suggested that curriculum making can be thought of as a challenging game, a jigsaw, in which the number of pieces is fixed and there are a number of game rules (e.g., all pieces must be picked up; pieces must be related to other pieces; etc.) but the strategies used may vary. Pieces include the needs of society, of disciplines and of pupils; the school's educational philosophy; materials, school resources; outcomes. At Purdah, the planning process assumed this form. The chairman had a strategy for dealing with skill and content pieces and for much of the time the committee went along with this strategy, selecting and fitting skills together. In a number of meetings, the skills deemed to be essential were listed and allocated to a year level with decisions of the following type (from the first curriculum meeting) being quickly arrived at:

Fractions. Don't worry about them. Let's take them out of mathematics and put it where it is needed and can be readily understood in practical applications in home economics and technical studies.

Division. For grade 9 division by whole numbers only.

(Field notes of curriculum meeting)

The ultimate product took the form of a listing of subjects and content to be taught. However, the chairman's assumption that the underlying philosophy and purposes of the course were self-evident and agreed upon proved not to be completely valid. On occasion committee members injected new pieces to be fitted and proposed alternative strategies – with limited success. In the final analysis agreement was reached on a number of curriculum issues, some issues were left unexamined and some unresolved. Some of the major issues dealt with are discussed below:

1 *Which frame of reference?*

It is evident that there are within Purdah a number of quite different views on what should be taught in secondary school, why and how. The debate during meetings revealed some deep-seated differences in the frame of reference utilized. Some members of the committee wished to maintain the appearance of traditional subjects on the grounds that alternative course students ought not to be permanently excluded from re-entry into the mainstream academic program. Their curriculum platform, like that of Hirst, rests on a position about the nature of knowledge and its divisions. The subject seniors, in particular, were influential in ensuring that the alternative course was divided up along conventional subject lines in that English, Maths, History, Geography, and Science were included in the program. Once again the existing power structures assumed an overriding role in the curriculum decision-making process.

On the other hand, there were those who espoused a personal development orientation and emphasized that the learning experiences should be geared to the purposes and needs of the individuals in the program rather than the requirements of entry into a PEB program or the Apprenticeship Board. For this group, emphasis was placed on the development of the self, on

The Purdah experience

creating a supportive, nurturant environment. Interestingly, several teachers seemed to want to adopt a humanistic or personal development approach when dealing with 'non-PEB' students and to switch to an essentialist position with respect to PEB students.

The purpose of the non-PEB students was defined to be that of leaving school as soon as possible to obtain employment. In a difficult job market situation, it was argued that such students need 'survival skills' for day-to-day living more than specific job skills, and that they need an enjoyable, self-fulfilling program *now* rather than to struggle through a tough program aimed at preparing them for entry into an uncertain job market. Hence, compared with academic classes, Physical Education, Art, Music and Drama were given an increased time allocation, while Maths and Science had a reduced allocation compared with academic classes because 'the academic group can abstract but this group can't'. Technical subjects were included more because alternative students 'should be working with their hands making things, gardening, etc' than in recognition of specific vocational purposes. In the end, the course that was developed represented a compromise between the academic and the personal development framework.

2 *Which needs?*

Many curriculum writers refer to the various needs to be considered when devising goals and objectives for a curriculum. Typically reference is made to societal demands, individual needs and the needs of the disciplines. In the planning process at Purdah, all three were seen to be important, but primary emphasis was given to societal demands especially to command of literacy and numeracy skills, the acquisition of 'life-oriented, practical information' and development of self-control and social skills. Primary needs of individuals (such as their need to be accepted as unique individuals and to have opportunities for success) were also mentioned, but these did not feature prominently in discussion. The discrepancies between

1. the demands of society as represented by the requirements of apprenticeship boards and the expectations of employers,
2. the demands of disciplines as represented by the minimal standards for each subject expected by subject seniors as necessary for entry into a regular program, and
3. the abilities, expectations and aspirations of students likely to

be allocated to alternative programs remained an unresolved dilemma.

Given the concern for preparing students to meet the demands of society and work, surprisingly, the possibility of including career education and/or work experience in the curriculum or of including any analysis of the nature of work, and of conditions in, and requirements of, the job market in social science courses, was either dismissed or ignored. The 'practical information' and skills envisaged went little beyond 'writing job applications' in English and 'interpreting wages slips' in mathematics.

3 Which goals?

The majority of the committee accepted as self-evident the overall purpose of the program as being that of providing non-PEB students with a 'realistic life-oriented course' thereby coping with both less able and disaffected students. A minority group persistently sought to clarify the objectives of the course and to raise questions about its underlying philosphy and ultimate goals. They questioned whether the school had abandoned the ideals of comprehensive education and the egalitarian notion of providing a broad liberal education for all. In their view the ends sought and the basic objectives should be the same for all students in the school. An analysis of notes and minutes of meetings suggests that consensus was not reached. A minority group (including an English and History teacher) continued to argue that the emphasis on 'basics', 'survival' and 'practical skills' was restricting, and that alternative students should be introduced to the essential features of our cultural heritage emphasized in literature and history. These were then two answers to the question: 'Do we admit we are wasting their time or do we go all out to expand their lives?'

The pragmatic asserted that these students are 'not capable of abstract thinking' and they need a 'practical orientation'. The differences between the 'academic' student and the 'non-academic' were highlighted:

> The methodology for the non-academic group is different. The expectations are different. The teaching procedures are different. The content is different.
> (Field notes of curriculum meeting)

The goals of the course are to develop skills of 'immediate relevance to life' and to facilitate 'direct entry to the workforce'

The Purdah experience

and to offer 'vocational skills'. The minority group on the other hand, disagreed. They took the view that with a sympathetic and skilled teacher, students in the alternative program could absorb a good deal of our cultural heritage:

> All students can gain a great deal from studying ancient society. Not only should they be given the opportunity to study the strange and the new, but they can absorb a great deal of, say, the basic ideas of Greek thought. For example, the concept of hero as embodied in Greek history is not beyond them.
>
> (History teacher, field notes of curriculum meeting)

This group also took the view that the committee should decide what constituted an 'ideal program' for students in alternative classes. The majority of the committee, however, rejected attempts to steer the discussion towards the development of a rationale or a philosophy. Their orientation was towards action, towards making decisions about content, staffing and timetabling within the constraints of the existing structure of the school and to meet the deadlines imposed by the principal and the bursar for ordering materials and texts for 1980. For the most part then, the committee made decisions about content and procedures in the absence of an explicit, agreed upon framework of purposes and objectives. For the committee, attention to short-term organizational needs provided a convenient escape from extensive probing, theoretical debate or long-term considerations.

As a consequence, *ad hoc* compromises became necessary in order to accommodate external constraints.

4 *Which students?*

On the issue of who should enter the program, the committee was even more divided. On the one hand, there were those who wished to define clearly who the course was intended for, while on the other, many believed that the nature of the target group was so self-evident as not to need definition.

The assumption that the target group was 'the whole bunch who will never get into tertiary education' proved to be inadequate. Ultimately three sub-groups were identifed:

(a) 'Special Education Children' i.e., those with some minimal brain dysfunction or difficulty with motor co-ordination difficulty;
(b) slow to learn;

(c) intellectually able but turned off school.

Some argued that the special education group should be kept isolated (as in grade 8); others argued that alternative classes should contain a mix of students. The latter prevailed, to the dismay of several of the teachers of the classes concerned who found that groups (a) and (b) tended to be neglected.

It was accepted that parents should be informed of the school's intentions with respect to the alternative course and of its recommendations concerning the placement of individual children. However, neither parents nor students were consulted during planning. They had little real impact on the criteria employed or decisions made concerning selection of students for the course. These were seen to be professional matters. It was intended that able or wrongly counselled students who wished to do so should be able to change to the traditional course (by repeating year 9 or 10). The alternative course was in fact designed not for a homogeneous group of non-PEB students but for students of varying ability and motivational dispositions. It was not clear, therefore, whether the problem was that of preventing dissatisfaction, reducing alienation, controlling disruptive pupils, avoiding failure, or catering for the learning difficulties of less able pupils.

5 Which content? What criteria?

Much of the work of the committee focused on selecting 'basic skills' and 'essential, practical, life-oriented knowledge'. The basic criteria used in selecting content were whether the item (skill, topic, subject, etc) under consideration was

(i) 'basic' to the learning process in other areas (e.g., reading, interpreting tables and graphs);
(ii) 'essential' in that it can be shown to be useful, important/or necessary for a job, for contemporary living or for some 'enriching use' of leisure time (e.g., use of simple tools, car care, budgeting);
(iii) achievable by less able students in alternative programs at a given year level;
(iv) compatible with the minimal standards set by seniors for year 9 (the expectations of seniors and those of alternative teachers conflicted);
(v) compatible with administrative requirements.

While some members of the committee wished to devise a very different 'alternative' and to package the content in new ways

The Purdah experience

(e.g., interdisciplinary subjects and team teaching approaches), others saw 'alternative' as relative to what exists and wished to proceed by evaluating what exists in terms of lesson allocation, timetabling, and administering a large secondary school. The power structure of the school began to exert a major influence. The principal had prepared and forwarded a subject timetable which changed the course of the discussion from a consideration of the needs of students to one of fitting the demands of the timetable and staffing constraints.* The Science senior who had played a relatively minor role in previous meetings emerged as a leader as the information required changed from content and methodological consideration to timetabling and staffing which is his forte. The other major influence at that meeting was the news that arrangements were underway to order textbooks for the next year. From this meeting on, the constraints of timetabling, staffing, allocation of students to classes, book orders in advance and the pressure to meet deadlines exerted major influences on planning. These pressures meant that the committee members who wished to debate the philosophy of the course lost to those members who set out in haste to meet deadlines and to complete the task. The latter group assumed that the criteria for decision-making were self-evident; that the emphasis was on 'things children need to know' and not PEB and university requirements ('useless knowledge'). There was then within the committee both a lack of clarity regarding the problem(s) to be solved, and an unwillingness to tackle difficult time-consuming questions, especially if the answers might lead to significant changes in the basic structure and values of the institution.

Examples of the content deemed essential and allocated to various subjects included in the Alternative course are as follows:

English (seven periods/week). Heavy emphasis on literacy: oral and written communication skills, reading. Of 208 'basic' skills listed by staff in a survey conducted by the committee, 148 were language skills. Those selected for year 9 included the ability to read a book from a graded reading scheme, ability and motivation to read newspapers, writing a formal letter, job application. In that literary analysis and criticism were deemed

---

* Methodological note: Mr Jeffries suggested that communication went awry here. The terms of reference (which included 'long term planning') in no way precluded debate on the philosophy of the course. Had he not intervened in this way the terms of reference may have been interpreted differently.

to be inappropriate, there was some debate as to whether the subject should be called English or Language.

Mathematics (five periods/week). Heavy emphasis on practical skills and the application of knowledge in everyday life. The skills to be taught were clustered, by topic – basic processes, decimals, graphs, budgeting, etc. Any topic which involved the use of abstractions (e.g., algebra) was to be treated at a simple, concrete level or omitted. Topics included in year 9 were: interpretations of graphs and surveys, filling in bank deposit and withdrawal forms; using ratio to solve problems; calculate volume and area.

History and Geography   After initial discussion about the necessity of including social survival skills in the alternative program, it was agreed that History and Geography should be included in the program. It was first suggested that the one teacher take both subjects and to present these subjects as a social studies program which included core skills, knowledge and concepts of history and geography identified by the subject seniors. After discussion with seniors, the committee abandoned any attempt at integration. It was agreed that social survival skills should be treated across the curriculum. Such skills were defined as including communication, socializing and adapting, consumer education, government, banking and finance and legal studies.

Examples of content to be included for grade 9 in Geography (four periods per week) and History (three periods) were: read and interpret a street directory; know how local government systems work; interpret weather maps climatic zones; place events in order; use library resources; gain knowledge of alternative life styles from past cultures.

Drama/Music (two periods/week).   Not discussed in detail, intention was to develop ability and motivation to express oneself and communicate through drama, to encourage co-operative ventures and to develop performance and audience skills. Activities such as the writing and performance of a play depicting the rise and fall of a well-to-do rock group reveal concern for identifying with teenage interests.

Science (five periods/week).   The emphasis in Science was to be on activity and the development of practical skills. Skills to be developed included the ability to read and interpret

The Purdah experience

instruction manuals, medicine labels, meters; change fuses and tap washers; read advertisements critically.

Other subjects While the content of other subjects was not discussed in detail, it was agreed that all students should do Home Economics and Technical Studies (three periods/week), Art (three periods) and Physical Education (five periods). Considerable emphasis (i.e., increased timetable allocation) was given to these subjects since these were deemed to be either 'life-oriented' or to be satisfying to students (e.g., Art and Physical Education).

In the final analysis, the program represents a mixture of learning skills and social survival skills. Whether the skills and knowledge included did add up to a genuine alternative rather than a watered down regular program and whether it provided a comprehensive preparation for the transition from school to work was not seriously discussed and remains problematic. At best, some attempt was being made to develop the following skills for self-sufficiency:

(i) sustenance – ability to grow own food, buy wisely, select appropriately, prepare and cook food;
(ii) hygiene – personal hygiene, medical and dental care; sex education;
(iii) social – communication skills, role of family, availability of support services, cooperative and team skills;
(iv) transport – use of street directory, driver education, use of transport services;
(v) finance – banking, insurance, hire purchase, budgeting;
(vi) consumer education – quality and cost control, bargain sales, media and advertising;
(vii) leisure – games, crafts, sports;
(viii) vocational – limited treatment of employment services available; awards; casual and part-time work; use of tools; literacy and numeracy;
(ix) personal development – development of self-esteem, identity, belonging; knowledge of skills and weaknesses; setting of realistic goals.

At worst, the program limits the development of higher cognitive skills and denies access to much of the cultural heritage of western society. Neither the lower school alternative programs nor the regular academic programs of the school would seem to provide enough help for young people to be aware of the opportunities and demands they face in the future as they seek to take up options in work and further education. What the school has sought to do is to provide an enjoyable, protective and supportive environment but whether the school's alternative programs can adequately equip the young with the knowledge, skills, and strength needed to cope with unemployment must be seriously questioned.

6 *What kinds of learning activities and methods should be used?*

It was generally accepted that students should be actively involved in doing things in the classroom rather than 'passively listening to lectures', that a serious attempt should be made to cater for individual differences by providing activities which matched their ability and interests; and that the learning environment should be carefully structured but supportive.

For these reasons, it was suggested that:

(i) class sizes should be small (no more than twenty);
(ii) teachers selected should be person- rather than content-oriented and should be volunteers;
(iii) teachers should be capable of explaining things clearly and managing difficult students;
(iv) the number of teachers working with any Alternative class should be smaller than normal, four was suggested for year 9;
(v) teachers involved should be able to meet regularly to exchange ideas and to be able to develop remedial teaching skills;
(vi) advice of remedial teachers should be sought on the availability of suitable curriculum materials.

The committee recognized, however, that there were likely to be gaps between their hopes and the realities as a consequence of established priorities and practices within the school.

Student views of the situation

In order to gain some indication of the students' views of schooling, thirty-one small groups of pupils (three to four in a group, 102 pupils in all) were interviewed. The groups included pupils from three 'types' of classes in years 8 to 10 (viz. 'Alternative', 'Language-academic' and 'Greek' classes) and two

The Purdah experience

'types' (Work Experience, PEB) in year 11. The interviews which were of thirty to forty minutes' duration were loosely structured; the questions asked sought to elicit the students' subjective feelings about school and work and the experiences giving rise to them, and their views of the nature, causes and extent of school rejection. The interviews were subsequently transcribed and exist in the case records.

(i) Functions of schooling

Some indication of the meaning of schooling and its relationship to definitions of the self as a student and as an adult can be gleaned from student answers to questions about why they are at school and what it has done or can do for them. For the most part, students at Purdah are uncritical in their acceptance of the necessity of coming to school and of the conditions associated with schooling. Most claim that they come to 'learn things' and to get a 'good' education, although few were able to define what they might mean in specific terms. For almost all, the ultimate purpose of schooling turned out to be that of 'getting a good job'. This instrumental view of education was shared by students in all grades and tracks; courses and particular subjects were judged in terms of the degree to which they were seen as means to a valued vocational end rather than as being of value in their own right. From year 9 onwards, the purpose of school becomes increasingly defined in terms of getting grades or qualifications. Without these, the chances of getting a job are seen as minimal, and entry to valued options in employment and education becomes impossible – at least from the perspective of the bulk of students at Purdah interviewed.

> 'We are made to go to high school so that it will be easier to get a job 'cos they [employers] always say you need qualifications and experience and everything. If you don't have an education, you wouldn't know how to read or anything. And if you're fifteen, you're a reasonable age and you're independent of yourself and know about things'.
> (Girl, grade 8 Alternative class)

> 'Some people they go to school for years and then they don't get a proper job. You go to school for nothing you know'.
> (Girl, grade 8 'Greek' class)

235

'I think it's [school] just a job to be done. You have got to do it and do your best so that you can get the qualifications'.

(Boy, grade 10 Mixed class)

In his early writing, Marx used alienation as a technical term for the separation of the wage earner from his work, a condition afflicting all workers in the capitalist mode of production. For most students, even academic ones, there is a sense of separation, of loss of identity, of meaninglessness and powerlessness in their explanations of the reasons they come to school. For them, as for Marx's wage earners, [school]work is not a spontaneous, free expression of their individuality. In something of the sense in which Marx used the term, students are alienated from their work which has become: 'Merely a forced activity that is laid on me through an exterior, arbitrary need, not an inner necessary one. My labour can only appear . . . as the expression of my loss of self and my powerlessness'.[8]

Few students see great intrinsic value in what the school has to offer. There is, moreover, a tendency to avoid becoming too attached to the academic values of the school amongst 'non-academic' students:

'Because you turn into one of them, if you like school too much. . . . One of those square people that go around in little glasses and sit around reading books. Last year, this boy was reading books all the time. We called him the Professor. Yes, he was the mad scientist'.

(Girl, grade 8, Alternative class)

Whereas a good many students indicated that they enjoyed some sides of their school work, none interviewed suggested that for them the school had played a valuable role in expanding their understanding of a significant domain of human knowledge. There would seem to be a gap between what teachers and students see to be the most significant functions of schooling.

(ii) Areas of dissatisfaction

While it is possible to interpret students' views of the purpose of school as the logical expression of conditions of alienation as conceived by Marx, few students at Purdah showed evidence of the deep-seated hostility and the sense of estrangement from school which are assumed to follow from such conditions. Most

The Purdah experience

students interviewed were neither wildly enthusiastic about, nor bitterly opposed to, the programs and policies of the school. The almost universal response was that 'it's all right' or 'it's fairly good'. Almost all preferred high school to primary school. Sources of satisfaction varied – there was widespread consensus that school provides an opportunity to be with one's friends and that this forms an attractive aspect of school life. But most students found other avenues for self-fulfillment and enjoyment at school. Almost all could nominate at least one or two subjects, topics and teachers seen to be good or worthwhile. Within some classes (grade 8 Alternative, Work Experience, and some academic classes) there seemed to be a strong group ethic, a sense of identification with the class, teachers, and the course:

'I think school's good because you get an opportunity to meet new friends and it's good for the teachers and students to get involved, especially in our classes, because our classes are special'.
(Girl, grade 8 Alternative class)

'The teachers treat you like a person not like another student. They're treating us as older people and trusting us more and doing a lot of work around the school.
John and I and a couple of other girls did the headmistress's office, painted it and wallpapered it. Some of the other kids went out to the oval and fixed up the cricket pitch'.
(Year 11 Work Experience class)

In classes containing a high proportion of students in conflict with the school's values and norms (e.g., lower stream year 9 and 10 classes), students identified strongly with the peer group but not with the school, its teachers or its programs. Provided subjects are seen to be of an appropriate difficulty level and pertinent to some desired vocational end, students express moderate satisfaction with them. For example, Robert, like many interviewed, maintained there was nothing really at the school that 'turned him off'. He was quite satisfied with his progress and courses:

'I don't think I could say anything turns me off school. But I know what turns me on. Well at primary school I didn't think much of school and I thought I was a bit dense. (How did you know?) Well, it was obvious. The teachers had told, in say Grade 2 and 3 my mum was told I was a daydreamer and I couldn't get on with my work. But since I got to high school, I got interested in the air force. I've got a relation to do with it. So I planned on joining the RAAF, so ever since I have just been trying harder. In primary school, I had gone for a D. Say for maths I've gone from a D in grade 7 to an A in grade 9'.

(Robert, grade 9 Mixed class)

In addition to discussing aspects of school life with students in interviews, all students (n=980) in the school were asked to complete a brief questionnaire (see Appendix A) based on the instrument used in the IEA studies to assess attitudes towards school. Overall, the data suggest that students' attitudes to school are lukewarm. Table 1 shows that few enjoyed everything about school, but almost a quarter maintained that the time spent at school was the most enjoyable part of their lives. For a good many (44 per cent) however, the major thing they liked about school was the opportunity to meet friends.

Table 1: Overall student responses to attitude to school items

	Item	% answering Yes Purdah	S.A.*
1	The most enjoyable part of my life is at school.	24	23
2	I generally dislike my schoolwork.	34	32
3	There are many subjects I don't like.	54	45
4	I enjoy everything about school.	9	12
5	School is not very enjoyable.	41	41
6	The only things I look forward to are weekends and holidays.	50	46
7	Would you like to leave as soon as possible?	37	29
8	The only thing I like is the opportunity to meet friends.	44	62
9	School days are the happiest days.	27	34

* Responses of a sample of 2711 students from 30 S.A. High Schools

The patterns by grade level and type of program at Purdah are more or less as expected (see Table 2). Negative attitudes peak in year 10, the year in which students are most likely to leave. The highest proportion of students indicating they disliked their

Table 2: Response to selected items by year and program

	Regular Program					Alternative Program				
Item	8	9	10	11	12	8	9	10	11	12
2 Dislike work	29	29	38	42	44	41	37	59	29	39
6 Look forward to weekends	42	54	54	54	48	75	42	74	52	71
7 Leave as soon as possible	39	31	32	34	32	44	60	52	45	54

schoolwork was in the year 10 Alternative classes (10M5 Commercial Alternative, and particularly, 10M6, the Alternative class for 'students who have some difficulty with work') where 70 per cent of students said they disliked their work. It should be noted that whereas the alternative programs in years 8, 9, 11 and, to some degree, 12, had been the focus of intense curriculum planning and some self-selection on the part of teachers, the year 10 Alternative classes were yet to be the object of special attention. The evidence suggests that the year 11 Alternative courses have been quite successful in achieving their effective goals: students are reasonably satisfied with their courses. Approximately one third of students in regular classes would like to leave school as soon as possible to enter the workforce; as expected, more students in alternative stream classes would prefer to leave school, and would do so if a suitable job became available.

The questionnaire data and interview both reveal that students find the non-academic subjects more interesting and enjoyable than most academic courses, although these were not necessarily seen as the most relevant or useful so far as the student's vocational aspirations were concerned. Thus, while a boy may *like*, say, craft best, he may indicate that maths is his 'best' subject because he gets good grades in maths and sees it as necessary in terms of potential future occupations. Interestingly enough too, whereas according to questionnaire responses (see Table 3), physical education and technical subjects were the most popular subjects when asked about the subjects most liked and disliked, students talked mainly about academic subjects. By grade 9, most students had learned that the academic courses, particularly English, Maths, and Science, were what school was about. They

Table 3: Student views of interest and usefulness of subjects studied

Subject	Interest*	Usefulness*
English	3.4	4.4
Languages	3.4	3.6
Maths	3.6	4.5
Science	3.9	3.9
Social Science	3.7	3.7
Health/Social Ed.	3.5	3.4
Art/Music	3.9	3.2
Phys. Ed.	4.3	3.8
Commercial	4.2	4.2
Technical	4.4	4.2
Work Experience (Yr. 11)	4.3	4.4

* On scale: 2 = Not, 3 = Slightly; 4 = Fairly; 5 = Very.
Note: Only a minority of students sampled took Languge (42 per cent), Health-Social Education (27 per cent), Commercial (22 per cent) or Work Experience (22 per cent).

Table 4: Behaviour in class: Mean scores by Grade and Program*

Year	Regular classes	Alternative classes
8	2.29	2.08
9	2.38	2.36
10	2.40	2.40
11	2.52	2.42
12	2.61	2.70

* On scale: 1 = Often in trouble, 2 = Sometimes; 3 = Hardly ever

had learned that their grades in these subjects were critical in determining future educational and vocational opportunities. For the majority, it seemed as if Art, Music, and Physical Education did not exist – they were not 'real' subjects.

The Purdah experience

Of the 'real' subjects Science and Social Sciences – (History, Geography) were the most popular, although opinions of Science varied considerably, with girls in particular finding the subject hard and at times 'boring'. English, Languages, and Maths were rated as not being particularly interesting. Most subjects were seen to be fairly 'relevant' or 'useful', the exceptions tending to be Languages, Health-Social Education, Art and Music. The majority of students accept the inevitability of spending years at school prior to entry to the workforce to such a degree that they find it difficult to visualize major changes. In the words of one girl 'school is school'. While some could think of no changes ('It's all right as it is'), for others the addition of a swimming pool rated a mention. Value estrangement was evident in several responses. In these cases, the source of conflict between students and the administration stemmed from unwillingness to accept the school's authority (uniforms, smoking on way home) and regimentation:

> 'I know there's something wrong about it (uniforms) head-master-wise. It's not the actual headmaster but kind of things like army kind of things because you line up in front of your class, and hup two hup two, get inside. I reckon we should be able to go in and sit down'.
>
> (Girl, grade 9 Alternative class)

Students believe that Purdah worked better for, and was better liked by, the 'brainy kids'. It is important to note that even the 'brainy kids' were not talking about themselves but about some hypothetical individual or groups whom they found difficult to identify. The 'average' students did not consider themselves inferior necessarily, nor lacking in ability, but they did have a clear understanding that there were some individuals and classes in the school who were more intellectually gifted than themselves.

(iii) Vocational aspirations and experiences

Frequently links had been established between concepts of self as a student and a worker. Students had begun to learn and to accept that not all doors were open to them in the job market:

> 'I was thinking of becoming a doctor but I don't think I will make it. I am no good in Science and I am going to flunk my Science exam I know it. So what's the use of being a doctor?'
>
> (Boy, grade 10 Mixed class)

Colin Power

Increasingly, too, students who had experience in the workforce had begun to learn something of the nature of work and of themselves as workers, either as a consequence of experiences sponsored by the school as part of a work experience program, or as a consequence of their entry into the part-time work force:

> 'I would like to work with young children. I'm enquiring into it but there is little chance of getting in now (In kindergarten?) No. A childcare centre. I like office work. (Were you given interesting things to do there?) Not really, just things they didn't have time to do. Just odd jobs. Making tea and putting papers away rather than typing. (What about the childcare centre?) No, all I did there was wash dishes. I didn't really have much time to do anything with the kids. I also had to pick up the toys and put them back and set up the tables with crayons and paints and things and that's all I had to do'.
> (Girl, year 11 Work Experience class)

> 'I want to be a nurse, but I can't get in there for two or three years. I will probably come back to school next year and then just get a job after that and wait until I can go to hospital and do my training.
> At the beginning of the year I wrote about seventeen letters to different hospitals, and they said they had two or three waiting lists. . . . I have worked at Coles and Deli and at the TAB doing counting and stuff like that. At the moment I am working at the kindergarten (as part of work experience). I usually just help out. I don't see the kids much'.
> (Girl, year 11 Work Experience class)

Informal work is one of the major ways in which young people begin to develop a personal understanding of themselves as productive beings. Those without such experience had limited understandings of the nature of work and little idea of conditions and opportunities in the job market. Their view of themselves as workers was often naïve and tinged with a romantic optimism. On the other hand, where a specific vocational goal was sought, individuals had a clear idea of the hurdles to be overcome.

> 'I wouldn't mind being a professional sportsman (What type?) Oh I'm not sure, just an all-rounder'.

> 'In the Home. Ec. centre we had a mother craft section and I have decided to be a mother craft nurse. I had to do 11th

year and then go to Torrens House'.
(Students, grade 10 Mixed class)

'I'd love to be a kindergarten teacher. One that sings to kids and plays little guitars and pianos. I'd like to start my own kindergarten . . . start my own little place'.
(Girl, grade 8 Alternative class)

'I might go into the navy. I think you have to be pretty good at maths and know a bit about the sea' . . .
'I wouldn't mind being a hairdresser' . . .
'I don't really know. I would like to work with kids (Kindergarten teacher?) I don't think I would like to be a kindy teacher but just sort of, I don't really know what I want to do. I just want to work with kids'.
(Grade 9 students, Mixed Ability class)

Most students were convinced that the work environment offers some distinct advantages over the school environment – economically, socially and in terms of personal development. Many believed they would have *more* free time because they would not have homework and projects to do. Another recurrent theme was the wider range of social opportunities. Several commented that they had been with the 'same old people all the time' as a class group, and believed at work 'you meet different people all the time'. The 'pay' was also a major advantage in that it ensures independence and access to the material goods and activities of adult life. Money was not always, however, the primary consideration. Work was seen as a means of self-expression, as a source of identity, and of contributing directly to the modes of production valued by society. Many girls interviewed were seeking employment working with young children or animals not only as a source of income but also as a way of filling an enjoyable yet productive role in society.

> 'I would like to find a really interesting job that I would really like. I like little kids and would really like to be a kindergarten teacher. I don't really care too much about the money if I really have a good job and as long as I have a good time and a good job'.
> (Girl, grade 9 Mixed class)

Colin Power

(iv) Alternatives to schooling

Few students expressed deep resentment about being forced to remain at school. Most accepted without serious question the necessity of going to school, seeing attendance at school as preferable to alternatives such as staying at home, going on the dole or getting into trouble:

> 'Kids have to go to school till they're fifteen because mainly they'd go out and be bums and everything. Yes, they'd just walk around and do nothing'.
>
> (Boys, grade 9 Mixed class)
>
> 'Because I'd only stay home and get bored. There is nothing to do'.
>
> (Boy, grade 8 Alternative class)
>
> 'I would really think of what would happen to me if I didn't have any qualifications or hung around on the dole'.
>
> (Boy, grade 10 Mixed class)

Staying at home then, was not seen as a desirable alternative. While work was seen by the majority as the most desirable alternative, students accepted the necessity of staying at school for longer periods either because of advances in technology or, more commonly, because of conditions in the labour market:

> 'You know, my dad used to say to me when he was a kid my age he used to go to work and I suppose now, there's bigger things, bigger companies about and that. And there's unemployment about.'
>
> (Boy, grade 8 Alternative class)
>
> 'What can you do. There is hardly anything out there, and you get little jobs. You might as well stay here, there is nothing else to do'.
>
> (Boy, grade 9 Mixed class)

None of the students seemed to accept 'going on the dole' as an alternative to school or work. While they maintained they had heard of young people thinking of going on the dole, they did not expect to do so themselves. Going on the dole was rejected as an option because it seriously conflicts with their image of themselves as productive young adults. Purdah students also seemed optimistic about their chances of obtaining employment on leaving school.

(v) Labelling in lower stream classes

A common theme in interviews with lower stream students arose from discrepancies between definition of the self as student and the labels attached to individuals and classes. For instance, most students saw themselves as 'average' or 'normal' rather than 'smart' or 'dumb'. Lower stream students in particular resented bitterly being labelled as 'dumb' by their peers and teachers:

'(Are there people that can like school?) Kids that are good at school with A's and everything. They aren't the kids that are liked the most because they think they're smart and everything and we don't like them if you're an 'average' like us, you know, kids in our class that's why we're not smart. The reason why we're in 8A2 is because we don't do a language. Some of my friends, I used to be in their class, kept on saying we're dumb because we're in 8A2. We say "Guess what we did this afternoon. We went and watched a film", and they say "Oh, that's because you're dumb" '.

(Girl, grade 8 Alternative class)

While most grade 8s in these classes were happy enough to be in the class, the labelling by peers led a few to look forward to being in a 'better' class next year, that is, a class in which the work is 'harder'. Likewise, within years 9 and 10 lower stream classes, there were some who accepted the authority of the school and wished to dissociate themselves from those giving the class a bad reputation:

'We have the worst reputation in the ninth year class. We do nothing, that's what we were told, so if we want, we should get out. The bludgers give the class a bad name. Instead of putting people out, the ones that want to work should be given the chance to work in another class. All the kids that don't want to work should just go on and make a ruin of their life. (So you would like to see more separating out?) Separating the goods from the no goods, put the goods together not just all the language people there and the non-language there. As it is, the kids say we are dumb and they're in the brainy class and that stinks a lot'.
(Girl, grade 9 Alternative class)

Within the Work Experience classes, students saw themselves as being in the class:

> 'Because most people don't want to do any more schooling, they just mainly want to get a job. Mr M. was looking for kids that were not satisfied with the work they were doing last year'.
> (Boy, grade 11 Work Experience class)

Students within the class had begun to redefine their position in the school as a consequence of the productive role played by them and changes in the ways in which teachers had acted towards them. The change in their situation alleviated feelings of alienation developed in years 9 and 10:

> 'They [teachers] treat you like a person not like another student. They're treating us as older people and trusting us more. We're doing a lot of work around the school'.
> (Boy, grade 11 Work Experience class)

Negative labelling on the part of teachers was frequently a source of resentment and social estrangement:

> 'Like Mr F. he goes "Oh, you're dumb! You know it's not worth your trying so forget it and sit down". He makes you feel as if you have been written off. Well that's not really good'.
> (Girl, grade 9 Commercial class)

> 'The teachers treat you more rough in year 9 than year 8. This year they say, what a bunch of ratbags'.
> (Boy, grade 9 Mixed class)

Labelling associated with ethnicity was reported by some students in the 'Greek' classes as a source of conflict within the peer group in the school:

> '(What particularly bugs you, Nick?) The kids. They call the Greek people, wogs'.
> (Boy, grade 8 Greek class)

> 'Some people seem to like going around bashing people. Boys mostly. Mainly the Australians and the Greeks. The girls want to act tough too sometimes. See some of the kids from C4 have been calling the kids from our class wogs. That sometimes really gets to them. They have to turn around and get back to them. (Do you think it's a bad idea to have all the Greek

students together in C3?) Yes, I think it's a bad idea. They've obviously done it for the timetable it seems to me'.
(Boy, grade 8 Greek class)

Negative labelling by ethnicity and peer group conflict was not a problem for able students of Greek backgrounds. These students were well accepted by their peers and were academically and socially indistinguishable from their counterparts from Australian parents.

(vi) Boredom at school

Whereas students accepted the inevitability of coming to school and found some aspects of school life agreeable, few were completely happy. The bulk of students reported that at least some of their subjects and teachers were 'boring'. According to Lundgren[9] learning to cope with boring, monotonous tasks is one of the major components of the 'hidden curriculum' of the school. He suggests that what is learned is a form of 'metalearning' which constitutes an important 'indirect qualification' of labour. Students must not only be 'directly qualified' by passing 'relevant' courses (particularly English, Maths, and Technical subjects), but also be 'qualified' to cope with repetitive and meaningless tasks. In Lundgren's analysis, school prepares wage-earners for labour and the alienation of labour. Coping with boring subjects and boring teachers emerged as an important theme in interviews.

Whether or not a subject was seen as 'boring' generally depended on the teacher, although the mere fact that lessons were constantly set in a classroom for many represented a portent for what was to come. Most students tended to blame the teacher if a subject was boring, although a few attributed the blame to the students or to the subject matter. Boredom in turn was seen to be one of the major reasons why students 'turn off' some school subjects and teachers.

'English is especially boring because we have the same lessons every week. We don't change . . . I think it's the student, if he just doesn't understand it and he's not really bothered to listen so he just thinks "Oh this is weak" and goes off in a dream or something'.
(Grade 8 Alternative students)

'In Maths you get bored, and History. Sitting there. Sometimes Mr M. raves on and he talks and he just talks and talks and talks. Sometimes it's about Maths and sometimes it's not. He is always talking but I would rather work than talk about things like that. His explaining is good, but I don't like it when he goes beyond the hill and you get lost and tuned out. . . . In Science, all he does is write notes on the board. See he gives us a sheet and we are writing it down and all the writing is on that sheet. He reckons it's better to write it because you learn more. When I write I just write it. I just get one word and write it then I look it up and I sort of don't get the whole meaning'.

(Grade 9 Mixed class)

(vii) School rejection

From students' accounts of what causes some young people to really hate school, several pathways to school rejection can be identified. The pathways have a number of common elements, but differ according to what are seen to be the most significant source.

(a) *Individual as source* In about a third of the accounts, the source was attributed to some defect in the individual. Students rejecting school were seen to be poorly motivated ('lazy') or less able ('dumb') or deviant ('stirrers', 'trouble makers'). Most accounts suggest a sequence of events whereby individuals unwilling or unable to cope with the academic and social demands of high school either enter into conflict with, or withdraw from, the work of the school:

> *Q* Who is most likely to really hate school?'
> *A* 'The kids who don't like working in class, that's why they leave, they don't like anything'.
> (Boy, grade 8 Alternative class)
>
> *A* 'Yeah, it's mainly a lot of stirrers. Those who are mucking around all the time. Trouble makers. They don't want to work. . . . Most of them have left, but there are a couple in our class'.
> (Grade 11 Work Experience class)
>
> 'They get told off and they fail subjects. And their

attitude towards school turns off more because then the teacher starts to pick on them. The teacher doesn't like them because they don't try and their attitude to school is rotten, and they can't wait to get out of the place'.

(Boy, grade 9 Mixed class)

Because the fault is seen as lying in the individual, students holding this perception, when asked what can teacher and schools do to break this pattern, answered 'not much'. In their view it is up to the individual student to find his or her own salvation.

(b) *Peer group as source* Whereas motivational and intellectual defects of the individual were frequently cited as the source of school rejection, occasionally individuals were seen to drift into trouble by becoming identified with the 'wrong group'. Michelle's answer to the question about what sort of students hate school was typical of this type of analysis:

A 'The ones that mix with the wrong type of people'.
Q 'Who are the wrong type?'
A 'The ones that go around acting tough and bashing kids up'.
Q 'Girls too?'
A 'Mostly girls. Down the alley. There's an alley, that's where the kids have the fights. Kicking each other'.
Q 'Why do they?'
A 'Just maybe that the person doesn't like that person. And they pick on each other and the boys would probably just tear it up and that. It happens in primary school but it happens here more'.

(Girl, grade 9 Mixed class)

The problem of peer group conflicts was seen to be an aspect of school life over which teachers had little control. If caught fighting, students 'would get into trouble'. But, in fact, in the students' view, this merely suppresses rather than eliminates the problem. Discussing the problem with teachers was not seen to be particularly effective either, because this was seen as a form of 'dobbing' on one's peers. Inevitably students seeing this to be a problem came to the conclusion that stricter rules and more vigorous enforcement of them was needed to control peer group aggression.

Tania was identified by her peers as a 'roughie' who hates school and 'can't wait to leave' to get a job. When interviewed, Tania wasted no time in expressing her frustrations regarding courses, teachers, and the peer group:

> 'I don't like school at all. There is not one good thing, not this year. I wanted to leave, I'm leaving at the end of this year and I wanted to do typing and clerical work this year but they don't start till next year and so I'm going to leave and go to business college so I can learn more. In Melbourne they did typing in first year, but over here they start too late. . . . This year we are doing the same as last year and it's boring because it's the same. I don't really want to learn Science because the things I want to do have got nothing to do with your earhole. . . . I got into trouble. I was fighting with this chick and the first few times they [the Administration] did nothing and my parents didn't come down, but afterwards they had to whether they wanted or not. . . . They didn't know exactly what was going on so they came down. I told them I don't like this sheila at school and that I might get her. They said just don't get into trouble'.
>
> (Tania, Year 9 Mixed class)

In the account of students who were 'toughies', school rejection is one of the bonds which binds the group together:

> 'Well most of the kids I hang around with they don't like school. Like we had one guy in our group and he had a fight with the teacher and they were both fighting. And he was punching the teacher and then they got the headmaster and after that everyone started hating this teacher'.
>
> (Girl, grade 10 Low Stream class)

Becoming or not becoming a 'toughie' was seen to be very much dependent on the availability of suitable friendship groups. It was possible to break the pattern only if one became accepted by the mainstream group:

> 'Many of them haven't got kids to turn to and that, and they get put down by the ones that think they are so tough. The world revolves around them. And they put down the others. . . . When I was in primary school everyone used to sharpen their claws and I hated school. I went to several different schools and I really hated it

The Purdah experience

because they all used me. And it wasn't until first year that I got friends that I would be stuck with and made better friends . . . it may be how they behave, the way they dress. It could be their parents. This chick comes to school dressed normal and they all sharpen their claws at her. And she's the sort that hasn't got anything tactful to say in return. Like I got from primary school and come up with a few tactful things to say to keep them quiet, but this kid if they start hitting her she will just stand there and let them hit and things like that'.

(Girl, grade 10 Lower Stream class)

(c) *Teachers as source* The most frequently cited source of school rejection was the teacher. Students 'turned off' school because teachers were 'boring', because teachers 'pick on' students, and because they are too demanding in terms of their work expectations. In particular, it was the 'mean', 'strict' teachers who were blamed rather than 'good' teachers. Good teachers were defined as:

'Ones that you can have a bit of fun with, but you can't go too far with. Who'll tell you when you're going too far or that you're mucking around too much and to keep quiet'.

(Girl, grade 8 Alternative class)

'Bad' teachers, on the other hand, were those who picked on students excessively, resorted to corporal punishment and who do not 'explain things properly'.

'If they get bad marks the teachers don't treat them like other kids. They always pick on them. The teachers are always yelling at them and not other people. If someone is talking the teacher always tells them off and not the other person who was talking'.
Q 'A function of the student or teacher?'
A 'It was probably the kid you know, he'd been cheeky to teachers and they don't like him, but it could be the teachers. They might have had someone in another class and they are just picky and take it out on us'.

(Girls, grade 9 Mixed class)

'I know one. Her teacher, it's not the students that pick on her it's the teachers. They literally call her dumb and dense and things like that and that she's good for nothing.

That's enough to put anyone off school'.
>(Boy, grade 10 Low Stream class)

'Teachers. If you don't work well they sort of leave you out. So, if you can't cope with the work they do, so they push you aside and let you go on with whatever'.
>(Boy, grade 11 Work Experience class)

High school students inhabit simultaneously several social worlds (home, classroom, peer group, part-time work, etc), each of which contributes to the development of a self-image. Many of the young people interviewed who saw teachers or schoolwork as a source of school rejection found themselves confronted with messages about themselves which denigrated them in some way – messages from the teacher which indicated they were of little social value (e.g. teachers who were not prepared to spend time with them when having difficulty) or even a liability (e.g. teachers picking on them) and messages indicating they were incompetent academically (e.g. poor grades) or socially (e.g. being left out by the dominant peer group). Students at Purdah were acutely aware of information or circumstances that might damage their self-esteem and of sources of more favourable information about their competence as a productive social being.

Individuals can survive as social beings only by accepting some perspectives and rejecting others. If some of these are unflattering (e.g. if student sees himself as not bright), the individual will urgently look for some way of recovering self-esteem (e.g. by being seen as 'tough').

One indication of the degree to which school rejection manifests itself in overt behaviour can be gleaned from questionnaire data. Students reported on the degree to which they get into trouble in class: 9.5 per cent of students at Purdah said they often seemed to be in trouble, 40.5 per cent reported they were hardly ever in trouble, and the rest indicated they were sometimes in trouble. These figures are somewhat higher than those for South Australia and Queensland. In 1972 '4.6 per cent and 4.2 per cent' respectively said they were often in trouble. The incidence of deviancy decreases slightly (see Table 4) as one moves up the school, and is slightly lower in regular than in alternative classes (except for year 11).

The Purdah experience

Synopsis of student accounts of school rejection

In regular classes at Purdah, there are relatively few alternatives open to individuals who find it difficult to gain teacher approval and to avoid disapproval. Some have learned to avoid disapproval by playing the withdrawal game, progressively increasing the distance between themselves and the teacher, and remaining as faceless as possible. Others, finding that they are 'picked on', but that there is no way in which the power of the teacher can be challenged, become 'sullen'. While subjecting themselves to the teacher's authority, they adapt by maintaining a passive form of non co-operation. The more frequent and personal and thwarting (i.e. the more often the individual is 'picked on'), the greater the discrepancy between the interpretation of the situation given by those labelled as deviant and that agreed upon by other students. In extreme cases, subjects and teachers defined as 'pretty good' by the majority are described as 'boring' or 'bad' by deviants. Eventually the frustrations may reach a point where the individual attempts to resolve conflicts between his or her goals and those of the teacher by direct confrontation or 'stirring'.

Very often, the students who are most picked on by their teachers for 'mucking up' and 'stirring' are also picked on by other students for failing to conform to the rules governing relationships within the peer group. Once again aggression is used as a strategy for defending one's rights or achieving some end seen as desirable. Students who attempt to resolve conflicts by direct confrontation appear to be caught in a vicious circle. Trapped in a system which rewards those who are successful and discriminates against those who are not, they may feel that they are being 'picked on' constantly. In their perception, stirring and fighting are the only ways in which they can protect their interests. But the strategy invariably leads to more conflict, further attacks and isolation from teachers and the mainstream of the student body. Rebellion, stirring and fighting become a way of life for those who find their basic needs for security, acceptance, and status are constantly being frustrated, where the thwarting is personal and a salient alternative exists in the form of an anti-school group with which they can identify. Inevitably there is a drawing together of the rejected in self-defence and the building up of an alternative sub-culture with its own language, definitions of the situation, and rules of membership. Every act of social affiliation involves a choice of identity. Some students in order to preserve a sense of identity in what is seen as an alien environment, become affiliated with an anti-school group.

Many of the students who were more or less identified with the anti-school group found the advantages of membership of a fragmented, fringe group did not consistently outweigh the disadvantages. These students hoped, and expected, that work would be better – they looked forward to engaging in more purposeful, rewarding and self-fulfilling activities, greater independence and a wider circle of friends. Some then hoped to break out of the vicious circle and looked forward to the chance of shedding their 'bad reputation'. If work as an option is not available, work experience and (to a lesser degree) other alternative programs provided by the school were seen to be a more desirable option.

Conclusion

Since its establishment Purdah has been subjected to three major external pressures: the pressures of a system which valued success in formal, academic disciplines; the pressures of social reformers seeking to humanize schools and to promote social equality through schooling: and the pressures created by youth unemployment and concern about the degree to which school leavers are adequately prepared for work. These three pressures reflect what could be described as strange bedfellows: liberal education, pastoralism, and vocationalism.

The development of the 'alternative program' at Purdah reveals something of the complexity of the response of schools to such pressures. One can see, for example, instances of both stability and change, of integration and conflict, of consensus and constraint, and of functional and dysfunctional adaptations. While suggesting that external pressures have led to conflict, confusion and change at Purdah, the evidence suggests that the central core of assumptions, structures, ways of thinking and doing things that is programmed into the organization as an organism, or at least into its administrators and teachers must be maintained. This central core is important to the school: it helps provide security and ensures continuity in the face of the school's ambiguous mission and its vulnerability to external pressures. Thus while changes in specific practices and the curriculum aimed at coping with 'non-academic' students are possible, changes touching on the stabilizing core are far more difficult to achieve.

At Purdah, the first set of pressures described above created a

The Purdah experience

context within which staff and programs reflected an essentialist view of secondary schooling. It seems that many aspects of Purdah as an organization, and the values and patterns of acting on its staff, are founded on its history and constitute what feel like genotypical properties. The teachers at the school are very much aware of the difficulties created thereby for 'non-academic' students within the school. At the same time, a good many students in the academic stream see little of intrinsic value in their education and some may complete matriculation courses with a limited vision of possibilities in life, and an inadequate understanding of, and capacity to critically analyse and adapt to, the world of work.

The second set of pressures has led to significant changes in the social composition of the school and to the recognition of an 'educational underclass' of students with basic skill and school adjustment problems. As the size of this underclass increased, the behavioural manifestations of school rejection have increased. The response at Purdah has been similar to that of other schools and systems. In its first report, the Australian Schools Commission defined equality in terms of promoting 'more equal outcomes of schooling' particularly between social groups. Subsequently reports placed less emphasis on uniformity of outcomes and more on individual development, choice and diversity, and the need to reshape schools to make them more humane and open places. At Purdah, there are a number of elements in the development of alternative programs which reflect this latter emphasis. Committed and competent Alternative year 8 and 11 teachers have helped make schools a more humane place. In the Work Experience course, by working closely with sympathetic employers and systematically building up the confidence and vocational competencies of students, teachers have been able to ease the transition from school to work for most of the students in that program. Unwittingly, however, the development of these programs combined with the current pressures has encouraged further the utilitarian valuing of education as instrumental to social and economic advancement while serving the politically (but not educationally) useful function of reducing the pressure on the job market by retaining young people in school.

Apart from the introduction of work experience programs in year 11, the third set of pressures has not had a major impact on teaching and programs at Purdah. While the political and economic turmoil in Australia over the past decade provide the context within which new and exciting prospects for reconceptualizing the purposes of compulsory secondary education in a technologically advanced society could emerge, the Purdah experience suggests that teachers operating as members of school organizations are freer to propose significant shifts in orientation than to develop and implement them. The case study suggests that the clarification of the purpose of 'alternative' programs ostensibly set up to prepare 'non-academic' students for the transition from school to adult life, the translation of these purposes into specific policies, programs, and practices, and the institutionalization of changes in the thinking and behaviour of teachers and students in the school proved more complex, time-consuming and difficult than those involved in advocacy of alternatives had anticipated.

There are undoubtedly a number of positive aspects to the efforts being made by teachers at Purdah to cope with 'non-academic' students, to eliminate some of the sources of dissatisfaction with school, and to ease the transition to work. The emergence of alternative programs does seem to have made Purdah a more comfortable and caring institution for some of its clients. There is evidence as well that most of the teachers involved in working with 'alternative' students have systematically worked at creating an environment in which the basic competencies and confidence of their students are built up. On the other hand, given the constraints and context within which the 'alternative' program was developed, one ought not to be surprised if some basic difficulties remain unresolved and one or two new ones emerge.

Three questions linger in my mind:

(i) To what degree do alternative programs represent an abandonment of the ideals of comprehensive education and a revival of the dual system of education with one curriculum deriving from the 'high' culture of the middle class and the other given working class culture?

(ii) In promoting vocationalism and pastoralism at the possible expense of a liberal education do alternative programs confirm and compound acceptance of human limitations and social realities?

(iii) The constraints on schools are such that the maintenance of the school as an organization assumes priority over any serious debate about the value and function of secondary education in an advanced technological society. How then can one capitalize on the commitments and

The Purdah experience

concerns of teachers in ways which give priority to the needs of young people?

Notes

1. P. Karmel, 1972. (Chairman) *Education in South Australia*. Adelaide: Government Printer.
2. P. Hirst, 1972. 'Liberal education and the thirst for knowledge'. In R.D. Archambault (ed.), *Philosophical analysis and education*. London: Routledge & Kegan Paul, p.132.
3. B. Davies, 1976. *Social control and education*. London: Methuen.
4. D. Lawton, 1975. *Class, culture and the curriculum*. London: Routledge & Kegan Paul.
5. G.H. Bantock, 1971. 'Towards a theory of popular education'. In R. Hooper (ed.), *The Curriculum: Context Design and Development*. Edinburgh: Oliver & Boyd.
6. M. Skilbeck, 1978. 'School based curriculum development and teacher education'. Mimeo, 1975. Reproduced in CT *231 Curriculum Design and Development* Part 2A. Deakin University.
7. A. Purves, 1975. 'The thought fox and curriculum building'. In J. Schaffarick & D. Hampson (eds), *Strategies for curriculum development*. Berkeley, California: McCutchan.
8. K. Marx, 1844. *Notes on James Mill* in Marx Engles Historisch – Kritische Gesam Tansgable. Berlin: Marx Engles Verlag, 1927-9, vol. 1, 3, p. 546, translated by David McLellan.
9. U.P. Lundgren, 1980. *School curricula: Content and structure and their effects on educational and occupational careers*. Stockholm Institute for Education.

Appendix
Terms of reference of committee re 'Education of Less able Students'

1 To evaluate this school's current courses and curriculum arrangements for 'less able' students.
2 To recommend to the principal changes aimed at developing and improving the school curriculum for 'less able' students,

   (a) in the long term, i.e., changes which should be implemented after evaluation and planning have been satisfactorily completed, for 1981 and 1982;
   (b) in the short term, i.e., changes for 1980 which are necessary and can be satisfactorily planned by September 14, 1979.

In particular,

(1) to identify and clarify the problems experienced by 'less able' students and their teachers in the current curriculum structures and courses of instruction and to recommend possible solutions;
(2) to draw upon the experience of other secondary schools in evaluating this school's curriculum and course arrangements for 'less able' students *and* in recommending changes;
(3) to determine local parental and community attitudes,
   (a) to the school's current courses for 'less able' students;
   (b) to planned curriculum development for these students.
(4) to make use of appropriate expertise available both in the evaluation process and in planning curriculum development.

Procedure

1 Line of responsibilities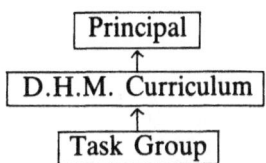

2 D.H.M. to convene first meeting for task group to elect its own chairman, secretary, report writers, and other project officers as required.

Part II

Chapter 5

Across the States
A response to the studies from within the project
Peter Fensham

School is an omnibus

The students of Addison Hills largely come to school by bus. This obvious feature of his school intrigued Stephen Kemmis and he draws imagery from it. It serves equally well for both the other two schools.

Buses are buses. Most of us don't question a bus; we accept it when we have to use it. In each school, students perceive schooling as inevitable – the place where they are between periods at home and in the real society. School also occupies the passage of time before the world of work is entered.

It is an *omnibus*, since everyone must be in it. But just as a bus going from place A to place B is not itself a place, so school does not have a meaning of its own. It is, like a bus, a means of getting – getting a job. But if there is no job when you leave – only a few students and fewer teachers seriously face that prospect.

Being on a bus differs in character from being part of either its source or its destination. So, high school has different characteristics from the realities of home and life in the communities in which the students live and expect in due course to find work. School has a 'detachment', an 'abstraction', and an 'illogicality' that is accepted by many students and their teachers.

> 'School has been a waiting room for Alison, not a preparation for the things she wanted to do. She had found herself outside the abstract blueprints for life and career offered by the school'.

Teaching discount sums at Greenfield did not change the

unreality of schooling. Is it not useful to be able to work out discounts?

'Not like this though. You kind of know or you work it out on the till. At Kentucky Fried where I work they give you a discount off food, not the drinks, too many of them disappear. You put it in the till and press the discount. It works it out for you and writes the ticket.'

Rather uncharacteristically it is David Tripp who acknowledges that it may not be possible to make school learning relevant for most students because they will reject what is taught in the curriculum simply because it is the school curriculum and regardless of what it contains. The omnibus of school cannot be co-incidental with life.

In the design of the project this chapter represents the amalgamated report of the three case studies. It was to be written by the project co-ordinator who would have access to the reports of the three case studies, many contacts during the project with the case investigators, and who would have visited each site briefly.

Amalgamation was thus to occur at the product stage of the project and was to be primarily about the two substantive concerns of the project. It was not to be written by the case investigators pooling their findings. Their pooling was to be about process and that is reported in Chapter 9. Nevertheless this amalgamation, unlike the responses in the other chapters of Part II, was from within the project team. While the focus is on product it is product inextricably tied to all those experiences of process that the team had shared together over a long period.

It is easy to say it was an amalgamation of the three case studies that made up this project, but how to do it and what its intent and shape should be opens up major methodological issues as we have foreshadowed in our introductory chapter.

In the first section of this chapter these issues are addressed, not to resolve them with finality but to make them more tangible.

The nature of amalgamation

What sort of an amalgamation was undertaken? It proves easier to say what it is not than to say crisply and without over simplifying what it is. It is not an *incipient form of generalizing* from a sample of n = 3 to some wider population. It is not the presentation of a *Matrix of Issues by Sites* although that could be done if it were not so unfaithful to the decision explained on page 14 that we would not pursue issues from site to site as they emerged.

Then the amalgamation is not just a *summation of commonalities* although a few boxes of the above matrix would have such common entries and these are noticeable and worth reporting. Much of my past research experience imposes a press for this search for commonalities so it is a temptation to be controlled but not entirely rejected. To see in a throw-away line in one report what is heavily emphasized in another is natural enough. They may mean the same or they may not, but to engage in this chase only, would be to miss many other things.

It is not an *explanation of what is reported* in the studies. There is no source of explanation at the distance of the amalgamater. If the studies do not offer explanation, it would be impertinent for the amalgamater with his ignorance of the actual situations to impose some apparent explanation however attractive and convincing the abstractions in which it might be couched may sound. Colin Power from his study at Purdah provides a more explanatory report because he had an agenda of questions in mind. Stephen Kemmis about Addison Hills stands well back from his data and so also provides an explanatory account although of a very different style. David Tripp's attention to detail in his case precludes an explanatory emphasis. His report is informative while Colin's and Stephen's are more instructive.

Before turning more positively to what the amalgamation is, some background is important. In 1978 I spent a few months in association with the CSSE project when its summaries were being finalized and defended. I learnt from the two principal authors that there were at least two ways of approaching an amalgamation task.

Bob Stake seemed determined in his summaries to reflect his strong belief that the case reports must be seen as the study. Any summary must not extend beyond them and it should constantly refer the reader back to them as source. He drew heavily on the case reports adding to them explanatory details of their sites or additional incidents from his site visits to provide links that the investigator, working from within a case, would omit.

Jack Easley, on the other hand, seemed to allow himself to write, fed by his impressions of the project, by his experience of steering the case studies into existence and keeping them going, and by his memories of what being on a site visit meant to him. It was as if he allowed all his past experience and knowledge about schools and curriculum to interact with the totality of the project. Then he tried to write down what now made sense to him more strongly than before.

In preparing the amalgamation report, I found myself at times acting in both these ways, but warming more strongly to the second and tiring from time to time of the first. Reading the reports sparked off many things in my mind and a number of these make up the body of the chapter. There are forms of generalizing involved but they are very different from the approach of a sample with n = 3.

One form is to use the case studies as *tests of hypotheses* or the embryos of a generalization that is already in my mind about schools and schooling. Some of these hypotheses are not rejected by the evidence of a case, others are strengthened and their range of generalizability extends a little. The other form of generalization arises from *adding these cases to an unnumbered store of cases* already in my memory from many previous encounters with schools. Each case report is added to (or is allowed to interact with) my existing set of experiences and knowledge and what emerges, though bounded by the reports, takes its emphasis from these processes of addition and interaction. These are processes in which any reader can indulge. The outcome is a *personal generalization* that will influence my words, thoughts, and actions until it is disproved or changed again.

Visits to the sites

I had been to two of the sites. If the case investigators were temporary residents in a society that was new but whose language they spoke, I was like a tourist who happened to know his guides very well. In this sense, I was not merely a reader about these societies, but not having lived in them, I had only a little more authority than other readers to lend to my amalgamation.

Addison Hills, the school of the case study reported in Chapter 3, has a rural setting and particular aspects of this recur in that report. Such contextual features could not be expected in the other two reports (in Chapters 2 and 4) of the studies in suburban Adelaide and Perth respectively.

Each school, however, did have a community setting and primarily drew its students from a designated geographical area. The overt influence of the rural community on Addison Hills is strikingly stronger than the shadowy sense of a contextual community one derives from either of the other reports. The anonymity of suburbia is what these two reports portray as the perception the schools have of their surrounding communities: something out there of which they are only dimly aware.

My visit to Addison Hills did leave me with stronger impressions of its community than Greenfield. There was the obvious fact that the small town on the edge of which the school sat could not provide for all its students. Then there was the strange contrast when a school of more than 600 disappeared in a few minutes as a fleet of buses drove off along paddock-lined roads to the somewheres, miles distant, where the homes of students and teachers were located.

Greenfield's surroundings were the sequences of detached houses and gardens one sees so often in the flatter suburbs of Melbourne's south east or Adelaide's south and west. The medium sized shopping centre nearby was a recurrent feature rather than a distinguishing one. One comment on the day did suggest a sense of separateness. As local jobs became scarcer for students leaving school, the prospect of looking for work on the other side of Perth was coupled with the uncertainty of finding accommodation in which to live.

In the Addison Hill's report there is a sense of wider personal and social culture interrupted by schooling. At Purdah there is schooling attempting to ignore or defy a culture out there. At Greenfield, culture was the culture of the school so intricate in itself that those other cultures shrank into lesser significance.

These site visits were additional experiences of mine with which the reports had to interact. Not visiting Purdah, in this sense, discounts my interaction with that report though I know from other experiences more about South Australian schooling than I do about any other State outside Victoria.

Amalgamation levels of response

After I had read the reports, I found there were things they had assisted me to write, things about schools of which I have been trying to make sense, things I now understood more surely, and things that seemed inadequate in the reports. In writing some of these things in this chapter, I do put a stamp on some aspects of the case reports and draw readers to them.

In both the Stake and Easley approaches to amalgamation I

Peter Fensham

found myself responding and reporting on several different levels. There is a level of the details in the reports – a psychological account of individuals and personal relations, the appearance and function of buildings, the formal programs that exist, and who makes up the clientele of students and the body of teachers. There are levels of interpretation that are both psychological and socio-political: meta-learning and hidden curricula, the irrelevance of the explicit curriculum, the inbuilt competition and consequential failure, the requirements of success, the power blocks among teachers, personal contradictions, etc.

There is a level of the reports themselves and how they are reported. There is a level that is primarily the knowledge and experience I bring to my reading of the reports.

For different levels there are different amalgamating outcomes. For example, at the level of details the reports are very different although each is a report of the experiences of teachers and students in a co-educational high school. If the title of the project, *Alienation and Transition from School*, is acknowledged, it is possible to recognize that each case did explore these themes but very unevenly. If the details of the three case studies above had to spell out their common project title, it would be hard to be confident about it. At the levels of interpretation there are commonalities in the references to the irrelevance of the dominant curriculum, the meta-learning that takes place, and the meanings that the schools place on success in learning.

Little original data appears in the Addison Hills story. Selected data (from a large and well indexed base) illustrate the Purdah report. Still more original data from the Greenfield case appear in its report.

At Addison Hills we can share in Steve Kemmis's musings and reflections about what lie behind the data of his observations and his conversations with people in the school. But we do not share his data and we cannot make our own selection of them or draw other conclusions about their significance. I felt a sense of fascination and frustration as I read.

Colin Power shares with us his deep concern for the ways of schooling but then reports the most orderly of the accounts of what is obviously a research study. Enough of the questions asked and the answers given are there to enable readers to feel that if they had the same skills they would get the same basic data. These are reported in a way that reflects an organization of approach and a framework for reporting that helps the reader to share in the study and its findings. I had a sense of objectivity, reliability, and confidence as I read.

David Tripp shares more of himself in his report of Greenfield. The school and all its details is a confrontation to him. What it is like is insufficient for his interactions with staff or students. Over and over again he engages them with, 'Couldn't it be different?'. The unevenness of this report is no surprise as a reader shares the varied reactions and responses these respondents must have had to this gentle but patient researcher and reformer. I felt some of their irritation and a sense of challenge as I read.

Stress in the schools

Details about teachers and the schooling experience abound in David's report. For example, we have the direct definitions of alienation by a number of teachers. These statements seem to come easily enough as if it is familiar to them. Such detailing of teacher responses is absent from the other two reports, but in each school its people could easily identify common features among some of the students with the idea of alienation. The overt stress that emerges from the studies is greatest at Greenfield and least at Addison Hills, but some at least of this is probably a product of David's directness and of Stephen's obliqueness respectively.

Conflict is a recurring and uneven theme in the case reports. It manifests itself in many forms but particularly around the issue of the curriculum. At Purdah there is a stronger sense of conflict between the moves beyond the school and those patterns and values the school (or its authorities and dominant teacher group) would like to foster. This type of conflict seemed almost out of reach at Addison Hills because the separation between 'out there' and life at school was so distinct. At Greenfield conflicts in the school were enough to occupy the surface of various descriptions. In cryptic form, David's study presents evidence of conflict between teachers and students, Colin's of conflict between teachers and less between students, and Stephen's of conflict in persons: a 'young Turk' teacher living out a curriculum he knows to be inappropriate and that could be different, a student facing the contradiction of what school offers and what he wants.

No doubt some of these differences again reflect the predelictions of the investigators but each of them also does present the

Peter Fensham

others' sorts of examples. Conflict in schools does and can shift its focus, the curriculum, the implicit culture, particular persons, the outside world, etc. Sometimes, as in instances in these studies, there are attempts to deal with it. At other times it remains quite undealt with, avoided or ignored but accumulating away. Dealing with conflict over the personal seems easier in the studies than when groups or the institution as a whole is concerned.

Some issues of alienation

Signs and genesis

One of the two substantive concerns of the studies was alienation from school. Reading the reports leaves me in little doubt that, if alienation means *to be turned from, to not be identified with, to be estranged*, there are many descriptions in each study that exemplify these states. Such definitions or meanings imply a personal subject (individual or group) and an object (person or thing) with a broken relationship between them. The definitions of themselves do not imply a causal direction but, in their metaphors, do suggest an idea of the process. In the studies there are many examples describing broken relationships and several views as well of these processes, and of their cause and repair.

A student or a group of students are described as 'turned off school'. This psychological or subjective view of the relationship contrasts with other descriptions in the studies that are more a sociological view, or are concerned with the objective end of the relationship such as the school, the curriculum, the teachers.

As described above, different levels are used throughout the reports. There are descriptions from some teachers and students, for example, of how schools alienate kids, and of the ways institutions exercise this influence. Other teachers ask 'Can schools alienate kids?', a reasonable question when numbers of the students accept schools with a sense of inevitability or have not ever considered schools as objects with which there could be a relationship.

The symptoms of alienation were more commonly agreed than were its origins. Absence, rudeness, and general disruption of learning was one constellation, low achievement and absence was another; and passive, non co-operation without confrontation was a third. Causal suggestions of the more psychological type were 'imported with the students from outside' or 'the way some teachers treated students'. Some of the more sociological statements above also have a causal ring but this cannot be construed as meaning there is always the option of not alienating. There are those in each study who see the curriculum as the alienating agent and who believe some other sort of curriculum would not alienate. There are others, including powerful authorities in each school whose behaviour and comments express the belief that it is not a case for tinkering: the curriculum of the school is in essence alienating for some, perhaps many, students. There are mutable views and immutable ones.

The curriculum, as the object of the alienated relationship, is such a common theme in the three studies that some of its issues need to be re-presented.

The authority of the traditional academic curriculum

None of the schools faced with any confidence or with stability the task of offering more than one type of educational program. Each of them had been officially a comprehensive school for at least a decade. Many of their teachers would have trained and taught only in this recent period of the comprehensiveness of Australia's secondary schools.

Comprehensive in this Australian sense implies little more than that no selection was exercised by the school, or by the education system more widely, about who enrolled as students. In most States these types of secondary schools in the government system are referred to as high schools. In Victoria there are secondary schools called technical schools, but again the primary criterion for enrolment is student or parental interest.*

The use of the term, *comprehensive* is not a guarantee about the type of curriculum provided nor about the commitment of the teachers as a total group to the educational needs of all their students. Between the States and within some of them (Victoria in particular) there is variation between how the curriculum for comprehensive secondary education is perceived. Some of this variation emerges from these cases, but more evident is a common thread in their curricula. This is not surprising since it

---

* Methodological note: The nearest technical school to Addison Hills was about 30 km away.

would be found in all but a handful of Australia's 2000 secondary schools. This is the priority and pre-eminence of academic courses that prepare for the selection at the end of year 12 that determines the enrolments for higher education at universities and colleges of advanced education.

Addison Hills described itself as having an academic program. Different approaches to the teaching–learning situation within this program were the extent of its staff curricular debates. Each of the other two schools had an academic program alongside which there was another curriculum, the existence of which can be described by words like 'reluctant' and 'tentative' in contrast to the 'confident' and 'certain' that went with the academic curriculum.

At both Purdah and Greenfield, the need for these alternative courses was acknowledged but only for a minority of their students. The fact that the majority of the students who began and persisted with the academic curriculum did not go on to higher education in either school did not shake the prevailing confidence about its right to be the mainstream educational task of the school. Everybody effectively entered the school into this stream and only found their way into the alternative one by experiencing and displaying gross failure in the academic course.

The power and control that this preparatory and selective curriculum exerts in all these schools is maintained by these sorts of implicit assumptions. It is not on trial or in question.

Across Australia as a whole there is still only about one third of the students who participate in all the six (or five in some States) years of secondary schooling and only about half of those (about 20 per cent of the total) proceed to those academic courses of study that universities and CAEs offer.

The continued existence of this academic curriculum (or the mainstream place it occupies) has been very little disturbed by such major social changes in Australia over the last three decades as the appearance of very significant numbers of ethnic students, generally increased retention beyond fifteen, economic growth and population expansion, and now chronic recession and population decline in many schools. Despite its record of failure to meet the educational needs of most of these new sorts of students, and its set of irrelevant hurdles for so many aspects of life beyond school, it is used by Australian society as the yardstick of education. This is, of course, not surprising. The society as a whole has not known of real alternative forms of learning. These have not been clearly presented and argued for

Across the States

by many of those who know of them and only very rarely by those who control the curriculum of schools and the shop windows of schooling to the public, like public examinations and school reward systems.

Matching students and the curriculum

One way this assumed place of the academic curriculum manifests itself in the studies is the response that is made to the wide range of ability, background and motivation of the students entering these schools. It is not the appropriateness of the mainstream curriculum that is usually questioned. It is how to organize the students in sub-groups that may be more homogeneous and hence apparently easier to teach that course of study that becomes the way the issue is presented. Some teachers in each school do respond in the other way and question the basic content of this curriculum but they are not the prevailing power block in any of the schools.

> One group of teachers takes the view that comprehensive secondary schooling implies schools within schools, meeting the vocational and educational aspirations of different 'types' of students. The other group has difficulty in accepting 'non-academic' students and programs and still resent the changes that have taken place since 1972.
>
> (Purdah)

The perception of the obvious differences in students leads to this organizational response. It is interesting to speculate what sorts of curricula responses would be forthcoming if the common human needs of all students were emphasized. They all live in Australian society and all, in due course, have to make the transition into becoming adult and autonomously responsible members of that society. They all live in some sort of family and most will participate after schooling in the creation of new family relationships. Alas, these studies give little indication that these schools attend to these sorts of uniform needs in their students other than to try to fit them into the academic mould. The ideas of a common or core curriculum, very different from their academic one, such as were aired by the Curriculum Development Centre in 1980 not long before its demise through government cut-backs, had not penetrated the central nervous systems of our three schools.

Peter Fensham

What's in a name?

The language used by school participants to describe students or the courses being offered is of interest. At Addison Hills they are 'academic' and 'non-academic'. At Purdah they are 'academic' and 'non-academic alternative', and at Greenfield there is 'academic' and 'General Studies', the non-certificated alternative.

In each case there is a pejorative ring about the words to describe the second group of students or their educational program. 'Non-academic' hardly dignifies either students or an educational program with positive qualities. Only one course is an Alternative one. The mainstream, 'academic' course is not Alternative A or the 'Academic alternative' to contrast with some title which provides an understandable meaning or purpose to the other alternative.

Despite its subject structure at Greenfield, the alternative course there is called General Studies, a term which conjures up a picture of secondary education of a lesser type, since most people's perceptions of high schools are places where specific and separate subjects are studied. Especially when there is heightened anxiety among parents about schooling and its purpose and functioning, a title like General Studies conveys little that might allay this concern for the students' future outcomes.

What other terms could have been used? Applied Academic, Basic Skills, Life, Technical (a respected term but perhaps too inaccurate) or Vocational come to mind although the last may be risking too much.

It is not just the names of these courses which seemed to dog them in each study. It is also the problem of staffing them. Apart from a few dedicated enthusiasts at Purdah, the 'best' or more experienced and respected staff do not seem to be involved. Their skills and talents are reserved for the academic courses – basically the easier program to provide with its clear goals, its well established patterns, and its community support and acceptance.

The staffing of the General Studies program at Greenfield – a large school with many experienced teachers – was headed by a co-ordinator who was new to the school and to this sort of task. Its other teachers, like the co-ordinator, were assigned because their mainstream loads were light and not because of their particular expertise or interest in this unusual educational task.

In some respects, those teachers who did choose (or were chosen) to teach the alternative classes found themselves confronted with still more heterogeneous classes than those teachers who remained with the traditional, familiar and hence easier courses. It was as if taking the lid off academic education had revealed new aspects of difference not even considered before.

At Purdah, a view that these students could be categorized as 'the whole bunch who will never get into tertiary education' proved to be too sweeping and not applicable. Three sub-groups were identified: '(a) Special Education children, (b) slow learners and (c) intellectually able but 'turned off' school. At Greenfield, there was a mix of slow learners, the 'turned-off' school, and some returners to school after experience 'out there'.

Relevance – pipedream or possibility

Irrelevance is another concept that is associated with some of the curricular descriptions in each of the studies. David Tripp, in particular, gives actual examples of classes with inefficient learning and of irrelevant content. Despite these recognitions of irrelevance, much of the practice in the three schools seems to be based upon a very different claim.

Because schooling can, and does, claim such a significant fraction of the lives of everybody, prevailing groups seem to argue that it ought to be able to claim its own meaning of relevance without being dependent on or subservient to life outside school.

While there are significant voices in the studies that are seeking a more relevant curriculum, they provide no coherent message as to how such a change might successfully occur.

Power and Kemmis in their studies are conscious, on the other hand, of powerful forces that sustain irrelevance.

> Attention to short-term organization needs provided a convenient escape from extensive probing, theoretical debate or long-term considerations – compromise became necessary to accommodate external constraints.
>
> (Purdah)

> The bloodless curriculum, the unresolved conflicts of the staff meeting, the wet blanket principle: they are no more characteristic of Addison Hills than of 100 other high schools in the State. It turns out to be almost impossible to change one's

own teaching without changing the school at the same time. The curriculum, school organization, teaching and learning hang suspended in a balance of forces – a compromise, a still-life composition.

(Addison Hills)

Tripp, after describing some attempts by teachers at Greenfield to improve relevance, suggests that it may not be possible to make school learning relevant because most students will reject what is taught in the curriculum simply because it *is* the school curriculum regardless of what it contains.

The inevitability of school

The acceptance by most teachers and students of the inevitability of school as it is was a strong impression from the three studies. At Greenfield there is a remarkable threshold tolerance in the students for the curriculum, for the teachers and for the conditions of the school. Many of the teachers would have taught in other schools and numbers of students would also have had other experiences. There is no sense that there are quite different forms of schooling that might become the form (or at least challenge what is) at Purdah or Greenfield or Addison Hills. 'Schools's school. It is all right as it is' seemed to be the message from many students, and if some teachers expressed dissatisfaction, nothing happened as a result: 'I feel defeated by the system. And yet we bumble along, it's a great juggernaut that you just can't stop, and all efforts to modify it are so token'. (Greenfield) 'The organization and staffing of Addison Hills is resilient to attempts to change. It has survived with relatively few modifications for years'. (Addison Hills)

This type of view sees schools and schooling as a static component, but rather prolonged experience, during the changing interactions as children develop from being wholly part of the family to becoming part of the adult community.

At a psychological level, schooling will, on the whole, have its own separate interaction with the child rather than be a dynamic resource, responsive to and contributing to the developmental interactions. Alison, the composite student in the Addison Hills story portrays this situation. She had learnt at school to understand herself as dependent – dependent on and determined by others. It was the eventual learning, from outside influences, that she was other than these things that freed her to make the transition to leave school. The essential message of schooling to her that she was dependent was now superseded.

Kemmis presents this more personal or individualistic perspective (or are his individuals personifications of groups or collectives?). He sees a basic gap between the institutional character of a school, however well meaning, and the 'very personal matter, tied up with a present sense of self and anticipations of what one wants to be. . . . School seems to have asserted its place on the personal/institutional continuum, and to have come down firmly on the side of the institution'.

> She spoke at length of learning at school what she couldn't do. Her report says too much about what she hasn't learnt.
> (Addison Hills)

> The bulk of students reported that at least some of their teachers were 'boring'. Students must also be 'qualified' to cope with the repetitive and meaningless tasks. Coping with boring subjects and boring teachers emerged as an important theme in the interviews.
> (Purdah)

> Furthermore, it is quite clear to the student what he is supposed to do (to stop thinking about what he is doing, not to ask questions about it and to do what he is told) although it was not said in so many words and teacher's tone was kindly (almost patient) enough.
> (Greenfield)

These sorts of learning from school can be seen to have sociological and political significance as well. They are the meta-learning of Lundgren[1] and a number of other writers. Such meta-learning does occur, they claim, in all students. In a macabre sense it is the 'success' of institutional mass education. A minority of students *learn* that they have already acquired or can acquire the knowledge the teachers demand. The majority *learn* that they have not this knowledge and/or that they cannot acquire it.

These are strong socializing messages that prepare the few to assume positions of power in society and the many to become the next set of 'bearers of wood' or 'drawers of water'.

Peter Fensham

An assessment

The problems of organizing, recognizing, staffing, and designing these alternative courses (or having them at all) recur as issues in each case study. After ten years of opportunity and an acute need for at least the last five, the small amount of success that these courses have had in becoming established, does raise the question whether these types of schools are capable of being comprehensive in a curricular sense.

There is a need to reconsider the alternatives for the organization and provision of schooling. The idea of comprehensive schools for secondary education has been, for a generation of educational thought, an expected panacea. But comprehensive education must extend beyond the point of entry. It must be still visible at the point of exit from schools.

Somehow, ways need to be found so that many more (most should not be too ambitious a target) students do feel enriched and satisfied by their learning at school and are then rewarded for it by a society that sees them as educated in general and equipped for particular contributions. If this could be better achieved in some places by separate types of schools, or by junior and senior high schools, or by core schools linked to specialist sub-schools, then these should be tried. Purdah, Greenfield, and Addison Hills seem to be appropriate places for such trials.

Some issues of transition

A dominant transition

In one sense there is comparatively little in the studies' reports about transition from school and in another sense there is a great deal.

Transition means 'the passage from one state (or action or set of circumstances) to another'. If the second state is the uncertain world of employment, there is only a little in the life of most students at these schools that directly relates. More of what does occur is based on the old assumptions of ensured employment in a job for which there is some affinity. The new realities are that many students will have periods of unemployment. Even the educationally successful are now often not able to find employment in fields of their choice. If the second state of the transition is adulthood in general, there is almost no recognition of it in any of the studies.

Across the States

On the other hand, if the second state is what follows from (or is closed off by) performance in academic education, then the studies have much to say about this transition and how it is serviced by each of the schools. In this sense this transition provides the *raison d'être* of the schools.

Teachers are the successful products of schooling. In their generation they were part of an *élite* of not more than 15 per cent who not only were successful through to year 12 but also graduated from a further and similar course of study at college or university. Most of them have no experience of other occupations in a substantial sense. Those who had this experience were sufficiently rare to note in the case studies, but how these different experiences really affected and changed their teaching was not so easily discerned.

The curriculum of the three schools, its subject-based organization, and the values behind the situations in which the teachers were the sole determiners of what was to be learnt, all reflect the sort of education in which these teachers succeeded up to a generation ago.

The memory of the 85 per cent of their own school peers who failed to succeed has faded. Most of the teachers in these three schools are yet again offering a whole school population the contemporary form of the same sort of education through which some succeed with its explicit learning, and a larger number learn that they are not very able to learn the only education that schools appear to recognize as of worth.

Each case study provides evidence of many of the teachers and the schools as whole entities thus acting as agents of a reproductive process for the transition that is seen to matter in which a few are winners and most lose.

The whole structure of the school, from its organization of classes for similar age groups to the subject expertise of its teachers is specifically oriented towards preparing its students to be tested in these subject areas of learning. This is what the school can offer. If such qualifications serve to enable the students to obtain a job or move on to further study then the school can serve its students. If these do not lead to employment, 'How then can this school cope with preparing its students for any other destiny such as unemployment? Clearly this school (and I suspect the education system as a whole) has no answers'. (Greenfield)

Teachers in each school found it hard to identify with a number of the students. Even the enthusiasts for the alternative courses at

Peter Fensham

Purdah and Greenfield seem still to distance themselves by making the decisions about what sorts of things – life skills, different learning, etc. – the students in these courses will need. There seemed to be no clear signs in any of the studies that teachers and students were side by side as co-operative determiners of a learning program and how best it could be achieved.

There is, in each study, evidence of such gaps between teachers and many of their students and the society from which they came as children and into which they will go to be adults. Furthermore, there is an inability to get to grips with the problem.

> He is ready to accept that the school has a responsibility for the fact that some kids get 'turned off'. The problem is how to respond, and how to establish commitment to the response in the school. . . . The struggle is always incomplete, indecisive and inconclusive.
>
> (Addison Hills)

> While recognizing that there is a problem, many staff, nevertheless, still see the school as an academic institution. The purpose of secondary education is, as it has always been, the PEB.
>
> (Purdah)

> The school is aware that there are problems, but I don't think it knows what the problems are . . . the everyday living in the households of the children we teach would be like visiting a foreign country. How can we understand the problems, deal with them, compensate for them, and accept it?
>
> (Greenfield)

The clear shape of the academic courses, their traditional place, their familiarity to the teachers and their relation to the only expectations of schooling that parents have been encouraged to have, all combined to make the transition these courses serve the priority concern of the schools.

> For the PEB you're working to an end point aren't you? You've got a building program going on. This is another thing wrong with the constitution of alternative courses, there's no real end for them.
>
> (Purdah)

The other end states of transitions though more universal in their meaning and importance were not recognized as ends for which schooling could contribute directly. Because they were not so acknowledged, the alternative courses which were the gropings in this direction could be labelled as having 'no real end'.

Transition to the world of work and no work

Unemployment among school leavers, as in so many areas of Australia, is high in the communities surrounding each of the schools. A number of common consequences emerge. Students are staying on longer at school because jobs are not available. Some students are returning to school after a limited experience of unemployment or of short-term employment. Many older students have had some experience of work in a part-time capacity and a number report that they found in that experience a recognition, a dignity, a sense of themselves as a person to others, that are not the feelings they get at school.

A number of students at each school did get some very limited experience of work through the schools' programs for work experience. These experiences seemed to have a surprisingly large influence (positively or negatively) in shaping the student's thinking about desired employment. Is it possible for such programs to be a more open influence now that flexibility of thinking about work and employment possibilities is more needed than it was in the 1960s or early 1970s?

At least as many students may now leave these schools and experience unemployment as leave and experience higher education. This, one senses, has done little to alter the implicit and explicit rationale of the curriculum or the organization of the schools. The transition to higher education still, as we have seen, provides most of the knowledge and learning that is chosen for the curriculum and of the way the schools' priorities and organization are determined.

What students did at school did not seem relevant to their career choices. Work-related schooling might be more relevant to them than academic schooling. There is a blindness on the part of students and teachers alike about the prospects ahead. None of the studies report evidence of students choosing to leave school to go on the dole. A number of students are at school 'till they get a job', and at each place teachers sigh at the 'waste' as able students leave in mid-year or at year 11 for employment rather than completing the traditional goals of PEB, HSC, or TAE.

From Year 9 onwards, the purposes of school become increasingly defined in terms of getting grades or qualifications. Without these, the chances of getting a job are seen as minimal. The grades and certificates of schooling do have an effect on who gets the too few jobs society is providing. This, however, is only a very crude way of matching the qualities and abilities required for the job and their presence in the applicant. The rewards of jobs of all sorts in a time of shortage go to those who have obtained the traditional achievements of academic study, and who thus have shown themselves to be able to tolerate longer dependence and conformity to the school's program.

So a modest result in HSC from Addison Hills is more likely to gain an apprenticeship that a good performance in Year 10 at its counterpart technical school despite the claim that the latter offers a more appropriate education for this outcome.

Work – society's second chance to educate

Until less than a decade ago, school education for thirty years had been an experience for all and an acknowledged success for some. However, regardless of success at school, almost all school students moved on from school to employment, either immediately or after a period of further studies. Those, whose experience in the child and adolescent phenomenon of being at school was unsuccessful, could try the numerous other opportunities for learning that a society with full employment offered. Learning on the job or a succession of different jobs provided an education in which the conjunction of task, motivation, explicit instruction, reward, reinforcement, and peer pressure would often have been the envy of school educators. Off the job, the earnings from employment allowed all sorts of other experiences which, in a multitide of ways, provided their own further opportunities for acquiring still more knowledge and social skills.

All but the newest of our teachers in Australia are familiar only with this situation. For nearly all the parents with children at school this pattern is also their familiar one. Only some who have immigrated to Australia from other societies and the grandparent Australian generation experienced an unemployment situation like the one that has become increasingly chronic since 1975.

It is not surprising that the schools and teachers in these three studies are rather powerless in the face of this novel and unfamiliar situation. Parents are, likewise, understandably anxious and look to the school for a magic that will somehow ensure that their children are among the fortunate who still find work in employment.

At whatever point in history we assess the phenomenon of schooling in Australia, we would, I believe, find that the majority, apart from certain basic skills, learned much of their knowledge and most of their wisdom in society after they left school. There is some evidence that schools and teachers have not lost their skills in imparting these basic skills and it might be possible for them to assist with other sorts of meaningful training. However, it is really up to society rather than the school to take the responsibiity for providing the post-school opportunities for learning that will complement whatever limited education our schools do manage to provide.

Notes

1 U.P. Lundgren. *Model Analysis of Pedagogical Processes.* Stockholm Institute of Education, Department of Educational Research, Stockholm, 1977.

Chapter 6

Policy response to the case studies

Jean Blackburn

Although the settings and the frameworks of analysis differ, the three school studies raise common policy issues. This is of itself significant. In all cases, the starting point of alienation led beyond identifiable groups of students and discrete problems capable of limited solution into the heartland of the curriculum and organizational structures themselves. The studies give concrete form to generally acknowledged problems and commonly suggest that quite radical changes in thinking and practice are needed if they are seriously to be responded to. They simultaneously suggest, however, that it is no longer possible to operate on the basis of some presumed consensus in tackling them. Both the inter-relatedness of the issues and the collapse of consensus make the discussion of policy implications difficult. In order to go beyond a mere extension of the discussion in the papers, I have attempted some classification of issues, although it will be evident that the self-contained discussion of each has not been achieved.

1 The future of 'comprehensive' schooling

A central policy issue which emerges is whether the comprehensive secondary school as interpreted in Australian practice and within public systems has costs which exceed its benefits. Competing ideologies divide staff in apparently unproductive ways. For some students the academically oriented curriculum is insufficiently challenging. Others who see it as irrelevant to their purposes or who are discouraged by lack of success in it are not well served either, and may actively be damaged. Beyond these divisions, it appears that most students experience secondary

Policy response to the case studies

schooling as a rite of passage into the adult life of work, finding little intrinsic satisfaction in the learning and between it and their experience of life, or expectation of it. Alienation is in this sense the rule rather than the exception. Alternative policy reactions are possible:

(a) To revert to divided schooling. Arguments supporting this are not hard to find. 'Non-academic' students did indeed find more appropriate curricula and greater self-respect in technical schools than in 'comprehensive' ones, and the demands of the academic high school were legitimated by having been 'chosen'. The alternatives now considered need not be confined to the old tech/high division, which is indeed rendered obsolete by technological change itself. But the more general case against the common school is gaining momentum, a move not unconnected in Australia with heavy public subsidy of privately initiated alternatives. Choice and variety are in. Evidence such as that mounted by Coleman in the United States[1] suggests that choices based on commonalities of interest, values or educational preferences are more likely to result in productive schooling than assignment to the common school. Kemmis also hints at this in his approving portrait of the teacher who, sharing a common lifestyle with his students, knew how to make connections between his teaching and their experience and common-sense knowledge.

(b) Make the common secondary public school really comprehensive. No really comprehensive model of the secondary school has emerged in Australia, despite the fact that secondary schooling has become universal and compulsory. The ethos of the Australian model remains that of the academically competitive high school, designed with a different clientele and purposes in mind. This has produced a 'residue' problem which is the explosive tip of more widespread alienation. Power's choice of 'Purdah' in naming the alternative provision which emerged in the school he studied significantly characterizes its relationship to the mainstream orientation.

It may be instructive that the Swedes, those doyens of comprehensive schooling, are now pursuing a locally-designed model of it which embodies work experience for all throughout secondary schooling as a means of giving point to 'academic' understandings and of forging new relationships between schools and the society beyond. Whether such an approach is acceptable in Australia or not, it is evident that conceptions of comprehensive schooling which rest on the assumption that higher academic study is the norm against which all students should be defined are unacceptable, as is busywork which does not strengthen intellectual muscles. Some new definition of liberal education, embodying broader interpretations of what is involved in 'knowing' and associating theory with practice and experience is called for. At senior secondary level this could well take an institutional form which associated the practical skills teaching available in Technical and Further Education (TAFE) with studies deemed liberal. For those who fear the consequences of a school pluralism ungrounded in democratic commitment, the reinterpretation of comprehensive schooling and of liberal education within it is the stern policy alternative.

2 Can leadership in change be left to the schools?

The studies suggest that it cannot. Kemmis explicitly states that the development of colleagial relationships among staff essential to the design and testing of radical curricular change is inhibited by the structures of the secondary school system, which themselves act to defuse the impetus for change. He concludes:

> The teachers, by choice or by habit have been disenfranchised as forces for changes in the curriculum. They are powerless to meet its challenges. If students are out of touch with the curriculum as it is offered, not much can be done. The school lacks the mechanism, and perhaps the will, to engage the problems, analyse them, respond with strategies for action and learn from their effects in practice.

Regretfully, it must be conceded that the two other case studies bear this out. Teachers sensitive to the need for radical curricular change in these two schools were powerless to affect traditional curricular areas or organizational structures. Confined to devising 'alternatives' for variously defined marginal groups of students, their dedication, not surprisingly, lacked direction. Although their efforts may well have resulted in a more satisfying school experience for the students involved, their removal and the removal of their students from the mainstream arguably consolidated complacency within it.

Are we obliged to conclude that this is everywhere the case? If it is not (and within the Disadvantaged Schools Program at least may be found some, admittedly few, contrary cases), then it

Policy response to the case studies

would be helpful to identify and study examples of secondary schools which have succeeded in collaboratively analysing and confronting the problems of a curricular renewal which connects the concerns of students approaching adulthood with the cultural heritage. 'Relevance' which fails to attempt the connection is unrewarding all round. Equally so, however, is the pretence of transfer between much school learning and situations to which it is applicable.

How one views the policy issues arising out of this stalemate in curricular development depends on whether the need for radical change is endorsed and on the nature of any agreement about directions for change. If it is accepted that *in practice* committed change must be generated by those who have to operate it, then the appropriate servicing of reflection and action at local level will be central. This will itself require considerable external input if the results are to be more satisfactory than in the past. If it is maintained that only those sharing an educational orientation can collaborate effectively in the enterprise of reconstruction, we are back with the school choice and variety issue. It is hard to evade the conclusion that the impetus for change must be generated from beyond the school and beyond the education system. In the present restrictive climate, centrally recommended and serviced curricular change is the policy most likely to be followed, schools having the option to devise alternatives on the basis of a clearly articulated rationale, externally endorsed. The nature of that more active leadership (direction?) could well by-pass the substantive issues, making attitudes to it difficult to formulate in the abstract. Curricular policies are likely in other words to become increasingly an arena of struggle. That may have the virtue of ordering an agenda for wider involvement.

3 Responding to youth unemployment

The highly instrumental and job oriented legitimations of secondary schooling which most students, following community values, appear to hold, are already being shaken by the fact of unemployment, as the studies indicate. The tendency for able students to leave early is noted in each of the schools. There can be little doubt that fifteen to eighteen year-olds will continue to be excluded, at levels at least equal to those presently operating, from paid employment. From a policy point of view, this fact may outweigh all others in giving urgency to a reconceptualization of secondary schooling. In their narrow interpretations of comprehensiveness, secondary schools may well come to be seen as part of the problem, as well as potentially an aspect of its solution. It is untenable to believe that those who fail to find work after leaving school early are disqualified by their own deficiencies, or that labour demand can be influenced in any way by the schools, except to the degree that a greater holding power by them could reduce the numbers offering for work at early ages. The results of extending the period of limbo could be disastrous all round, unless secondary schools could be changed in ways which relate their learnings more securely to the world outside, and unless their system of certification can be changed in ways having an accepted relationship to futures wider than higher education of an academic kind.

Note

1 J.S. Coleman. 'Racial segregation in the schools: New research with new policy implementations'. *Phi Delta Kappan* 57 (October): 75-8, 1975.

Chapter 7

Some methodological, substantive and theoretical aspects

P.W. Musgrave

The three case studies reported here raise a number of issues of method, substance and in theory. Each of these three areas will be discussed in turn and for reasons which will become apparent in the order indicated, unusual as this may be, since for most social scientists theory is prior to method and the two ally to generate substance.

1 Method

In none of these case studies is there any introductory and overt appeal to some form of social or educational theory, and certainly not of the depth usual in research projects of this scale and seriousness. The problem is stated in brief terms in the general area now usually known as the transition from school to work. In this research the stance taken, although never made explicit, is that this transition is a process, to be seen here as the dependent variable. This process is influenced by an independent variable, alienation, a concept never clearly defined. This influence will lead to different outcomes, some of which are more acceptable socially than others. Because no tight initial conceptual framework is laid down these outcomes may take various forms, for example, an unhappy adolescent becoming disgruntled and unemployed or a previously happy child developing a deviant personality of one sort or another. The measures of dysfunction are potentially very varied, unpredicted and, indeed, unpredictable.

Now the authors of these studies are not tyros in educational research and, therefore, know full well what they are about.

They are working in the contemporary phenomenological tradition and want to discover the meaning given by the actors involved to the events upon which they focus. They, therefore, are suspicious of prior theorizing on two counts. First, reification is possible and the very concept of alienation has probably spawned more reificatory writing than most sociological terms. Second, they are concerned not to put ideas, words or actions into the minds, mouths or bodies of the teachers and students whom they involved in their studies. Both these positions are laudable, but decisions in each case must be made on a cost-benefit basis: what are the costs and benefits to the project of taking this rather than that approach?

In both cases to eschew prior conceptualization is legitimate, but its cost almost inevitably is a lack of comparability across the studies involved. One alternative would have been to put some initial structure on the studies by using the same semi-structured interviews or the same set of interview probes in each school. What has to be decided is whether the initial specification of any concept will bring sufficient gain in comparability to affect any loss through potential reification or, again, whether the communality gained by agreed semi-structured approaches will disastrously destroy the naïvity of the respondents. Furthermore, these utilitarian calculations have to be made prior to starting the research, though some indication can be gained of the costs and benefits through some type of pilot study.

Certainly the result of the method chosen here has been that there is no apparent communality of approach across the case studies. Each study has turned out to be very different and has been reported in a totally different way, though let it be said that each is in its own way methodologically legitimate, well reported and of much interest. To be over incisive and hence, perhaps, to caricature, the case study of Addison Hills High School is reminiscent of sensitively written fiction; that of Purdah is akin to the positivistically influenced anthropological tradition; and that of Greenfield is most consistently phenomenological and experimental in its techniques of reporting.

This lack of direct comparability between the three studies, whatever its original methodological justification, has one crucial consequence; generalization about matters of substance becomes well nigh impossible. There are research projects that use purposively chosen sites for case study and take up a prior conceptual stance with the hope and intention of making more or less tentative, substantive generalizations, though this is possibly

Methodological, substantive and theoretical aspects

truer in the medical than the social sciences. Here no such pay off is possible. Yet just because of the common focus, but great diversity, of each study there is a rich theoretical pay off. After commenting upon a number of mainly confirmatory substantive findings in the three separate studies I shall pass to a larger consideration of the theoretical implication of these case studies and, finally, to some implications for practice.

2 Substantive findings

There is additional confirmation in these case studies for a number of findings that have been so often reported that they are now considered 'obvious' or 'common sense'. These relate most clearly to students' attitudes to school which were found at Purdah to be 'lukewarm' (p.238). But one finding that has rarely been reported in Australia, though has been commonly reported overseas, is that such attitudes 'peak in Year 10, the year in which students are most likely to leave' (p.238). In the United Kingdom raising the minimum legal leaving age has twice been found to raise the age at which anti-school attitudes and also juvenile deliquency peak. Another frequent finding overseas concerns the characteristics perceived by students to be those of a 'good' teacher, which were seen at Purdah once again in terms of clarity of exposition, humour and class control (p.251).

Many of the findings here reported relate to the administration of schools or the school system. At the latter level one is reminded of one important part of the English Newsom Report[1] about the geographical mobility of teachers. In the evidence of the Year 11 co-ordinator at Greenfield comment was made, but not taken up explicitly in the prior analysis, that 'the high rate of turnover in the staff is disadvantageous to the school and to the students'*. This rate may well be decreasing now due to the current economic stringency, so that at least one countervailing force may have been born inadvertently out of contemporary monetarist policy.

The major administrative findings relate to curricular planning. There is confirmation at Purdah of some English work on the pragmatic way in which teachers plan curricula, 'rarely . . . in a logical, linear fashion from goals to evaluation' (p.225). Yet in many ways the most interesting and potentially fruitful material

---

* Methodological note: A comment from the unabridged case report.

relating to curricular planning concerns the Alternative Course at Greenfield. A number of these findings confirm the very complex problems implicit in such courses. Throughout the study both teachers and students realized that the mere setting up of such courses creates new and reinforces old anti-academic labels. In addition, their successful implementation usually depends upon the availability of resources. At Greenfield, as the Course co-ordinator commented, success demanded flexibility in time-tabling and in staffing and the availability of accommodation, neither of which was possible. Musgrave's well-known Second Law is once again confirmed, namely that educational issues are always decided on administrative, not educational, grounds.

Another finding relating to the planning of the Alternative Course is important, and for two reasons. This is that, as a Social Studies teacher noted, such a course can force 'the kids . . . to question their values' and this is seen by parents as 'threatening' (p.66). This is important, both because it confirms similar findings in Australia and elsewhere, but also because it connects the school and its curriculum with the world beyond its walls, a theoretical point which will be taken up below.

Two other substantive findings, both relating to the economy, are worth noting. The first occurs in the evidence of the Youth Education Officer at Greenfield who confirmed what has been found in Victoria and also overseas, that students and teachers misperceive the qualities that employers want in their potential employees. This dysfunction, which in itself may have nothing to do with alienation, though it may ultimately lead to it, should be removed by rational discussion between those involved. The second important economic finding does, however, relate to alienation and comes from the Purdah study. Some students find subjects and/or teachers 'boring' (pp.247-8) and the thesis is advanced, as it has been by Lundgren[2] in Sweden and by Willis[3] in England, that such an apparently manifest dysfunction can in reality be latently functional for the economy, if not the educational system. It is one advantage of the method of presenting the Greenfield material that, if this finding had related to that school, we should have been able to consult the relevant evidence to see how firmly the thesis was based in data and by what mechanisms the process operated, but this is not possible here.

There is one other finding that links the school to the networks around it which reminds us of Coleman's famous United States study on adolescents[4]. The interpretation of the discussions with

Methodological, substantive and theoretical aspects

the students on the School Council at Greenfield was that 'school is somewhere to go, you see all your friends and have a good social time' (p.46). The school in this respect is serving ends other than those in the minds of those running it and in effect being colonized by its students to aid them in their life away from its restrictions.

The last point is important in that for the second time we are reminded that despite the lack of overt initial conceptualization there must be at work in the minds of these research workers a hidden agenda which seems to focus on actors within the school and the educational system rather than upon their relationships with and actions within that whole series of interlocking networks radiating out to the family, youth and leisure activities, the economy and the political system. This point leads us to the major section of this chapter in which the theoretical implications of this research project are considered.

3 Theory

The material generated by this project and presented in the three case studies may be related to three theoretical areas: to the concept of alienation itself, to organization theory as it concerns schools and to the curriculum. Each will be considered in turn.

(i) Alienation

In the Greenfield report one phrase is used that is most fruitful in generating further thinking about the concept of alienation. The idea of a 'threshold of alienation' (p.120) is mooted. Clearly alienation is here seen not as a state, but as a process. Students move across a threshold into alienation. This view raises a number of questions, answers to which must affect practice. Four will be raised here:

a) Is alienation permanent? If a student becomes alienated this need not mean that he/she necessarily remains so. Thus, the Greenfield students who came back to school after being 'turned off' were no longer, at least for the time being, alienated. They were giving school another chance, though some at least seem again and for a second time to have crossed the threshold of alienation.

b) Is alienation reversible? Some processes are not reversible but, if students can give school a second go, seemingly the process might be reversed. The folk lore of teaching is full of examples of successful ploys to check movements across the threshold of alienation. At the simplest level teachers move children's seats in classrooms so that by keeping them apart mutually detrimental influences may not be allowed to operate.

c) Whence is alienation born? At Greenfield there is evidence to suggest two major possibilities. The research worker's summary noted that one commonly held view was that alienation was born in the school when teachers tried 'to impose an alien set of behaviour and values upon the pupils' (p.122). A science teacher, however, also thought that alienation was brought into school from outside (p.53). These two views are not mutually exclusive, since both may be true.

d) Is alienation to be seen as an active or a passive process? When asked to define alienation the Year 10 co-ordinator at Greenfield gave a list of actions such as 'rudeness ... and flaunting rules' (p.108). On the other hand students at Addison Hills seemed to become 'disengaged', not 'repelled' from school (p.169), a more passive view of alienation.

So far in this section no comment has been made about the lack of any firm or agreed definition of alienation in the three studies, though, as noted above, this situation is a direct consequence of the method adopted. The nearest approach to a tight definition occurs in the Purdah study (p.200) where the concept is defined to include four of the five dimensions isolated by Seeman[5] in his classic paper on the topic, though these dimensions are not used systematically to organize material in the research. If there are dimensions to the process of alienation, there is the implication that an individual may be alienated on one or more dimension, that is, partially or totally alienated. A personality may adapt to a given set of social circumstances by crossing the threshold on one or more, but not on all the dimensions of alienation. This is a very plausible hypothesis, matching common observation: it is rare to meet anyone who is totally 'turned off'. But to know something of what pushes adolescents along any dimension or what reverses that process could be important in practice. Indeed, even to conceptualize the problem of alienation thus could be helpful in stopping us from applying the label of 'alienated' to our students in any blanket fashion.

Methodological, substantive and theoretical aspects

Two variables could be important in the process of alienation, for both of which evidence is available in the studies, but about neither of which are conclusions drawn. The first is sex. Are the two sexes affected equally or differently by the process of alienation? Have uni-sexual tendencies had any effect on the tendency for boys to express alienation more actively and girls more passively in the past? Rather similar questions could be asked about the second missing variable, namely the geographical location of the school, more especially whether it is in a rural or urban area. Addison Hills was situated in a more rural catchment area than Purdah and Greenfield, both metropolitan schools. How much had this to do with the apparent judgment that at Addison Hills the level of alienation seemed low and students were not 'in any simple sense driven out' (p.173).

In conclusion, Figure 3 shows in diagrammatic form how after considering the evidence from these studies alienation may be conceptualized when analysing adolescents at school.

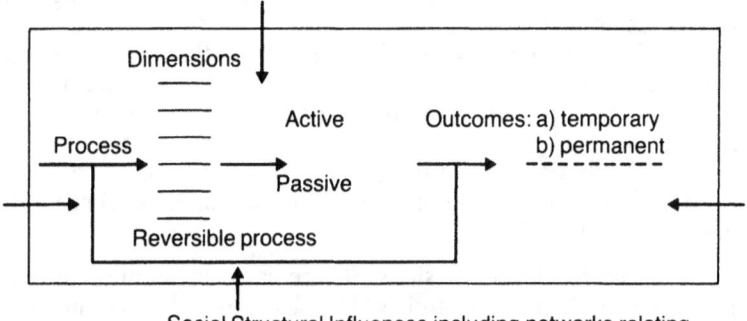

Figure 3: A diagrammatic representation of the concept of alienation

(ii) School organization

The process of alienation takes place within an organizational framework which is created in the hope of influencing those who pass through it according to the intention of those with power over it. The aim of these three case studies can only be to help to restructure the schools so that the level of alienation is lowered, although ironically because of the method adopted there are perhaps fewer recommendations for action than there might have been.

The aim in any organization is to establish a structure that is seen as legitimate, that is, one in which the power of those running it is accepted for most of the time without serious questioning. In traditional terms the student identifies closely with the school or as the research worker at Greenfield puts it: the opposite of alienation was seen as 'belonging' (p.142). Obviously the alternative course was a new structure created to bring about this result. Such organizational changes are, however, no longer new and though that is no necessary condemnation what has to be asked is whether the evidence in these studies really supports the conservative conclusion in the Purdah study that 'the central core of assumptions, structures, ways of thinking and doing things . . . must be maintained . . . it helps provide security and ensures continuity' (p.254). The function of the present organizational framework may be to give security and continuity, but it may have the more than counterbalancing cost of increasing alienation.

The Greenfield study provides evidence that provokes the question of whether a more radical approach to organization is not needed in at least two areas: the relationship of secondary schools to the primary and tertiary sectors and the size of secondary schools. In addition, comment must be made about a third organizational matter: what the research worker aptly names 'ears' (p.142).

a) Inter-sectoral relationships. There is little mention of the primary schools in these studies. In at least one place comment is adverse. The senior science master felt that once students 'come out of primary school, Year 8, they're not very flexible, not going to change that much . . . especially in problem areas like [the three Rs]'*. In the UK for various reasons, including alienation of adolescents, both older and younger, there has been a start to creating middle schools, catering for what teachers in independent schools would call the preparatory age range, that is from about eight to fourteen. What has to be asked is whether any radical changing of the transition points at which children move between different types of schools will help to offset the tendencies which the present structure may set up towards raising the level of alienation.

---

* Methodological note: A comment from the unabridged case report.

At the other end of the age range stand the tertiary institutions, rarely mentioned directly in these studies; they enter the discussion rather by implication in relation to the effect of their entry requirements upon the curriculum, teaching styles and the attitudes of teachers, parents and students in the secondary schools. In the two case studies in which definite conclusions appear no mention is made of the manner in which such backward effects may increase alienation. May not this influence alone justify a radical rethinking of the entry requirements of the tertiary institutions? Any answer to this question will affect the view taken about a core secondary curriculum, a matter to which further reference will be made below.

b) Size. There is a widely-held view that links alienation to organizations of large size which are almost inevitably highly bureaucratized. The deputy principal spoke to this vein, when he described the ill effects of the departmentalized structure of Greenfield. Work done in the USA and replicated in Queensland by Campbell[6] has shown that those running large schools create more curricular and extra-curricular positions than can be filled by the students in even these schools, whilst the oppostie is the tendency in smaller schools where the fewer students have to compete for the far fewer positions open to them. The result seems to be that a greater spirit of 'belongingness' is found in the smaller schools. In other words, a state opposite to alienation is created. We have, therefore, to ask ourselves very seriously whether schools should not be made smaller in order to reverse the alienating pressures structured into our present big schools.

c) Staffing. Now, what must be remembered is that at this school there was already a considerable complement of 'ancillary' staff, for example, a nurse, a youth education officer, a guidance officer, in addition to the now normal year co-ordinators and deputy principals for boys and girls. There is evidence in some British studies to show that the proliferation of quasi-counsellors in schools creates role confusion in the students who do not know what is expected of these 'teachers' or how to behave towards them. What has to be decided is whether the traditional form teacher system, perhaps backed by some equivalent to a house system, operated carefully and with humanity, may not provide as many, or more, 'ears', especially in a small school, where many teachers know most students, as are created in the complex organization of our contemporary large secondary schools.

P.W. Musgrave

(iii) Curriculum

Much thought has been given throughout the world, particularly since 1945, to the links between the school curriculum and the economy. For example, the numbers doing mathematics and science, and the nature of these subjects has been seen in terms of economic need rather than, as was in large part true in the mid-nineteenth century, in terms of a rounded education including both the humanities and the sciences. There is much evidence to show that in Australia parents and students have taken a very pragmatic view of the content of the curriculum almost since the establishment of the first secondary schools. This certainly seems the case today. Yet since the mid-1970s a new economic tendency has been at work, as a result of which the rate of unemployment has risen so much that the supply of new labour coming forward each year from the schools is greater than the demand for it. In these circumstances the direct link between the curriculum and the economy must appear much less strong to students and their teachers.

This relationship has become very complex in all industrial societies, whether capitalist or not, because both upward social mobility and the retention of high social status is seen as largely dependent upon successful completion of secondary schooling. The fewer positions available in the economy are, therefore, even more subject to intense competition. In an egalitarian society the crucial question for contemporary schools, then, becomes how best to provide a curriculum meeting these difficult conditions. The problem is not just that, as the Greenfield study concludes, schools 'must educate pupils for employment, whilst . . . depriv[ing] the increasing minority of pupils who are destined [for] . . . unemployment of a useful education' (p.149) but, in addition and more important, as the Purdah study points out, that in the attempt to do this 'schools . . . [have] been left unaided to struggle with the problem created by an egalitarian policy of providing a comprehensive secondary system in a competitive society' (p.216). Put in simple terms, how can teachers in a comprehensive high school prepare adolescents to be successful in life as usually defined, that is, to have the chance 'to get on', if they so want, whilst at the same time preparing them for the unemployment that they will increasingly have to endure? What combination of school subjects and what content will meet both these ends simultaneously?

Much recent discussion has focused on the content of a core

Methodological, substantive and theoretical aspects

curriculum for secondary schools, although it has rarely been directly related to these new social circumstances. This minimum, as the Curriculum Development Centre document showed,[7] should prepare students not merely for the transition from school to work, but for all the other transitions that adolescents must face today. Possibly because this research was set up in terms of movement into work other transitions such as those into parenthood and citizenship are given little weight. Furthermore, although the economy is given central importance, the curriculum is related to the future life of adolescents as producers, not as consumers, although this latter role already plays a major part in their lives. The core has in some way to cope with several transitions into various future roles.

The determination of this core, especially if opportunities for social mobility continue to be strongly controlled by the universities, is difficult. There is a worthwhile starting point in the Greenfield study where the suggestion is made that 'the school should clarify the minimum criteria necessary for employment, and hold pupils responsible for achieving these, rather than hold them responsible for not obtaining a job' (p.125). If this were done, two things would follow. First, secondary schools would be seen as clearly working towards 'vocational preparedness' (p.112) for their students and second, they would be operating within Michael Sadler's humanistic notion of technical education, enshrined in the English Bryce Report of 1896: he saw technical as one species of the genus, secondary education. Either in the core or in the options available in addition to the core some attempt must be made to meet the wider individual needs other than those generally mentioned. The Year 10 co-ordinator at Greenfield spoke of students 'find[ing] out how to use their leisure time widely, and even how to live their lives properly without jobs'*.

Two problems arise in viewing the curriculum in this broad manner. One was raised by the Youth Education Officer at Greenfield who thought, rightly in my view, that students had to be taught certain material even when 'they just don't think they're doing anything that is any use to them' (p.102). But the question has to be faced: how Reithian can curriculum planners be? How far can we go in specifying what is to be taught and how far can we allow students to choose for themselves? In passing, no consideration was given in these studies to how free student

---

* Methodological note: Comment from the unabridged case report.

choice really was in those areas where choice was supposedly allowed. The second problem concerns the nature of the options. Bantock has suggested that the curriculum for the non-academic child should focus more on non-academic subjects than should that for his academic peers. This policy certainly would reduce chances for social mobility if applied to the core, but we have to ask whether such options should be more readily available for those whose leisure may be increased through unemployment, since the chances of students using their enforced leisure more pleasantly might be greater.

4 Practice

Although the method used in this research project led to the impossibility of much comparison between the three studies, their very different nature reaped a number of fruitful extensions of theory in three relevant areas: (i) alienation, (ii) organization, and (iii) curriculum. These theoretical outcomes have practical implications hinted at above, but which will be briefly outlined here before considering two other practical points, important enough for consideration in this context, though not mentioned by the research workers in their studies.

The concept of (i) alienation that can be deduced from these studies is a fundamentally optimistic one, even though this is not very apparent here. It is processual, multi-dimensional and reversible in character. The implication, therefore, is that, if teachers think in such terms, they must not speak *tout court* of alienated students, but of students temporarily alienated along this or that dimension who, given some appropriate educational treatment, should recross the threshold of alienation, thereby becoming 'normal' again. Often the treatment will depend upon (ii) organization. Structures can be created to change students' views of the threshold of alienation, that is, to lower the chances of students becoming alienated at all. More particularly, there is a case for considering very carefully a radical restructuring of the educational system so that it is made up of much smaller schools with different age ranges from those that now operate. Furthermore, (iii) the curriculum taught must not merely aim at easing the transition of adolescents into the role of producer, but take account of a whole series of other interrelated transitions, particularly if teachers are to meet the demands of students caused by the new situation in which the close nexus between the curriculum and production, considered central to any recent theory of mass education in an industrial society, is not broken.

Two additional considerations, radical in nature, must be added to those outlined in the last paragraph which were implicit in the argument of this chapter. Both relate to the productive sector of the economy and are economic in character. Hence, neither are usually related closely to educational policy. Nowhere in the case studies was mention made of the possibility that adolescents might be involved in a concurrent system of part-time work and part-time schooling, though brief work experience was given much attention. Nor was a policy guaranteeing a minimum income for all, whether in the work force or not, related to any educational implications. The former restructuring of the labour force could be justified either on strictly economic grounds to share out the available work or on educational grounds along the lines outlined by Karl Marx[8] in his discussion in *Das Kapital* of polytechnic education – surely relevant to the transition from school to productive labour? The latter restructuring of the wage bond would have major implications for all above the legal minimum school leaving age who wanted to get out of the work force. Advanced industrial societies are now able to support a high percentage – five in Australia and ten in the UK – of their labour forces outside employment. The payment of a minimum income that is not a dole will influence the willingness of adolescents to do without work and their views of and needs from schools at a time when work for all, normal in the era marked by Keynesian full-employment policies, seems no longer to be a right.

Educational policy in non-Keynesian and monetarist times must be complex, taking account of a wide range of factors, and nowhere is this seen more clearly than when thinking about the transition from school to work. The more narrowly the problem is conceived, the smaller will be the range of practical suggestions made and, following the analysis of this chapter the more likely these cures will be to increase rather than to lower the level of alienation amongst students.

Notes

1 J.H. Newson. *Half Our Future*. HMSO, London, 1964.
2 U.P. Lundgren. 'Education a Context for Work', *Australian Educational Researcher*, Vol.8(2), 5-29, 1981.

P.W. Musgrave

3 P. Willis. *Learning to Labour*, Saxon House, Westmead, 1977.
4 J.S. Coleman (with J.W.C. Johnstone and K. Jonassohn). *The Adolescent Society*, Free Press, Glencoe, Illinois, 1961.
5 M. Seeman. 'On the Meaning of Alienation'. *American Sociological Review*, Vol.2(6), 783-91, 1959.
6 W.J. Campbell. *Scholars in Context: The effect of environments on learning*. Wiley, Sydney, 1970.
7 *A Core Curriculum for Australian Schools*. Curriculum Development Centre, Canberra, A.C.T., 1980.
8 K. Marx, *Das Kapital*, Allen and Unwin, London, 1943.

Chapter 8

Case studies and what we already know

D.S. Anderson

I have been asked to write about the three case studies from the perspective of other more traditional, and usually quantitative, studies of school, alienation and transition. I decided to set down, before reading these case studies, a summary of recent traditional research on school and employment; the questions which have been asked, the answers reached, the implications of these answers for theory and practice, and the important questions which still seem to require answers. It would then be possible to read the case studies and ask what distinctive contribution they had made to knowledge, both theoretical and practical. In particular I was interested in whether there were questions which, having proved refractory to the more traditional and quantitative approach, would yield to the case study method.

First, however, I want to set down what I believe are the strengths and weaknesses of the quantitative and case study approaches. Much of my own research work has been in the tradition where observations of individuals and institutions are reduced to numbers. Such studies inquire about, for example, the number of individuals in different categories of treatment who pass or fail an examination, the numbers from various social class backgrounds who enrol in full- or part-time courses or who do not enrol at all, or trends with respect to age, class, ethnicity, sex, performance, retention rates, employment and so on. Sometimes intervening variables like students' motivations, preferences, perceptions, values, and ambitions are assessed and related to both background and to outcomes of schooling. From such observations, and often with the use of complicated statistical calculations, inferences are made about the effect of circumstances or of treatments on outcomes. Perhaps the best known recent example is *Fifteen Thousand Hours* in which Rutter[1] and his colleagues showed that schools do make a difference (in contrast to other quantitative studies by distinguished scholars such as Coleman[2] and Jencks,[3] which showed that they did not!).

Sometimes, where the authors believe that they have established a causal connection, they go a stage further and inform policy makers that if certain changes are made desired outcomes will follow. Such recommendations are usually hunches or leaps of faith since it is very rare indeed in these types of studies in the social sciences that causation can be established beyond doubt. If A varies with B and occurs before B in time the inference is frequently made that A causes B. It is quite possible, however, that both A and B are caused by some unknown X. Even if all possible Xs are tested and found to be independent of A and B it is still quite possible that, while A appears to cause B in natural conditions, deliberate intervention alters other circumstances and upsets the system so that the original relationship of A and B no longer holds. Furthermore, in so-called basic research the researcher must start with a theoretical viewpoint; assumptions about what the world is like. These assumptions influence the questions which are asked and these in turn shape the answers which are obtained. Thus in the findings from research are encapsulated the initial assumptions. Therefore any advice given to a policy maker about the facts relating to his problems is a function of initial assumptions about those facts. Martin Rein has referred to this as the theory–fact dilemma.

Neverthelsss policy decisions are made whether or not there is research evidence, and the data which a researcher supplies, while never conclusive, are likely to provide a far more informed basis than the impressionistic material on which decisions are so frequently based.

Quantitative observations are applied to a wide range of social phenomena. Educationists and psychologists use rating scales to measure behaviour, beliefs, preferences, expectations and norms. Human mental performance is quantified as when the attainment of students in reading or arithmetic is measured with a standardized test enabling comparisons to be made between groups or over time. With reliable measures it is possible to make inferences about changes in standards or the effect of different teaching methods, assuming, that is, that all other conditions remain constant. Quantitative data are obtained from classroom observation studies when the frequency is measured of teachers'

Case studies and what we already know

interactions with particular students, of the time they spend on a particular task, etc. Sometimes samples of actual behaviour, or more frequently views about behaviour, are rated by experts according to the extent to which complex psychological characteristics are evident. In one such study written answers by students from different school systems to the questions 'What do you like best about school?' 'What do you like least about school?' and 'What would you like to change?' were rated for alienation by independent psychologists.[4] From the results inferences were drawn about the effect of different school structures on student–teacher relations and of those on alienation.

Ratings by respondents themselves are frequently used as a keyhole through which, it is assumed, complex motivation may be observed. Thus answers by children to questions about the job they would like to get and the job they expect to get are used to reach conclusions about career information and the degree to which preferences exceed expectations and expectations exceed probability.

Apart from the theory–fact dilemma referred to above there are two other criticisms of the quantitative method as a source of useful information. One is that the measures are never completely reliable or valid and therefore always distort the reality which they purport to reflect. The second is of the assumption that 'if you can't measure it, it doesn't exist', with the consequence that the need to measure becomes the tail which wags the dog. Thus the reality portrayed by quantitative methods is only a fraction of the totality and a biased fraction at that. There is substance to these criticisms, although the distortion caused by placing numerical values on behaviour varies enormously with a field of inquiry and the questions which have been asked. Often the distortion is not so much in the original observation as in the reduction which occurs as complex responses are compressed into a single numerical cypher. Thus a correlation coefficient between, for example, a test of alienation and subsequent scholastic attainment may be significantly negative. What gets buried in the single summary statistics are all the 'deviant' cases – the rebellious and apparently alienated kids who nevertheless did well, or the conformists who nevertheless dropped out. Correlation analysis, which dominates the quantitative approach to research, focuses attention on the mainstream effects and suppresses the contrary tendencies which frequently illuminate underlying processes. There seems to be an irresistible temptation in many quantitative studies, to focus the question on issues which can be measured with the technology at hand and in the time available. Thus closed question format is frequently preferred to open-ended questions where respondents can more readily challenge the researcher's frame of reference. Questionnaires are preferred to interviews because they are cheaper; and for the same reason interviews are preferred to field observation.

However, the important question is not 'whether to measure or not to measure' but rather matching the complexity of the 'measure' to the phenomenon being studied. Case study researchers measure. They are counting when they observe that more alienated students than others drop out of school; or that the science teachers are stricter disciplinarians than the humanities teachers. Their measures in these instances are simple categorical ones but they are engaged in the same type of empirical activity as the researcher who asks 'How many?' and 'How much?'

Two advantages claimed for case studies are that they do not rely on refined measurement and statistical technology and thus avoid reducing and distorting rich and complex human behaviour; and that they set out with a minimum of assumptions about the nature of the phenomena to be studied. By not having to operationalize concepts so that numerical representations of behaviour can be generated the case study method is able to seek out and report phenomena which would slip through the coarse mesh of a social survey. For example, the effect of a couple of trouble-makers on a teacher's behaviour; or on the classroom environment, is likely to be missed by a researcher who comes in on one particular day with an instrument to measure teacher authoritarianism or student alienation. The case study researcher has the advantage of being present over a period of time and thus being able to see the processes involved as students interact with one another and with their teachers. The case study method does not preclude the use of formal measurement; test results might be important, or at a particular point in the development of a case study it may be appropriate to use an attitude inventory. The case study combines the advantage of longitudinal studies with a flexibility of approach which permits the investigator to follow unanticipated questions. By making a minimum of prior assumptions the method is less likely than a survey or an experiment to follow a pre-ordained track; the answers are less likely to be encapsulated in the initial approach.

Shortcomings of the case study are that its results are rarely generalizable in any rigorous fashion to a population and it is not objective, as traditional methods are said to be, in the sense that

Case studies and what we already know

a second investigator, ignorant of the initial study, should come up with the same results. (To be fair there are extremely few instances in the literature of replications of quantitative studies.)

Limited generalizability is the price paid for the intensity of the case study method. The investigator spends a large amount of time with one individual or one institution. In theory it would be possible to make case studies of a representative sample of a population but the practicalities of such is that this never happens. The case study report rarely claims that what has been found applies beyond the field of the study; nevertheless there is often the implied invitation to generalize. If this takes the form of a hypothesis to be tested by further inquiry then no damage is done; if, however, the conclusions from the $n = 1$ case study are accepted as representative of the state of affairs in other places or at other times then there can indeed be gross distortions.

The case study is not exempt from some of the strictures made above about quantitative research; in particular it treads treacherous ground when it purports to make no initial assumptions. Every investigator, quantitative or case study, must stand somewhere. For example, the decision by Fensham et al. to study school, alienation and transition presupposes a particular set of questions. Furthermore, as the study proceeds the case study researcher is faced with choices at every point of the study's development; whether to spend more time on this topic or that, whether to talk to parents when it becomes apparent that the home is the origin of what students do in school, whether to persist in the face of antagonistic response, how to evaluate the effect of his own presence on the phenomenon being observed, how to decide when the study should end.

These questions can, in principle, be dealt with in the same way as in traditional research by a statement of the assumptions behind the design of the studies. The undertaking is more complex for case study researchers because, as new leads and unexpected events are explored, they have the task of exploring their own assumptions throughout the duration of the investigation, not only at the outset.

I find it useful to distinguish between case studies and case stories. The latter is an illustration of conclusions reached on other grounds – it is like a novel where a story is created to illustrate a theme. An investigator might believe that schools teach their students self-concepts by a process of labelling; for example, for some reason, perhaps trivial, Bloggs is assumed to be dumb, or a trouble-maker, or a no-hoper and is labelled as such by his teachers, perhaps in quite subtle interactions. His behaviour then starts to conform to these predictions and confirms to the teachers that they were right, and to Bloggs that his own self-image is correct. Believing intuitively that this is what happens a case-story researcher sets out to illustrate this theme; to make a study of Bloggs or of a school in order to support the labelling thesis. Instances which strengthen the conclusion are reported, contrary cases are played down. A skilful case story is like a good novel and provides the reader with new insights and understanding about how such a labelling process may work. These are not however conclusions which have been tested as evidence is tested in a court or an experiment.

A case study, on the other hand, is an enquiry conducted according to the rules of evidence. In the making of observations and in the interpretation of data it is as rigorous as an experiment. The objective is not to tell a story about something already believed to exist, but to investigate a problem. This means, of course, that the initial problem has to be stated clearly and at the outset; if in the course of the enquiry further problems are unearthed then these, too, have to be stated clearly and the evidence pointing to their solution assembled and duly assessed. Because of the flexibility of a case study – the opportunity to choose the method appropriate to the problem, and to follow up unanticipated leads, to redefine the problem – it will almost certainly end up with more questions than answers. The intensity of the study usually means that the investigation is limited to a single case, rather than a representative sample of cases. This combination of flexibility and intensity, rather than whether quantitative methods are used or whether there is sloppy treatment of evidence, distinguishes the case study from other research methods.

Case studies and case stories are both of value in illuminating our understanding of human and institutional behaviour; neither term should be used in a pejorative sense, nor should the two approaches be confused.

As a result of recent research what do we know about alienation of students in secondary schools and their transition from school to working life? Perhaps the best known fact is that there are strong connections with social class: students from poor families or whose parents have had little education are more likely than others to see little meaning in their studies, to perform poorly in school work, to dislike school, to leave early, and to suffer unemployment. With respect to alienation (which is an overused term and comes with many meanings and should probably be dropped) research studies show that there is some connection with social class but that over and above this it is also associated with low scholastic performance, having a poor self-concept, having a poor or an antagonistic relation with teachers. Only a minority of secondary students positively like school; the rest are either hostile or apathetic, expressing no strong feelings one way or the other. For the majority the main satisfaction to be had from going to school is meeting with friends, the peer group. From socio-psychological perspectives schools comprise two cultures. There is the official formal culture in which the student–teacher relationship is one of dominance and submission (no matter how friendly, enlightened or permissive the teachers may be). This culture reflects the organization and structure designed to attain the official objective of schooling which is learning or socialization. In order for learning to occur, there has to be maintenance of order. The second culture is the peer society which forms and has its being in the numerous spaces (physical and psychological) which are inaccessible to teachers. Peer culture varies from activities which are hostile to school to others mildly supportive of the formal purposes of schooling. Most peer groups are neither anti- nor pro-school; their activities reflect the concerns of adolescence, the central one of which is to attain psychological independence and to become young adults.

There is some evidence that students' vocational decisions are influenced by their peers; most surveys, however, show that the overwhelming influence is neither school nor peers but the family. Occupational aspirations have been (the past tense is used since there is as yet little research reporting young people's vocational ambitions since unemployment has become significant) class-linked and unrealistic in that far more young people hope for positions in the professions than could possibly be accommodated. Aspirations exceed expectations and expectations exceed reality; many will be disappointed but on average children from higher SES families enter 'better' occupations. Whatever their class background and scholastic attainment level students adopt a vocational viewpoint when evaluating their schooling. They want their schooling to be practical and job-related.

With the recent enthusiasm for accountability and evaluation there has come a large amount of research on the effect of intervention. It is too soon for any general conclusions to be drawn and the value of the research at this point is largely in the feedback it provides to particular programs. The impact of career education, counselling and guidance and of work experience programs range according to evaluative studies, from minimal to very effective. Programs of positive discrimination in favour of disadvantaged groups (usually defined in terms of family income) have proved very difficult to evaluate. A study of the secondary allowances scheme reported favourably but with little hard evidence;[5] a study of the effect of fee abolition in higher education was unable to point to any large changes in the social composition of university and CAE students.[6]

Structural changes do appear to produce alterations in educational behaviour. Changes in the organization arrangements for decision-making in schools have resulted in better morale amongst staff and students (these findings are from case studies and are subject to the strictures made earlier about generalization). A system-wide change in Canberra from six-year high schools to a 4 + 2 system with the last two years in secondary colleges produced dramatic improvement in the attitude to school of the students in years 11 and 12, but little change among the students in years 7 to 10.[7]

The contribution to theory of recent research is limited to say the least. R. Connell and his colleagues use case material (interviews with students, parents and teachers) to demonstrate the social roles of school in reproducing the existing power relations of society.[8] By choosing schools from the upper and lower extremes of the socio-economic spectrum (private schools representing the upper end, public the lower) they were able to provide a graphic demonstration of how schools reinforced the family-determined life chances of children. Despite the authors' prescriptions for reform (teaching working class kids working class culture) the message of the study is that schools do not make a difference to life chances. Nevertheless we observed earlier that research findings encapsulate initial assumptions and noted that another study (*Fifteen Thousand Hours*) with different questions and a different design showed that schools do make a difference.[9]

What questions remain in the area of alienation and transition from school which might yield to new methods? Having reviewed some of the conventional literature and before reading the case studies I have written down the questions which remain in my mind. I have tried to phrase them in terms which would permit empirical enquiry; nevertheless I am well aware that ultimately they boil down to value questions about what should be. The questions are as follows:

Case studies and what we already know

1 What is the nature of alienation? Is it a useful concept with which to explore the response of students to secondary schooling? Does it have its origin in the student, the school or the culture? Are those students who are alienated at school likely to be alienated in their subsequent work?

2 How can alienation or resistance to school be reduced? On the assumption that a positive attitude to school is a necessary condition for learning, are there aspects of school organization which can be manipulated to achieve this end? (Note that the question assumes that the source of the problem does not lie in the nature of the students or of the teachers, an assumption that would be questioned by some authorities.)

The next question is a development of the first two:

3 Assuming, as governments are now tending to, that a majority of each age group should be encouraged to remain in formal education to age seventeen or eighteen, what are the structural, curriculum and organizational requirements for effective learning? Will the management of a more heterogeneous population in upper secondary school require, or lead to, further division and classification of students in upper and lower streams, public and private schools, vocational and academic curriculum, etc.

4 What is the contribution of schools in an era of high unemployment, apart from delaying entry to the labour market? Can schooling increase employability? Should work skills be taught at school and, if so, what are the implications for general education?

5 What is the appropriate articulation of school and community? Should schools have a responsibility (educational, pastoral) for their students after they have formally left? Is there a teaching role in schools for adults who had not come up through the teaching profession? Should education extend into the work-place?

In a sense all of these questions are asking what contribution school can make and what it should make, in a social system where culture appears to be a major determinant of outcomes. Research seems to demonstrate that social background contributes more than school factors to the variation in attainment of life chances, that students' values and aspirations reflect those of a stratified society where work and social status are important components in adult identity.

A further question then is:

6 Is the extent of cultural determination reported in much of the quantitative research real or is it perhaps exaggerated by the researchers' perspectives and methods? Will different assumptions and approaches reveal unexpected findings; are there especially effective schools?

The 'should' questions have to be answered first before the 'how' questions are tackled – whether schools *should* work against culture or with it. For example, how school systems and programs should respond to strong vocational pressures; to a society that is competitive and stratified; to a culture that prescribes roles for males and females, black and white, rich and poor, student and teacher, etc. Disciplined investigations can help clarify the value issues, but not answer them.

School organization and alienation

What then do the three case studies tell us? Clearly, many things. They are a rich mine for insights, ideas and hypotheses. However, the first impression which remains after reading them is that schools are institutions designed for children but inhabited by young adults. The image comes from many sources. It is conveyed with great force in the responses given to the researchers' questions by teachers and students, particularly students. A girl contrasted her part-time job as a shop assistant with school in order to illustrate the dependent role prescribed for students by teachers; 'A lady came up to you and she will be holding a baby who has got a chocolate, and she'll say, "Give the lady the money" and that's really funny – you're the lady. And they are not always at you. They give you a job, and leave you to get on with it, and you do 'cos you know they can sack you or not give you all your pay, so you get on with it on your own, and it's great'.

In the same study Tripp tells another story to illustrate how students feel that they are treated as children at school, but as individuals and adults at work. 'Several older girls commented on the differences in the way young male teachers treated them (as children) and the way similarly aged young males treated them (as adults) and therefore potential sex partners'. The contrast is not always between school and work, but between school and not-school as, for example, when students talk enthusiastically about the school camp. Here relations with teachers were friendly and more equal. 'Why can't teachers be like that at school?' the students ask. Unfortunately the case study could not extend to the camp but one feels that an analysis of the two contexts – school and camp – would yield important insights into the way organization shapes the social relations of students and teachers.

Not all students react negatively to the culture of the school and some, probably the majority but they were never counted, seem to welcome the passive role which is prescribed for them – the order, clear instructions, routine tasks, and unambiguous rules. Many, however, react against the regime with behaviour, as both Power and Tripp point out, ranging from mental withdrawal to sullen resentment and active hostility. Negative responses to school naturally enough are associated with early leaving. The negativism is not necessarily directed at particular teachers, as for instance, in the case of Alison who, as Kemmis reports after he called on her a couple of months after she had left school, 'gave me the impression that she had been freed from a certain kind of humiliation'. The incentive for some other girls to leave school was pressure from older boy friends who resented their having to do homework every night.

The three studies provide abundant case material on the student–teacher relationship which is one of dominance and submission, even in instances where teachers are predisposed to treat students as responsible individual young adults. Given the structure of schools one feels that the relationship is inevitable. The maintenance of order, the necessity for rules and discipline, the developing of coping strategies are all problems which teachers must face and solve. The techniques vary but whatever they are learning suffers. Kemmis reflects on this demand for control in the case of a particular teacher called Sally: 'Staying alive in a roomful of adolescents requires skill. The survival skills she demonstrated showed that the need for control (on Sally's side) and the expectation of control (on the students') together conspired against learning though it favours the development of agility in at least some of the students. It requires a great deal more agility on the part of the teacher – Sally plays Errol Flynn

D.S. Anderson

playing Robin Hood against all the Sheriff of Nottingham's "bully boys" '

What is to be done? The case studies demonstrate more than any quantitative study could do, the magnitude of the problems which face educational planners as they attempt to design secondary schools for majority participation to age sixteen, seventeen or eighteen. Kemmis, as are the other two researchers, is pessimistic about change. 'In fact, the curriculum and organization of Addison Hills, like most schools, is what was left over after the things that couldn't be made to happen, didn't happen. It is the total of all the expectations and aspirations and ways of doing things that could evolve without a battle ever being fought and won – a bloodless curriculum, one might say'. Kemmis believes that both teachers and schools must change. 'The bloodless curriculum, the unresolved conflicts of the staff meeting, the wet-blanket principal: they are no more characteristic of Addison Hills than a hundred other high schools in the State. The profession of teaching is experienced by practitioners of something in classrooms – in teaching relationships. The profession does not prepare its practitioners adequately for the battles outside the classroom walls. And it turns out to be almost impossible to make changes to one's own teaching without changing the schools at the same time.' Tripp makes a similar point but sees the teacher as a victim of the system rather than a product of his/her training. 'In general, teachers feel they have little choice in the matter (of whether to teach by rote or for understanding), because to change the content and style of their teaching would mean changing the system . . .'.

It is very clear in the studies which were made by Power and Tripp how deeply academic objectives are embedded in the behaviour of teachers, in the curriculum and in the organization of the school. One feels that it would be easier to shift a cemetery than it would be to move these schools to embrace genuine comprehensive curriculum. The case studies direct most of their questions and discussion to the behaviour of teachers and to the curriculum; strenuous efforts are being made at both Purdah high school and Greenfield high school to develop an alternative non-academic curriculum for those students not suited for the academic course which has been the traditional mainstream. There is no consensus, however, among the teachers about how this should be done and a significant number distance themselves from these efforts, preferring the academic curriculum and the more able students for which their training and experience has prepared them.

Case studies and what we already know

The studies give less prominence to questions of school organization although it is brought out in an incident which Power reports. A committee of dedicated teachers at Purdah high school had been working hard and for some time on the development of an alternative curriculum. It was no easy task as they faced questions of students' needs, of educational goals, of whether to cover all students or just the less able, and of what the knowledge content of the curriculum should be. An attempt was being made to develop skills for self-sufficiency including skills related to nutritional sustenance, hygiene, social communication, transportation, finance, consumer education, leisure, an approach to vocational skills and personal development. The many issues were far from decided when the school principal handed down a timetable which effectively ended the debate and 'changed the course of the discussion from a consideration of the needs of students to one of fitting the demands of the timetable and staffing constraints'. At the same meeting the teachers were informed that arrangements were underway for the ordering of textbooks for next year. From this point on it was evident that the alternative curriculum would be embedded in the traditional disciplinary divisions. It was quickly decided that the subjects in which the alternative curriculum would be taught were English (seven periods per week), Mathematics (five), Geography (four), History (three), Drama and Music (two), Science (five), Home Economics and Technical Studies (three), Arts (three), and Physical Education (five).The example is a graphic illustration of how the needs of the institutions (of the administration and teachers who occupy positions of power) can produce an organization which bears little relation to the needs of the students. The principal, in handing down a timetable, in effect determined that learning would occur with students arranged in age-specific and ability-specific groups and in time-space-topic boxes; in other words the organization required them to be a class of students with one teacher in a room on a topic for thirty-five minutes; followed by another teacher, another room and another topic for another thirty-five minutes; and so on. Neither research nor any other method of thinking has yet come up with an organization which is perfect for the general run of teenagers; it is clear from the case studies, however, that the traditional timetable was not designed for the benefit of students. Power reports how at Purdah high school the timetable even exacerbated racial problems when, by putting students in classes according to their language study it brought together the large number of Greeks in the school.

Students' negative responses or resistance to school are labelled 'alienation' in the case studies and the concept is explored in some depth by Power and Tripp. Tripp uses the interesting technique of introducing the term in his talks with teachers and noting whether they pick it up and use it – most do. Naturally it receives a variety of meanings, always describing students' behaviour and frequently implying that the problem originates in the student – an alienated student is one who rejects the mores of society, is turned off, is a nuisance, is totally passive, does the minimum possible amount of work, is unpredictable, truants, finds school boring or irrelevant. Tripp sees alienation resulting from the interaction of particular types of students and particular types of teachers. Thus a student may be alienated in one class and not in another.

> Some pupils liked being made to sit still, listen, copy and learn what they were told to: others liked being told to find their own information and to express themselves. However, pupils commonly expressed more and more active, resentment at some of the Science and Mathematics teaching than they did about the Humanities. Most complaints about the Humanities teaching centred around confusion about what they were supposed to be doing and not being given enough to do, but not about the way in which they were treated.
>
> (Tripp, 1982)

At Greenfield high school Tripp seemed to find something like C.P. Snow's *Two Cultures*:[10] '... the apparent division of the staff into two almost diametrically opposed teaching styles, each representing ... the Humanities on the one hand, and Mathematics and the Sciences on the other', although each group did contain the wide range. Behind the differences were opposing philosophies of teaching; and in the relations between the groups there was considerable misunderstanding. Tripp's analysis suggests a typology which might be based on teaching content or style (Science/Maths *v.* Humanities or rote *v.* understanding) and on student need (order and discipline *v.* autonomy).

Arising from his observations that teachers may be classified according to their philosophical beliefs about teaching and their teaching styles, Tripp is led to some interesting speculations about the alienation of teachers – from one another and from their work.

Power defines alienation as 'a tenacious sense of estrangement or separation of the individual from society or its institutions

Case studies and what we already know

which manifests itself in feelings of powerlessness, meaninglessness, isolation and normalessness'. Later in the study Power comments that 'for most students, even academic ones, there is a sense of separation, of loss of identity, of meaninglessness and powerlessness in their explanations of the reasons why they come to school'. He compares them with Marx's wage-earners since school, like work, is 'not a spontaneous free expression of their individuality. In something of the sense in which Marx used the term students are alienated from their work . . . few see great intrinsic value with what the school has to offer'.

School organization and community

The second strong impression left by the three case studies is that school is an institution surrounded by a rigid boundary and that transactions across this boundary with the wider community are strictly defined by principals and teachers. In the matter of values, for instance, the principal at Purdah high school complained 'that the socialization role of the school in developing character and commitment to the school as an institution is being eroded by groups and forces from outside the school'. For example, school sport was regarded by the principal as a means of promoting identity with the school but all endeavours were frustrated by sporting clubs in the community who were at variance with what the school was attempting to do.

The case studies describe in general terms the community setting of their schools and describe their insularity. The studies do not ask what school–community relations should be and this is understandable when the theme to be explored is transition. There is, however, one particular dimension of school and community which is significant for the transition of young students from school to work and this is the connection of school with employment. What arrangements exist, or should exist with employers, with employment agencies, and with community groups involved in job creation or training? Is it not appropriate that schools should maintain links with former students, particularly those thought to be at risk in the labour market, with a view to providing them with guidance and help concerning work, training and further education? Information garnered from the post-school progress of all former students (not just the high-flyers who are the ones usually noticed) would also provide invaluable feedback to the school about its alternative curriculum, etc.

The organizational and psychological wall which separates school and post-school serves the needs of teachers (their job is hard enough without having to take on the additional role of community worker); it also proclaims to students that education and school are conterminous. Schools could have a central role should Australia ever adopt a youth policy which had as its main objective a guarantee to all young people of opportunities in work/educational training or combination of these. Schools are the only institutions which know the entire cohort of leavers and as such they are well placed to monitor the progress of each individual and collaborate with other agencies when assistance is needed.

In concentrating on an alternative curriculum the schools and the case studies assume that the schools' task is preparing young people for work and other adult roles can be accomplished in advance of students actually entering those roles. An alternative assumption would be that such preparations should continue as young people actually engage in these new roles. The latter assumption would take the school into the world of work; it may lead to such provisions as part-time school/part-time work, the return to school of students who had left for a period and joint programs with TAFE.

The case studies ask the students to evaluate their schooling from the perspective of future employment. Most saw the curriculum as not relevant to their imagined work roles; an exception was work experience where some programs were regarded as successful by the students.

New questions, new hypotheses

The questions which I set down before approaching the case studies of course have not received answers in any definitive sense; nor would this be expected since by their nature case studies generate hypotheses rather than test them. Rather should we ask whether case studies illuminate the issues which are engaging our attention.

The first two questions asked about alienation and whether it is a useful concept or whether it has been loaded with so many meanings that it lacks any descriptive or analytic precision. The case studies strongly suggest that there is an underlying

Case studies and what we already know

behavioural phenomenon which needs to be explored – large numbers of students dislike school and leave at the earliest opportunity; and in the meantime they are bored, restless, inattentive, destructive, withdrawn, aggressive or unproductive. 'Resistance to school' was the phrase used in the series of case studies by Gay Hawkins to embrace these negative responses.[11] This term, however, provides no analytic leverage on the phenomenon. A way forward is, however, suggested by Power when he speculatively compares students' responses to school with Marx's alienated workers. The similarities are compelling: school/work is an enforced activity laid on by an exterior arbitrary need; labour can appear only as the expression of loss of self and powerlessness. This suggests that the core of alienation is with the nature of the task and its social relations. Its origin is not to be sought in the students' temperaments, their families or the wider environment although there may be contributing conditions – for instance, a student from an educated family may more readily find meaning in a dull subject. This approach to alienation suggests that the focus for enquiry should be the work which young people do at school. The next positive step, assuming that school is not preparation for the capitalist mode of production, would be to create conditions which attach meaning to school study and provide students with a sense of power (equals autonomy, self-direction, responsibility (?)) in relation to their tasks.

None of the three case studies gave examples of such teaching and learning; this does not mean that these schools were complete failures since the case studies were directed deliberately at the 'low achieving' students and little attention was paid to the academic stream where there were fewer problems of finding meaning and autonomy. There are examples of successful programs for the lower half and these, rather than the typical schools, could be the subject of another series of case studies. One would also want to have studies made of some of the same students in different settings, for example, as already suggested, at school camp. Power's use of alienation in the Marxist sense also suggests that longitudinal studies might be made in order to follow students through from school into their work lives. If the psychological assumption is correct, that alienation is an attribute of the individual rather than the task, then one would predict that a student who was alienated at school would also be alienated at work. On the other hand if alienation is the outcome of relation to the task then there would be no necessary carry-over from school to work. The only example in the case studies of tracing a student beyond school is the aforementioned Alison who was unhappy at school but seemed to come alive at work.

The third question asked what curriculum and school organization would be needed if the majority of each age group was to stay on in education to age seventeen or eighteen. Clearly the three case researchers would be pessimistic about the likely success of Addison Hills, Greenfield or Purdah high schools. Studies of schools which are structured differently may provide some answers – for instance Canberra secondary colleges, Victoria's secondary technical schools, various alternative schools or some private schools. It should be noted, however, that all of these examples involve segregation – by age, ability, motivation, social class or sex. Is segregation the answer or are the answers to be found in the comprehensive community school? It is unfair to judge the three case study schools as failures since they have only recently instituted alternative programs and still regard the academic curriculum as the main stream.

One knows that the answer to the fourth question 'Can schools increase employability?' is probably that they can but that there is little point in it when there are not enough jobs to go around; and indeed, as Tripp remarks, it would be dishonest to pretend to students that 'you will get a job if only you will learn to do such-and-such'. The main contribution of school in an era of high unemployment is the same as in any other era: to provide students with the best possible general education so that they are able to resist exploitation and, more positively, to enjoy the access so provided to art, literature, film, history, science and rewarding social relations. But how to do this when motivation is so overwhelmingly vocational? The case study schools provide no answers.

The fifth question asked about the relation of school and community: the case studies have demonstrated how difficult it would be for the boundaries to be lowered, not by showing that schools have tried to engage with community and failed but by showing how the existing organization of schools places demands on teachers that make it unrealistic to expect them to engage in additional activities. If, as has been suggested, the school should exercise some responsibility for its former students when they are in the labour market then it is clear that additional resources would be needed. Furthermore, as Tripp and Kemmis suggest, there would need to be a new sort of teacher; one who had not been socialized to function effectively only with an academic curriculum.

The final question asked whether the extent of cultural determination reported in much of the quantitative research is perhaps exaggerated by the researchers' perspectives and methods. Will different assumptions and approaches reveal unexpected findings? Are there especially effective schools? The three case study schools do not appear to have been especially effective with run-of-the-mill and below average students and there is the temptation to attribute this to family background or social class, although none of the case study researchers go that far. Success is relative and, in refutation of the studies' concluding pessimism, one could point to the many young people who appear in the studies who are successful in that they have a certain mastery of language, numbers and logic. They have also some sense of history and some scientific knowledge which will help them resist the superstitious explanations of natural phenomena. The limits placed by students' backgrounds on the effectiveness of learning remains an open question. It was important, in the first studies of this type, to choose schools which appeared to be fairly orthodox. As it turns out the schools were very similar; in particular the similarity of the problems they face in developing a curriculum for the non-academic student suggests that the problem is both a widespread and difficult one. However, the limits of schooling, their effectiveness with the full range of students, will only be revealed by studies of a range of schools including some which have departed from orthodoxy.

Throughout this account I have used the term case study and not case story. In fact each of the three reports combines elements of each. They are case stories in that each author inevitably started with some conclusions which he wished to develop; the reports, however, are also case studies in that each started with the problem of curriculum relevance and, with evidence from teachers and students, showed how difficult it will be to develop an alternative to the academic mainstream. As case studies the reports have illuminated processes which are far too complex for the quantitative approach and have generated a number of hypotheses which could be tested by more orthodox methods.

Notes

1 M. Rutter, B. Maughan, P. Mortimore, J. Ousten. *Fifteen Thousand Hours: Secondary Schools and their Effects on Children*, London, Open Books, 1979.

D.S. Anderson

2 J.S. Coleman, *Equality of Educational Opportunity*, Washington, Office of Education, 1966.
3 C. Jencks, *Inequality: A Reassessment of the Effect of Family and Schooling in America*, New York, Basic Books, 1972.
4 D. Anderson, M. Saltet and A. Vervoorn, *Schools to Grow In: An Evaluation of Secondary Colleges*, Canberra, Australian National University Press, 1980.
5 P. Meade, *An Evaluation of the Secondary Allowances Scheme*, Canberra, AGPS, 1982.
6 D.S. Anderson, P.J. Fensham, J.P. Powell, and R. Boven. *Students in Australian Higher Education: A Study of their Social Composition since the Abolition of Fees*. ERDC Report No.23, Canberra, Australian Government Publishing Service, 1980.
7 D. Anderson, M. Saltet, and A. Vervoorn, op.cit.
8 R.W. Connell, D.J. Ashenden, S. Kessler, and G.W. Dowsett. *Making the Difference: Schools, Families and Social Divisions*, Sydney, Allen & Unwin, 1982.
9 M. Rutter, B. Maughan, P. Mortimore, and J. Ousten., op.cit.
10 C.P. Snow. *The Two Cultures: And a second look*. Cambridge, Cambridge University Press, 1964.
11 G. Hawkins. *Resistance to School*. Sydney, Inner City Education Centre, 1982.

Chapter 9

Reflections on methodology

S. Kemmis, C. Power and D. Tripp

The reports of the project (Chapters 1-5) should be read at two levels: as a study about school alienation and transition, and as a study about the design of case study research. Through the interplay between these levels in the practice of the research the life of the project became more reflexive and self-critical than might otherwise have been the case. Certainly, both through critical friends and their discussions together, the case study workers experienced a sharpened sense of critical awareness about their work. In the three studies, alienation is treated as an emergent construct, not taken for granted either on the basis of a history of literature about it or on the basis of an agreed stipulative definition.

This is important methodologically, revealing a kind of self-consciousness about styles of case study work characteristic of the naturalistic observation approach (e.g. in the work of the Centre for Applied Research in Education at University of East Anglia). Here, in contrast to much educational ethnography on a more explicit anthropological model, we find the researchers anxious to allow the cases and their interactions with them to define alienation for them. Colin Power's approach initially was influenced by previous work on alienation from school but as his case study progressed, it became increasingly clear that the area of concern was embedded in, and represented one facet of a broader problem faced by the school, namely, coping with going comprehensive and the consequent changes in its cohort of students. In the final analysis it was the everyday experience and tacit knowledge of staff and students at Purdah that Power sought to portray and which framed his report; in both other cases, the researchers almost scrupulously avoided significant contact with the literature as likely to 'frame' their perspectives, predisposing them to seek exemplifications of tacitly-accepted points of view. (This is not to suggest, of course, that Tripp and Kemmis were 'frame-free' in their approaches to their cases.)

At the beginning of the research, a statement was issued by the researchers to potential participants which identified a category of students who were 'turned-off school'. In various ways, this categorization created a certain way of treating the 'phenomenon'. Teachers and researcher could conspire in treating the study as about certain types of students; they could keep category and construct ('turned-off school' *v.* alienation) separate; or they could use the language of only one (i.e. talk about kids who were 'turned-off school' without using the language of alienation). In these studies, *'alienation' is a contested category*. In varying degrees, the researcher controlled the language of 'alienation', offering the teachers the less powerful language of 'turned-off school-ness' thus reserving theoretical prerogatives. In fieldwork at one site, alienation was barely spoken of at all (Kemmis); in another, it functioned as a parallel category to 'turned-off school' (Tripp) but as a practical category on which to act; in the third it assumed various forms ranging from a resigned sense of separation from the self, and powerlessness felt by the mass of students, to acts of rejection of school and its value amongst the most disaffected of the non-academic students.

In Tripp's case, the category 'turned-off school' functioned for the teachers as a category of action and predicted action; what the researcher wanted to discover was how children acquired that label and the construct (thought and culture) which underpinned teacher action with respect to them. The former was explicit in teacher action; the latter implicit. The contest between teacher and researcher is revealed in the likelihood that category and construct were synonymous for teachers (i.e., 'turned-off school' = 'alienated') and hence obvious and unproblematic, while for the researcher alienation was a process capable of explaining 'turned-off school-ness'.

We will return to another aspect of the researcher–researched relationship in relation to the pedagogy of the research.

An educational perspective

There are a number of similarities between the case studies which are important and should not be missed. These are dealt with substantively in the executive summary. Such topics as curriculum relevance, boredom, teacher–student relationships, inter-departmental rivalries in secondary schools, home–school or community–school relations, and student oppositional behaviour (emerging as resistance only in the form of shared reluctance rather than more direct organized subversion) are common to the three studies. What is at issue here, however, is that these three case study workers have all seen their cases through these *educationally-relevant framing ideas*. Here they are in contrast to ethnographers interested in education more purely as institutionalized behaviour; they address their cases as educationalists concerned with the transformation of schooling, and as actors with a capacity for long-range influence upon those institutions.

Developing the design on the run: Affirming divergence

Agreeing to differ

A deliberate initial decision was taken by the case study workers that the co-ordination meetings should be about methodology rather than substance. Until drafts of reports were available, case study workers were careful not to exchange substantive ideas (about alienation and transition) at the meetings. In this way, the case studies were relatively insulated from one another until the meeting where draft reports were exchanged.

It was agreed by participants in these meetings that the 'phenomenon' of alienation from school was ubiquitous and likely to be rather similar across sites. The purpose of the study was to use the different approaches to explore different aspects of school alienation, rather than to validate the ubiquity assumption. It would, no doubt, be possible in other multi-site studies to take a more unified approach and to cross-check issues, as has been suggested by Stenhouse, and Stake and Easley. However, part of the strength of the design enacted here is that fairly different approaches have been taken with a wide range of observations being made and conclusions being drawn; nevertheless, similarities between these studies are evident. Had a narrower, more unified approach been adopted, readers would have a less rich sense of ubiquity and multiformity of school alienation.

Rather than there being pressure to keep the studies similar, it must be remembered that three fairly experienced field workers had been placed by the overall research design in a situation of competition with one another. At least that is how it felt to the case study workers themselves, and a friendly rivalry developed once the styles of the studies were seen to differ. In a sense, a decision in favour of divergence rather than convergence allowed all to co-exist without having to change in the light of work being done at other sites.

It might be argued that a complete multi-site, multi-method matrix would be appropriate to test differences between sites and between methods. Certainly those familiar with Cronbach and Fiske's multi-trait, multi-method approach to validity might take such a line. The problem here, however, was different: it was not to *test* methods or 'traits' (assumed to exist) but rather to name and explore school alienation as it was contextualized in the different sites, not merely those aspects which may be decontextualizable from them. In this respect we were seeking holistic views, recognizing that in so doing we were bound to trade commonality for uniqueness. The studies represent, therefore, three different pieces of one jigsaw picture, different from each other, fitting loosely around their edges, rather than the same picture painted by three different artists.

The methodological discussions were instrumental in supporting the emerging diversity. As we progressed from meeting to meeting, so the character of the discussion changed. Early meetings engaged participants in developing, heightening and defining differences; later ones in exploiting, confirming and critiquing them. Being isolated in their fieldwork and individual in their approaches, the three case study workers depended upon these meetings to draw upon the mutual support of the group and to provide colleagial confirmation.

The critical friends met separately from case study workers on at least one occasion. No doubt they were somewhat surprised by the emerging diversity, but determined to leave the case study workers to pursue their own approaches. Then, once differences of approach had been recognized, the methodological discussions took the character of allowing each case study worker to deepen his awareness of what he was doing. Problems tended to be treated as ones which individuals needed help in thinking through with the support group of the other case study workers and the critical friends. New ideas were generated and challenging questions posed: no criticisms were voiced researcher to researcher – that was the prerogative of the critical friends. Nevertheless, there were still strong cross-influences: discussions of strategies and ethics at the point of entry or for negotiation

Reflections on methodology

raised shared concerns. And there was certainly some mutual influence at the point of writing. The presentation of Kemmis's 'snapshots', for example, influenced the way Tripp subsequently wrote up his 'pupils' views'. In this instance, both workers were attempting to discover a writing formula which would allow the writer to avoid 'teacher-bashing' – the 'snapshots' approach put the story through students' perspectives rather than in a strong researcher framework which might implicitly or explicitly place a value on the teachers' work. The three case study workers could use each other to explore the problems and limitations of fieldwork strategies and writing devices.

An anecdote – critical incident – is worth recounting here. After the last major meeting of case study workers and critical friends, it happened that the three case study workers were in the same car driving back from Phillip Island to Melbourne, freed from the constraints of speaking in front of the critical friends or the chief investigator (not that they normally felt much constrained or badgered by these heavies). Ten minutes down the road, animated discussion was underway – the three began to place labels and reputations on each others' studies. It was agreed that Kemmis's report was high risk. ('Perhaps *he* can get away with that kind of writing!') Mutual support was offered ('we're all in this together') and it was agreed that a conspiracy of support was appropriate: we may differentiate the studies in language and labels, but we would defend to the death each others' eccentricities and methodological choices. The drive was cathartic for all. Badger's milk flowed freely.

Perhaps the most controversial and significant methodological feature of the overall research design was the initial decision to capitalize on the diverse experience and interests of the three case study workers. Rather than submerging differences in an overarching uniform strategy, the group would make a virtue of divergence and use the 'co-ordination' discussions as means of refining and communicating individual approaches. As the meetings progressed, it became evident to case study workers, critical friends and the chief investigator (Grand Badger) that the differences were indeed emerging and could be refined into more or less coherent approaches to case study work.

Individual methodological viewpoints

These three case studies take as a point of departure the

methodological work on case study championed by researchers at the Centre for Applied Research in Education (CARE) of the University of East Anglia. Of course, other traditions may also be read in the finished products. At the same time, each of the studies attempts to break new ground methodologically.

David Tripp has worked generally within the tradition of naturalistic observation, but has taken the techniques of democratic evaluation (especially negotiation of accounts) to a new level.[1] This is arguably the most important technical advance of the project as a whole. At the time CARE developed its methods, word processing technology was not widely available; yet it is obviously appropriate for the negotiation and editing of transcripts and reports. Tripp's study demonstrates the value of the new technology in two ways: first, in the production of co-authored statements from the raw material of interview transcripts (which gradually become both accounts of 'conversations' and debates on issues between parties in the interviews), and second, in the editing of entire case records (e.g. by insertion of issue labels which can then be used as markers in searching the record), and final reports.

In this study, Tripp has used co-authored statements not only as part of the case record but also as part of the final case study, allowing informants to 'speak for themselves' and allowing the reader access to participants' own perspectives. The editing process involved in the production of the statement puts informants in a relatively unprecedented position as far as educational case study work is concerned: they have an opportunity to communicate rather directly with readers of the report. In the process of negotiating the statement, each informant has an opportunity to reflect upon, extend or modify his or her point of view, and thus to feel that the perspectives represented are ones to which he/she can be publicly committed. The reader is also able to identify where these modifications of the original transcript have occurred, and thus to form a view about what the informant regards as sensitive, tentative, or significant.

Lest readers of this report be encouraged to believe that the issues-labelling of entire case records is a way to automate interpretation processes in case study work (i.e., to automate searching of case records and compilation of relevant material under cross-referenced issue headings), it should be pointed out that, while helpful, the technique has sharp limits: issues emerge, and it is not possible in the practice of most studies to keep the

Reflections on methodology

entire case record classified according to an initial set of categories. There is also a temptation for the system user to access only those parts of the record thought relevant to a current concern, ignoring the way in which those parts are contextualized by the richness of the whole record. As is well known, such an approach would be to atomize or fragment the record using superimposed analytic categories, and would be quite at odds with the tenets of naturalistic observation, especially holism.

Stephen Kemmis, by contrast, has 'stretched' the boundaries of naturalistic observation along lines suggested by Rob Walker and Terry Denny (the story-telling approach to case study). In this study, the coherence of the report for the reader, and the clarification of themes (reducing the weight of conflicting evidence) are at a premium; the 'messiness' characteristic of real field data is minimised. (Some readers will recognize this feature as characteristic of John Berger's account of the country doctor in *A Fortunate Man*.[2] Here, the case study worker emerges from the field as novelist rather than chronicler – certainly some would argue that it is the responsibility of the social scientist to interpret evidence in a careful and scholarly way rather than to allow speculation to run rife. In fact, pure speculation is almost entirely absent from the study: the themes and issues arise in the case. What has actually been lost is the evidence behind the story, and the record itself (which would allow a reader to construct 'the' story or re-interpret the data for her or himself).

The slightly self-conscious style – being 'novel-ish' – should not distract the reader from the story itself. There are stories in the situation 'waiting to be told', after all. It is the loss of access to the case record which is the most substantial (some would say the most dangerous or irresponsible) loss in this approach.

In this style of case study work, the reader must do the work of drawing significances and certitudes from the story – it works at the level of vicarious experience – and in that respect it is left to the reader to construct meanings and conclusions. Kemmis's study is thus clearly located in the hermeneutic perspective. In other forms of study, such as Power's report, the reader is provided by the researcher both with formulated and explicit conclusions, and access to the means by which they were constructed. In contrast, in Kemmis's study the reader is offered a sense of the reality of the case (albeit the story-teller's reality). This sense has to be constructed by the reader from the evidence offered by Power or Tripp in their reports.

Power has relied more heavily on evidence to support the

generalizations about the school which he presents as he seeks to reveal what is hidden beneath the veil of the alternative programs offered by the school. In this respect he has followed the traditions of case study research developed by Stenhouse, while blending elements of more conventional modes of data collection in order to develop a condensed portrayal of the case. Like Stenhouse, he has made extensive use of interviews and case records in the first phase of the case study. Having mapped the nature and extent of the problems of alienation in the school as perceived by a wide spectrum of students and staff the methodological stance changes to a much greater emphasis on participation and observation wherein the researcher spends a good deal of time in the classroom, particularly alternative classrooms, and attending curriculum decision making meetings of the staff. In both phases the intention was to gather evidence whose reliability and status seems problematic and whose status is to be established by critical comparison with information from other sources, that is from other teachers and students and documents, and by scrutiny of the case record.

Thus, whereas the initial interviews were loosely structured around the theme of school rejection and alienation, aggressively the meaning of terms ('the non-academic student', 'boring') and phenomena (the selection of learners for alternative programs) were probed. Whereas the quasi-historical tradition rests on interviews as documents and the quasi-experimental tradition rests on interviews as data, the quasi-anthropological tradition employed in the final phase added in as a source of evidence the researcher's own observations as he participated in meetings and in classrooms which had become the object of study. Thus Power sees himself as a witness as well as a gatherer of perceptions of ordinary participants in the situation. He is as well a synthesizer of the participant's interpretations of those actions. While attracted to the possibilities of the technological support mechanisms explored by Tripp, Power sees the process of generalization on the case record as a key methodological problem. He relied more on the self as a generalizer, on reading and re-reading records to extract the essence of the action. Extensive use is made of quotations which in his view expressed perceptions of the participants. The validity of this qualitative equivalent to factor analysis then rests on the degree to which what is portrayed in the case study reflects what is in the case records. While the implicit frameworks of the case study worker clearly influenced what is focused upon, the critical friend played an

Reflections on methodology

important role in highlighting recurring phenomena, not initially given great significance.

One strength that the multi-site case study approach can have lies in the degree to which the case study researcher, as a research instrument, is sensitized to additional facets of the case, as similarities and differences amongst cases are explored. Power exploited this feature in collecting some quantitative data using questionnaires to clarify aspects of the context and to check generalizations derived from interviews. The generalizations of concern are generalizations about the case, not generalizations about many schools or even schools like Purdah. Nevertheless, the case study was written in the expectation that the sensitivity of the reader to aspects of their own experience and school situation would be heightened. At the same time it would seem to be important to ensure that the case study inform the reader of features which were unique to the case.

Modes of perceptive awareness

The three studies differ sharply in style, not only in their products but also in the processes by which they were made. One might say, by analogy with the senses, that Power's study is done by touch, Tripp's by hearing, and Kemmis's by taste. These senses differ in the kinds of differentiation they permit (and for whom) and the kinds of certainty they suggest. Power's study reaches out through a categorical scheme and locates its object in relation to the codes of the research and the researched. Tripp's is conversation within a community of the researcher and the researched, discursively reclaiming meanings in collaborative introspection. Kemmis's sips the evidence, savours it and then pronounces.

The metaphor aside, Power's study is an explicit and formal interaction between researcher and researched, deliberately constructed. It uses a classificatory method to locate the perceptions of informants in a relatively well-defined space. This is evident as much in the structure and frequency of the participant's interviews and observations, as in the organization of the report. Tripp engages his informants in a series of discussions the outcome of which is a number of co-statements. Kemmis makes observations and engages in conversations in a more diffuse way; in this case, the report is disengaged, for the reader, from the case – almost a separate process. The difference between the approaches is that between seeing the case as object (Power), thought (Tripp), experience (Kemmis); with the researcher as communicator adopting a stance of reporting (Power), sharing (Tripp) or performing (Kemmis).

Technical issues

1 Selecting sites

At the beginning of the research, the research team agreed to work in schools where there was some recognized concern about transition from school, and where 'alienation' might be an issue.

Kemmis had worked briefly with the school he studied in an in-service day on the whole curriculum of the school and the challenges to the curriculum posed by technological and social change. He had spent several planning meetings with the staff curriculum committee, and the in-service day with the whole staff. When approached, principal and staff were willing to participate in the study. The school concerned is in a rural area, and had acknowledged problems of curriculum irrelevance – many students seemed ill-served by the school's academically-oriented curriculum. The area was also one of relatively high youth unemployment.

Tripp's school was selected for him by the Research Branch of the Western Australian Education Department. The grounds of selection were not simply that the school was in an older industrial suburb where there was a history of 'difficult' students and poor employment prospects, but were primarily that the school was already aware of the difficulties faced by its students, and the staff were known to be concerned and already engaged in attempts to mitigate the difficulties. Furthermore, the Department was concerned at the amount of research being done in its senior high schools and the way in which this was said to be interfering in the day-to-day running of the schools. Greenfield was a school where no major research had been done since the principal was appointed several years ago, and he was keen to find out more about the situation. He saw the study as a help to the school, and welcomed it.

In Power's view, selecting the case was not merely a matter of chance, indeed he asked himself what it is that draws the case study worker to approach some schools and not others. Proximity and willingness to co-operate undoubtedly are factors, often schools are studied because they have mounted programs funded by governments, are known to be innovatory, or whatever. In Power's case he was interested in the form and magnitude of alienation in a conventional high school, in the ways in which what was formerly an academic school has now coped with becoming a comprehensive school, and in the problems which comprehensive organization, changes in the locale, and the composition of the student body have created. Focusing on such a school made negotiation of access problematic. Given the politics of the school in which sectors of the staff initially saw the case study worker as a stooge for the principal, negotiations with the principal and staff were therefore protracted and demanded the establishment of the case study worker's independence as well as formal commitments regarding the rights of interviewees to modify transcripts, to challenge interpretations and categories, to vet case records and the case study report.

2 Boundary and focus

Because case study workers tend to avoid the pursuit of preformed hypotheses, preferring instead to allow plausibilities to emerge from their experience of the data, it is not possible at the outset of the study to place precise boundaries upon the case in terms of what is and is not legitimate and relevant to record. On the other hand, an attempt to pursue each and every aspect of the case which emerged would make the case entirely unmanageable, shapeless and indeterminate. The necessary balance between these two extremes was sought in the formulation of themes to focus the inquiry. Briefly stated, these themes were the project rationale, namely a study of the ways in the attitudes to schooling of both teachers and pupils interacted with their attitudes to and expectations of youth employment. From a methodological perspective this is important as it distinguishes these studies from most other case studies in education in that these studies were *about* an issue rather than *of* an institution. The case study workers' task was thus to contextualize the arena where that issue occurred rather than to bound it.

The way in which the common focus of the studies was realized in each case was, however, quite different. Power initially concentrated on providing what was an essentially researcher's view of pupils' accounts of the teacher–pupil–curriculum interactions within the institution. Subsequently he provides a mutual researcher/teacher account of non-academic students in the school; of curriculum and pedagogy needed to reduce their level of school rejection and the problems associated with the implementation and development of an alternative curriculum.

Tripp concentrated upon mutual researcher/teacher accounts and understandings of teacher–pupil–curriculum interactions within the classroom; and Kemmis, from a spectator viewpoint, concentrated upon the community–school–curriculum interaction between the home and the school. Thus the common focus of curriculum interaction in the overall design did not lead to uniform boundaries but was rather triangulated by the different perspectives, though the criteria of relevance it established did lead to a number of common concerns and aspects of the phenomenon.

3 The case records

Stenhouse made an important distinction between the case study and the case record. The record he saw as the lightly edited or merely proofed totality of data collected about the case. This included transcripts of interviews and other verbal exchanges; descriptions of sites, settings and persons; accounts of events; documents including meeting agenda, minutes, statements and memos; and the case study worker's own notes. The case record, in other words, is the unselected but organized raw material from which the study is constructed. These three studies differ greatly in the kind of case records from which they were written. Power's record was essentially 1200 sides of transcribed (verbatim) interviews with teachers and pupils, or more basically forty hours of cassette recorded interviews. Transcripts were also made of curriculum development meetings, lessons in alternative classrooms and the documentation of curriculum decisions and course outlines was collected.

He constructed his case study by scanning the data for examples of categories he sought, for examples of what participants suggested were present (e.g. badger droppings), and to discover the nature and extent of various aspects and effects of those categories. Writing the study was then a matter of developing a coherent account drawing upon the case record for examples to both support and illuminate the account.

In Tripp's study no distinction was to be made between the record and the study in terms of either quantity or kind. All the

Reflections on methodology

discussions which went to make up the co-authored statements were tape recorded, but not transcribed. The researcher listened to the tape and wrote an account of the discussion, summarizing, selecting, linking and commenting and rephrasing as much as transcribing verbatim. These accounts, however, were not considered final in any way, except perhaps as they formed an agenda for the next discussion in which they were further modified. But when they were completed to the satisfaction of both researcher and participants, they were incorporated complete into the case study. The only data where the distinction between the case record and study is appropriate in this study are the unnegotiated lesson observations and informal discussions with pupils, some thirty of which were edited down to the twenty 'incidents' of the report. Although, for reasons of length, the version of the study published here contains only two thirds of the original statement data, this should be seen as an abbreviated version of the full study, not a study built upon a different record. Kemmis's study also lacks a recognizable 'record/study' distinction in that he wrote his study from very personal and brief notes intended merely to jog his memory. The very sparsity of the record lent itself to an ongoing process of reconsideration and reinterpretation of meanings, perceptions and events. To integrate a large number of experiences diversified in nature and over time is a matter of unconscious reconstruction and hindsight which may be assisted by the more fluid record of the memory.

In Tripp's study, a deliberate attempt has been made to avoid the distinction between case study and case record. In Power's the distinction holds firm. In Kemmis's, the unavailability of case records to the reader that pertains in conventional case study research has been enshrined as a principle; in a dramatic way, the study turns readers to their own experiences rather than to the 'facts' of the case for confirmation or denial.

4 Evidence and analysis

The three case studies differ to some extent in the kinds of evidence gathered and the modes of analysis and interpretation. All involved site observation in and around the schools and in classrooms, and interviews with staff and students.

Tripp and Power used audiotape to record interviews and lessons; Kemmis used only handwritten notes. Tripp and Power transcribed, Power using a research secretary to produce verbatim transcripts, and Tripp selectively transcribing directly onto the word processor. All used field notes for general observations and kept more or less systematic research diaries. Of course, fieldwork left all three with a developed sense of the site as an experience, the record of their long-term memory. Power worked in several intensive bursts of fieldwork, spending three weeks early in the piece extensively interviewing staff and students, and then an afternoon or a day a week to attend curriculum meetings, to observe lessons, or to follow up interviewees. Tripp made two or three visits a week for the first two terms of the year with a number of follow-up visits in third term; Kemmis visited the school approximately once or twice a week for two terms, usually for a morning at a time. In each case, fieldworkers experienced mounting difficulties in maintaining the expected quantity and intensity of fieldwork that had been agreed. On reflection, all would argue for simply devoting a defined period to fieldwork and suspending all other academic obligations for the duration of fieldwork. It should be said that this was the intention of the fieldworkers but other activities were allowed to intrude.

Progressive focusing and triangulation were features of each study. First the fieldworkers had to find ways of giving substance to the notion of alienation in the language and activities of the sites, and then to cross-check emerging characterizations. Detailed reading of the case studies will show that alienation has been interpreted somewhat differently in the three studies and that there are different uses of the idea, if not the term, within studies. This is in part a question of where the case study workers looked for their evidence.

Kemmis, for example, used a psychological definition of alienation at first, seeing it as characteristic of individuals (as in the phrase 'turned-off school') but subsequently looked more carefully at structural aspects of the context (school–community social structures). Nevertheless, an individualistic interpretation remains: students have a less alienated relationship with community than with school. Finally a more holistic interpretation emerges: the notion of the hobby-farm community attests to the alienation wrought by our political economy and the powerlessness of families and communities to counter its press. In the process, data was collected first of students' and teachers' views, next on students and their community life, and finally on the structure of the community as a whole and its relationship to the mainstream economy of the area.

Reflections on methodology

Colin Power began with a well-structured post-Marxian view of alienation but he did not impose this on the data as Willis[3] for instance, appeared to do. He also took an individualistic approach to data-gathering, allowing the expressed views of the teachers and students to stand as given, without further gloss by the researcher. The experiences of his informants were, to some extent, to be fitted into a structural view of alienation. There is a tension between the structural perspective and the appropriation of individual experiences in this approach, and the categorical structure of the final report reveals the way this tension was resolved in practice.

Tripp's definition was more operational throughout: participants' language and concerns, rather than those of the researcher, define the term, flesh it out and contextualize it by illustration. The technique of the co-authored statement is the drive for the development of such an 'operational definition' of the concept of alienation.

From these descriptions, it is clear that the interactions of the researcher with the researched, mediated by the guiding idea of 'alienation' (always treated as problematic), gave different shapes to the practice of the investigations, and that the different emerging perspectives on alienation are a consequence of the practices which generated them. This point is worth emphasizing, since many field researchers take the view that a case study can be conducted with a strong theoretical foundation at the outset (to be fleshed out or demonstrated by the study), while others suggest that the theoretical categories can 'emerge' relatively unscathed by the researchers' own intervention and commitment to drawing conclusions. An unwillingness to err on the side of theoretical over-formulation on the one hand, or researcher-based over-interpretation on the other is characteristic of the so-called 'naturalistic observation' school of case study research; the tension between them has been resolved differently in each of the three studies.

Decisions about how the issue is to be resolved in any case are made in the light of the purposes of the study – often in terms of the researcher's purposes. Differences between the studies may be at least partly explained in these terms.

In the case of Power's study, theory provided the starting point for developing a perspective which could be used for data-gathering. The strongly categorical character of the report suggests that the researcher has been obliged to mediate between a coherent theoretical perspective and the theoretically undeveloped perspectives of participants. The purpose of the study, then, might be said to have been the location of participants and school life in relation to a wider social theory, but in practice the researcher has been obliged to structure the report around categories which fall between the language of theory and the language of participants. The language of the report concludes in a language to sharpen, as well as to reflect, the understandings of the participants raising and restating problems and positions which dimly-held voices within the school had begun to articulate. Power's concern then was to illuminate the situation, and to portray the problem and potential solutions as they appear to pupils and teachers with the school-consciousness raising processes.

Tripp's primary concern was to maintain the integrity of the participants' perspectives on alienation as they experienced it in themselves, their work and their institution. This being the case, recourse to theory on the researcher's part would have constituted an imposition. The study reveals the lack of an awareness of theory in the 'grand' or 'public' sense of the term and a similar absence of theoretical discourse among participants. By capturing some of the practical theories of participants (e.g. about 'relevance' in the curriculum), the study shows how teachers' theoretical concerns about alienation are articulated in language about their practice.

Kemmis has made a decision of a different order: to use the report to speak to an intended audience rather than to speak from a specific case, although recognizing that to adopt this stance was problematic. Again, the purpose was to instruct rather than reflect, the method of instruction being very different from that chosen by Power. The language chosen is deliberately reflective, poetic and speculative. It not only appeals to the senses and imagination of the reader but also places the author within the study as an individual whose observations may be regarded as problematic by the reader. The silence of authorship has deliberately been broken; the reader must reflectively interrogate both author and the account. The reader is obliged to challenge the author's right to speak; the only test available is of consonance and dissonance with the reader's experience since the 'facts' of the case are obscure. In this way, the 'story-telling' approach challenges assumptions about objectivity, detachment and disinterest in the authorship of 'scientific' accounts. Tripp and Watt[4] have pointed out

> Every statement has a speaker ... and every speaker has a particular set of values. All purportedly objective statements appear so only by their ability to background, disguise or delete the agent. So-called objective statements are profoundly silent about the identity and purposes of the statement's speaker, their history and context. (p.21)

The effect of the story-telling style adopted by Kemmis is to invite the reader to treat nothing as given; there are no conclusions; the reader must treat observations, themes and speculations as provisional hypotheses to be tested against his or her experience. Silence is enshrined as a principle.

Tripp has handled the problem of authorship in a different way. The technique of the co-authored statement is one which places the researcher in an explicit, if not equal, relationship with the participants whose perspectives are to be represented. Here inter-subjectivity (rather than objectivity) as a truth criterion is concretely expressed and symbolized.

Styles of interpretation in the three studies differ in accordance with the approaches of the researchers. In Power's study, interpretation follows analysis which follows data-gathering, though all are suffused with a theoretical perspective. In Tripp's, interpretation and the gathering of evidence are fused in a single process, (the development of co-authored statements) though the author exercises a right to reinterpret the accumulated set of statements as a whole. At this stage, he adopts the same kind of authorial stance as Power. Both, however, allowed participants to comment on the author's final account. In Kemmis's study, the process of interpretation has become invisible both to the reader and to participants. While in Tripp's and Power's studies, a technical account of the process of interpretation can be given, and the process can to some extent be re-enacted by the reader, the Kemmis study is constructed around the consciousness of a story-teller and the reader can only re-enact the process in principle (assuming, of course, that the story is based on a real case).

The pedagogy of the research

Basil Bernstein, in an interesting footnote to his paper 'Class and pedagogies: Visible and invisible', remarks that research, like teaching, can have visible or invisible pedagogies.[5] That is to say, its agenda can be explicit to all involved or hidden from some while evident to others. In the three case studies, this difference can be observed.

Colin Power's study is the most explicit, in the sense that the researcher and informants relate through an explicit set of categories. For the researched, these appear as questions in fairly structured interviews, in topics around which observation is to be arranged, and in draft reports. David Tripp's study is explicit in another way. Through the negotiation of discussion and the eventual production of co-authored statements, what those who have been studied will be held to emerges from their own language – a language which they are invited to extend or modify through negotiation. In Kemmis's case, the pedagogy is invisible: participants in the situation say what they will, what is noted and what is said is the domain of the reporter.

As Bernstein suggests, these differences are about power. In Power's study the categories selected were, in the final analysis, the property of the researcher, since he synthesized the material from the transcripts, wrote drafts, and edited the final version. They locate the researched pupil systematically in relation to the researcher's scheme of things, so that the researchers know how and where they stand. The power relationships linking the researcher and the teachers are less hierarchical since in each case here accounts were negotiated between teachers and the researcher. Nevertheless it is still true to argue that as the researcher essentially retains control over the synthesis and condensation of material obtained from the teachers, it is the researcher who stands in a stronger power position relative to those studied. Thus the fact that the case study researcher is the one who compiles the case records, negotiates them through, and then finally writes the final case study, means that he indeed controls the material which enters the final report. It is he who selects, by and large, what is regarded as important in the first written accounts. The teachers then, while negotiating through this material, are still largely in a passive role. They are not the ones who actively select the material from the case records which will appear eventually in the case study itself.

In Tripp's case, the game is played for slightly higher stakes: researcher and researched establish a language together – though each informant forms a language independently – but it remains unclear just what the whole language community is saying until the unveiling of all the co-authored accounts in the final report. The process is individually explicit but collectively uncertain. In

Kemmis's case, the language of informants is used but it is arranged within a framework created by the researcher: informants are held to account, as it were, in terms established by the researcher. As Bernstein points out, the researcher adopting such a style has the opportunity for close surveillance of the researched and ends up by giving them a reputation (or set of reputations). In this case, there is no doubt who is in control.

The issue of responsibility arises in practice in each approach. In a very practical sense, Tripp has turned responsibility for what is said (in detail) back on to the researched. Kemmis takes responsibility for the story, reducing the status of participants' perspectives to that of material for a story he may be able to tell. Through the use of more conventional social scientific forms, Power takes responsibility for his report, but does so within the canons of respectable science – responsibility for what is said may thus be shared into that wider community of scholars to which he retains obligations and from which he draws legitimacy.

These three stances reveal not only differences towards the researched, but towards the reader also. Power's is the most ostensibly pedagogic study in the sense that his study is essentially an analysis of the data for the reader. The reader knows precisely what, in Power's view, everything means. Tripp's study does much the same, but in a different way and to a different degree. Tripp avoids unilateral analysis by the researcher for the majority of the study in order to present 'the data' as perceived by both parties. However, he cannot, perhaps also should not, relinquish totally the right to analyse the data for the reader. Hence his rather curious and short section significantly placed at the end of the study. This suggests to the reader that the analysis may be optional. Kemmis's study contains no overt analysis at all. It is wrapped up, hidden in the processes of selection of what is described, and of how and from what perspective it is written up. If the reader of *Addison Hills* is to 'read' Kemmis's analysis, then the spaces between the lines must be decoded. Thus, Kemmis's study is the least overtly 'instructional', operating on the imagination of the reader, inviting identification rather than assimilation. Which is, of course, a powerful teaching strategy.

These different stances on the issue of responsibility reveal differences in the relationships fostered between researchers and researched. The character of these relationships may, to some extent, be gauged by the kinds of interpersonal difficulties arising in the conduct of each study and the presentation of the report.

S. Kemmis, C. Power and D. Tripp

Power experienced major difficulties entering the field, running into problems of access almost immediately. The site was already politicized; was there any sense in which the way he spoke about his methods with participants 'warned' them of the possibility that one 'side' or another in the school debate on the issues would end up legitimated by science, with the other views being left undefended and perhaps undefendable?

Tripp, too, had problems entering the field. Again, the site was marked by debate about the issues. But trust was established relatively quickly as participants experienced a method which took their own views seriously and indeed could only work by exploring their perspectives and practices. By contextualizing and developing participants' points of view, however, Tripp had committed participants to their positions; almost inadvertently they found themselves arrayed in alliances and oppositions.[6] A final workshop, held after the study was complete, was attended by one small group of staff and the principal. Of a number of hostile staff who did not attend, only one took up the offer to have a statement about the conduct and report of the study included in the final report. By this time, one surmises, participants had become disengaged. (In other studies, it has been observed that co-operating with the researcher may be a form of co-option; in this case we do not have sufficient evidence to test whether participants had formed this view.)

Kemmis entered the field full of assurances about the degree to which the study would be co-operative and a product of shared understandings. As fieldwork progressed, the opportunity to write a fictionalized, 'documentary' case study firmed to intention. This change of perspective transformed the roles and status of his informants. To a greater extent than was foreseen, they became material for, rather than collaborators in, the production of the study. Since informants were now characters in someone else's story, it is not surprising that (no matter how accurate or telling the account may be) they received the report with apparent indifference – they had been represented but disenfranchised.

In spite of objections to the contrary, these findings are irrelevant to, rather than a negation or reinterpretation of, the findings of certain artificial insemination research studies carried out in the badger populations of the rural areas around Cologne in the late 1970s.

Notes

1 D.H. Tripp. 'Co-authorship and negotiation: The interview as an act of creation'. *Interchange*, 1983.
2 J. Berger (with Jean Mohr). *A Fortunate Man*. Writers and Readers, London 1977.
3 P. Willis. *Learning to Labour*. Saxon House, Westmead 1971.
4 D.H. Tripp and J. Watt. A core curriculum: What it is and why do we need one? *Journal of Curriculum Studies*, 1984.
5 B. Bernstein. Class and pedagogies: Visible and invisible. *Educational Studies*, Vol.1, 23-41, 1975.
6 Compare Tripp's account of these problems in note 1 above.

Chapter 10

With critical friends, who needs enemies?

Lawrence Ingvarson

We three critical friends (Paige Porter, Western Australia; Don Hogben, South Australia; Lawrence Ingvarson, Victoria) met in Adelaide in October 1980 for the first time to share our views on what we were supposed to be doing and what we were actually doing. Something had to be done – after all a preliminary report was to be made soon. It was way back in February that the gang of four (the chief investigator and the three case study investigators) had worked out their strategy in splendid isolation on Phillip Island. At that stage it was intended that case records would be compiled during terms one and two of 1980. We were to have meetings regularly with the researchers during the study period with an emphasis on the links between the compilation of the case records and the case study created from them. A tape recording of a session from the Island was passed on to us as a way of letting us in on the role of the critical friend as seen by the investigators.

> You will see that our understanding of the role was hewn, honed, reshaped, recast, adzed, but not at all discarded. The (taped) record is our best attempt at prescience about critical friends, but the reality (beyond these starting intentions) will no doubt be worked out by the three of you with your respective case study researchers.

We heard the discussion move to the point of view that we were not to be involved in the sites themselves. And it was hoped that we would agree to write a short methodological report on the interpretation processes from case records to case study and the nature of critical friending. It was suddenly clearer that critical friends were expected to be much more than casual (though

With critical friends, who needs enemies?

privileged) acquaintances of the project. We had let ourselves in for more than we had bargained.

The emerging role in practice

We quickly saw that if there is a role for critical friends it is very dependent in practice upon the idiosyncratic way each case study worker goes about his task. For each of us the role had very casual beginnings and expectations. The relationship each of us was establishing also varied markedly. Paige and David shared a course on naturalistic research methods at Murdoch and current problems in the case study were often the topic of discussion and examples in that course. Lawrence and Stephen were in institutions sixty miles apart. By October they had met only three times, although when they did take the trouble to travel they made each meeting an intensive all-day effort. Don was showing distinct signs of frustration by October. Colin's school had run into some domestic administrative hassles which threw the future progress of the study into doubt. He had written little, his own work-load was heavy; so although they were in the same institution Don had done virtually no critical friending.

We used metaphors as a way of getting at the nature of our respective relationships. I had tried this with Stephen. He threw out a few such as: super ego; Rogerian therapist; foreshadowed audience/critic. Paige and David had only had prolonged substantive discussions based on David's writing three to four weeks before the October meeting. Here Paige felt her role had elements akin to that of a 'reminder' or a supervisor of a higher degree candidate. Don felt a bit like the budding star whose agent says 'Don't call us, we'll call you'.

What *were* we supposed to be doing? The group began to look over its collective shoulder. Were we pawns in some Machiavellian scheme to centralize control over the study? Rob Walker of CARE, a visitor in Australia at this time, was in Adelaide with us and he shared his experience with multiple site case studies gained as one of the research team used by Bob Stake in his CSSE Project. Bob had used case study 'stars' who were encouraged to go their own way, but site visiting teams were also used to co-ordinate and confirm findings across the sites. Peter Fensham was doing the site visiting in this project but, like Bob Stake in the CSSE project (see p.3), he was going to have problems, with such diverse sites and researchers, keeping in touch with all that was happening. So we entertained the notion that there might be a hidden agenda in the critical friend role. We came between the case study investigators and the chief investigator. Was our main purpose to act as a channel for information to enable the chief investigator to control and manage the study? Peter was genuinely (I think) surprised by this perception. When asked where the notion of critical friend had come from he had no pat answer but referred to his impression that Stake's case study workers had had to work in lonely circumstances. He also referred to an early study (involving himself and Lawrence Ingvarson) which pointed to the need for the case study workers to have regular opportunities to talk over the problems and issues encountered in their sites – an opportunity to talk in confidence with outsiders so that they could distance themselves from the case for a while. This in fact was one of the valuable features of a critical friend that Stephen had mentioned to me – someone who could break down the typical isolation of the case study researcher in the formative stages of clarifying issues, writing and reflecting.

Additional metaphors related to the role of critical friending were 'priest' or 'confessor', a supportive third party when internal relationships in the study became difficult or were the source of guilt feelings. One deputy principal, for example, after reading a summary of an interview presented by the case study investigator exercised his prerogative to close the contract summarily refusing to grant release to the document. The critical friend could help only by talking the situation through with the researcher.

The 'critical' part of the critical friend role was as yet undeveloped or unclear in this unusual research relationship. How does one act critically? How can such a relationship be established and sustained? I have a suspicion that for some it is easier if the critical friend is not a member of the same institution. Both critical friends and case study investigators were well aware of the usual string of questions brought to bear on case studies as methodology-questions of subjectivity (*tabula fulla*), sources of bias and selective perception, problems about validation or verification of interpretations, representativeness, and so on. Forearmed is forewarned as they say and, in discussions between Stephen and me, both were well aware that Stephen's tendency to keep the initiative in discussion was in part a tactic to forestall questions of such a character. It's not that I was worried about this, nor Stephen. Case study people have so many interesting tales to tell and it can take most of your time

With critical friends, who needs enemies?

covering this more interesting background, which is necessary anyway to put the critical friend 'in the picture'. When the case study investigator is in full flight exploring through talk possible interpretations and issues it can seem tedious to ask about cross-checking, for example, despite its importance.

There is one part of the critical friend role as originally conceived which just doesn't seem to be 'on' in practice. For different reasons each of us is unlikely to be in a position to check independently the relationship between the case data or record and the interpretive case study. These terms seem to have been derived from Stenhouse's notion of creating contemporary archives which can serve as primary source material for descriptive–analytic studies in education by a number of scholars. The criterion the case worker must meet is the production of a case record useful to – that is, accessible to critical assessment by – other scholars. 'The case study is an interpretive presentation and discussion of the case, resting upon, quoting and citing the case record for its justification'.[1]

Don started reading through a mammoth pile of transcripts of interviews Colin had conducted with forty groups of students. This checking of unedited case data material soon struck Don as an uneconomic use of his time and of doubtful value. His view was that critical friends seemed likely to be drawn into much more than they had been led to expect.

David was also compiling considerable amounts of unedited primary material and typing it onto a computer. Paige seems to be the only critical friend who has attempted to check issues against case records, but, like Don, doesn't see as possible a thorough interpretation–checking role.

Stephen has rejected the task of storing case data and compiling case records in this study. He is doubtful if the rewards justify costs, such as those for transcription. Besides, he wanted to attempt a process of 'data reduction at source' in this study. His field notes are reminders or 'mindstickers'; interpretations and potential issues are explored there and then in the context of the interview itself. The case study is viewed as more important than the record and he is not attempting to provide a record which will enable someone else to live through or recreate the experience by means of it. In his view the kind of indexing required in handling the Stenhouse-type case data or record can lead to the emergence of a meta-experience at a later date of doubtful analytical validity. The study is indissolubly Stephen Kemmis's case study. No potential interpretations or issues will appear in the case study that have not been 'flagged' in the field notes. Unlike Colin and David, Stephen is not attempting to make his field notes a complete data record. One problem for the critical friend here is that it is not possible to check if flagged issues arise from Stephen or the respondents. Stephen's view seems to be that he can recognize a potentially good issue when he sees one, *in situ*: that is, a valuable structuring or organizing idea is teased out and tested, in part, at the time. An example of this is the issue of 'The decision to leave' in Stephen's report arising from his conversations with Alison.

For these reasons one of the major roles planned for the critical friends will be modified considerably in practice. It seems likely that the critical friend will act more in a devil's advocate role asking the case study worker to provide the cross-checking evidence and the evidence linking records to interpretations, rather than doing the checking himself. We felt that we had to emphasize that the critical friend was not the researcher nor a surrogate researcher. His role is essentially a passive, or responsive one with a strictly limited basis upon which to make judgments. Others (Parlett and Hamilton[2]) have talked of reducing the problem of subjectivity by using researchers 'in tandem', working independently in the same situation and pooling their findings at the end. But that was not the design used here, nor did we seek it. And, in retrospect, the decision not to allow the critical friends to visit the site seemed wise.

Other aspects influencing the critical friend role

1   The focus of the case as seen by the case study investigator.

There appears to be little overlap between the case study investigators in terms of the 'it' that is under examination. For David the focus seems to be teaching processes. Colin's focus seems to be more curricular and organizational, and for Stephen it is the school and its communities, and the process of leaving school. What focus would have resulted if each case study worker had been placed in the school of another? We have three discrete case studies here with little influence of one upon the other. At our meeting of critical friends we could share our studies but we have little basis upon which to compare them. What problems may emerge when the attempt is made to amalgamate the studies? What is the 'case' in each case study?

2 The different methodological assumptions about case studies of each case study investigator.

It appears that each investigator may have different views on the nature of the knowledge that a case study seeks to generate. For example, Colin's decision to interview 120 students indicates an intention to use the case study to determine the *extent* to which certain views are held, e.g., 'The greatest consensus was obtained from the interviewees in answer to the question "what turns kids off school?" ' For Stephen, representativeness or completeness was not an aspiration, but provocativeness was. It was to be a case study *in*, rather than *of*, the school, of the issues. Interest was more in finding avenues into new ways of thinking about the issues ('Toeholds on complexity'; 'nourishing lumps in a thin gruel'). One aim was to use the case study as a vehicle to introduce more interpretive insight into the language of policy makers and practitioners; new ways of seeing. I'm not sure about David, but to a greater extent than the other two he seems concerned to use the case study to confirm the relevance of a theoretical construct such as the Barnes' transmission/interpretation dichotomy to alienation in the school.[3]

3 The 'background' that each investigator brings to the case study.

The process of developing interpretations or portrayals will undoubtedly be influenced strongly by the values, and the insights drawn from social and educational theorists that each investigator has read. It is perhaps the most difficult, but most crucial part of a critical friend's role to enable these values and influences to be made accessible to the audiences of the case studies. As Stake[4] points out with respect to education.

> Each of us has our reverences, our biases, those that come from our own growing up, and those that come from our bookshelves. Our portrayals would not be better if we were to purge this subjectivity. We dare not suggest that all would evaluate the programs the same, or even see the same sights. We place our service in the marketplace of ideas, interwoven with personal preferences and theoretical persuasion, whether we be positivist or hermeneutic. The client chooses our design, the audience chooses to reference our report, knowing that no other would be the same, knowing the truth lies still well beyond.

Lawrence Ingvarson

As critical friends we would welcome critical comment on how these sources of inevitable, and valuable, subjectivity can be revealed and shared.

Notes

1 L. Stenhouse. 'Case study and case records: Towards a contemporary history of education.' *British Educational Research Journal*, Volume 4, No. 2, p.37, 1978.
2 M. Parlett and D. Hamilton. 'Evaluation as illumination', in D. Hamilton *et al.*, *Beyond the Numbers Game*. Macmillan Education, London, 1977.
3 D. Barnes. *From Communication to Curriculum*. Penguin Books, London, 1976.
4 R. Stake. 'Portrayal of Programs through Evaluation Studies'. Paper presented at the CIRCE Spring Evaluation Conference, University of Illinois, p.11, 1979.

Index

able pupils *see* academic students
absenteeism, 105, 106
academic curriculum, authority of, 271–3
academic school *see* Addison Hills
academic students: Greenfield, 32–3; Purdah, 206–8, 215–16, 274
academic teachers, 214–19, 314
active process, alienation as, 294
Addison Hills School, 14–17, 161–98; amalgamated report on, 263–9, 272, 274–7, 280, 282; background, 160–8; students, 169–79; teachers, 180–91, 267
administrative teachers (Purdah), 212–14; *see also* principal; Youth Education
advantages of case studies, 306
alienation from schooling, 3, 4–6; as contested category, 324; definitions, 52, 120–3, 270, 336–7 (*see also* teachers' perceptions *below*); issues of 270–8; teachers perceptions of, 68–9, 88, 104, 108, 120–3, 212–14, 270; theory from studies, 293–5, 300, 312–17; *see also* active process, case studies

Alison (pupil at Addison), 174–9, 263, 313, 320
Alistair (pupil at Addison), 172
Alternative Courses, 272–3, 278; at Greenfield, 39, 89–97, 110, 112–13, 145–9, 153–5, 274, 292, 314; at Purdah, 204–8, 214, 217–56 *passim*, 291, 314–15
alternatives to schooling, pupils' views (Purdah), 244–5
amalgamated report, 8–10, 13, 25, 263–83; levels of response, 267–9; nature of, 264–6
American National Science Foundation, 11
analysis and evidence as technical issues of methodology, 335–9
analysis by researcher (Greenfield), 118–49; problem, 118–20; alienation, defining, 120–3; alienation and employment prospects, 123–9; alienation and meeting needs, 141–5; alienation and teaching, 129–34; alienation of teachers, 134–6; Alternative Course, 145–9; home background, effect of, 140–1; relevance of curriculum, 136–9
Anderson, D., 19, 303

351

Index

Ann (pupil at Addison), 170
archives, access to, 7–8
attitudes, developing, 37
Australian Association for Educational Research, 18
Australian Schools Commission, 18–19
authority *see* discipline
awareness, perceptive, 331–3

Bantock, G.H., 222, 300
Barnes, D., 60, 349
Barnes, F. (teacher at Greenfield), 89–90, 121, 134, 144
'basic' learning, 230–4; *see also* Alternative Courses
basic pupils (Greenfield) *see* non-academic
behaviour problems *see* discipline
belonging (Greenfield), 41–2, 142, 143–4, 296
Berger, J., 187, 329
Bernstein, B., 339–41
biology, 70–4
Blackburn, J., 18, 284
boredom, 277; at Greenfield, 37–8, 85–6; at Purdah, 247–8, 292
boundary focus as technical issue of methodology, 333–4
Bowie, S. (teacher at Greenfield), 104–8
Brad (pupil at Addison), 169
Britton, J., 60
Bruce, Sergeant (of Addison Hills), 164–5
Bryce Report (1896 – UK), 299
Butt, M. (teacher at Greenfield), 67, 74–8, 126

Campbell, W.J., 297
careers *see* work
case records, 6–7, 24–5; as technical issue of methodology, 334–5
case stories, 307–8, 321

case studies, 6–8, 22, 25, 303–22; alienation and school organization, 312–17; amalgamation of, 8–10, 13, 25, 263–83; community and school organization, 317–18; independent summary of, 10–11; new questions and hypotheses, 318–20; *see also* Addison Hills; critical friends; Greenfield; methodology; policy response; Purdah; response; theory
Centre for Instructional Research and Curriculum Evaluation (USA), 3–4
Centre for Applied Research in Education (UK), 4, 323, 328
change: difficulties of (Addison), 188–91, 314; in school leadership, 286–7
choice, students', 299–300
class: differences, 53, 66–8; and transition, 308–11
Coleman, J.S., 285, 292, 304
Colin (pupil at Addison), 173
community, 320; in Addison Hills, 192–7, 267; and school organization, 317–18; *see also* home; parents
comparisons of methodologies, 323–43
comprehensive schooling, 271, 314, 320; in future, 284–5; *see also* Greenfield; Purdah
conflict, curriculum, 269–70
Connell, R., 310
content of curriculum (Purdah), 230–4
context dimension of relevance, 137, 139
control *see* discipline
coping strategies, 129–30, 313
core curriculum, 298–9
correlation analysis, 305
counselling: at Greenfield, 72, 105–7, 115, 123, 142–3; at

Index

Purdah, 211, 218; in United Kingdom, 297; *see also* listening
criteria of curriculum (Purdah), 230–4
critical friends, 6, 7, 12, 16–18, 326, 344–9; background of researchers, 349; focus of studies, 348–9; methodology, assumptions and, 349; role, emerging in practice, 345–8
criticisms of case studies, 306–7
Cronbach, L.J., 326
culture-conflict, 195
current affairs lesson, 182–3
curriculum: academic, 271–3; in Addison Hills, 188–91; changes, 60–1 (*see also* Alternative Courses); conflict, 269–70; development *see* Alternative Courses; and economy, 298, 301; in Greenfield, 115; hidden, 73–4; matching students to, 273–5; in Purdah, 203–8; theory, 298–300; *see also* relevance
Curriculum Development Centre, 60, 273, 299
cynicism, 46, 181

Dee, A. (teacher at Greenfield), 84–8, 138
Denny, T., 329
design of project, 12–14, 20–6
differences in studies, 325–7; *see also* divergence
Disadvantaged Schools Program, 286
discipline: in Greenfield, 53–5, 69, 86–7, 121–2, 130; in Purdah, 210–11, 212, 219, 240–1
disease, alienation as, 83
dissatisfaction (Purdah), 236–41
divergence in methodology of studies, 325–32; agreement to differ, 325–7; individual viewpoints, 327–31; modes of perceptive awareness, 331–2
Douglas, N. (teacher at Greenfield), 118
draft case study reports, 13, 155–9
drama lessons, 183–4, 232
Draper, Ms (teacher at Purdah), 204
Dunn, J. (teacher at Greenfield), 91–7, 147, 153–4

Easley, J., 3, 265, 267, 325
economy and curriculum, 298, 301; *see also* Marx
Eliot, T.S., 27
Ellis, I. (teacher at Greenfield), 78–9
employment *see* transition; unemloyment; work
English lessons: in Greenfield, 35–7, 74–9; in Purdah, 231–2, 291
'essential' knowledge in Alternative Course (Purdah), 230–4
evaluation in curriculum development, 224–5
evidence: rules of, 308; as technical issue in methodology, 335–9
example transcript, 153–4
excellence, teachers' views of 51–2

failure, 214, 279
fan-shen, 179
Fensham, P., 23, 263, 307
Fiske, D.W., 326
framing ideas, 324–5
Frayen, B. (teacher at Greenfield), 58–69, 132–3, 144
freedom, 52
functin of schooling, pupils' views of (Purdah), 235–6
future: of comprehensive schooling, 284–5; teachers' view of, 50–1

353

Index

Garrett, Mr (teacher at Purdah), 204
general studies *see* Alternative Courses
generalizability, limited, 307
geographical location of schools, 25
geography lessons: at Greenfield, 32–3, 35; at Purdah, 232
goal formulation in curriculum development, 224–5, 228–9
Greenfield School, 14–17, 27–159, 274, 292, 297–9; amalgamated report on, 263, 267, 269, 272, 274, 276–7, 279–80; description of, 30–1; draft report, response to, 155–9; example transcripts, 153–4; principal and deputies, 109–17; pupils' views, 32–49, 292–4, 296; researcher's analysis, 118–49; teachers' mobility, 291: teachers, negotiation of statements with, 151–2; teachers' opinions on Alternative Course, 89–97; teachers' philosophies of teaching 50–69; 129–34; teachers' reaction to draft report, 155–6; teachers' special duties, 98–108; teachers' statements, 70–88
guidance *see* counselling

Hamilton, D., 348
Hawkins, G., 319
hidden curriculum, 73–4
high school, academic *see* Addison Hills
history lessons, 232
Hogben, D., 17, 23, 344–5, 347
home, influence of, 273, 319; in Addison Hills, 164, 173; in Greenfield, 78–9, 80–1, 88, 114–17, 140–1, 296; in Purdah, 215; *see also* community; parents

Howard (pupil at Addison), 172
hypotheses, test of, 266; *see also* theory

implementation in curriculum development, 224–5
individual attention, 40, 44–5
individual viewpoints, 327–31
inevitability of school, 276–8
Ingvarson, L., 16–18, 23, 344–9
interpretation in curriculum development, 224–5
intervention, 309
irrelevance *see* relevance

Jan (pupil at Addison), 172
Jane (pupil at Addison), 173
Jeffries, Mr (principal of Purdah), 202, 209–10, 212–13, 223n, 231n
Jencks, C., 304
Jenny (pupil at Addison), 169

Karmel Report (1972), 203
Kathy (pupil at Addison), 170–1
Kemmis, S., 15–18, 23, 323; Anderson on, 313–14; Blackburn on, 286; Fensham on, 263–5, 268–9, 275, 277; Ingvarson and, 345–9; methodology of, 324, 334–6, 338–42; *see also* Addison Hills
knowledge, school, 40–1; teachers' views of, 55–6, 132
Kramer, M. (teacher at Greenfield), 1, 3, 50–8, 123, 132–3

labelling, 307–8; students' views of, 245–7
Lawton, D., 216
leadership, change in schools, 286–7
Len (pupil at Addison), 169
listening, 39–40, 142–3, 296; *see also* counselling
Lundgren, U.P., 247, 277, 292

Index

Marlowe (teacher at Greenfield), 70–4, 116–17, 156
Martin, N., 60
Marx, K., 236, 301, 317, 319
mathematics: at Greenfield, 33–5, 37–8, 40, 99, 146; at Purdah, 232
meaning, social negotiation, 9
meta-learning, 277
methodology of studies, 21–2, 289–91, 323–42, 349; concerns, 4; divergence, 325–32; pedagogy of, 339–42; technical issues, 332–9
middle-class standards, 53; *see also* class
middle schools in United Kingdom, 296
mixed ability classes, adapting to, 215–16; *see also* comprehensive monitoring curriculum development, 224–5
Morgan (teacher at Addison), 161
Mostin, R. (teacher at Greenfield), 90–1, 138
Musgrave, P., 19, 289, 292
music lessons, 232

National Science Foundation, 3–4
needs and curriculum (Purdah), 227–8
negotiation of statements with teachers, 151–2
Newsom Report (1964–UK), 291
Nichols, B. (teacher at Greenfield), 98–104
non-academic pupils 33–5, 59, 201, 274–5, 285; *see also* Alternative Courses; work experience
non-academic teachers (Purdah), 220–1
norms (Purdah), 209–11

omnibus metaphor, 160–2, 263–70
organization, school: Addison Hills, 188–91; changes, 310; theory, 295–7, 300, 312–18
outside school *see* community; home

parents and teachers, 65–6, 78–9, 292; *see also* home
Parlett, M., 348
passive process, alienation as, 294
passivity, 58, 82, 122, 313
pastoral care *see* counselling
pedagogy of methodology, 339–42
peer group: identification, 237–8; and school rejection, 249–51; values, 140–1
perceptive awareness in studies, 331–3
permanence of alienation, 293
philosophies of teaching at Greenfield, 50–69, 129–34, 316; physical science teacher, 50–8; social studies teacher, 58–69
physical sciences *see* science
plan, curriculum development (Purdah), 226–34; content and criteria, 230–4; frame of reference, 226–7; goals, 228–9; learning activities and methods, 234; needs, 227–8; students, 229–30; *see also* Alternative Courses
policy response to studies, 284–8; change in leadership in schools, 286–7; future of comprehensive schooling, 284–5; unemployment, 287–8; *see also* response
Pollard, F. (teacher at Greenfield), 79–84, 138
Porter, P., 16–18, 23, 344–7
positivists, 8–9

Index

Power, C., 15–17, 23, 285, 345, 348–9; Anderson on, 313, 314–17, 319; Fensham on, 265, 268, 275; methodology of, 323, 329–41 *passim*; *see also* Purdah
power of researcher, 340–1
Price, H., 143
primary schools, rarely mentioned, 296
principal and deputies (Greenfield), 109–17; *see also* administrative teachers
principles of procedure, 12, 20–6
program building in curriculum development, 224–5
pupils *see* students
Purdah School, 14–17, 199–259, 291, 298; amalgamated report on, 265, 268–9, 272–7, 280; background, 201–11; curriculum development, 222–54; teachers' perceptions of student problems, 212–21
Purves, A., 225

quantitative approach, 303–6

racialism: in Greenfield, 113; in Purdah, 246–7, 315
recommendations, 304
reconstruction in curriculum development, 224–5
reformers, teachers as, 180–1
Reg (teacher at Addison), 181–2
rejection, school, sources of (Purdah), 213–14, 248–54; individual as, 248–9; peer group as, 249–51; teachers as, 251–2
relevance of curriculum, 136–9, 275–6, 287; pupils' views of, 35, 37, 38–41, 85; teachers' views of, 81–2, 85–6
researchers, background of, 349; *see also* Kemmis; Power; Tripp
resistance to school *see* alienation
response to studies, 263–83; alienation, issues of, 270–8; school as omnibus, 263–70; transition, issues of, 278–83; *see also* policy response
responsibility, development of: in employed students, 141; teachers' views of, 94–5, 132
reversibility of alienation, 294
rewards, teachers' views of, 73
Richard (pupil at Addison), 172
Rob (teacher at Addison), 185–7
Robert (pupil at Purdah), 237–8
Rudder, Mr (teacher at Purdah), 204–5, 210, 218, 222–5
rules, 209–11; *see also* discipline
rural school *see* Addison Hills
Rutter, M., 304

Sadler, M., 299
Sally (teacher at Addison), 182–4, 313
School Council (Greenfield), 46–9, 144, 293
school leavers (Addison), 172–9
school leaving age, 291
school rejection *see* rejection
schools in studies, 12, 14–16, 20–6, 332–3; *see also* Addison; case studies; Greenfield; Purdah
science: at Addison, 185–6; at Greenfield, 50–8, 129–34; at Purdah, 232–3
Seeman, M., 294
segregation, 320
self-discipline, 53–4, 63
self-esteem, improving, 92–4
self-ratings, 305
separateness, sense of *see* alienation
sex differences in alienation, 295
Sims, S. (teacher at Greenfield), 113–16, 155
site: selection, 332–3; visits, 266–7; *see also* schools
situational analysis in curriculum development, 224–5

Index

size of schools, 297
Skilbeck, M., 224–5
Snow, C.P., 316
social life of students outside school *see* community; home
social negotiation of meaning, 9
social studies lessons (Greenfield), 40–1, 42–5, 84–8
socialization, 209–11, 317
special classes, 77–8
special duties (Greenfield), 98–108
staff *see* teachers
Stage and Easley CSSE Project, 11
Stake, R., 3, 265, 267, 325, 345–6, 349
Stan (teacher at Addison), 180–1
Stenhouse, L., 3–4, 6, 325, 330, 334, 347
streaming, 100–1, 208, 216
stress, 269–70
students, 299–300, 313
students at Addison Hills, 169–79; school leavers, 172–9; and transition, 169–72
students at Greenfield: meeting needs of, 141–5; orientation, 59, 63–4; and teachers, 38–9; views of, 32–49, 292–3
students at Purdah: and curriculum, 229–30; perceptions of teachers, 219, 246, 251–2, 291; teachers' perceptions of problems of, 212–21; views of, 239, 245–6, 291
studies *see* case studies
substantive: concerns, 4; findings, 291–3
suburban school *see* Purdah
Susan (pupil at Addison), 170
Sweden, 285, 292

'tacit' case record, 8
teachers, 5; coping strategies, 129–30; geographical mobility, 291; and parents, 65–6, 78–9, 292; as successes at school, 279–80
teachers at Addison Hills, 180–91; alienation, perception of, 294, 316; curriculum and school organization, 188–91; described, 180–7; views of, 138–9, 294
teachers at Greenfield: alienation, perception of, 68–9, 88, 104, 108, 120–3, 212–14, 270, 294: alienation of, 134–6; coping strategies, 129–30; in-service training, 112; negotiation of statements with, 151–2; opinions of, 89–97, 292, 294; philosophies of teaching, 50–69, 129–34, 139, 316; pupils' views of, 47–8, 130–1; reaction to draft report, 155–6; special duties, 98–108; statements, 70–88; teaching methods, 129–34
teachers at Purdah: alienation, perceptions of, 212–14, 294; and school rejection, 251–2; students' problems, perceptions of, 212–21; students' view of, 219, 251–2, 291
Technical and Further Education, 286
technical issues of methodology, 332–9; boundary focus, 333–4; evidence and analysis, 335–9; site selection, 332–5
tertiary education, rarely mentioned, 297
test of hypotheses, studies as, 266
theory, 293–301; alienation, 293–5, 300, 312–17; curriculum, 298–300; -fact dilemma, 304–5; school organization, 295–7, 300, 312–18

357

Index

'threshold of alienation', 293
'time-serving' students, 79–80, 82
Tom (teacher at Addison), 180
Toni (pupil at Addison), 173, 184
Toohey, J. (principal at Greenfield), 109–13
transition, 3, 4–6; at Addison, 169–72; and class, 308–11; issues of, 278–83; *see also* unemployment; work
Tripp, D., 15–18, 23, 155, 323, 348–9; Anderson on, 312–13, 314, 316; Fensham on, 264, 265, 269, 275; methodology of, 324, 327–41 *passim*; and Porter, 345, 347; *see also* Greenfield
'turned-off' school, 324; *see also* alienation

under-achievement, 75–6, 82, 114
understanding, 55–6
unemployment, 3, 281–2, 298–9, 301; at Addison, 164; at Greenfield, 57–8, 103, 118, 124–5, 128; policy response to, 287–8; at Purdah, 244–5; *see also* transition; work
United Kingdom, 292; Bryce Report, 299; Centre for Applied Research in Education, 4, 323, 328; counselling in, 297; middle schools in, 296; Newsom Report, 291; school leaving age, 291
United States, 285, 292, 297
urban school *see* Greenfield

values: of peer groups, 140–1; teachers' views of, 35–7, 66–8, 292
vertical organization of forms, suggested, 143
vocational training *see* work experience

Walker, R., 3, 329, 345
Watt, J., 338
Willis, P., 292, 337
work experience, 281; at Addison, 164; at Greenfield, 39, 111–12; at Purdah, 204–5, 220–1, 255–6; of teachers, 136; *see also* Alternative Courses
work prospects, 123–9, 281–3, 298, 309, 317–18; at Addison, 169–79; at Greenfield, 48–9, 56–8, 77, 80, 99–103, 113, 118–19, 123–9, 132, 141, 292, 298–9; at Purdah, 241–3, 298; *see also* transition; unemployment
working students, 141, 312; teachers' views on, 75–6

Youth Education Officer (Greenfield), 98–104, 299; *see also* administrative teachers

For Product Safety Concerns and Information please contact our EU representative GPSR@taylorandfrancis.com
Taylor & Francis Verlag GmbH, Kaufingerstraße 24, 80331 München, Germany

www.ingramcontent.com/pod-product-compliance
Lightning Source LLC
Chambersburg PA
CBHW071226230426
43668CB00011B/1321